Emotions at Work

Emotions at Work

Theory, research and applications for management

Edited by
Roy L. Payne
School of Psychology, Curtin University of Technology,
Perth, Western Australia
Cary L. Cooper
Lancaster University Management School, Lancaster, UK

John Wiley & Sons, Ltd

Copyright © 2001 John Wiley & Sons Ltd, The Atrium, Southern Gate, Chichester,
West Sussex PO19 8SQ, England

Telephone (+44) 1243 779777

Published in paperback August 2004

Email (for orders and customer service enquiries): cs-books@wiley.co.uk
Visit our Home Page on www.wileyeurope.com or www.wiley.com

Other Wiley Editorial Offices

John Wiley & Sons Inc., 111 River Street, Hoboken, NJ 07030, USA

Jossey-Bass, 989 Market Street, San Francisco, CA 94103-1741, USA

Wiley-VCH Verlag GmbH, Bochstr. 12, D-69469 Weinheim, Germany

John Wiley & Sons Australia Ltd, 33 Park Road, Milton, Queensland 4064, Australia

John Wiley & Sons (Asia) Pte Ltd, 2 Clementi Loop #02-01, Jin Xing Distripark, Singapore 129809

John Wiley & Sons (Canada) Ltd, 22 Worcester Road, Etobicoke, Ontario, Canada M9W 1L1

Wiley also publishes its books in a variety of electronic formats. Some content that appears
in print may not be available in electronic books.

Library of Congress Cataloging-in-Publication Data

Emotions at work: theory, research and applications for management/edited by Roy L. Payne
and Cary L. Cooper.
   p. cm
   Includes bibliographical references and index.
   ISBN 0-471-98759-X (cloth)
1. Work—Psychological aspects. 2. Emotions—Social aspects. I. Payne, Roy. II. Cooper, Cary L.
BF481 .E56 2001
152.4—dc21

British Library Cataloguing in Publication Data

A catalogue record for this book is available from the British Library

ISBN 0-471-98759-X (hbk)
ISBN 0-470-02300-7 (pbk)

Project management by Originator Publishing Services, Gt Yarmouth (typeset in 10/12 pt Times)

This book is printed on acid-free paper responsibly manufactured from sustainable forestry, in
which at least two trees are planted for each one used for paper production.

Dedication

Janice M. Beyer, a dedicated scholar and pioneering leader in the field of management, passed away on 20 June 2001. The chapter in this book represents one of her last publications and the only piece focusing on the topic of emotions. Within these pages, Jan shares some thoughts about an emotion that her autobiography (Beyer, 1996) shows she cared very deeply about—the feeling of belonging. This personal interest in "belonging" might offer some explanation for her sustained professional interest in the subject of culture. If so, then this chapter represents a small tribute to who Jan was as well as what she studied. She would no doubt be very pleased to know of the book's dedication. While we will continue to learn from her, those who had the good fortune of knowing her will miss her dearly.

Beyer, J.M. (1996) Performing, achieving, and belonging. In A. Bedeian (Ed.) *Management Laureates: A Collection of Autobiographical Essays*, Vol. IV, pp. 39–84. Greenwich, CT, JAI Press.

Houston, Texas

David Niño

Contents

About the editors

Roy L. Payne graduated in psychology at Liverpool University and has spent most of his career as a researcher and teacher in business schools and psychology departments in the UK. He is currently Professor of Organizational Psychology at Curtin University of Technology, Perth, Western Australia. His work has led to publications in major international journals on organizational structure and climate/culture, and he has also published extensively in the occupational stress area. The latter publications include four books co-edited with Cary L. Cooper which have been widely cited in the occupational stress literature. These remain active areas of interest, as well as more recent work on trust in organizations.

Cary L. Cooper is Professor of Organisational Psychology and Health in the Lancaster University Management School, Lancaster University, UK. He is President of the British Academy of Management, Fellow of the Academy of Management, and recipient of the Academy's 1998 Distinguished Service Award. He has published in an extensive range of journals and books on stress, health and well-being in the workplace and was founding editor of the *Journal of Organizational Behaviour*. He is a Fellow of the British Psychological Society, Royal Society of Medicine, and the Royal Society of Health.

List of contributors

Janice M. Beyer PhD. When this chapter was written, Janice was The Harkins and Company Contennial Chair in Business Administration, and Professor of Sociology and Communication Studies at the University of Texas at Austin (please see dedication at the beginning of this book). Her publications include two co-authored books entitled *Implementing Change* and *The Cultures of Work Organizations* and over 80 articles on topics such as organizational design, commitment, ideologies and values, charismatic leadership, rites and ceremonies in organizations, the sociology of science and the structure of universities, human resources policies and practices, and the utilization of organizational research. Her most recent research focused on the use of metaphors and evocative language in the business press, relationships between various forms of employee attachment (e.g. organizational commitment and identification), and socialization of experienced employees. Professor Beyer served as Editor of the *Academy of Management Journal*, as President of the Academy of Management and of the International Federation of Scholarly Associations in Management, and as a member of the Editorial Boards of the *Administrative Science Quarterly* and the *Journal of Quality Management*. She is a Fellow of the Academy of Management and holds a PhD in organizational behaviour from Cornell University.

Harold H. Bloomfield MD, *1337 Camino Del Mar Suite E, Del Mar, CA 92014, USA*
Harold Bloomfield is a Yale-trained psychiatrist and award-winning psychological educator who has been a vital part of many important medical and self-help movements worldwide. The author of 19 books, including the best-sellers *How to Survive the Loss of a Love* and *Making Peace with Your Parents*. His expertise has been featured in numerous national publications, and on scores of national television shows, including Oprah, 20/20, Good Morning America and CNN. His latest and most important book to date is *Making Peace with Your Past*. Dr Bloomfield has been a leading advocate for Emotional Literacy and is

one of the co-founders of the Foundation for Education of Emotional Literacy (FEEL).

Arthur P. Brief PhD, *A B Freeman School of Business, Tulane University, New Orleans, Louisiana 70118-5669, USA*
Arthur Brief received his PhD from the University of Wisconsin-Madison in 1974 and currently is the Lawrence Martin Chair of Business at Tulane, A. B. Freeman School of Business, with a courtesy appointment in the Department of Psychology. He is also Director of the William B. and Evelyn Burkenroad Institute for the Study of Ethics and Leadership in Management. Prior to his move to Tulane in 1989, Professor Brief was on the faculties of several other schools including, most recently, New York University's Stern School of Business. In addition to lecturing throughout the United States, he has taught organizational behavior in Chile, Finland, France, Italy, Mexico, People's Republic of China, Taiwan, and elsewhere internationally. His books, among others, include *Task Design and Employee Motivation, Managing Job Stress, Productivity Research in the Behavioural and Social Sciences, Meanings of Occupational Work: A Collection of Essays*, and, most recently, *Attitudes in and Around Organisations*.

Graham Burrows AO, *Department of Psychiatry, University of Melbourne, Austin and Repatriation Medical Centre, Heidelberg, Australia 3084*
Graham Burrows is a Professor of Psychiatry at the University of Melbourne, Director of the Psychiatry and Psychology Clinical Service Unit at the Austin & Repatriation Medical Centre, and Chairman of the Mental Health Promotion Unit. He has an extensive psychiatry practice and many years of research and clinical service provision in psychiatric services for the community, most notably for depression and suicide. He has a particular interest in the prevention of mental health problems and mental health education and promotion. He is Chairman of the Mental Health Foundation of Australia and Chief Editor of *Mental Health Australia*.

Susan Cartwright, *Manchester School of Management, University of Manchester, Institute of Science and Technology (UMIST), PO Box 88, Manchester M60 1QD, UK*
Susan Cartwright is a Senior Lecturer in Organisational Psychology at the Manchester School of Management. She is a chartered psychologist, and is the author of seven books and over 50 scholarly articles. Her interests are in the areas of occupational stress and organizational change. She has authored a major report on stress for the European Commission.

Yochi Cohen-Charash, *Department of Psychology, University of California, Berkeley, CA 94720, USA*
Yochi Cohen-Charash is currently completing for PhD in the Department of Psychology, the University of California, Berkeley. She earned her MSc, in management from Tel Aviv University, and her MA in psychology from the Uni-

versity of California, Berkeley. Her research interests revolve around the role of emotions in organizational life, focusing mainly on discrete emotions, such as envy, jealousy, guilt, fear, and greed. She also studies fairness in organizations.

Cary L. Cooper, *Manchester School of Management, University of Manchester, Institute of Science and Technology (UMIST), PO Box 88, Manchester M60 1QD, UK*
Cary Cooper is BUPA Professor of Organisational Psychology at the Manchester School of Management, and Pro-Vice Chancellor of the University of Manchester Institute of Science and Technology. He is President of the British Academy of Management, Fellow of the Academy of Management, and recipient of the Academy's 1998 Distinguished Service Award. He has published in an extensive range of journals and books on stress, health and wellbeing in the workplace and was founding editor of the Journal of Organizational Behaviour. He is a Fellow of the British Psychological Society, Royal Society of Medicine and the Royal Society of Health.

Carsten K.W. de Dreu PhD, *Department of Psychology, The University of Amsterdam, Roetersstraat 15, 1018 WB Amsterdam, The Netherlands*
Carsten de Dreu is Professor of Organizational Psychology at the University of Amsterdam (The Netherlands). He received his PhD in social psychology from the University of Groningen (The Netherlands) and was visiting researcher at the University of Illinois at Urbana-Champaign and Yale University. He is co-editor of *Using Conflict in Organisations* and *Group Consensus and Minority Influence* (Blackwell, forthcoming) and he has published over 50 journal articles and book chapters on interpersonal and group negotiation, minority–majority influence and team innovation.

Ian Donald PhD, *Centre for Investigative Psychology, Department of Psychology Department of Psychology, University of Liverpool, Eleanor Rathbone Building, Bedford Street South, Liverpool L69 7ZA, UK*
Ian Donald is Reader in Organizational Psychology at the University of Liverpool, UK, where he is also director of the Safety Research Unit. He has a Masters in Environmental Psychology from the University of Surrey, and a PhD from Aston University Business School, where he was also lecturer in Applied Psychology. He has researched and published in a wide range of areas of organizational and environmental psychology, adopting both qualitative and quantitative methodology. Among many research and consultancy projects for major Blue-chip organizations, Ian has carried out national and international studies of office environments, exploring related management processes and meaning. His current interests are in organizational culture as shared conceptualizations, and their relationship to emotion, safety climate and culture, organizational change, and stress, particularly amongst workers in Hong Kong. Most of the research is undertaken from a social cognition perspective, including the role of scripts,

personal meaning, and emotion. Ian is also International Co-editor of the *Journal of Environmental Psychology*.

Rose Evison, *Change Strategies, Springbank, 20 Tomcroy Terrace, Pitlochry PH16 5JA, Scotland*
Rose Evison has worked as an independent consultant helping organizations and individuals change for over 25 years. She is qualified as a practitioner in occupational and counselling psychology and has wide-ranging experience in all types of organizations. Her approach focuses on developing skills that are needed to improve job performance. Specializing initially in interpersonal and cognitive skills, after extensive experience in counselling and personal growth, she added the skills of emotion management to her repertoire. She designs change processes that take operating situations, skills, and dysfunctional emotional responses into account with practical strategies for modifying all three. Using these methods, she has naturalized, within organizational development, change processes regarded as "clinical" in other contexts. She continues to work with development programmes, teams and individuals from her new base in Pitlochry, Scotland.

Stephen Fineman, *School of Management, University of Bath, Bath BA2 7AY, UK*
Stephen Fineman is Head of Research and Professor of Organisational Behaviour in the School of Managment, University of Bath. As well as researching emotions at work, he has published in the areas of work experience, work stress, unemployment and the greening of organizations, mainly from a social constructionist perspective. Recent books include *Emotion in Organisations*, *Experiencing Organisations*, *Organising and Organisations* and the *Business of Greening*.

Agneta H. Fischer, *Department of Psychology, The University of Amsterdam, Roetersstraat 15, 1010 WB Amsterdam, The Netherlands*
Agneta Fischer is Professor of Gender, Culture and Management at the University of Amsterdam (The Netherlands). She received her PhD in theoretical psychology from the University of Leiden (The Netherlands). She has published journal articles and book chapters on gender and cultural differences in emotions, regulation of emotion, the social context of facial expressions, and gender and management. She edited *Gender and Emotion* and is co-author of the *Social Context of Emotions* (Psychology Press, forthcoming) with Brian Parkinson and Tony Manstead.

Elizabeth Gray, *E501 Seashore Hall, Department of Psychology, University of Iowa, Iowa City, IA 52242, USA*
Elizabeth Gray is a doctoral student at the University of Iowa in Personality and Social Psychology. Her current research interests include (1) how basic personality traits are related to important real-world criteria, such as sleep and academic performance; and (2) the longitudinal stability of temperament and personality in young adults.

Peter Herriot, *The Empower Group, Century House, Priestley Road, Basingstoke, Hants RG24 9RA, UK*
Peter Herriot works for The Empower Group, where his main areas of expertise are career management and the employment relationship. He is concerned to relate academic and practitioner perspectives on work and organizational psychology. He is author of several books, including, most recently, *The Employment Relationship: A Psychological Perspective.* He has just completed his period of editorship of the *European Journal of Work and Organisational Psychology*, and is an ardent Europhile.

Maurice King, *Research Consultant, Vasse Research Institute, VRI BioMedical Ltd, Level 4, David Maddison Clinical Sciences Building, corner of King and Watts Streets, Newcastle, NSW 2300, Australia*
Maurice King was Professor of Psychology (1972–1997) at the University of Newcastle (NSW) where he fostered an interdisciplinary research group in medicine and science on brain–immune interactions. In 1997, he became Director/Professor of the Institute for Behavioural Research in Health at Curtin University of Technology, Western Australia. The Institute focuses on pure and applied research in psychoneuroimmunology. He retired from Curtin University in January 2000 and is currently Research Consultant to Vasse Research Institute.

Richard Lazarus, *Department of Psychology, University of California, Berkeley, CA 94720, USA*
Richard Lazarus obtained his BA in 1942 from the City College of New York. After military service in World War II, he returned to graduate school in 1946, obtained his doctorate at Pittsburgh in 1948, taught at Johns Hopkins and Clark Universities, then came to Berkeley in 1957, where he has remained. Lazarus has published over 200 scientific articles and 18 books, both monographs and textbooks in personality and clinical psychology. In 1966, *Psychological Stress and the Coping Process*, which is now considered a classic, appeared. In 1984, with Folkman, he published *Stress, Appraisal, and Coping*, which continues to have worldwide influence. In 1991, he published *Emotion and Adaptation*, which presents a cognitive–motivational–relational theory of the emotions. He became Professor Emeritus at Berkeley in 1991, in which status he continues to write and publish research on stress, coping, and the emotions.

Sarah MacCurtain, *Department of Personnel and Employment Relations, College of Business, University of Limerick, Limerick, Ireland*
Sarah MacCurtain teaches Organisational Behaviour at the University of Limerick. Her research interests are the roles of trust and reflexivity in determining conflict patterns within top teams, gender and careers, and emotional intelligence. She was involved in the Price Waterhouse Cranfield research project between 1997 and 1998, exploring differences in human resource strategies over the last five years in Greenfield sites. She is currently involved in a research project

on top management teams, trust and innovation and has worked on a consultative basis with several Irish and multinational firms. She is a qualified user of the Myers–Briggs Type Inventory. She is a co-author of *Effective Top Teams*.

David Niño, *Assistant Professor of Management at the University of Houston – Clear Lake*.
When this chapter was written, he was a doctoral candidate under Janice Beyer's supervision in the Department of Management at the University of Texas at Austin. His research with Janice Beyer has appeared in the *Journal of Management Inquiry* and as a chapter in S. Srivastva and D.L. Cooperider (Eds) *Organizational Wisdom and Executive Courage*. His dissertation research provides an in-depth study of how tacit organizational rules shape and constrain patterns of knowledge sharing in a large and rapidly changing high-technology organization. David holds a BA in philosophy, a BBA in Finance, and an MA in Latin American Studies from the University of Texas at Austin.

Roy L. Payne, *School of Psychology, Curtin University, GPO Box U 1987, Western Australia 6845*
Roy Payne graduated in Psychology at Liverpool University and has spent most of his career as a researcher and teacher in business schools and psychology departments in the UK. He is currently Professor of Organizational Psychology at Curtin University of Technology, Perth, W. Australia. His work has led to publications in major international journals on organizational structure and climate/culture, and he has also published extensively in the occupational stress area. The latter publications include 4 books co-edited with Cary L. Cooper which have been widely cited in the occupational stress literature. These remain active areas of interest as well as more recent work on trust in organizations.

Jared Rosen, *WholeLife Inc., 101 Lucas Valley Road, San Rafael, CA 94903, USA*
Jared Rosen has been a pioneer in the field of emotional self-management. As a psychotherapist and researcher, he investigated the connection between breath, emotional resistance, stress, and disease. He has taught public workshops throughout the USA and internationally since 1989. Additionally, he has developed unique training programs and implemented them in hospitals and treatment centers. Mr Rosen developed Whole Self-Management, a cutting-edge stress-management program taught to corporate executives. Currently, he is the CEO of Whole Life Publishing and the executive director of the Children's Emotional Literacy Project. He is the co-author of the forthcoming book *Emotional Power* written along with best-selling authors Harold H. Bloomfield MD and Ayman Sawaf.

Ayman Sawaf, *WholeLife Inc., 101 Lucas Valley Road, San Rafael, CA 94903, USA*
Ayman Sawaf visionary executive and entrepreneur, is the founding chairman of the Foundation for Education of Emotional Literacy (FEEL), a non-profit or-

ganization devoted to the advancement of emotional intelligence in business, education, families and society. He founded and was the chairman and CEO of Enchante Ltd which developed emotionally intelligent new programming with Warner Brothers and Norman Lears Act III Productions. Enchante published the first Emotional Literacy program for children consisting of 21 books. Mr Sawaf is also one of the creators of the EQ map, and is co-founder of Advanced Intelligence Technologies. Mr Sawaf has created and managed successful businesses in the USA, Europe, and the Middle East. Currently, he is the chairman of Whole Life Publishing.

Robb Stanley BSc(Hons), DClinPsy, *Department of Psychiatry, University of Melbourne, Austin and Repatriation Medical Centre, Heidelberg, Australia 3084*
Robb Stanley was born and educated in New Zealand, he joined the staff of the University of Melbourne Department of Psychiatry in 1979 and holds the position of Senior Lecturer responsible for two graduate psychotherapy diploma programmes. He is currently Secretary/Treasurer of the International Society of Hypnosis and Treasurer of the International Society for the Investigation of Stress. He has authored or co-authored approximately 60 publications and has particular interests in emotional processing and cerebral activity, anxiety disorders, anorexia nervosa, clinical hypnosis and cognitive–behavioural psychotherapy. His personal interests include cooking, travel, and horse racing. He currently co-owns seven race horses.

David Watson, *E11 Seashore Hall, Department of Psychology, University of Iowa, Iowa City, IA 52242, USA*
David Watson is a Professor of Psychology at the University of Iowa. His primary research interest is in the area of mood, and how it relates to basic traits of personality. He is also interested in the dysfunctional emotional processes that characterize a wide range of clinical syndromes, including the mood and anxiety disorders.

Howard M. Weiss, *Department of Psychological Sciences, Purdue University, West Lafayette, IN 47907, USA*
Howard Weiss is Professor of Psychological Sciences at Purdue University. His research focuses on emotions in the workplace, primarily guided by the framework of Affective Events Theory which he developed with Russell Cropanzano.

Michael West, *Organizational Studies, University of Aston Business School, Aston Triangle, Birmingham B4 7ET, UK*
Michael West is Professor of Organisational Psychology at the University of Aston Business School. He has been a member of the Corporate Performance Programme of the Centre for Economic Performance at the London School of Economics since 1991. He has authored, edited or co-edited 12 books including *Effective Teamwork, Developing Creativity in Organisations* and the *Handbook of Workgroup Psychology*. He has also written more than 120 articles for scientific

and practitioner publications, and chapters in scholarly books. He is a Fellow of the British Psychological Society, the American Psychology Association (APA), the APA Society for Industrial/Organizational Psychology, and the Royal Society for the Encouragement of Arts, Manufacturers and Commerce. His areas of research interest are team and organizational innovation and effectiveness, and the organization of national health services.

Preface

This book was prompted by a request from the publishers for an update of the books we had edited previously on stress in the workplace: *Stress at Work* (1978), *Current Concerns in Occupational Stress* (1980) and *Causes, Coping and Consequences of Stress at Work* (1988). Whilst that was tempting, it seemed to us that the late 1980s/1990s had brought a renewed and broader concern with emotions of all kinds. There was a growing interest in the more positive emotions such as happiness, and Michael Argyle's book *The Psychology of Happiness* (1987) is an exemplar of that work, as well as a burgeoning interest in the nature of emotion itself. Ekman and Davidson's book *The Nature of Emotion* (1994) contains works by the leading scholars in the field and it illustrates vividly the debates raging amongst them. There is, of course, a very large literature on stress at work that deals with a restricted range of the negative emotions. There is a huge literature on positive emotion, captured in the concept of job satisfaction, but many other emotions have largely been ignored in work psychology, though the influential work of Weiss and Crapanzo (1996) on affective events theory in the workplace, heralded the developing interests of both academics and managers. The interests of the latter were also strongly stimulated by Goleman's *Emotional Intelligence at Work* (1998). With this activity in the background, it was decided to broaden the book to deal with a comprehensive range of emotional experiences.

The title *Emotions at Work* is deliberately ambiguous, hence the subtitle "Theory, research and applications for management". The title does, of course, convey the central focus of the book which is on emotions in the workplace, but the other possible meaning of "emotions at work" is a concern with the processes involved in the production of emotional experience. The first part of the book is entitled "The nature of emotion" and it introduces the reader to what is known about emotions and the processes that bring them into being. Chapter 1 is by Robb Stanley and Graham Burrows from the Department of Psychiatry at Melbourne University. They define emotions and list some of the main emotions described by workers in the field. They also describe the emotional process, strongly linking emotion to motivation and behaviour. The chapter also deals with the function of emotions in this overall process, describing the range of positive and negative emotions and their significance in detecting conditions which may be of clinical significance. The conceptual and empirical difficulty of being precise in this field is strongly signalled.

These difficulties are perhaps suggested by the need to have a chapter solely on the distinctions between emotion, mood, and temperament. Chapter 2 is by Elizabeth Gray and David Watson from the Department of Psychology at the University of Iowa. They present a thorough review of the literature on the three and use the concepts of duration, focus on the object/situation, intensity of the emotional experience, the frequency, the function, and the type of the state to differentiate between them. They finally offer an integrative schema, starting with a distinction between positive and negative affect and then defining emotions, moods, and temperamental traits that arise within the two broad states. It is convincing in its parsimony and clarity.

The nature of emotions is further explored by Richard Lazarus and Yochi Cohen-Charash from the Department of Psychology of the University of California at Berkeley. This chapter examines the main epistemological approaches to the study of emotions and does so specifically focusing on the work that has been carried out in work organizations. A total of 15 discrete emotions are defined and each is considered in the context of stress and coping in work situations. The theoretical emphasis is on the need to approach the study of emotion within a cognitive–motivational and relational meaning framework. This tool can be effectively used to "ask, about each adaptational encounter at work, what might have brought an emotion about, how it is coped with, and what the consequences might be" (p. 75). Having explored the variety of emotions and provided classifications of those that are relevant to the workplace in particular, we are immediately faced with the question, "How well can we measure these different emotional states?"

Part II of the book is called "Measuring and assessing emotion at work." It continues the concern with processes by concentrating on the biological correlates of emotion in Chapter 4, which is by Maurice King who was Head of the Institute for Behavioural Research in Health at Curtin University in Perth when the chapter was written. The history of biological studies of emotions commences with Darwin, William James and W. B. Cannon and moves through the limbic system, brain opiates, psychoneuroendocrinology, and brain imaging. It moves on to psychoneuroimmunology and lists the main indictors of emotional activity and how they may be measured. The role of the brain is also described briefly but comprehensively. It is concluded that "... while the central nervous system generates emotional perception, it does so only in concert with the peripheral nervous system, so that measuring peripheral system variables makes pragmatic sense" (p. 98). The last part of the chapter considers the practicality of collecting data on physiological, endocrinological, and immunological activity in the workplace. It concludes that such measures do seem capable of helping to distinguish between cognitive and emotional reactions, and in helping to discriminate between different emotions.

Reading Chapter 5 by Roy Payne may well convince the reader that the psychological sciences could do with all the help they can get from the biological sciences.

The chapter concentrates on self-report measures of emotions and moods. The recent debate about the size of the correlation between measures of positive and negative affect is presented as well as frameworks for classifying emotional experiences. A number of measures that have been used in work organizations are described. They include measures of emotion and mood, and it is indicated where some measures can easily be adapted to assess them as well as temperament. Whilst there is much work on positive and negative affect, and a reasonable amount on anger, the chapter calls for more work on emotions such as envy, jealousy and guilt, and describes some measures developed by clinical psychologists that might be adapted for use in work organizations.

Having prepared the way, the book begins to move into the heart of its focus on work organizations and Part III is concerned with "Organizational influences on emotion". Part III commences with a blockbuster history of affect at work by Howard Weiss from Purdue University and Art Brief from Tulane University. Having briefly set the intellectual context in the early 20th century, they describe how a paradigm of research into the dissatisfied worker developed in the 1930s and how '... the end of the decade saw the study of affect at work become the study of job satisfaction by way of questionnaire" (p. 142). The correlates of job satisfaction ruled for the next 30 years and the 1960s became the golden age of job satisfaction research. The work of all the major players is described (Herzberg, Vroom, Locke, Cain Smith, Loftquist and Dawis), but their works are presented as the strands that make a history, with the emphasis on story. The 1970s is seen as a period of consolidation with major reviews but few new ideas, except for Salancik and Pfeffer's introduction of the idea that satisfaction is much affected by the processing of information generated in the work context. The 1980s brings a shift towards a broader interest in the nature of affect, as well as a strong concern for the influence of temperament on job satisfaction and other indices of psychological well-being. The role of cognition in the affective process also becomes a developing theme as well as the way in which culture/climate can influence affect in the workplace. The authors also identify the trend to a broader interest in affect and the development of emotional intelligence as characterizing the 1990s. The key themes, and how they have played a part in bringing job satisfaction research into the 21st century, are eloquently presented in the discussion.

The role of culture in developing and sustaining emotions in work organizations is the focus of Chapter 7 by Janice Beyer and David Niño from the Graduate School of Management at the University of Texas at Austin. They explore how cultures:

- manage the anxieties posed by uncertainties;
- provide ways to express emotions;
- encourage and discourage the experience of emotions;
- engender identification and commitment;
- produce ethnocentricism.

They do this by summarizing a recent and dramatic event on the campus of Texas A&M University. Students were building a large bonfire, continuing the tradition of associating it with the annual football game against their arch rival the University of Texas. The bonfire collapses, 12 people are killed and 27 injured, some very seriously. As the story unfolds, the authors use it to provide vivid and dramatic examples of the positive and negative emotional forces that cultural identification can produce.

The strength of people's identification with their colleagues is the focus of Chapter 8 that examines "The origins and consequences of emotions in organizational teams". The authors are Carsten de Dreu, University of Amsterdam, Michael West of Aston Business School, the University of Aston in Birmingham, UK, Agneta Fischer who is also at the University of Amsterdam and Sarah McCurtin, University of Limerick. Having established the power of the drive in human beings to belong to groups, and the positive and negative emotions that can arise from those drives, the authors show how feeling that we belong to a team has a protective effect on the frequency of experiencing negative emotions. They then tackle the question of how well group identification, and the emotions attached to it, can control the nature and quality of the interpersonal processes that develop in a team. This leads to an interest in their relationship to team performance including team creativity.

"Feeling out of control" could well be used as an operational definition of stress. As is pointed out above, it is also crucial to good teamworking. It is such a central concept to understanding the nature of organizations, and the effect they have on people's experience, that it was deemed worthy of a chapter all of its own. Steve Fineman's chapter (Chapter 9) is entitled "Emotions and organizational control." Steve is at the School of Management at Bath University, UK. The chapter starts with the argument that the best organizations function on pure rationality, and emotion is controlled out of the equation. Having raised doubt about the validity of this assumption, the author explores how managers in organizations actually exert control, and how their workers attempt to control them. The second half of the chapter uses descriptions/accounts of the visit of a pollution inspector to an organization, and what it is like to be a doormat for a senior broker in the financial services industry. It provides an excellent example of the use of qualitative methods to research emotions in organizations.

Having established the problematics of emotions in organizations, Part IV of the book is concerned with "Managing emotions in the workplace". Chapter 10 is by Rose Evison who is a psychologist and consultant in personal development and interpersonal relationships, currently resident in Pitlochry, Scotland. The chapter focuses on how to help individuals manage "the production and enhancement of emotional states associated with optimizing performance, and minimizing emotional states associated with performance decrements or health hazards" (p. 241). The chapter distinguishes functional emotional responses (FER) from dysfunctional emotional responses (DER) and examines the role of learning, in shaping them. It draws on emotional theory to indicate how they may be changed, which leads to recommendations about how they can be managed both by the individual and by managers of other individuals.

Cary Cooper and Sue Cartwright's chapter (Chapter 11) focuses more on the organization level and concentrates on stress and destructive emotions. They are from the Manchester School of Management at the University of Manchester Institute of Science and Technology. They indicate the different actions that managers in organizations need to take, depending on whether their strategy is primary prevention (reducing the causes of stress), secondary prevention (improving people's capacity to manage stress and their emotional reactions to it), or tertiary prevention (providing support to people who have stress through counseling and other forms of intervention/support). The chapter concludes with a section on the broader implications of creating healthy work environments and the importance of considering the needs of small and medium enterprises.

One aspect of the work environment that has not been widely considered in stress research itself is the physical environment. Chapter 12 is by Ian Donald who is an environmental psychologist at the University of Liverpool. Ian concentrates on offices as physical environments. In discussing the nature of emotion in organizations, he draws on the concept of emotional labour and how different theories of organization might influence it. Academic and architectural interest in how office design might influence emotions and behaviour is a relatively recent phenomenon, and Ian points to an emphasis on function rather than psychological effects in the design of most offices. The office as status symbol is treated in some depth and the loss of its role in open planning. There is also a section on the role of lighting in influencing mood. In looking to the future, Ian ponders on the home as office and the emotional consequences that trend might bring about.

The final part of the book is about "Emotions and the future." The first chapter (Chapter 13) in Part V is by Peter Herriot who lives near London and practises as an occupational and organizational psychologist. Peter emphasizes the social nature of emotions and how the employment relationship is fundamentally social in nature. The changing nature of the employment relationship is outlined and the potential differences that are developing between senior managers in organizations and the rest of the people they employ. The expectations for compliance, for difference (the need to develop a competitive advantage) and for change (the organization's ability to adapt and be flexible) are considered in some detail. Some surprising comments occur: "It is not so much that it is the survival of the fittest that is the order of the day, rather it is the survival of the biggest" (p. 319). This leads to a somewhat pessimistic view of future employment relationships for the majority of workers, though Peter concludes this is not inevitable if senior managers manage with intelligence and a concern for the emotional consequences of their actions.

Emotional intelligence and the future are the focus of the final chapter (Chapter 14). Ayman Sawaf, Harold Bloomfield, and Jared Rosen are consultants with Whole Life Expo in the USA. Their chapter is entitled "Inner technology: emotions in the new millennium." This chapter too considers how changes in the economies of the world are changing the requirements of effectively dealing with the changes. Emotional intelligence, and shared emotional intelligence in particular, are seen as vital assets. The chapter examines how emotional intelligence develops in both individuals and in organizations. The acronym FIRE is used to convey the importance of integrating Feelings, Information, Responsibility, and Energy to meet the challenges of the future. The chapter is both polemical and practical, in keeping with the aim of the book to move from theory to practice. The authors encourage us to stop being guilty for feeling emotions, to stop feeling shameful for being alive, to stop hiding from grief and sorrow, and to forgive others so that love can become the engine of our actions, and "emotions the modem to the soul" (p. 341).

The book itself is a modem to information—we hope you have good feelings about it.

References

Argyle, M. (1987) *Psychology of Happiness*. London: Methuen.

Cooper, C.L. and Payne, R. (1978) *Stress at Work*. Chichester: J. Wiley.

Cooper, C.L. and Payne, R. *Causes, Coping and Consequences of Stress at Work*. Chichester: J Wiley.

Ekman, P. and Davidson, R.J. (1994) *The Nature of Emotions: Fundamental Questions*. New York: Oxford University Press.

Goleman, D.P. (1998) *Working with Emotional Intelligence*. New York: Bantam Books.

Weiss, H.M. and Cropanzano, R. (1996) Affective events theory: A theoretical discussion of the structure, causes and consequences of affective experiences at work. In B.M. Staw & L.L. Cummings (Eds) *Research in Organizational Behaviour: An Annual Series of Analytical Essays and Critical Reviews*, Vol. 18, pp. 1–74. Greenwich, CT: JAI Press.

August 2000

Roy Payne and Cary Cooper

Part I

The nature of emotion

Chapter 1

Varieties and functions of human emotion

Robb O. Stanley and Graham D. Burrows
*Department of Psychiatry, University of Melbourne, Austin
and Repatriation Medical Centre, Australia*

THE NATURE OF EMOTION

The concept of emotion is central to all aspects of human experience and yet the concept is quixotic when it comes to defining what emotion is precisely. Many aspects of emotion are described differently depending on the context. Like other aspects of human experience there are often common-sense understandings and theoretical definitions that do not precisely match, and yet without precision research into the nature of normal and abnormal emotional reactions is compromised.

When considering the nature of emotions, the components of subjective experience, verbal description, accompanying physiological response, motivational influences, behavioural expression, and consequences need to be considered. The components may be consistent with each other or there may be discrepancies between them. Depending on their orientation, some researchers view emotions as primarily biological and physiological (Panksepp, 1988) while others view them as primarily psychological (Lazarus, 1991).

The subjective experience of emotional states is only available to us via the verbal descriptions that are applied. The language used to describe emotions varies considerably from person to person, as do individual familiarity with emotional states. Some people are cut off from their emotions while other people are dominated by their emotions. Some are expressive of their emotions while others seldom show significant emotions. Does this mean they experience

Emotions at Work. Edited by Roy Payne and Cary Cooper.
© 2001 by John Wiley & Sons, Ltd.

them differently? Or has personal experience, biological differences, or cultural acceptance simply altered the expressive component of emotions? Because of the complexities of subjective experiences and expression emotions are difficult to study.

Emotions and feeling states direct attention to events, thoughts or stimuli, organize perceptual and thought processes, as well as activating and motivating many, if not most, aspects of human behaviour. The central role of emotion in human functioning applies both to interpersonal (or social behaviours) and personal solitary behaviours. Whether in the social, work, family, or solitary sphere of human endeavour, human emotions and affects direct much of our functioning. The universal nature of the principal emotions and the presence of recognizable emotional states within animal behaviour underscore both the biological and the adaptive functions of emotions. In spite of the universality of emotional states, there is considerable debate over the precise nature of the fundamental emotions.

The expression of emotion also has a significant secondary role in complex social communication, indicating to the observer not only the impact of contemporary events but also the likely response of the person being observed. The expression of anxiety may communicate to an observer the desire to avoid or escape, joy the likelihood of persisting and anger an intention to defend.

Emotions vary in terms of whether they are positive or negative experiences, in arousal and intensity (i.e. strongly aroused to weakly aroused), reactivity (i.e. whether easily aroused), centrality (i.e. whether they dominate consciousness or are peripheral experiences), and, of course, the situations that arouse them (i.e. universal situations to highly idiosyncratic situations). Given the multidimensional nature of emotional experiences and of emotional expression, it is not surprising that the boundaries of when an emotional reaction is considered inappropriate, pathological, or representative of a psychological or psychiatric difficulty are poorly defined. Emotional reactions that are extreme in relation to the situation, or that persist beyond a reasonable time, or that are attached inappropriately to the situation, may each be labelled as pathological or representative of a psychological or psychiatric difficulty. The boundaries of what is excessive, too persistent, or inappropriate are not fixed and are subject to interpretation.

Emotions are associated with a range of other related states, such as feelings, affects, and temperaments. All these form related aspects of our general emotional functioning. While having a degree of independence, immediate feeling states are responsive to the situation but also related to the other emotional realms of affect, emotion, and general temperament. The precise nature and delineation of emotions, affects, and temperament are seldom agreed upon, the concepts varying from researcher to researcher.

WHAT ARE OUR BASIC EMOTIONS?

Clearly, while there are many words to describe emotional experiences, the range of emotions are not endless. Most researchers agree there are a limited number of emotions, although the precise number and nature of our basic emotions remain in dispute. The most influential theorists in this debate come from the biological and social psychological perspectives.

Broadly speaking, there are approaches to emotion that emphasize the biological nature of emotional processes (Izard, 1977), others that focus on the cognitive processes whereby emotion is subordinate to the information processes of the human mind (Kagan, 1994). Other approaches emphasize the developmental nature of emotions and their role in facilitating learning, behaviour change, and development (Sroufe, 1996). There are those who view emotions in terms of their functional involvement in the interaction between the individual and his environment (Barrett & Campos, 1987). Others view emotions as social or cultural labels defined by the circumstance in which they occur (Abu-Lughod & Lutz, 1992). The difficulties considering the nature of emotions arise from the complex nature of the process of emotional arousal.

Izard (1984) and colleagues have persuasively argued on the basis of observable, distinct and recognizable neuromuscular expressions (facial) of emotion that there are ten basic innate emotions. These "differential emotions theorists" propose the ten basic emotions are biologically distinct. The manner of their expression may be modified through childhood into adult life with the maturation of the underlying biological structures, muscles, and nerve connections. The wide variety of labels humans apply to their emotional experience in adult life is seen as resulting from the various combinations of these "basic emotions". While the ten basic emotions are seen as comprising the basis of all human emotional expression, what elicits the emotion will be determined and changed with learning and an interaction with cognitive or the information processes involved.

The ten basic emotions identified by the differential emotions theorists are:

- interest–excitement;
- enjoyment–joy;
- startle–surprise;
- distress–anguish;
- rage–anger;
- disgust–revulsion;
- contempt–scorn;
- fear–terror;
- shame–shyness–humiliation;
- guilt–remorse.

The way an individual expresses emotions may be modified by family, social, and cultural influences. Learning in all its various forms plays a significant role in determining what is considered the socially or culturally appropriate emotional expression in a particular situation.

Those theorists interested in the cortical circuitry of the emotional systems of the brain (Panksepp, 1988) propose, on the basis of the brain circuitry, that there are four basic emotions, anger, fear, sorrow, and joy. Other affective states are seen as representing complex interactions between these basic emotional systems. This approach proposes there are a limited number of underlying primary emotional circuits within the brain that have a "command circuit design ... (and) bring a variety of brain functions into rapid coherence to generate coordinated behavioural, physiological and hormonal states" (Panksepp, 1988, p. 49). From an evolutionary viewpoint, Panksepp (1988) acknowledges the possibility that the affective properties of various stimuli activate one of two particular systems, a generalized pleasure system that is based on things that help sustain life and a generalized aversion based on events incompatible with sustaining life. Within these two general systems, Panksepp (1988) proposes four to five primary command systems (1) the foraging–expectancy–curiosity–investigatory system, (2) the anger–rage circuit, (3) the anxiety–fear circuit, (4) the separation–distress–sorrow system and perhaps a fifth one a "social–play" circuit. This biological evolutionary approach to emotion does not deny secondary learned cognitive elaborations of the primary systems.

The approach of Panksepp (1988) is also consistent with the emotional processing model of Davidson (1992) and his colleagues, who have proposed that the processing of emotional events involve either positive or approach activity or negative avoidant activity. They propose that different parts of the brain and information processes are involved in the approach and the avoidant emotions. In their view, the approach–avoidance motivational axis underlies all emotional responses, with left and right hemisphere anterior regions being differentially involved in emotional responses and cognitive style.

The various perspectives in the debate over whether there are basic emotions are outlined in Ekman and Davidson's (1994) discussion. While there is still considerable debate, those involved in this field agree on the need for greater data and that our level of knowledge in this important field remains rudimentary. The labels used to describe emotional states may be used idiosyncratically and have considerable culturally defined influences, but there is also consistency in the physiological component of responses in relation to environmental events (Ekman, 1994).

THE EMOTIONAL PROCESS

Considering the nature of emotions involves examining each stage of a complex multi-stage process (Figure 1.1). It is necessary to examine the events that elicit emotional responses and the detection of those events and the perceptual processes that determine how those events are processed. With the perception of an

Eliciting event → Detection of the event
        → Change in basal arousal (orienting and preparing to respond)
        → Appraisal of the significance of the event (interpretation)
        → Emotional response consistent with the interpretation
        → Subjective experience of the emotion
        → Change in motivation
        → Motivated behaviour
        → Secondary appraisal of the significance of the response

Figure 1.1   Stages of an emotional response

event, there is a change in the base level of arousal. This is more than an orienting to the change in stimulation, as it may also involve the initial learned or genetically encoded interpretations (e.g. danger, etc.). There is evidence that humans may be pre-programmed to respond to certain events such as heights and small fast-moving animals (e.g. spiders, mice, rats, etc.). The major contribution to our emotional response comes with the interpretation of the significance and nature of the event. Whether an event is perceived as threatening or enhancing of well-being is based on cognitive processes of interpretation. These processes are learned and set against past experiences and beliefs. The emotional response, including the physiological responses, subjective awareness, and behavioural intention, follows the appraisal of the situation. The subjective experience of the emotional state flows on to motivation to behave in pre-programmed or learned ways. The behaviour designed to deal with the situation motivated by the resulting emotional state follows.

At each stage of the process of emotionally responding there is constant feedback that attempts to restore the organism to balance or homeostasis. At the same time, each stage of the emotional response is subject to its own interpretation and from this a secondary emotional process, similar to that just described, commences.

The elicitors of the emotional response may be an external event or an internal process. Internal processes include our own thoughts, images from memory or changes in bodily sensations. Events may be responded to because we have an innate sensitivity (such as with the perception of heights) or because of learned experiences (previous traumatic events).

A change in arousal state prepares us for the response. The degree of change will be influenced by our basal state when the event occurs. The arousal change from a stressed individual may be considerably amplified when compared to the response from a relaxed individual.

Our appraisal of the event is the most significant component of our emotional responses. Perhaps more than any other animal, the complex nature of our interpretations, taking into account our beliefs about our world and about ourselves, allows a complex of emotional responses. As noted earlier, there is a range of elaborate emotional responses available to the adult human well beyond the basic emotions discussed earlier. Contradictory emotional responses may also be experienced from the same events.

FUNCTIONS OF EMOTIONS

For the individual, emotions are viewed by most researchers as having an adaptive purpose or function, with either a protective or a nurturing function. This overriding adaptive function of protecting from negative consequences and maximizing positive consequences was identified early in the study of emotion in Freud's *Beyond the Pleasure Principle* (Freud, 1920). Through essentially biologically programmed processes, emotions activate protective mechanisms or behaviours in situations of danger, threat, or loss, as well as the processes involved in seeking out ways of meeting, in a nurturing way, human needs.

For human beings in the 21st century, emotional experience, physiological accompaniments, and behavioural responses are often manifest in situations that do not require the protective actions of primitive humans. Being biologically wired into our neurotransmitter systems, the emotional state remains, however, available for a protective purpose should the need arise. Most of us do not experience real threat or danger, but a socially or individually created perception of threat, danger, or loss, the result of interpretive cognitive processes. Similarly many of the basic needs are met and activation of additional nurturing is above and beyond basic human requirements.

Emotions and feeling states direct attention to relevant events, thoughts, or stimuli, organize perceptual and thought processes, as well as activating and motivating many, if not most, aspects of human behaviour. The central role of emotion in human functioning applies both to interpersonal (or social behaviours) and personal solitary behaviours. Whether in the social, work, family, or solitary sphere of human endeavour, human emotions and affects direct much of our functioning. The universal nature of the principal emotions and the presence of recognizable emotional states within animal behaviour underscore both the biological and the adaptive functions of emotions.

What are the functions served by emotions? Not all consequences of emotions are functional, some may be unintended and the long-term consequences may differ from those in the short term. Similarly, asking the question of the functions of emotions, we need to consider the differences between functions for the individual versus functions for the social group within which the individual operates. Emotion may be protective of an individual's well-being, but also a form of communication as far as the social group is concerned. Asking "What are the functions of emotions?" may also lead to asking "When is emotion dysfunctional?" and "Where are the boundaries between functional and dysfunctional?"

Emotions, when provoked by the interactions with the environment or from internal processes, organize attention toward the relevant events and away from others deemed to be less relevant. Having shifted attention to what is perceived to be the emotion-eliciting event(s) and, as a result of the interpretation of the nature of that event, emotions activate affective and behavioural programmes consistent with the interpretation. The arousal of motivation based on the interpretation of the event is usually connected with behaviours that communicate the emotion to others and those designed to resolve the presenting situation. Perceptual and cognitive organization (attention shift), social communication, arousal of motivation, and precipitating behaviours (biologically determined as well as learned), that have the purpose of resolution of the situation, are all the adaptive functions of emotions. Because of the individual variations in arousability and learned responses, as well as the constant feedback from one aspect of emotional experience to the other, the emotional expression observed by others may be complex and variable.

Emotions allow us to communicate to others verbally, non-verbally, and behaviourally the impact events have on us. Emotions observed in others may activate empathic emotional experiences in the observer. They may allow the observer to engage in solution-focused actions without having to emotionally experience the event themselves.

The cognitive–behavioural perspective, which dominates contemporary thinking about dysfunctional emotions, views emotional responses as the products of interpretations of the psychosocial world. Anxiety is always at some level a result of perception of threat. Anger, in its various forms, is a result of a perception of attack or threatened loss. These are the two sides of the "fight or flight" mechanism. Unhappiness is about loss or threatened loss of sources of satisfaction, self-esteem, and safety. Depression is viewed as the result of beliefs, whether valid or not, that the person's psychosocial world is punishing, that their well-being is threatened, that there may not be a solution to this adversity, and that it represents personal failure. Guilt arises from blaming ourselves for the adversity of others, while joy arises from perceived success or satisfaction in meeting needs, in achievement, or affiliation.

EMOTIONS AT WORK

In the workplace, as in all aspects, emotions may serve to motivate, organize, direct, and activate behaviours, but also may be disruptive to the other appropriate work-related and social behaviours. Broadly, both positive and negative emotional states have the capacity to enhance or interfere with work-related behaviours. Success and achievement may motivate but, if it fulfils the individual's needs, prior success may mean that motivation for further success diminishes. Mild anxiety or even unhappiness may motivate for change. Significant anxiety or unhappiness that reaches the state of clinical depression may severely interfere with work and social functioning.

Emotion may also disrupt by distracting the individual from the task at hand. It may disorganize cognitive processes and behaviour, making information processing and complex behaviours ineffective. Decision making and problem solving may be interfered with either directly as the arousal disorganizes information processes, or indirectly as a result of being a distraction from the task at hand.

Emotion may precipitate other consequences, such as alcohol misuse, that interfere as secondary processes in effective functioning.

In the past, the workplace was promoted naively as an emotion-free environment with decisions being made on an unemotional rational basis only. The denial of emotional factors in the workplace is not realistic. The failure of the workplace that attempts to suppress emotion, and the realization that a positive emotion may be beneficial to work outcomes, lead to both employee-assistance programmes and teambuilding, and rewards-based work practices.

Emotional states may be communicated directly via verbal and behavioural means, inferred from facial and bodily communications, or indirectly inferred from behaviours. Irritability or risk-taking behaviours may be the indirect expression of unhappiness, while alcohol or drug abuse a communication concerning unhappiness, depression, or anxiety.

THE PRINCIPAL EMOTIONS IN THE ADULT

Adults can experience and discriminate between a large variety of complex emotional states. These emotional states arise from interactions between internal and external experiences and manifest themselves, in differing degrees, in subjective experience, physiological changes and behaviour. They may be short lived or persistent, largely dependent on internal processes or largely a response to external events. Emotional states may have a positive or negative impact or valence and may vary in intensity from mild to extremely intense. They may be appropriate or inappropriate to the situation provoking them. The appropriateness may be in terms of the situation, the intensity, or the duration.

If inappropriate to the situation or inappropriately intense or persistent, emotional states may represent a clinical problem. Most of the research on emotional states has focused on negative emotions, as in their extreme forms they are problematic because they interfere with the individual's functioning.

Perhaps surprisingly, research shows (Bradburn, 1969) happiness is not the opposite of unhappiness; in fact, they may be independent dimensions. It is not possible to feel happy and unhappy at the same time. The relationship between the positive and negative valence is an inverse relationship but only a moderately inverse relationship (Kammann & Flett, 1983). The intensity of emotions are positively related; that is, those who report feeling most intensely positive are also those who feel most intensely negative (Diener, Sandvik, & Larsen, 1985). The sources of positive feelings, while they may vary dependent on cultural situations, have been identified by Argyle (1987) as feeling associated with extroversion, education, employment, positive life events, and satisfying leisure. Negative emotional states are associated with proneness to anxiety (neuroticism), low social status, poor health, low self-esteem, being female, and stressful life events.

SATISFACTION

A number of research studies have identified a general dimension of well-being made up of a "thoughtful appraisal of quality of life as a whole, a judgement of satisfaction with life" (Argyle, 1987, p. 5). Satisfaction, like many emotional states, is a relative matter. The level of personal satisfaction is compared with past levels or with what is believed to be the experiences of others. The domains that determine satisfaction may also vary and depend upon personal priorities. Priorities may vary between domains of relationships, family, personal recognition, finances, job, health, self-esteem, and achievements.

Satisfaction is an extremely important emotion in the workplace. It is complex and may represent a combination of positive emotions. Satisfaction may be dominated by a focus on relationships (affiliation) or achievement of goals (and recognition), or by combinations of these. This means that some people in their workplace are dominated by the quality of their relationships, by their acceptance by others, or their disapproval. These workers may be gregarious in seeking out the company of others, or, alternatively, easily distressed by their apparent non-acceptance of rejection by others. Approval is a primary motivation for these individuals, either in the form of seeking the approval of others or fearing their disapproval. At the other extreme is the worker whose satisfaction is determined be their own approval for having succeeded, rather than by others' recognition of their success. These people may be relatively insensitive to others' emotions, and prone to seeking success and achievement at all costs.

HAPPINESS AND JOY

Satisfaction is one of the positive emotions humans experience. Joy and elation, excitement and interest, and contentment and comfort are other positive emotional states experienced by adults. Happiness and joy are not just the absence of unhappiness.

Positive emotions are associated with pleasures. Some pleasures deal with satisfying human needs and wants, and changing or decreasing unpleasant physical states, such as the needs for food, drink, warmth, and rest. Some pleasures involve the stimulation of pleasure centres of the brain, releasing pleasurable experiences, such as with sex and exercise (known to release endorphins). Others' pleasures are more of a social nature, affiliation, recognition, etc. Less easy to explain are the positive emotions associated with music, reading, personal achievement, and aesthetic experiences, which do not seem to reflect appetite-related nor social needs.

People seldom complain of too much joy or happiness although disinhibition and an extreme elevation in mood may be a problem for family, friends, and co-workers.

STRESS

The term "stress" is often used as though it is a description of an emotional state or even a disorder. It may be used as an apparent diagnosis; as a description of the state of psychological or physical distress; as the precipitant of sub-clinical and clinical disorders; or to describe the situations that evoke discomfort. This wide use of the term lacks precision and interferes with research and communication.

More appropriately, stress should be used to refer to the highly individualistic process whereby personally significant events are found to evoke a distressing response. The psychological and/or physiological response, not the conditions that evoke it, is more reasonably what we refer to as "stress". Even restricting the use of the term to the presence (acknowledged or otherwise) of a distressing response to personal, social, or environmental conditions, the term has a variety of uses. Stress may refer to a temporary unpleasant affect, or to a symptom of some more significant disturbance or a more clearly defined clinical syndrome (medical, psychological, or psychiatric).

"Stress" itself is a process and not strictly an emotion. The various contributors to the individual's stress response include environmental and lifestyle factors; the individual factors, including emotional reactivity, subjective thinking about problem situations, coping strategies available, self-esteem, learned responses, and the availability of social supports.

Not all stress is negative, although clinically we reserve the term for that which causes distress. As an acute response to the environment (and for some people even the repeated acute response), stress may be a motivating force to action, it may act as a useful and even sought-after stimulant to problem solving and productivity. In this way, we need not assume stress is always problematic. The concept of "eustress" has been introduced to describe the difference between this positive motivating pressure, on which some thrive, and the "distress" which we are commonly referring to in talking of the stress that appears in the clinical situation. Where the subjective distress is persistent, severe, or chronic, the activation of the ongoing sense of threat may result in a clinical syndrome, most commonly anxiety, or if the sufferer feels powerlessness to cope, a depressive disorder may be precipitated.

Where there is persistent or chronic physiological arousal, stress may result in physical damage to bodily processes unable to re-establish balance in physiological processes through homeostasis.

As a clinical problem, stress occurs when the demands being made on the person by the situation exceed, or are perceived by that individual as exceeding, their ability to cope. In other words, stress is experienced when the demands of the situation are threatening or perceived as threatening the individual (or in some situations the hyperarousal occurs because of excessive responses to information overload), or if the demands of the situation are perceived to exceed the coping mechanisms available (in reality or as a result of their beliefs and expectations about their coping abilities). It is by this process that psychological and physiological hyperarousal is experienced as the acute stress response (Lazarus & Folkman, 1984). The distressing psychological (affective) state of threat or impending threat, and the physiological impact that is distressing in the acute state, disturbs and is potentially damaging of the homeostatic functioning of bodily and psychological processes alike, particularly if repeated.

The occurrence of the stress response is highly individual. While we may agree on certain events, such as tragedies which are stress producing for almost everyone, there are a whole range of events that do not fall into this class. What may be simply problematic and challenging for one person may be threatening and highly stressful for the next. The personal relevance and availability of coping mechanisms are the key factors, again making it even more sensible to define stress by the response rather than the problematic situation. The distress response will therefore relate to individual personality characteristics and flexibility; the life experiences and life history; other ongoing problematic or challenging situations; the availability of suitable coping strategies to resolve problematic situations; the patient's confidence in putting these into effect and their ability to tolerate partial solutions to challenging situations.

"Stress", as a process, can activate the arousal of vigilance, in search of the maximum possible information to facilitate problem solving, or activate the already existing coping mechanisms to deal with the perceived situation. This enhancement of the processes to deal with the situation is a positive contribution to resolving the challenge perceived as confronting the individual. If a solution is not evident, this stress response can activate the processes necessary for escape from the perceived threat. If problem solving or escape is not seen as possible, an individual's perception of threat and/or of a lack of effective coping mechanisms to deal with the threat, may result in a level of subjective or physiological distress (often experienced as anxiety). Repeated or chronic experience of such distress may evoke a sense of powerlessness and depression.

It needs to be noted that there is a very large individual variation in the responses to the challenges of life and the perceived threat that comes from being unable to, or believing you are unable to, effectively solve the presenting problem. First, there is wide individual variation in whether a situation is perceived as problematic. Second, the existence or belief in coping strategies available varies widely. Both of these factors, plus the personal history of confronting difficult or distressing situations, alters the perception of threat as well as the perceived ability to "cope". Some have a lowered threshold for perception of threat because of their earlier experiences in childhood and early adult life. If threat is perceived, whether real or believed, there is considerable individual variation in how it affects the individual. There appears to be considerable individual variation in how the repeated arousal to this perceived or real threat affects psychological and physical health.

Psychological or physical hyperarousal, caused by this perceived imbalance between the situational demands and the coping mechanisms, leads to a wide range of subjective feelings (i.e. tension, anxiety, irritability, anger, depression, guilt, overstimulation, etc.); acute physical symptoms of stress (in the skeletomuscular, cardiovascular, respiratory, gastrointestinal and genitourinary systems); the neuropsychological effects on concentration, memory, learning and problem solving; and personal and social behaviour (including habit disorders, drug and alcohol abuse, risk-taking behaviours, gambling, and antisocial behaviours).

The individual variation, most likely the result of genetic predispositions (although it is not impossible that it has been acquired through conditioning), manifests itself by some patients responding primarily within one biological system while another patient manifests the stress response in a different manner. For some, the cardiovascular response is the acute (and most likely chronic) response, while for others it may involve primarily psychological or respiratory or muscular responses. Any combination of systems manifesting acute stress can present in the primary care setting.

FEAR AND ANXIETY

Anxiety is a normal emotion experienced at some time by virtually all humans. It represents threat or danger, whether that is perceived or a reality. Anxiety is designed to motivate the seeking of solutions to the perceived danger. In its acute form, the perception of threat to our existence, well-being, or ability to cope results in an alerting response and the "flight or fight" response.

The immediate signs of anxiety are well recognized, but there is considerable variation in how each individual experiences or expresses anxious feelings. For some, anxiety, in both its normal and abnormal forms, is represented and experienced primarily as a subjective emotional state with an internal sense of apprehension, worry, excessive alertness, poor concentration, overactive and uncontrollable thought processes, and, in the more extreme states, a sense of fear or panic. For others, the experience of anxiety is primarily present as a physical state with a sensation of tension, elevated heart rate, blood pressure, sweating, muscle tension, and gastric or urinary activity. Such signs may be accompanied by nausea, headaches, dizziness, and a plethora of physical symptoms. Alternatively, anxiety may manifest itself primarily through behaviours, such as difficulties in sitting still, excessive talking, procrastination, avoidance and distraction, and self-medicating use of alcohol or sedating drugs either illicit or prescribed. Any or all of the subjective, physical, and behavioural signs of anxiety may be present.

Clearly the distinction between normal and abnormal anxiety needs to be established. Normal anxiety serves a useful and protective function in some situations, and, through changed motivation, anxiety may be performance enhancing. On the other hand, abnormal anxiety (too intense, protracted, or attached to situations without a cause) serves no useful purpose, and is associated with an inability to function at a satisfactory level. While anxiety is common in its extreme forms, it may present as an anxiety disorder (i.e. phobia, panic, obsession, etc.).

Anxiety is often specific to a situation, as with a phobia, but it may also be general to a wide range of situations, or habitual without specific eliciting situations.

Abnormal anxiety is also far too common. The prevalence, course, and age of onset of anxiety disorders vary according to the particular disorder. Nevertheless, it has been estimated that perhaps as many as 10% of the population may experience anxiety severe enough to qualify as an anxiety disorder.

FEARS AND PHOBIAS

An estimated 5–10% of the population may be afflicted with phobias. Specific phobias are more common than agoraphobia or social phobia. A specific phobia involves fear that is triggered by the presence or anticipation of a specific object or situation. The most common fears and phobias involve inappropriate anxiety in response to heights, blood, the dentist, closed-in spaces, dogs, or spiders.

Agoraphobia is literally "a fear of the marketplace", a debilitating fear of being away from what are perceived to be safe environs. It is not a common condition, but can significantly interfere with employment and social functioning. Most commonly, safety is only experienced at home and anxiety is overwhelming when even short distances from home "safety". Often, people with agoraphobia may be unable to work because of anxiety; however, some find home and work the "safe" environments and may manage to function only within these two environs. Others with agoraphobia turn to sedating drugs or alcohol to "cope" with the "threatening" work situation.

Social anxieties are common, many people experience anxiety when they are in a social situation. They may use alcohol to facilitate the social relationship. Social anxieties commonly reach phobic proportions. These phobic responses involve persistent and excessive anxiety in one or more social or performance situations. They are particularly associated with the presence of unfamiliar people or where public scrutiny may be possible. The individual often fears the evaluation of others and humiliation. They may fear having an anxiety (or panic) attack or behaving in a way that is embarrassing or humiliating, such as shaking or blushing. The most common forms of social phobia revolve around public speaking or eating, but they can also present as a difficulty in using public toilets.

UNHAPPINESS, SADNESS, GRIEF, AND DEPRESSION

Unhappiness, sadness, and grief are common human emotions. In a significant number of people it turns to depression. Where does happiness become unhappiness? Is there neutrality in-between? What is the starting point at which unhappiness or sadness become depression and at what point does commonly labelled depressed mood become clinical depression? There is no clear delineation and yet the definition of these boundaries is essential for our understanding of the causes.

Unhappiness and sadness may be interchangeable terms, and refer either to the experience of loss or of an absence of satisfaction. We are usually unhappy when we perceive the world as not meeting our needs, or desires, or when previously experienced satisfactions are taken from us. Receiving adverse experiences also results in unhappiness, sadness, and common, as opposed to clinical, depression.

Grief is perhaps easier to specify. It is experienced as a normal emotional response to real or perceived loss (of another person, significant other, lifestyle, job, or contributor to self-esteem). When normal grieving becomes abnormal and problematic depends somewhat on cultural values and definitions. If grief is "excessive" or prolonged or inappropriate to the situation, it may be considered a clinical problem.

The signs of unhappiness and depression are well known, including a sense of dysphoria, sadness and loss. There may also be a combination of other signs including a flatness or non-reactivity of mood, little enthusiasm, energy for or interest in normally motivating situations, irritability, poor concentration, decreased interest in food and sex, disturbed sleep, weight loss or gain. Self-depreciation, guilt, self-abuse and suicidal thoughts, impulses or feelings may be less easily identified, as they may be hidden from family, friends, peers, colleagues, and workmates. Some people continue to function in one environment, while ceasing to function poorly in others. At work, unhappy and depressed persons may, for a significant period, hide their distress, while they struggle to function in other contexts, such as at home or with their hobbies or interests. Relationship difficulties, erratic behaviour, anger, alcohol, and illicit drug use may all be signs of the depressed state. Risk-taking behaviour may also represent the expression of personal distress with a lack of concern over their safety or well-being.

Depressive disorders requiring clinical treatment are common and associated with significant morbidity and mortality. Lifetime prevalence rates have been estimated from US epidemiological studies at 17%. In studies conducted elsewhere (e.g. in New Zealand) similar rates have been reported. In women, depression appears to be about twice as prevalent as it is in men, and there do not appear to be significant differences between racial groups. While the mean age of onset of depressive disorder is about 40 years, an onset between 20 and 50 years of age may occur. Furthermore, depression may be present from childhood or it may occur in old age. Depression is associated with an increased incidence of suicide. Annual suicide rates in depression are three-to-four times higher than that of other psychiatric disorders and 20 to 30 times higher than the rate for the general population.

While, on the one hand, severe depression is usually readily recognized, milder forms of the disorder are often difficult to differentiate from emotional changes associated with daily life. Bereavement, job loss, divorce, and other stresses of life, which might result in a reactive depressed mood of short duration, do not

constitute a diagnosis of depressive illness. Depressed mood of itself is not sufficient for a diagnosis of depressive disorder. It is often associated with other
emotional difficulties and clinical disorders (e.g. anxiety disorders).

Major depression is a syndrome consisting of a number of symptoms, one of
which is persistently lowered mood. Together with cognitive and vegetative
symptoms, the presence of depressed mood constitutes a diagnosis of depressive
disorder. Other features of depression can include disorganized thinking, delu-
sions, early morning wakening, decreased libido, and constipation. A family
history of depression, a previous episode of depression or of hypomania (an
excessive elevation of mood) provide additional evidence to support a diagnosis
of clinical depression. To date, there are no laboratory tests that can confirm a
suspected diagnosis of depression. Of the symptoms of depression, it is usual to
require at least three or four of the symptoms, together with either depressed
mood or loss of interest or pleasure, to be present every day for a minimum of
2 weeks before a diagnosis of clinical depression can be made. Furthermore, the
symptoms should cause significant distress or impairment in social, occupational,
or other important functions of the patient's life.

Sometimes, the first manifestations of depression are the changes in efficiency in
the workplace, poor concentration, and forgetfulness. Changes in motivation and
a lack of enjoyment of previously enjoyed activities, social withdrawal, irritability,
and, at times, risk-taking behaviours such as gambling, alcohol, or drug use are all
manifestations of unhappiness.

ANGER/RESENTMENT

Angry feelings are the other side of the "flight or fight" mechanism. Anger is an
adaptive emotion designed to activate self-protection at times of perceived attack
or threat. Anger is a defensive response to particular events and revolves around a
perceived threat to safety, well-being, self-esteem, or threatened loss of status,
possessions, or relationships of particular personal value. Intolerance, irritability,
anger, and rage are on a continuum. The normal range of angry responses include
subjective experience of anger, an increase in physiological arousal, focused attention on the provoking situation, motivated behaviour to both decrease the
aroused state and to deal with the situation to remove the perceived threat of
loss or danger.

Seldom in normal life is a threat to safety actually experienced. More likely, the
threat may be to perceived self-esteem. Interference with achievement or relationships, while not a threat to safety, may provoke angry responses. Barriers to
achievement or the recognition of achievement may provoke angry responses at
the perceived cause of the interfering barrier. Interference with relationships and
affiliation may threaten loss of the relationship, particularly in the person with

poor self-esteem for whom such a threat of loss or interference takes on enormous significance.

Anger and resentment can also be carried from one situation to another, or be expressed indirectly rather than directly to the threatening situation. Uncooperative behaviour and attitudes may reflect such an indirect expression of anger. In the workplace, inhibitory processes of what is acceptable or will be tolerated may interfere with the expression of angry feelings.

CONCLUSION

The variety of emotional responses ranges from normal reactions to the abnormally persistent, intense, or inappropriate. The boundaries between the normal and abnormal are poorly defined, as the appropriateness, duration, or intensity are open to considerable interpretation. This makes the study of both ends of the spectrum, the normal emotional response, and the clinical problem difficult. The words used in describing emotional states are also influenced by personal, educational, and cultural influences. Variable manifestations in any combination of subjective experience, physiological response, and behavioural expression makes the study of this important field difficult. Agreed definitions and standardized ratings of severity improve research endeavours, but remain based on agreements that have no external criteria to confirm them.

Emotions were developed in primitive mankind to serve adaptive functions of protection from danger or loss and nurturance of biological and social needs for the individual. Emotion is central to all aspects of human experience. Emotions and feeling states direct attention to events, thoughts or stimuli, organize perceptual and thought processes, as well as activating and motivating many, if not most, aspects of human behaviour. The central role of emotion in human functioning applies both to interpersonal (or social behaviours) and personal solitary behaviours. Emotions also serve as a means of communication within a social group, and yet the purpose served by emotions in the 21st century remains tainted by the requirements of the adaptive functions of primitive mankind. The precise nature and delineation of emotions, affects, and temperament are seldom agreed upon, the concepts varying from researcher to researcher. The lack of precise agreement on the existence of basic emotions, what they might be, the process of modification with experience, and the boundaries between normal and abnormal emotion makes their study more difficult.

REFERENCES

Abu-Lughod, L. & Lutz, C. (1992) Introduction: Emotion, discourse and the politics of everyday life. In C. Lutz & L. Abu-Lughod (Eds) *Language and the Politics of Emotion*, pp. 1–23. Cambridge, UK: Cambridge University Press.

Argyle, M. (1987) *The Psychology of Happiness*. London: Methuen.

Barrett, K.C. & Campos, J.J. (1987) Perspectives on emotional development II: A functionalist approach to emotions. In J.D. Osofsky (Ed.) *Handbook of Infant Development*, 2nd ed. New York: Wiley-Interscience.

Bradburn, N.M. (1969) *The Structure of Psychological Well-being*. Chicago: Aldine.

Davidson, R.J. (1992) Emotion and affective style: Hemispheric substrates. *Psychological Science*, **3**, 39–43.

Diener, E., Sandvik, E., & Larsen, S. (1985) Age and sex effects for emotional intensity. *Developmental Psychology* **21**, 542–546.

Ekman, P. (1994) All emotions are basic. In P. Ekman & R.J. Davidson (Eds) *The Nature of Emotion*, pp. 15–19. New York: Oxford University Press.

Ekman, P. & Davidson, R.J. (1994) *The Nature of Emotion*. New York: Oxford University Press.

Freud, S. (1920) *Beyond the Pleasure Principle*, Standard Edition **18**, pp. 3–64. London: Hogarth Press.

Izard, C.E. (1977) *Human Emotions*. New York: Plenum.

Izard, C.E. (1984) Emotion-cognition relationships and human development. In C.E. Izard, J. Kagan, & R.B. Zajonc (Eds) *Emotions, Cognition and Behavior*. New York: Cambridge University Press.

Kagan, J. (1994) On the nature of emotion. In N.A. Fox (Ed.) *The Development of Emotional Regulation: Biological and Behavioral Considerations*, Monographs of the Society for Research in Child Development Vol. 240, No. 59, pp. 7–24. Chicago: University of Chicago Press.

Kammann, R. & Flett, R. (1983) Affectometer 2: A scale to measure current level of general happiness. *Australian Journal of Psychology* **35**, 259–265.

Lazarus, R.S. & Folkman, S. (1984) *Stress, Appraisal and Coping*. New York: Springer-Verlag.

Lazarus R.S. (1991) *Emotion and Adaptation*. New York: Oxford University Press.

Panksepp, J. (1988) Posterior pituitary hormones and separation distress in chicks. Abstracts, *Society for Neuroscience*, **14**, 287.

Sroufe, L.A. (1996) *Emotional Development: The Organization of Emotional Life in the Early Years*. New York: Cambridge University Press.

Chapter 2

Emotion, mood, and temperament: similarities, differences, and a synthesis

Elizabeth K. Gray and David Watson
Department of Psychology, University of Iowa, Iowa City, USA

Emotions, moods, and temperaments clearly play important roles in our daily lives. They are crucial to our interpersonal relationships, our careers, our selves, and our interactions with the environment. Not surprisingly, therefore, these concepts are quite familiar to most psychologists and, indeed, to most people. Nevertheless, most people—and even most psychologists—actually would find it quite difficult to define them precisely and to distinguish them from one another. These concepts obviously overlap substantially, in that they all can be linked to subjectively experienced feelings, but what exactly are they, and how do they differ from another? Moreover, what implications do they have for understanding the everyday experience of people in important contexts, such as the workplace? The basic goal of this chapter is to clarify the nature of these familiar, but somewhat fuzzy, concepts. In it, we will provide a scientific analysis of these concepts and detail their importance for psychological research and for understanding daily experience. We will discuss each of these concepts in turn, relate them to each other, and then examine the interrelation among all three. We conclude by offering an overall framework to guide research and assessment in this area.

Emotions at Work. Edited by Roy Payne and Cary Cooper.
© 2001 by John Wiley & Sons, Ltd.

EMOTION

Humans are acutely aware of emotion in their life through their own direct experience. Everyone knows how it feels to be frightened at the thought of someone following you, filled with joy at the news of a birth, disgusted at the smell of sour milk, or overcome by sadness at the break-up of a romantic relationship. We are familiar with these intense feelings, as well as the concomitant thoughts and physiological changes, and our subsequent behavioral responses. However, the fundamental nature of these emotions remains somewhat mysterious. Why do we have these emotions, and what is their function in our lives? How are they organized, and how do they relate to one another?

Before we can examine these issues, we first have to define the concept of emotion itself. Although there currently is no consensually accepted view of this construct, most researchers in this area stress certain common themes in their definitions. In their textbook, for instance, Carlson and Hatfield (1992) define emotion very generally as "a genetic and acquired motivational predisposition to respond experientially, physiologically, and behaviorally to certain internal and external variables" (Carlson & Hatfield, 1992, p. 5). Similarly, Watson and Clark (1994a) define an emotion as "an organized, highly structured reaction to an event that is relevant to the needs, goals or survival of the organism"; they note further that each emotion "represents a response to specific types of events, and each gives rise to characteristic forms of adaptive behavior" (Watson & Clark, 1994a, p. 89). Finally, Levenson (1994) characterizes emotions as "short-lived psychological-physiological phenomena that represent efficient modes of adaptation to changing environmental demands" (Levenson, 1994, p. 123). On the basis of these definitions, it is clear that emotions are (1) innate, biologically hard-wired systems that (2) promote the survival of the organism by (3) facilitating efficient, adaptive responses or reactions to changing environmental circumstances.

With regard to this second aspect, all emotion theorists agree that these systems are highly adaptive and serve many purposes in our lives. One important function of emotions is to provide information (Clore, 1994). Emotions provide information to the self by way of thoughts and feelings: they guide us to take action, to approach or avoid an object or person, and they color our judgments and decisions. Emotions also can provide important information to others about our current state; facial expressions, for instance, vividly convey our current experiences to others in a highly efficient manner (e.g. Ekman, 1982). Finally, emotions provide us with information about our position in the environment and in relation to others (Levenson, 1994).

Emotions also help to shift attention and to alter associative networks in memory (Levenson, 1994). Indeed, another key function of emotion is to focus attention on a specific aspect of the environment that may require action or decision (Clark & Watson, 1994; Clore, 1994). Through this narrowing of attention, an organism can more easily determine the relevance or irrelevance of an event (Frijda, 1994). If the event is judged to be irrelevant, then no further response is likely to be necessary. In contrast, if the experience is judged to be highly relevant, it is further evaluated as either positive or negative (Nesse, 1991); once these determinations have been made, the organism is ready to propel itself into actions designed to promote its survival.

Because emotions supply information, focus attention, and signal relevance in situations, they are highly adaptive; indeed, they are essential to the survival of the organism (e.g. Clark & Watson, 1994; Frijda, 1994). They allow the organism to respond quickly, decisively, and vigorously in the face of a novel or threatening situation (Frijda, 1994). Any given emotional response may have multiple functions depending on the consequences, point of reference, and context considered (Averill, 1994). Note, moreover, that although the basic *systems* themselves are highly adaptive, this by no means suggests that all of our affective *responses* are functional and adaptive. Indeed, as we ponder the course of our daily lives, it is painfully obvious that each of us is capable of responding to situations and stimuli in dysfunctional and counterproductive ways (Clark & Watson, 1994).

Many theorists have further extended this analysis by positing specific evolutionary/adaptive functions for basic emotions such as fear, anger, disgust, and happiness. For example, it has been suggested that fear acts to protect organisms from threat or danger, anger enables them to defend themselves and their resources, disgust keeps them safely away from noxious and poisonous substances, and happiness serves as a reinforcer to motivate consummatory behavior (e.g. Frijda, 1994; Izard, 1992).

At this point, however, we must confront two ongoing controversies within the emotion literature. One important disagreement concerns which emotions should be considered "basic"; in fact, at a more fundamental level, some theorists have questioned whether some emotions truly can be considered more basic than others. Starting with the seminal work of Darwin (1872/1965), most traditional models in this area have posited the existence of a relatively small number (i.e. from seven to eleven) of discrete, fundamental emotions. Furthermore, a core set of emotions—joy, interest, surprise, fear, anger, sadness, and disgust—are recognized by most theorists and are included in almost every model (see Ekman & Davidson, 1994; Watson & Clark, 1994a).

But what makes a given emotion (such as fear or disgust) "basic" or "fundamental"? As part of his Differential Emotions Theory (DET), Izard (1992) outlined three components that are necessary to define an emotion as basic. According to Izard, a basic emotion must have (1) a distinct, innate neural substrate, (2) a unique and universally recognized facial expression, and (3) a specific subjective feeling state. In a related vein, Ekman (1992) argued that the basic emotions are those that evolved through natural selection because they serve essential biological and social functions; he offered defining criteria that were quite similar to those of Izard, positing that a basic emotion is characterized by a unique facial expression and by a highly distinctive pattern of autonomic nervous-system activity. Defined in this manner, the evidence suggests that six emotions (fear, anger, sadness, disgust, surprise, joy) perhaps can be characterized as basic or fundamental. It is noteworthy, however, that Ortony and Turner (1990) have challenged this view, arguing that we currently lack compelling evidence to establish that these emotions—or any emotions, for that matter—are more fundamental than others. They have broadly challenged the traditional model of basic emotions and have suggested that it may be impeding progress in this field.

An even more fundamental controversy concerns the specificity versus non-specificity of emotions. As we have seen, most traditional models posit the existence of seven to eleven specific emotions. Not surprisingly, researchers in this tradition emphasize the importance of assessing and analyzing each of these emotions separately. They argue, for instance, that fear and anger represent highly distinctive states that necessarily must be measured and analyzed separately from one another. In sharp contrast, however, an increasing number of researchers have called for an alternative, *dimensional* view of emotions (e.g. Russell & Feldman Barrett, 1999; Tellegen, 1985; Watson & Tellegen, 1985). In essence, dimensionalists argue that emotional experience is largely non-specific in nature; for example, self-ratings of fear and anger actually are strongly positively correlated with one another, such that these emotions are not clearly distinguished from one another in everyday life.

Although some of the earlier models argued for the existence of three major dimensions (see Watson & Tellegen, 1985), affect researchers gradually converged on a two-factor structure. Two alternative structural schemes currently play an important role in this literature. First, Russell and his colleagues have proposed a model that is based on the general dimensions of *pleasantness versus unpleasantness* and *activation* or *arousal* (see Russell, 1980; Russell & Feldman Barrett, 1999). Second, Watson, Tellegen, and their colleagues have articulated a scheme based on the broad, non-specific factors of *positive affect* and *negative affect* (see Tellegen, 1985; Watson & Tellegen, 1985; Watson, Wiese, Vaidya, & Tellegen, 1999). Because this scheme has also played a prominent role in the mood and temperament literatures, we will present it as an overall organizing framework toward the end of the chapter.

We must also emphasize that these two approaches to emotion (i.e. general dimensions versus specific, discrete emotions) are not fundamentally incompatible with one another. Indeed, as we will discuss in greater detail on pp. 36–39, our structural scheme is *hierarchical* in nature, positing the existence of both (a) general higher order dimensions and (b) more specific, lower order affective states. Thus, this structural model is encompassing and is able to subsume and synthesize all of the research in this area.

EMOTION AND MOOD

The experience of *emotion* is often confused with the closely related phenomenon of *mood*. These two constructs are similar in that they both involve subjectively

Table 2.1   Emotion, mood, and temperament: conceptual distinctions

	Emotion	Mood	Temperament
Duration	Brief, short term, spontaneous onset, lasting seconds unless stimulus persists	Long term, pervasive, changing state of mind, lasting minutes to days	Lifelong, trait-like; stable over periods of months to years
Object	Focused on a particular object or event; response system	Unfocused	Applied to pertinent situations or events
Intensity	High intensity/activation	Low to moderate intensity/activation	—
Frequency	Infrequent occurrence	Frequent, continuous, changing occurrence	Stable and organized throughout development
Function	Adaptive, to focus attention, provide information to the organism	To instigate, facilitate, sustain, and modify active engagement with the environment	Influences emotional reaction, cognition, and behavior
Type entity	Brief state	Longer term state	Trait or disposition, individual difference variable

experienced affective states that can be broadly characterized as either pleasant (positive) or unpleasant (negative); moreover, these affective states reflect the current status of the organism as it interacts with its environment (Parkinson, Totterdell, Briner, & Reynolds, 1996). Moreover, it appears that moods and emotions may contain some common components and be controlled by similar processes (Parkinson et al., 1996). Because these constructs do share many similarities, they have often been researched together under the more general label of *affect*. Affect is a more general psychological construct that refers to mental states involving evaluative feelings; that is, states in which a person feels good or bad about what is happening to them (Parkinson et al., 1996). Because of this, the conceptual/taxonomic schemes discussed in the preceding section (i.e. basic emotions, dimensions) actually are models of affect that can be applied to both moods and emotions (Parkinson et al., 1996).

Although they both are exemplars of the broader construct of affect, moods and emotions are characterized by several important differences. These differences include comprehensiveness, duration, frequency/intensity, and pattern of activation (Davidson, 1994; Ekman, 1994; Watson & Clark, 1994a). A summary of these distinctions can be found in Table 2.1. We will discuss each of these differences in turn, as they help to clarify important aspects of these concepts.

First, although moods and emotions both involve subjective feeling states, the former concept is much broader and more inclusive; that is, mood refers to *all* transient feeling states, not simply those feelings that accompany specific, discrete emotions such as fear, anger, and joy. There are at least three ways in which the concept of mood is more inclusive and encompassing than that of experienced emotion. First, moods include many important and commonly experienced feeling states that reflect milder, attenuated versions of the classic emotions. For example, people frequently report feeling annoyed and irritated (subthreshold manifestations of anger), nervous and tense (mild forms of fear), and cheerful and pleasant (attenuated versions of joy). Second, the concept of mood encompasses mixed, blended states that represent complex combinations of more basic affects. For instance, when beginning a new relationship, a person might experience mixed feelings of joy, excitement, and fear. Finally, the concept of mood subsumes important low-activation states (such as fatigue and relaxation) that signal the absence of a strong emotion.

A second basic difference is that moods typically have a much longer duration than emotions (Davidson, 1994; Ekman, 1994; Watson & Clark, 1994a). The reaction to an emotion-provoking event is designed to be strong and intense; it also, therefore, is intended to be quite brief, lasting only for a few seconds, or minutes at the most. Izard (1991), for instance, states that "expressions of emotions are brief (lasting on the average approximately 1/2 to 4 or 5 seconds)" (Izard, 1991, pp. 80–81). A mood, on the other hand, can last hours or even days. For example, whereas the full emotion of fear may last for only a few seconds or minutes, feelings of nervousness and apprehension can persist for several hours (e.g. as one anticipates giving a public speech).

A third difference is that moods are experienced more consistently and frequently than emotion. True emotional reactions occur rarely and briefly while moods fill much of our everyday life. Ekman (1994) suggests that "in at least a weak sense, moods may always be present. Moods provide the affective background, the emotional color, to all we do. Emotions can be viewed as phasic perturbations that are superimposed on this background activity" (Ekman, 1994, p. 52). Similarly, Watson and Clark (1994a) argue that "waking consciousness is experienced as a continuous *stream of affect*, such that people are always experiencing some type of mood" (Watson & Clark, 1994a, p. 90; emphasis in original). In other words, emotions refer to the intense, high-activation states that occur quite infrequently, but that exert a profound influence on us when they do occur. In contrast, mood typically involves the longer lasting, low-activation feeling states that comprise the basic stuff of our everyday experience.

Lastly, moods and emotions are influenced by somewhat different processes and stimuli. As was noted on p. 22, emotions usually are considered to be *response* systems that are activated by certain eliciting stimuli: fear is a response to threat or danger, anger is a reaction to frustration or insult, disgust is a response to a noxious substance, and so on. Emotions prompt the organism into action or decision; they therefore have an object, a specific goal. The broader implication of this view is that emotions do not arise randomly without good reason. As Izard

(1991) put it, "all emotions, as contrasted with drives, are noncyclical. One does not become interested or disgusted or ashamed two or three times a day in rhythm with ingestion, digestion, and metabolic processes" (Izard, 1991, p. 44). Moods, on the contrary, are not so much a reaction that is triggered by an event, but more a summary of our affective state (Watson & Clark, 1994a). The existing data clearly indicate that moods are strongly influenced not only by external events and experiences, but also by various internal processes; furthermore, because of these important endogenous influences, mood states *do* show strong cyclic patterns of variation, a topic we return to shortly.

MOOD

In a 1936 article, Ruckmick (cited in Wessman, 1979) noted the general lack of scientific research on mood. This neglect persisted until the 1970s; since 1980, however, there has been an explosion of interest in this topic. Similar to emotion, mood is a concept that is very frequently used, but is often misunderstood. Moods, in fact, can be especially hard to understand because they are often subtle and shift slowly with no clear beginnings or ends (Thayer, 1996).

Before turning to other issues, it is important to define this concept more precisely. Thayer (1996) characterizes mood "as a background feeling that persists over time" (Thayer, 1996, p. 5). Similarly, Watson and Clark (1994a) define mood as "a transient episode of feeling or affect" (Watson & Clark, 1994a, p. 90). Parkinson et al. (1996) argue that "mood is an undirected evaluative mental state which temporarily predisposes a person to interpret and act towards a wide variety of events in ways according to its affective content" (Parkinson et al., 1996, pp. 9–10). From these definitions, we can infer that moods typically involve feeling states of mild to moderate intensity that wax and wane gradually over time; unlike emotions, they usually cannot be linked to a specific precipitating event or experience, but rather reflect the cumulative effect of multiple inputs (including both internal endogenous processes and external events).

How do we explain the continuous presence of moods in our everyday lives? Why do we experience these feelings, and what basic functions do they perform? Similar to emotions, moods clearly serve both informational and motivational functions (Morris, 1989; Parkinson et al., 1996; Schwarz & Clore, 1983). According to Parkinson et al. (1996), moods primarily influence people to "evaluate and act toward events in particular ways" (Parkinson et al., 1996, p. 72). Moods monitor and shape our lives by playing a critical part in instigating, facilitating, sustaining, and modifying active engagement with the environment (Mayer & Gaschke, 1988; Morris, 1989; Wessman, 1979). Wessman (1979), for instance, argued that mood alters the way in which a person "appraises and becomes engaged with [one's] world" (Wessman, 1979, p. 75).

As these examples indicate, mood theorists emphasize that moods influence how people interpret and appraise the events of their lives; indeed, Ekman (1994) argues that "the primary function of moods ... is to modulate or bias cognition. Mood serves as a primary mechanism for altering information-processing priorities and for shifting modes of information processing" (Ekman, 1994, p. 52). Ekman's argument is supported by a considerable body of data indicating that cognitive and memory processes are strongly influenced by mood (Bower, 1981; Schwarz & Clore, 1983; Thayer, 1996). The evidence establishes that people are more likely to attend to—and to learn more about—events that match their current mood state; similarly, they recall information better if their current mood is congruent with the mood they experienced when they originally learned the material (Bower, 1981). Other data show that mood affects the decision-making process, judgment and reasoning tasks, and the processing of persuasive messages (Parkinson et al., 1996; Schwarz & Clore, 1983). In a related vein, Thayer (1996) argues that thoughts and moods form an interactive and integrated process. He emphasizes that moods and cognitions typically are in synchrony (i.e. congruent with one another). For instance, negative thoughts of helplessness and pessimism typically accompany negative feelings of sadness and depression; conversely, positive thoughts of confidence and optimism typically co-occur with positive feelings of excitement and enthusiasm (Thayer, 1996).

Similar to emotions, moods are primarily adaptive and promote the survival of the organism (Thayer, 1996; Watson et al., 1999). Thayer (1996) emphasizes that moods operate as messenger systems that provide important signals to the organism. At certain times, they indicate an abundance of bodily resources and a general readiness for action; at other times, they signal that energy stores are depleted and that rest and recuperation are required. Moods thus provide feedback regarding our changing levels of energy and tension. They let us know when to preserve our resources and when to act, when to be cautious, and when to invest in new projects and expenditures (Thayer, 1996).

Moods serve as filters in our lives; they are at the core of our being and influence almost every area of our lives (Thayer, 1996). In fact, moods are general summaries of our physiological and psychological functioning; unlike emotions, they reflect all the internal and external stimuli that currently affect us (Thayer, 1996; Watson & Clark, 1994a). Not surprisingly, therefore, mood fluctuations have been linked to an enormous array of variables, including daily life events, circadian rhythms, and the weather (Clark & Watson, 1988; Cunningham, 1979; Stone, 1981).

Given the range of possibilities, it is important to consider the basic classes of factors that determine the quality and level of mood (Parkinson et al., 1996). An examination of these influences can help us to understand the vicissitudes of mood. To organize and understand these potential influences, Watson and Clark (1994a) offered a conceptual scheme that classifies them into four basic categories. These broad categories include (1) *exogenous factors* (i.e. short-term external events and experiences), (2) *endogenous rhythms* (i.e. internal biological processes that give rise to recurring cycles of mood), (3) *traits and temperaments* (i.e. stable individual differences in the tendency to experience mood states), and (4) *characteristic variability* (i.e. stable individual differences in the intensity of mood experiences and in the extremity of our mood fluctuations). Other researchers have used similar classification schemes, such as distinguishing between internal versus situational factors, or between external versus personal factors (e.g. Parkinson et al., 1996). In the interest of brevity, we will restrict the current discussion to two broad categories: internal and external influences.

Countless studies have examined external situational influences on mood; the accumulating evidence clearly indicates that mood is systematically influenced by a broad range of external factors, including social interaction and stressful life events (Clark & Watson, 1988; Eckenrode, 1984; Parkinson et al., 1996; Thayer, 1996; Watson, 1988). For instance, in a study of daily mood among Japanese college students, Clark and Watson (1988) showed that social activity was highly correlated with fluctuations in positive mood (e.g. feelings of energy, enthusiasm, and cheerfulness), but not negative mood (e.g. feelings of nervousness, dissatisfaction, and irritability). This link between positive mood and social activity is quite robust, and since has been replicated by other investigators using a variety of research designs (see Berry & Hansen, 1996; Thayer, 1996). In contrast, negative mood is more strongly related to minor daily stressors, and to health problems or complaints (Clark & Watson, 1988; Eckenrode, 1984; Watson, 1988).

Other studies have examined potential environmental influences, including various aspects of the weather, and factors such as noise, odors, and crowding (Clark & Watson, 1988; Parkinson et al., 1996; Watson & Clark, 1994a). The evidence indicates that mood is affected by a number of environmental factors, such as changes in the ionization of the atmosphere (Thayer, 1996). In addition, Cunningham (1979) demonstrated that sunny days were associated with elevated levels of positive mood, as well as increases in prosocial behaviors (e.g. helping and tipping; see also Schwarz & Clore, 1983). Finally, reductions in the photoperiod (i.e. the length of the daylight hours) during the winter months have been linked to increases in depressed mood in individuals suffering from Seasonal Affective Disorder (SAD) (see Parkinson et al., 1996; Schnurr, 1989; Thayer, 1996).

In thinking about external influences on mood, it is important to consider the issue of control. Many of these external variables are controllable; for instance, people have a certain degree of control over their sleep patterns, their consumption of sugar and alcohol, and their schedule of exercise and physical activity. Other external events, however, are beyond our human limits to control. This latter type would include such factors as the weather, the changing of the seasons, and certain types of stressful life events (e.g. getting a flat tire on the way to an important appointment). This distinction between controllable and uncontrollable events is important for two related reasons. First, it has profound implications for the causal conclusions that can be legitimately drawn from mood research. In the case of uncontrollable events, causality is relatively straightforward; for instance, it is much more likely that the weather affects our mood than vice versa. In the case of controllable events, however, causality becomes much less clear. For example, does exercise lead to an improved mood, or does being in a good mood increase the likelihood of exercise?

Second, controllable events play a key role in *mood regulation,* a process that recently has attracted considerable interest among mood researchers (e.g. Parkinson et al., 1996; Thayer, 1996). People are not simply passive observers of their moods; rather, they can take an active role in changing their moods by employing some type of mood-regulation strategy. For instance, a person may be able to self-regulate his or her mood by modifying behaviors such as sleep patterns or drug intake, or by actively engaging in some mood-altering activity (e.g. exercise, a sugar snack). Sometimes these strategies will fail, but at other times they may be quite effective; indeed, something as simple as a 10-minute brisk walk or a short nap may help us to salvage a terrible day (Thayer, 1996). Current formulations emphasize that mood regulation involves two basic steps: (1) the initial evaluation of mood and (2) a deliberate or active effort to change mood (Parkinson et al., 1996). The first step involves being consciously aware of our current mood state, which leads to the recognition that change is desirable. The second step requires the selection and implementation of a mood-regulation strategy to induce a more desirable state (Parkinson et al., 1996). Numerous strategies have been suggested for mood regulation, including thinking pleasant thoughts, relaxation techniques, exercise, listening to music, and the use of stimulants such as caffeine (Parkinson et al., 1996; Thayer, 1996).

The second broad category of mood factors includes internal, biological influences. Some of the most commonly researched internal influences are (1) physiological reactions, (2) circadian rhythms, and (3) the menstrual cycle in women; we will discuss each of these influences briefly. Most of this research, still in its early stages, is correlational; it is still too early to be able to theorize about causal links or direct cause and effect relationships (Parkinson et al., 1996).

As we have seen, mood serves as a general summary of a person's current state, so it therefore makes sense that it is influenced by variables (i.e. exercise, food, drugs, and sleep) that directly influence our internal biological condition (Hendrick & Lilly, 1970; Thayer, 1996). The evidence regarding exercise is especially clear and consistent: moderate exercise has been shown to both reduce negative mood (e.g. feelings of tension) and to enhance positive mood (e.g. feelings of energy and enthusiasm) (Clark & Watson, 1988; Thayer, 1996; Watson, 1988). Conversely, reductions in the quantity and/or quality of sleep are associated with increased tiredness and substantial decreases in positive mood (Thayer, 1996). Finally, the effects of food are quite complex and difficult to summarize briefly; for example, a sugar snack has been shown to produce an initial increase in positive mood, which then is followed by a rapid decline (Thayer, 1996).

Second, moods reflect the influence of endogenous circadian rhythms. More specifically, positive moods show a robust and well-defined circadian cycle over the course of the day. Positive-mood levels are quite low upon awakening; they then rise throughout the morning and remain elevated throughout the rest of the day, before declining again in the evening (Clark, Watson, & Leeka, 1989; Watson

& Clark, 1994a; Watson et al., 1999). Moreover, this cyclic variation in positive mood has been linked to two endogenous rhythms; one rhythm regulates body temperature, whereas the other controls the sleep–wake cycle (Watson et al., 1999). Desynchronization of these rhythms—as seen, for instance, in response to shift work or severe sleep deprivation—may lead to significant disturbances in mood (Bonnet, 1985; Parkinson et al., 1996; Scott, 1994).

Third, research on the menstrual cycle has been inconclusive. Strong mood effects have been attributed to this cycle, both in the popular media and in clinical lore; indeed, many women believe that it exerts a powerful influence on their mood (Thayer, 1996; Watson & Clark, 1994b). Nevertheless, the empirical data are surprisingly varied and inconsistent. On the positive side, Schnurr (1989) cites evidence for an increase in negative affect in the luteal phase prior to menstruation; in addition, Thayer (1996) reports a finding of higher negative affect during menstruation. On the negative side, however, McFarland, Ross and DeCourville (1989) found no systematic changes in mood across the various phases of the cycle. McFarlane, Martin and Williams (1988) reported that women who were taking oral contraceptives experienced a less pleasant mood during the menstrual and follicular phases of the cycle, but that normally cycling women showed no systematic menstrual effect. Finally, Watson and Clark (1994a) report relatively modest menstrual effects in most women.

Innate individual differences in temperament represent another potentially important biological influence on mood. This is perhaps the most researched area of mood influence; in fact, personality variables generally are considered to be the best predictors of mood (Parkinson et al., 1996; Watson & Clark, 1992; Watson et al., 1999). In particular, positive and negative affect show strong and robust correlations with extroversion/negative affectivity and neuroticism/negative affectivity, respectively (e.g. Diener, Smith, & Fujita, 1995; Watson & Clark, 1992; Watson et al., 1999). We now consider temperament—and its relation to mood—in greater detail.

MOOD AND TEMPERAMENT

Similar to mood and emotion, the concepts of mood and temperament show both important similarities and differences (see Table 2.1 for a comparison of the three constructs). As noted on p. 21, mood and temperament are similar in the sense that they both have subjectively experienced feelings as a centrally defining component. Beyond that, however, they differ in at least three related ways: the state/trait dimension, duration, and organization/stability (Goldsmith, 1994).

The state/trait distinction is probably the most basic and simple difference between mood and temperament. Mood reflects our current state of mind, whereas a temperament displays the basic characteristics of a trait. A state is a temporary, situational response that is easily changed and is highly reactive to environmental influence; Tellegen (1985) defines a state as a "comparatively short-lived process ... manifested as short-term intra-individual fluctuations" (Tellegen, 1985, p. 684). Similarly, Lazarus (1994) asserts that an affective state "usually refers to a transient reaction to specific kinds of adaptational encounters" (Lazarus, 1994, p. 79). In contrast, a trait is a dispositional construct that reflects more permanent and stable aspects of the self (Lazarus, 1994); Tellegen (1985) describes a trait as a "durable disposition ... that reflect[s] individual differences" (Tellegen, 1985, p. 684). Thus, a mood reflects a person's current frame of mind in the immediate present, whereas a temperament represents his or her typical reaction. The distinction between a mood and a temperament perhaps was best expressed by the great Roman orator Cicero (cited and translated by Eysenck, 1983), who stated in his *Tusculan Disputations* that:

> some men are prone to fear, others to another disorder, and consequently we can talk in some cases of an anxious temper, and hence of anxious people, but in other cases of irascibility, which is quite different from anger. It is one thing to be irascible, quite another thing to be angry, just as an anxious temper is different from feeling anxiety. Not all men who are sometimes anxious are of an anxious temperament, nor are those who have an anxious temperament always feeling anxious.
>
> (Eysenck, 1983, p. 114)

This state/trait distinction clearly suggests another key difference between mood and temperament, namely, duration. Because moods are state-like experiences, they are situational in nature and, therefore, are temporary. Moods, although longer in duration than emotions, still are relatively short-term experiences, typically lasting for no more than a few hours or days. In contrast, because it is trait-like, a temperament is a lifelong disposition that shows substantial stability over years, even decades. Indeed, traditional models in this area emphasize that temperaments are at least partially heritable and already are present at birth (Goldsmith, 1994; Watson & Clark, 1994b).

Finally, temperament reflects a more organized and stable structure than mood. Temperament is reliable and recurring, whereas mood is evanescent and ever-changing. Temperament as a stable structure becomes firmly established and subsequently influences emotion, thinking, and behavior in an organized and consistent way (Goldsmith, 1994; Watson & Clark, 1994b; Watson & Walker, 1996). In contrast, moods reflect more flexible systems that are constantly being influenced by the internal and external factors discussed earlier.

TEMPERAMENT

As was the case with emotion and mood, the concept of temperament has proven difficult to define precisely. However, although specific definitions have varied considerably across theorists, there does appear to be some general consensus on the criteria that characterize temperament (see Strelau, 1998). As noted by Strelau (1998), the most common features in defining this concept are that temperament: (1) refers to behavioral characteristics on which individuals differ systematically; (2) is relatively stable and is characterized by cross-situational consistency; (3) has a biological basis, and (4) refers mainly to formal characteristics of behavior or reactions (e.g. intensity, energy, strength). Davidson and Ekman (1994) offer a working definition of temperament, proposing that it reflects "early dispositional differences that are associated with emotional reactivity" (Davidson and Ekman, 1994, p. 95). Rothbart and Ahadi (1994) offer an overlapping conceptualization, defining temperament as "constitutionally based individual differences in reactivity and self-regulation, influenced over time by heredity, maturation, and experience" (Rothbart and Ahadi, 1994, p. 55).

Although the terms "temperament" and "personality" are sometimes used interchangeably, they clearly are distinguishable concepts. Temperament is similar to the concept of personality in that both involve stable, trait-like characteristics. Personality traits, however, are not necessarily biologically based or heritable; they may reflect biological influences, environmental factors, or some combination of the two. In contrast, temperament is a development construct that is based on the assumption that these individual differences are at least partly heritable and present at birth (Buss & Plomin, 1984; Rothbart & Bates, 1998; Strelau, 1998; Watson & Clark, 1994b). Temperaments therefore are restricted to biologically based dispositions, such as the basic emotional traits of positive and negative affectivity (Buss & Plomin, 1984; Watson & Clark, 1994b); put differently, temperaments are the elementary and fundamental traits that influence the subsequent development of broader individual differences in personality (Caspi, 1998; Strelau, 1998).

In addition, Rothbart and Bates (1998) have noted that temperament can be further distinguished from personality in that the latter encompasses individual differences in skills, habits, and social perceptions of self and others, which are influenced by temperament but are best viewed as separable processes. Ultimately, the domain of personality traits is much broader, and goes far beyond temperamental characteristics in scope.

Nevertheless, the general traits of personality—most notably, those comprising the "Big Three" and "Big Five" models—do show strong and consistent relations with temperamental constructs; indeed, several of these traits meet the biological and genetic criteria that define temperaments (Clark & Watson, 1999). Specifically, it is now generally accepted that the two traits common to the Big Three and Big Five models—extroversion and neuroticism—essentially represent dimensions of temperament (see Clark & Watson, 1999; Watson & Clark, 1992). The evidence for the other traits is less definitive, but a growing body of research suggests that the dimension of disinhibition versus constraint in the Big Three—as well as the corresponding traits of agreeableness and conscientiousness in the Big Five—also can be viewed as primarily temperamental dimensions (Clark & Watson, 1999; Costa & McCrae, 1992; Strelau, 1998). In fact, of the basic traits comprising these general structural models, only openness may not represent a temperament.

Four types of evidence support the claim that traits such as extroversion and neuroticism represent biologically based dimensions of temperament (for a general discussion, see Strelau, 1998). First, twin and adoption studies have established that individual differences on these dimensions are strongly heritable (Caspi, 1998; Clark & Watson, 1999; Rothbart & Bates, 1998). Second, these traits have shown universality across cultures (Costa & McCrae, 1992; McCrae & Costa, 1997). Third, individual differences on these dimensions arise very early in life, for reasons that cannot be explained entirely by environmental factors (Buss & Plomin, 1984). Fourth, these traits show impressive levels of stability across development (Clark & Watson, 1999; Derryberry & Reed, 1994; Strelau, 1998).

Temperament is often measured and studied in young children, and the concept plays an important role in the developmental literature. This focus is unsurprising, because temperamental dimensions clearly have crucial implications for personality development (Rothbart & Ahadi, 1994). Empirical studies of temperament in infancy and childhood have identified numerous dimensions of temperament, including positive and negative affectivity, activity level, effortful control, persistence, and soothability (Rothbart & Ahadi, 1994; Rothbart & Bates, 1998). It is noteworthy that these dimensions define a factor structure that is remarkably similar to those identified in adult studies of temperament and personality (Clark & Watson, 1999; Rothbart & Ahadi, 1994). For instance, Digman and associates have replicated the Big Five structure in a series of studies in which teachers rated the characteristics of elementary-school children (Digman, 1994, 1997). Similarly, studies of the Children's Behavior Questionnaire (Rothbart & Ahadi, 1994) consistently have identified three higher order factors that closely resemble the Big Three (Clark & Watson, 1999; Rothbart & Ahadi, 1994).

When identified early in life, these temperament variables also tell us much about an individual in later years. Temperamental variables assessed in childhood have been shown to predict personality traits in young adulthood (Caspi & Silva, 1995); interpersonal functioning in adults (Newman, Caspi, Moffitt & Silva, 1997); the development of attachment styles; and depressive mood, drug use and alcohol abuse in adulthood (Rothbart & Ahadi, 1994). Temperament shows stability through development (Derryberry & Reed, 1994) and is considered to be the origin of personality (Rothbart & Bates, 1998). In this regard, Caspi (1998) has outlined six mechanisms that guide the process of elaboration from early temperament to adult personality (Caspi, 1998). These mechanisms—learning process, environmental elicitation, environmental construal, social and temporal comparisons, environmental selection, and environmental manipulation—occur as part of the ongoing interaction between individual and environment over the course of development (Caspi, 1998).

As with emotion and mood, the construct of temperament also raises questions about importance and function. The answer here is not as simple, for the range of research is much greater; in fact, the functional roles that are assigned to temperament appear to differ somewhat across the child-versus-adult literatures (Strelau, 1998). In childhood, the significance of temperament primarily is expressed in social interaction (Strelau, 1998). Thus, temperament is seen as important in infant–caregiver interactions, in schooling, and in susceptibility to behavior disorders (Buss & Plomin, 1984; Rothbart & Ahadi, 1994). For adults, temperament is viewed as exerting a powerful influence across a much broader range of contexts, including work and occupational functioning, drug and alcohol use, academic performance, sexuality, interpersonal relationships, life satisfaction, health, and in coping with stress (Clark & Watson, 1999; Newman et al., 1997; Strelau, 1998). In general, the functional significance of temperament is apparent "when the individual is confronted with difficult situations and extreme demands" (Strelau, 1998, p. 336).

Unlike emotion and mood—which have received serious scientific attention only recently—temperament has been studied and theorized about since ancient Greece (4th century BC) (Clark & Watson, 1999; Strelau, 1998). The first real model of temperament was the theory of four humors developed by Hippocrates (see Clark & Watson, 1999; Strelau, 1998). In its original form, the theory posited four basic fluids, or humors, within the body. The relative proportions of these fluids—black bile, yellow bile, blood, and phlegm—determined the health and vitality of the individual (Strelau, 1998). Extending this view, Galen later proposed that a predominance of one of the humors resulted in a characteristic emotional style or temperament which formed the core, respectively, of four basic personality types (indeed, the word *temperament* derives from the Latin "to blend", so that differences in the blend of humors were equated with differences in temperament; Digman, 1994). The *sanguine* or cheerful, active temperament reflected an excess of blood; the *melancholic* or gloomy temperament reflected an excess of black bile; *choleric* or angry, violent types had an excess of yellow bile; and an excess of phlegm was associated with the *phlegmatic* or calm, passive temperament.

This early theory was followed by numerous theories of temperament by many well-known early psychologists, anthropologists, and philosophers including Immanuel Kant, Wilhelm Wundt, Carl Gustav Jung, Ivan Pavlov, and William Sheldon (Strelau, 1998). It is humbling to admit, therefore, that contemporary psychology has come full circle and rediscovered the wisdom of this ancient taxonomic scheme. Indeed, the Greek observation that there were four main temperaments maps remarkably well onto the four quadrants that emerge from crossing the Big Two personality dimensions—neuroticism (versus emotional stability) and extroversion—that are common to the Big Three and Big Five models. Thus, the stable extrovert is sanguine, the neurotic extrovert is choleric, the neurotic introvert is melancholic, and the stable introvert is phlegmatic (Eysenck & Eysenck, 1975). These two dimensions are found in all major models of temperament and personality and clearly comprise a basic organizing scheme for research in this area.

EMOTION, MOOD, AND TEMPERAMENT: AN OVERALL FRAMEWORK OF AFFECT

Emotions, mood, and temperament are related—but distinct—concepts. We have reviewed the nature of these interrelations by examining each concept, both individually and in comparison with the others. We now will provide an overall synthesis of this domain by presenting a robust and comprehensive structural framework that encompasses all of them.

As we have seen (p. 25), mood and emotion both involve subjectively experienced feeling states; accordingly, they often have been lumped together under the broader label of affect (Parkinson et al., 1996; Watson & Tellegen, 1985). These two research traditions differ, however, in that emotion theorists typically have emphasized the importance of specific, discrete emotions, whereas mood theorists have focused primarily on two broad, non-specific dimensions. As noted earlier, the most prominent dimensional scheme is based on the general factors of negative affect (i.e. the extent to which a person is non-specifically experiencing aversive states such as fear, sadness, anger, and guilt) and positive affect (i.e. the extent to which someone is non-specifically experiencing pleasant states such as cheerfulness, enthusiasm, confidence, and alertness). These two dimensions are quite robust, and consistently have emerged as general factors in analyses of self-rated mood (Diener et al., 1995; Mayer & Gaschke, 1988; Meyer & Shack, 1989; Watson & Clark, 1997; Watson & Tellegen, 1985).

One notable strength of this two-dimensional scheme is that it can easily be expanded into a more elaborate hierarchical model that includes both general and specific affects (see Watson & Clark, 1997; Watson & Tellegen, 1985; Watson et al., 1999); that is, each of the higher order dimensions can be decomposed into several correlated—yet ultimately distinct—specific affective states. Thus, the general negative-affect dimension can be decomposed into discrete negative emotions such as fear, anger, and sadness, whereas the broad positive-affect dimension can be subdivided into specific positive emotions, such as cheerfulness, confidence, and attentiveness. In this simple two-level model, the higher order level reflects the overall *valence* of the affects (i.e. whether they represent negative or positive states). In contrast, the lower level of the hierarchy reflects the specific *content* of the mood descriptors (i.e. the unique, distinctive qualities of each specific type of affect).

This hierarchical scheme neatly organizes the traditional foci of the emotion (i.e. the discrete affects) and mood (i.e. the two non-specific dimensions) paradigm into a single structural framework. It is noteworthy, moreover, that this same basic structure has been identified in ratings of both short-term mood states and longer term affective traits (e.g. Clark & Watson, 1999; Watson & Clark, 1992, 1994a; Watson et al., 1999). In other words, this same basic structure also characterizes the affective core of temperament. This suggests, in turn, that this structural framework—centered around the general dimensions of negative and positive affect—can synthesize the concepts of emotion, mood, and temperament into a single overall conceptual/analytic scheme.

Figure 2.1 offers a schematic representation of this integrated model of emotion, mood, and temperament. As noted on p. 36, the valence dimension occupies the highest level of the hierarchy; at the next level, it is subdivided into the separable and distinctive dimensions of negative affect/temperament and positive affect/temperament, which have long been the focus of the mood and temperament literatures. Finally the discrete emotions, the central concern of emotion theorists, sit at the base of the hierarchy. Figure 2.1 further extends this model by suggesting parallel concepts from the mood and temperament literatures that correspond to each of these basic emotions.

This argument is further supported by extensive data establishing strong and systematic links between mood and emotion, on the one hand, and temperament, on the other. Specifically, as noted on p. 31, individual differences in negative affect are strongly correlated with neuroticism, but are more weakly related to extroversion; conversely, individual differences in positive affect are more strongly related to extroversion than to neuroticism (Berenbaum & Williams, 1995; Costa & McCrae, 1988; Diener & Emmons, 1984; Diener et al., 1995; Larsen & Ketelaar, 1991; Meyer & Shack, 1989; Watson, 1988; Watson & Clark, 1992). For instance, across combined samples with an overall N of 4,457, Watson et al. (1999) obtained a correlation of 0.58 between neuroticism and trait negative affect, and a correlation of 0.51 between extroversion and trait positive affect. Thus, neuroticism/negative affectivity and extroversion/positive affectivity represent the essential starting points for any comprehensive model of emotion, mood, and temperament.

Before leaving this topic, we must address one unresolved issue. As noted on p. 24, two alternative two-dimensional schemes currently play a prominent role in the emotion literature: One focuses on positive and negative affect, whereas the other is based on the general dimensions of pleasantness and activation (Russell, 1980; Russell & Feldman Barrett, 1999). Can this pleasantness/activation scheme also be synthesized into our overall framework?

Yes, it can. As is discussed by Watson et al. (1999; see also Russell & Feldman Barrett, 1999), these dimensions can all be put into a single two-factor space. More specifically, they can be organized into a circumplex model in which affect descriptors are systematically arranged around the perimeter of a circle. In essence, this affect circumplex contains four bipolar dimensions (pleasantness, positive affect, activation, negative affect) that are spaced 45° apart.

This circumplex model was originally outlined by Russell (1980), and later modified by Watson and Tellegen (1985). Since its introduction, it has exerted a dominant influence on the mood literature. It is important to note, moreover, that key aspects of this circumplex are well established and clearly reflect robust properties of moods and emotions (see Watson et al., 1999). Nevertheless, it has also become quite clear that the circumplex does have a few flaws, and that it actually fails to fit the data well (see Watson et al., 1999, for a review of problems with the model). In response to these problems, Tellegen, Watson,

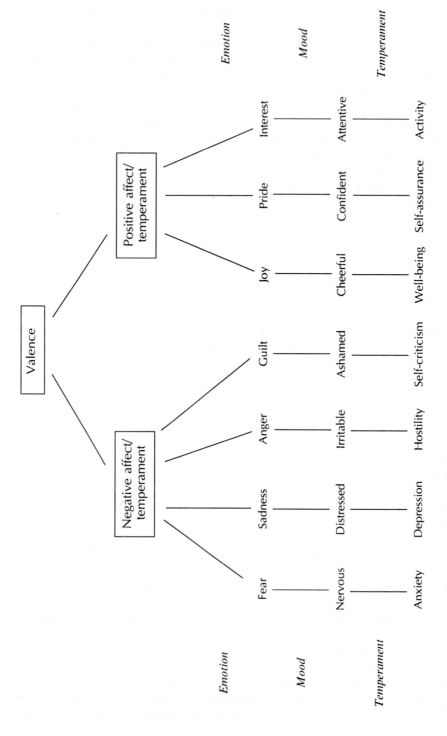

Figure 2.1 An overall framework for the structure of affect: emotion, mood, and temperament

and Clark (1999) recently presented an expanded, three-level hierarchical scheme that retains the basic features of the original model but allows for a better fit for the data. This expanded model is quite similar to the two-level hierarchical model discussed on p. 37; in fact, the only major difference is that a superordinate bipolar dimension of pleasantness (i.e. feeling cheerful and happy) versus unpleasantness (i.e. feeling sad and gloomy) sits at the apex of the hierarchy at a level above positive and negative affect. The addition of this third level improves the fit of the model, in part, by modeling the low-to-moderate correlations that typically are observed between measures of positive and negative affect (see Tellegen et al., 1999; Watson et al., 1999).

This expanded, three-level hierarchical scheme provides an elegant synthesis of the mood, emotion, and temperament literatures; it also subsumes both of the major dimensional models that currently are prominent within the mood literature. We therefore offer it as a general framework for theory and assessment to guide future research in this area.

REFERENCES

Averill, J.R. (1994). Emotions are many splendored things. In P. Ekman & R.J. Davidson (Eds) *The Nature of Emotion: Fundamental Questions*, pp. 99–102. New York: Oxford University Press.

Berenbaum, H. & Williams, M. (1995) Personality and emotional reactivity. *Journal of Research in Personality*, **29**, 24–34.

Berry, D.S. & Hansen, J.S. (1996) Positive affect, negative affect, and social interaction. *Journal of Personality and Social Psychology*, **71**, 796–809.

Bonnet, M.H. (1985) Effect of sleep disruption on sleep, performance, and mood. *Sleep*, **8**, 11–19.

Bower, G.H. (1981) Mood and memory. *American Psychologist*, **36**, 129–148.

Buss, A.H. & Plomin, R. (1984) *Temperament: Early Developing Personality Traits.* Hillsdale, NJ: Lawrence Erlbaum Associates.

Carlson, J.G. & Hatfield, E. (1992) *Psychology of Emotion.* Fort Worth, TX: Harcourt Brace Jovanovich College Publishers.

Caspi, A. (1998) Personality development across the life course. In W. Damon (Series Ed.) & N. Eisenberg (Volume Ed.) *Handbook of Child Psychology*, Vol. 3, *Social, Emotional and Personality Development*, 5th ed., pp. 311–388. New York: Wiley.

Caspi, A. & Silva, P.A. (1995) Temperamental qualities at age three predict personality traits in young adulthood: Longitudinal evidence form a birth cohort. *Child Development*, **66**, 486–498.

Clark, L.A. & Watson, D. (1988) Mood and the mundane: Relations between daily life events and self-reported mood. *Journal of Personality and Social Psychology*, **54**, 296–308.

Clark, L.A. & Watson, D. (1994) Distinguishing functional from dysfunctional affective responses. In P. Ekman & R.J. Davidson (Eds) *The Nature of Emotion: Fundamental Questions*, pp. 131–136. New York: Oxford University Press.

Clark, L.A. & Watson, D. (1999) Temperament: A new paradigm for trait psychology. In L.A. Pervin and O.P. John (Eds) *Handbook of Personality*, 2nd ed., pp. 399–423. New York: Guilford Press.

Clark, L.A., Watson, D., & Leeka, J. (1989) Diurnal variation in the positive affects. *Motivation and Emotion*. **13**, 205–234.

Clore, G.C. (1994) Why emotions are felt. In P. Ekman & R.J. Davidson (Eds) *The Nature of Emotion: Fundamental Questions*, pp. 103–111. New York: Oxford University Press.

Costa, P.T., Jr & McCrae, R.R. (1988) Personality in adulthood: A six-year longitudinal study of self-reports and spouse ratings on the NEO personality inventory. *Journal of Personality and Social Psychology*, **54**, 853–863.

Costa, P.T., Jr & McCrae, R.R. (1992) Four ways five factors are basic. *Personality and Individual Differences*, **13**, 653–665.

Cunningham, M.R. (1979) Weather, mood and helping behavior: Quasi experiments with the sunshine samaritan. *Journal of Personality and Social Psychology*, **37**, 1947–1956.

Darwin, C.R. (1965) *The Expression of the Emotions in Man and Animals*. Chicago: University of Chicago Press. (Original work published 1872.)

Davidson, R.J. (1994) On emotion, mood, and related affective constructs. In P. Ekman & R.J. Davidson (Eds) *The Nature of Emotion: Fundamental Questions*, pp. 51–55. New York: Oxford University Press.

Davidson, R.J. & Ekman, P. (1994) Afterword: How are emotions distinguished from moods, temperament and other related affective constructs? In P. Ekman & R.J. Davidson (Eds) *The Nature of Emotion: Fundamental Questions*, pp. 94–96. New York: Oxford University Press.

Derryberry, D. & Reed, M.A. (1994) Temperament and the self-organization of personality. *Development and Psychopathology*, **6**, 635–676.

Diener, E. & Emmons, R.A. (1984) The independence of positive and negative affect. *Journal of Personality and Social Psychology*, **47**, 1105–1117.

Diener, E., Smith, H., & Fujita, F. (1995) The personality structure of affect. *Journal of Personality and Social Psychology*, **69**, 130–141.

Digman, J.M. (1994). Child personality and temperament: Does the five-factor model embrace both domains? In C.F. Halverson, G.A. Kohnstamm, & R.P. Martin (Eds) *The Developing Structure of Temperament and Personality from Infancy to Adulthood*, pp. 323–338. Hillsdale, NJ: Lawrence Erlbaum Associates.

Digman, J.M. (1997) Higher-order factors of the Big Five. *Journal of Personality and Social Psychology*, **73**, 1246–1256.

Eckenrode, J. (1984) Impact of chronic and acute stressors on daily reports of mood. *Journal of Personality and Social Psychology*, **46**, 907–918.

Ekman, P. (1982) *Emotion in the Human Face*, 2nd ed. Cambridge, UK: Cambridge University Press.

Ekman, P. (1992) Are there basic emotions? *Psychological Review*, **99**, 550–553.

Ekman, P. (1994) Moods, emotions, and traits. In P. Ekman & R.J. Davidson (Eds) *The Nature of Emotion: Fundamental Questions*, pp. 56–58. New York: Oxford University Press.

Ekman, P. & Davidson, R.J. (Eds) (1994) *The Nature of Emotion: Fundamental Questions*. New York: Oxford University Press.

Eysenck, H.J. (1983) Cicero and the state-trait theory of anxiety: Another case of delayed recognition. *American Psychologist*. **38**, 114–115.

Eysenck, H.J. & Eysenck, S.B.G. (1975) *Manual of the Eysenck Personality Questionnaire*. San Diego, CA: Educational and Industrial Testing Service.

Frijda, N.H. (1994) Emotions are functional, most of the time. In P. Ekman & R.J. Davidson (Eds) *The Nature of Emotion: Fundamental Questions*, pp. 112–122. New York: Oxford University Press.

Goldsmith, H.H. (1994) Parsing the emotional domain from a developmental perspective. In P. Ekman & R.J. Davidson (Eds) *The Nature of Emotion: Fundamental Questions*, pp. 68–73. New York: Oxford University Press.

Hendrick, C. & Lilly, R.S. (1970) The structure of mood: A comparison between sleep deprivation and normal wakefulness conditions. *Journal of Personality*, **38**, 453–465.

Izard, C.E. (1991) *The Psychology of Emotions*. New York: Plenum Press.

Izard, C.E. (1992) Basic emotions, relations among emotions, and emotion-cognition relations. *Psychological Review*, **99**, 561–565.

Larsen, R.J. & Ketelaar, T. (1991) Personality and susceptibility to positive and negative emotional states. *Journal of Personality and Social Psychology*, **61**, 132–140.

Lazarus, R. (1994) The stable and unstable in emotion. In P. Ekman & R.J. Davidson, (Eds) *The Nature of Emotion: Fundamental Questions*, pp. 79–85. New York: Oxford University Press.

Levenson, R.W. (1994) Human emotion: A functional view. In P. Ekman & R.J. Davidson (Eds) *The Nature of Emotion: Fundamental Questions*, pp. 123–126. New York: Oxford University Press.

Mayer, J.D. & Gaschke, Y.N. (1988) The experience and meta-experience of mood. *Journal of Personality and Social Psychology*, **55**, 102–111.

McCrae, R.R. & Costa, P.T., Jr (1997) Personality trait structure as a human universal. *American Psychologist*, **52**, 509–516.

McFarland, C., Ross, M., & DeCourville, N. (1989) Women's theories of menstruation and biases in recall of menstrual symptoms. *Journal of Personality and Social Psychology*, **57**, 522–531.

McFarlane, J., Martin, C.L., & Williams, T.M. (1988) Mood fluctuations: Women versus men and menstrual versus other cycles. *Psychology of Women Quarterly*, **12**, 201–223.

Meyer, G.J. & Shack, J.R. (1989) Structural convergence of mood and personality: Evidence for old and new directions. *Journal of Personality and Social Psychology*, **57**, 691–706.

Morris, W.N. (1989) *Mood: The Frame of Mind*. New York: Springer-Verlag.

Nesse, R.M. (1991, November/December) What good is feeling bad? The evolutionary benefits of psychic pain. *The Sciences*, pp. 30–37.

Newman, D.L., Caspi, A., Moffitt, T.E., & Silva, P.A. (1997) Antecedents of adult interpersonal functioning: Effects of individual differences in age 3 temperament. *Developmental Psychology*, **33**, 206–217.

Ortony, A. & Turner, T.J. (1990) What's basic about basic emotions? *Psychological Review*, **97**, 315–331.

Parkinson, B., Totterdell, P., Briner, R.B., & Reynolds, S. (1996) *Changing Moods: The Psychology of Mood and Mood Regulation*. London: Addison Wesley Longman.

Rothbart, M.K. & Ahadi, S.A. (1994) Temperament and the development of personality. *Journal of Abnormal Psychology*, **103**, 55–66.

Rothbart, M.K. & Bates, J.E. (1998) Temperament. In W. Damon (Series Ed.) & N. Eisenberg (Volume Ed.) *Handbook of Child Psychology*, Vol. 3, *Social, Emotional and Personality Development*, 5th ed., pp. 105–119. New York: Wiley.

Russell, J.A. (1980) A circumplex model of affect. *Journal of Personality and Social Psychology*, **39**, 1161–1178.

Russell, J.A. & Feldman Barrett, L. (1999) Core affect, prototypical emotional episodes, and other things called *emotion*: Dissecting the elephant. *Journal of Personality and Social Psychology*, **76**, 805–819.

Schnurr, P.P. (1989) Endogenous factors associated with mood. In W.N. Morris (Ed.) *Mood: The Frame of Mind*, pp. 35–69. New York: Springer-Verlag.

Schwarz, N. & Clore, G.L. (1983) Mood, misattribution, and judgments of well-being: Informative and directive functions of affective states. *Journal of Personality and Social Psychology*, **45**, 513–523.

Scott, A.J. (1994) Chronobiological considerations in shiftworker sleep and performance and shiftwork scheduling. *Human Performance*, **7**, 207–233.

Strelau, J. (1998) *Temperament: A Psychological Perspective*. New York: Plenum Press.

Stone, A.A. (1981) The association between perceptions of daily experiences and self- and spouse-rated mood. *Journal of Research in Personality*, **15**, 510–522.

Tellegen, A. (1985). Structures of mood and personality and their relevance to assessing anxiety, with an emphasis on self-report. In A.H. Tuma & J.D. Maser (Eds) *Anxiety and the Anxiety Disorders*. Hillsdale, NJ: Lawrence Erlbaum Associates.

Tellegen, A., Watson, D., & Clark, L.A. (1999) On the dimensional and hierarchical nature of affect. *Psychological Science*, **10**, 297–303.

Thayer, R.E. (1996) *The Origin of Everyday Moods: Managing Energy, Tension and Stress*. New York: Oxford University Press.

Watson, D. (1988) Intraindividual and interindividual analyses of positive and negative affect: Their relation to health complaints, perceived stress, and daily activities. *Journal of Personality and Social Psychology*, **54**, 1020–1030.

Watson, D. & Clark, L.A. (1992) On traits and temperament: General and specific factors of emotional experience and their relation to the five factor model. *Journal of Personality*, **60**, 441–476.

Watson, D. & Clark, L.A. (1994a) Emotions, moods, traits, and temperament: Conceptual distinctions and empirical findings. In P. Ekman & R.J. Davidson (Eds) *The Nature of Emotion: Fundamental Questions*, pp. 89–93. New York: Oxford University Press.

Watson, D. & Clark, L.A. (1994b) The vicissitudes of mood: A schematic model. In P. Ekman & R.J. Davidson (Eds) *The Nature of Emotion: Fundamental Questions*, pp. 400–405. New York: Oxford University Press.

Watson, D. & Clark, L.A. (1997) Measurement and mismeasurement of mood: Recurrent and emergent issues. *Journal of Personality Assessment*, **68**, 267–296.

Watson, D. & Tellegen, A. (1985) Toward a consensual structure of mood. *Psychological Bulletin*, **98**, 219–235.

Watson, D. & Walker. L. (1996) The long-term stability and predictive validity of trait measures of affect. *Journal of Personality and Social Psychology*, **70**, 567–577.

Watson, D., Wiese, D., Vaidya, J., & Tellegen, A. (1999) The two general activation systems of affect: Structural findings, evolutionary considerations, and psychobiological evidence. *Journal of Personality and Social Psychology*, **76**, 820–838.

Wessman, A.E. (1979) Moods: Their personal dynamics and significance. In C.E. Izard (Ed.) *Emotions in Personality and Psychopathology*, pp. 71–102. New York: Plenum Press.

Chapter 3

Discrete emotions in organizational life

Richard S. Lazarus and Yochi Cohen-Charash
University of California, Berkeley, USA

Since the 1960s, there has been a tremendous growth of interest in research and theory in the arena of work stress. This was brought about by an increasing awareness that stress has a complicated relationship with important human values, such as subjective well-being, somatic health, and the functional efficiency of individuals and business organizations; it can facilitate these values as well as impair them. There have been many groundbreaking books on the subject of work stress, which focus on both organizational and personality variables. These include among others the classic early work of Kahn, Wolfe, Quinn, Snoek, & Rosenthal (1964), and the highly respected series edited by Cooper, Kasl, & Payne (e.g. Cooper & Payne, 1980, 1991), of which the present volume is the latest.

Psychology and other social sciences have also become more comfortable with subjective epistemological and meta-theoretical outlooks that are alien to radical behaviorism and logical positivism, its main philosophical underpinning. We are better prepared now than in the past to recognize ubiquitous individual differences, interactions among multiple variables, and a systems-theory approach to research. There is also beginning to be some limited understanding and acceptance of the importance of relational meaning, which is discussed on pp. 53–56.

Although there are a growing number of exceptions, what has not happened in organizational research and theory is a widespread recognition that the discrete emotions experienced at work constitute the coin of the realm in our understanding of the struggle of employees to adapt to organizational life. Better than any other source of information, the emotions can reveal the dynamics of this

Emotions at Work. Edited by Roy Payne and Cary Cooper.
© 2001 by John Wiley & Sons, Ltd.

struggle. The main purpose of this chapter is to develop the rationale for a theoretical research emphasis on discrete emotions in organizational life and the conditions that bring them about.

We begin by offering a brief analysis of epistemological and meta-theoretical perspectives that are or could be used in the study of stress, emotions, and coping at work. This is followed by a brief account of a cognitive–motivational–relational approach that includes arguments in favor of the study of discrete emotions and of a narrative research strategy (Lazarus, 1999a). After that, we examine recent outlooks and research. Finally, a discussion is presented of some of the important emotions in organizational life, which is the ultimate objective of this chapter.

EPISTEMOLOGICAL AND META-THEORETICAL PERSPECTIVES

These perspectives deal with methods of research and ontological assumptions that shape our approach. Main-effect research and three alternative approaches—interactional, conditional trait, and narrative—are examined briefly below.

Main-effect research

The search for *main effects* looks at either work setting or personality variables as sources of organizational stress. This was once the focus of organizational stress research but is, in our view, an unsatisfactory strategy because the two sets of causal variables, the work environment and personality, are kept separate. Work settings are, in effect, not integrated with personality variables to form meaningful functional relationships between the person and the organizational environment.

This violates the essence of cognitive–motivational–relational theoretical analyses of stress and emotion (Lazarus, 1991a), which view emotional reactions as dependent on the *relational meanings* constructed from relationships between persons and environments. It is not the person or the work environment alone that are responsible for stress and distress in organizational settings but the functional juxtaposition of both.

Researchers who study work stress today have increasingly begun to recognize this position, which is relevant to efforts to reduce stress by changing the conditions of work (see Morris & Feldman, 1996 for a review of emotional labor; Ruh, White, & Wood, 1975, for empirical data consistent with our position). The effort to change work conditions without considering personality variables, such as goals, beliefs, and resources of individual workers, is frequently counterproductive (Lazarus, 1991b) because it is likely to benefit some individuals but harm others. This statement does not apply, of course, to exploitative, destructive, and severely inhumane work conditions, which are commonly referred to as sweat-shops that should be eliminated if we are to have a humane society.

A research approach and pattern of application in which individual person characteristics are taken into account remains the most desirable approach to work stress. Although this might seem too costly for large organizations to under-take, trying to make working conditions better without taking individual differ-ences into account is likely to be largely unsuccessful and more costly in the long run than doing it right.

It should be possible to group like-minded individuals, say, by means of cluster analysis of personal–environment relationships, which might be much less costly. Environmental changes could then be made on the basis of relationship clusters to improve the person–environment fit for each subgroup. Research could then help evaluate the consequences of these changes. To our knowledge, this has not really been tried programmatically.

The interactional approach

Main-effect research has lost favor, and modern research increasingly deals with *interactions* between personality and work-setting variables. Nevertheless, inter-action refers only to a method of statistical analysis rather than an effort to evaluate the way work experiences are conceived and interpreted. Relational meanings are crucial to a cognitive–motivational–relational version of emotion theory and represent a higher level of abstraction than main effects or statistical interactions (Lazarus, 1998a, 1998b, 1999a). Clinical case study provides a good model for what we are saying because it tends to emphasize person–environment relationships and their individual meanings.

The conditional-trait approach

In personality psychology, making a psychologically meaningful connection between personality traits and environmental conditions is often referred to as the *conditional trait approach* (e.g. Wright & Mischel, 1987). Traits, such as goal hierarchies, beliefs, and personal resources make certain classes of environmental conditions functionally equivalent. Examples include the celebrated research of McClelland, Atkinson, Clark, and Lowell (1953) on achievement motivation and the more recent meta-analysis of Barrick and Mount (1991) on the relationship between the personality dimensions of the "Big Five" and job performance.

The narrative approach

Lazarus (1999a) has recently made a case for the advantages of a *narrative approach* to the emotions. This approach has recently come into prominence. In this approach, each emotion must be viewed as representing a distinctive dramatic plot or story. What this strategy of theory and research requires at a minimum is a descriptive portrait of the prototypical, or at least normative, story for each discrete emotion. This story contains antecedent and outcome variables, which could integrate the descriptive aspects of this approach with traditional cause-and-effect analysis. The work of Shaver, Schwartz, Kirson, and O'Connor (1987) on emotion prototypes illustrates both the descriptive and analytic side of a narrative approach.

One reason for turning to the narrative approach is disenchantment with systems-theory research. The main source of disenchantment is the large number of variables that must be dealt with in a systems approach and the unlikely prospect of simultaneously encompassing a sufficient number of them in research to fully evaluate the system and its subsystems. Mathematical models can only be used with a modest number of variables, which is a limitation that has long plagued psychological and economic forecasting. Beyond purely exploratory research, these models should be used only in longitudinal or prospective studies because cross-sectional research cannot prove causal influences.

A second reason for favoring a narrative approach is confusion over variable-centered and person-centered research. The former seeks external causal variables, the latter, personality and its descriptive characteristics. From the standpoint of sources of data, the mistake is often made of thinking of variable-centered as objective and person-centered as subjective.

The difference between biography and autobiography offers an analogy. A biography is thought of as objective in that it is put together by an outside observer, but it also frequently draws on first-person accounts. An autobiography is considered subjective because it is written through the eyes of the person whose life is of interest, but it usually draws on objective as well as subjective sources of data. The person writing it makes an effort at detached objectivity, though this often turns out to be an affectation. Therefore, the distinction becomes muddied. Variable-centered research can be either (or both) objective and subjective, and the same can be said for person-centered research. Emotion narratives can effectively combine variable- and person-centered research as well as objective and subjective data sources without confounding the data from the two types of analysis (see Lazarus, 1999a).

Before proceeding, it would be desirable to present a brief summary of the cognitive–emotional–relational theoretical approach on which the present account rests (for more detailed accounts see Lazarus, 1991a, 1998a, 1998b, 1999a and Lazarus, 1995). For those who are not familiar with the theory, the summary below could serve as a useful preamble to the later discussion of emotions in organizational life, which takes up roughly the second half of the chapter.

THE COGNITIVE–MOTIVATIONAL–RELATIONAL APPROACH

Five basic issues are reprised below. They have to do with (1) a discrete category approach to emotion; (2) the interdependence of stress and emotion; (3) the role of individual differences, appraisal, and relational meaning; (4) the role of coping and its efficacy; (5) the relative importance of process and structure.

1. A discrete-category approach to the emotions

The most widely adopted approach these days is to divide emotion into a number of discrete categories, each of which tells a different story about a person's ongoing adaptational struggles. Although any list of emotions is arguable, it should probably include anger, anxiety–fright, sadness, guilt, shame, envy, jealousy, relief, hope, happiness/joy, pride, love, gratitude, and compassion. Emotion theorists differ about how many emotions there are, and which ones are most worthy of programmatic study. Regardless of the exact list, a primary empirical and theoretical concern is to identify the most important emotions and describe their distinctive characteristics, antecedent causal variables, and consequences.

The discrete-emotions approach should be contrasted with the dimensional approach, which had been dominant in the past (beginning with Wundt, 1905, continuing with Schlosberg, 1941, more recently Russell, 1980, and others too numerous to mention). The dimensional approach consists of a factor-analytic attempt to identify the minimum number of dimensions that can account for the greatest amount of emotion variance. Three illustrative dimensions generated from this approach are positive–negative, tension–relaxation, and activation–quiescence.

It is difficult to imagine an emotion without an intensity dimension or without reference to a distinctive content or quality. For this reason, the intensity dimension is retained in the discrete approach but is examined only within each emotion category (e.g. by measuring the intensity of a given display or experience of anger, anxiety, and so forth). In the discrete approach, intensity is subordinated to an emotion's qualitative content, whereas in the dimensional approach discrete content categories are subordinated to emotional dimensions and provide little in the way of theoretical interest. Except for the recent period of radical behaviorism, discrete emotions have dominated philosophical and psychological thought ever since the ancient Greeks. It is also the way most lay people intuitively think about emotion when they talk about the topic.

When contemporary organizational researchers have shown interest in emotion, it is centered mainly on negative and positive affectivity as broad composites; that is, emotions are viewed as temporary or stable general states of positively toned or negatively toned affectivity, which influence the experiences of people at work and which, in turn, are influenced by work experiences.

Affect usually has a somewhat restricted meaning in that it refers to subjective experience in contrast with emotion, which is always embodied. And we use the common term affectivity because it implies a composite of emotions better than the word affect does, which implies differences among the emotions. Note too that the composite approach is more similar to a dimensional stance than one that is concerned with discrete emotions.

Nowadays, organizational research on emotion, as we view it, takes three main forms: research on positive and negative affectivity as dispositions that affect attitudes and behavior; research on positive and negative emotional states, such as moods and the behavior that flows from them; and research on emotion work, which deals with how emotions are shaped and regulated to accommodate organizational demands.

Positive and negative affectivity as dispositions   Researchers have examined the relationship between positive and negative affectivity as dispositions and work behavior and attitudes (George, 1990). Negative affectivity has been found to be associated with greater stress, depression, and somatic complaints at work (George, 1990) and more negative attitudes toward job and life (Staw, Bell, & Clausen, 1986). People high in negative affectivity have also been found in jobs that are low in autonomy, task identity, skill, significance, and feedback from management (Spector, Fox, & Van Katwyk, 1999), findings that seem indicative of how job choice is influenced by emotional dispositions. A relationship has also been found between dispositional affectivity and performance; that is, positive affectivity leads to more accurate decisions, better interpersonal relationships, and higher managerial potential than people low in positive affectivity (Staw & Barsade, 1993).

The belief that a happy worker is more productive than an unhappy one has lost some of its cachet, because it has not been consistently found empirically. Staw and his colleagues provide evidence that there is stability of attitudes towards one's job over time (Staw & Ross, 1985; Staw et al., 1986), and they say that affective dispositions should not be dismissed prematurely. They suggest that it would be more useful to view happy and unhappy as personality dispositions rather than as a consequence of our life situation. This change in strategy, they believe, should lead more consistently to positive results with respect to the relationship between dispositional affectivity and job performance (see, however, Davis-Blake & Pfeffer's, 1989 critique of this position).

Research on moods   A second form of organizational research on affect has focused on moods, especially positive moods, and work behavior (George & Brief, 1992, 1996; Isen & Baron, 1991). It has been found, for example, that people in a positive mood engage in higher levels of prosocial behavior (George, 1991), and that when the mood of group leaders is positive, it is associated with a better performance by the group (George, 1995).

Research on emotion work   A third form of organizational research deals with the ways role expectations and role performance influence affectivity at work. This research reverses the causal relationship between affectivity and attitudes and behavior; rather than focusing on how emotions affect behavior, it examines how role demands and organizational culture affect emotions as displayed. It also tends to emphasize affectivity as displayed rather than subjectively experienced (Ashforth & Humphrey, 1993; Morris & Feldman, 1996; Rafaeli & Sutton, 1987, 1989; Sutton & Rafaeli, 1988; Van Maanen & Kunda, 1989). Somewhat different from research on positive and negative affectivity and on positive and negative emotional states, research on emotional labor tends to focus on discrete emotions. As such, it is a first step in recognizing the importance of discrete emotions, rather than the broad categories of negative and positive emotions.

For example, Sutton (1991) describes the organizational norms regarding emotions that bill collectors, say, ought to express, and identifies rules for displaying urgency, warmth, anger, and neutrality. Moreover, the choice of the expressed emotion depends on the emotions displayed by debtors, such as anxiety, indifference, friendliness, sadness, and anger. Thus, although research on emotional labor does not altogether focus on discrete emotions, it makes use of them to help explain the phenomena of emotional labor.

We have three serious complaints about the emphasis on emotional dispositions, and with the grouping of emotions into positive and negative affectivity. First, with respect to emotional dispositions, and given what we have said at the outset of this chapter about main-effect research, we are wary of an exclusively dispositional emphasis, especially if it is adopted without reference to the role of environmental factors. We are also wary of an exclusive emphasis on the environment without reference to dispositional variables.

Besides, although affective dispositions and situational variables undoubtedly correlate with behavioral and emotional outcomes, these correlations tend to be low. In our judgment, the traditional trait approach will do less well in helping us understand and predict what happens in adaptational struggles than the conditional trait approach. For an in-depth examination of this issue, as it applies to coping, see Lazarus (1998a).

Second, when it comes to grouping emotions together as positive affectivity in contrast with negative affectivity, we also need to be quite wary. That stress should refer to only negatively toned emotions and be contrasted with positively toned emotions, as polar opposites, is a frequent but faulty assumption. Negatively toned reactions (e.g. stress) are often an integral feature of positively toned emotions, and vice versa, positively toned reactions often accompany negatively toned emotions.

It is, therefore, a mistake to make too much of the contrast. The affective tone of each emotion is always uncertain across transactions and for diverse individuals. We usually forget too that the distinction between negative and positive depends on whether the criterion for emotional valence is its subjective feel, its social consequences, or the antecedent conditions arousing the emotion (see also Lazarus, 1991a, 1993).

Third, and most important from our standpoint, grouping negatively toned emotions together and contrasting them with positively toned emotions diminishes the extent to which each individual emotion is considered distinctive with respect to its antecedents, subjective experience, and behavioral consequences. The differences among discrete emotions may be more important (or at least as important) for understanding problems of adaptation than the similarities within each grouping or between them. As you will see on pp. 54–56, these differences create a rich and useful analytic tool for understanding most of life's adaptational struggles.

Because each emotion has its own adaptational story-line or plot, lumping them together into opposing groups of positively toned and negatively toned reactions is not the most desirable research strategy. The same could be said about stress, which is commonly treated as a unidimensional variable ranging from low to high. When stress refers to a continuum of affective arousal, as it most often does, degree of stress becomes comparable to negative affectivity, both of which fail to provide a sufficiently rich portrait of the complex qualitative struggle of a person to survive and flourish.

We suggest that the discrete emotions provide the most useful source of information about the fate of an adaptational process (Lazarus, 1991a, 1993, 2001). If we know that an individual is experiencing any of the 15 different emotions (see Table 3.1), much more will be learned about the appraisal and coping process than by employing simpler metrics for emotion, such as degree of stress or positive and negative affectivity. Thus, if the dominant emotion is anger, we are dealing with a different kind of recurring adaptational drama than would be the case if the dominant emotion were, say, anxiety, guilt, shame, envy, jealousy, and so forth.

The views of Weiss and Cropanzano (1996) represent an exception to organizational psychology's emphasis on positive and negative affectivity. These authors examine current theoretical approaches to emotion, both discrete and dimensional, but they appear to move toward a discrete approach when they write:

> If it is affect we are after then we must recognize that affective reactions have their own phenomenal structure. For example, a person may be angry, frustrated, sad, or ashamed. All are negative affective reactions yet they may result in quite different behavioral consequences. The possibility that meaningfully distinct affective experiences occur at work has been ignored by researchers accepting job satisfaction as a measure of affect.
>
> (Weiss & Cropanzano, 1996, p. 5)

2. The interdependence of stress and emotion

In the past, two separate research literatures have become established, one centered on stress, the other on emotion, which, given their interdependence, is illogical and counterproductive. Many scholars who tend the garden of stress seem blissfully unaware of the research and thought of those who work in the garden of emotion, and vice versa. Instead, stress and emotion should be treated as a single topic. Stress generates emotional consequences but emotion encompasses all the phenomena of stress. What we mean by the interdependence of stress and emotion, therefore, is that stress always implies emotion, so it is useful to think of it as a part process—an important part, to be sure—of the broader state of mind that we call emotions.

This is a position that has been argued by Lazarus (1993), who maintains that the cognitive–motivational–relational rules for both concepts overlap substantially. So he set about expanding his stress theory (Lazarus, 1966; Lazarus & Launier, 1978; Lazarus & Folkman, 1984), which was centered on individual differences and the concepts of appraisal, coping, and relational meaning to the emotions (Lazarus 1991a, 1999a). In Subsection 3, we summarize key concepts of that theory. Coping, which is also a key concept, is taken up separately in Subsection 4.

3. Individual differences, appraisal, and relational meaning

These concepts are central to the approach to emotion we are presenting here. The essential principles are threefold.

(a) *Inter-individual and intra-individual differences* in emotional reactions are ubiquitous even under similar environmental conditions and, therefore, must be explained and dealt with theoretically. No two emotional encounters are ever identical, either between individuals or within an individual, under different environmental conditions and at different times.

(b) An emotional reaction depends on an *appraisal* of the significance for well-being of what is happening. We emphasize the verb form of appraisal, which is *appraising*. This has the advantage of placing our attention on the cognitive action rather than the cognitive result. In any case, appraising helps to explain individual differences by making reference to the cognitive–motivational–relational process whereby relational meaning is constructed from an adaptational encounter.

The fundamental premise of appraisal theory is that we evaluate every event in our lives that is perceived with respect to its significance for our well-being. The function of emotions is to facilitate adaptation though, if the appraisal is unrealistic, it can have the opposite effect. Appraising is the conceptual key to our emotions; it both shapes and reflects the way we cope with our emotions and the life conditions that bring emotions about. An appraisal is a joint product of an individual's distinctive personality and the demands, constraints, and resources of the environmental conditions being faced.

(c) *Relational meaning* is expressed in the concept of the *core relational theme*, which is a terse, composite, integrative synthesis of six separate appraising components—namely, goal relevance, goal congruence or incongruence, type of ego-involvement, options for coping, coping potential, and future expectations. These six components of the appraising process are combined in the person's mind—how we don't understand well as yet—into a single idea or theme, which integrates the separate partial meanings into one complex, unified meaning or gestalt.

This makes it possible to evaluate the significance of the person–environment relationship so rapidly that the appraising process seems almost instantaneous (Lazarus, 1999a), despite the complexity of the information and evaluations about the personal significance of the environmental display and what the person must do to cope. Ironically, it takes more time to read a core relational theme than it takes the mind to grasp and assimilate what it signifies, which illustrates that it is not the slow process of deciphering words that counts but the overall meaning that can usually be instantly sensed.

Because of the process of appraising, different kinds of adaptational encounters, regardless of their details, may share a common relational meaning, such as a particular kind of harm, threat, challenge, or benefit. These encounters are also likely to result in shared thoughts about the possibilities for coping. If we think of the similarities and differences among encounters in terms of their relational meanings, we can readily see why two individuals may display and experience the same emotional reaction even when environmental conditions vary, and different reactions even when conditions are the same.

The relational meaning is distinctive for each emotion. From this standpoint, there is an implacable logic to the emotions (Lazarus & Lazarus, 1994). If we have made a sound analysis of the relational meaning underlying each emotion and if we know the cognitive–motivational–relational antecedent process, then we have a good chance of accurately predicting the emotion that flows from them. And, vice versa, if we know the emotion that is being experienced or displayed, we should be able to reason backward to the relational meaning and the cognitive–motivational–relational process that generated that emotion in the first place.

Table 3.1 provides a plausible core-relational theme for each emotion.

Although controversies exist over some of the relational meanings underlying each of the emotions, there is also remarkable agreement about most of them among appraisal theorists (see Lazarus, 1991a). So we ask you to suspend, for the time being, any doubts about the details of the core-relational themes for each emotion and act as if our characterizations of them could be provisionally sound. Regardless of whether they are the best choice of relational meanings for each emotion, which is to some extent an empirical question, they are quite likely to apply in part or in whole.

There is another feature to the core-relational theme (or relational meaning) that should serve as an important practical caution. If we take seriously the point made on pp. 51–52, that so-called positively valenced emotions often contain negative features and so-called negatively valenced emotions often have positive features, then we must confront a major logical problem. In making a list of positive emotions (e.g. hope, love, happiness, and pride), and another list of negative emotions (e.g. anxiety and anger), we have, in a sense, oversimplified the core-relational themes for each emotion. This is because we have neglected the positive features of the negative list and the negative features of the positive list.

Let us consider a few examples—namely, love, happiness, pride, anger, and

Table 3.1 The core-relational themes for each emotion

Anger	A demeaning offense against me and mine.
Anxiety	Facing uncertain, existential threat.
Fright	An immediate, concrete, and overwhelming physical danger.
Guilt	Having trangressed a moral imperative.
Shame	Failing to live up to an ego-ideal.
Sadness	Having experienced an irrevocable loss.
Envy	Wanting what someone else has and feeling deprived of it but justified in having it.
Jealousy	Resenting a third party for loss or threat to another's affection or favor.
Happiness	Making reasonable progress toward the realization of a goal.
Pride	Enhancement of our ego-identity by taking credit for a valued object or achievement, either our own or that of someone or group with whom we identify.
Relief	A distressing goal-incongruent condition that has changed for the better or gone away.
Hope	Fearing the worst but yearning for better, and believing the improvement is possible.
Love	Desiring or participating in affection, usually but not necessarily reciprocated.
Gratitude	Appreciation for an altruistic gift that provides personal benefit.
Compassion	Moved by another's suffering and wanting to help.

hope. Many experiences of *love* are quite negatively valenced, and even the same relationship, which could justifiably be called loving, may have both positive and negatively toned features on different occasions. For example, when love is unrequited, the person who loves may suffer great distress, and when a lover senses that the love is in jeopardy, threat rather than happiness is apt to be the ruling mental state.

When a person appraises *happiness* as vulnerable to a change for the worse, or this mental state is in danger of being changed for the worse by subsequent conditions, and when others take offense at our good fortune, this emotion is unlikely to be a totally positive experience. Rather, it will often be mixed with negative emotional features that arise from the threat of undesirable changes. The same applies to *pride* when viewed by others as a personal putdown.

Similarly, *anger*, which is usually regarded as a negatively toned emotion, can under certain circumstances be an important source of gratification and be subjectively experienced as positive. By being angry we are apt to feel less helpless or frustrated and more in command of our situation and ourselves because we are doing something to overcome or avenge the social slight we have suffered. In effect, this emotion, which is usually treated as a negative emotional experience—probably because of its damaging social consequences rather than its subjective feel—should not be regarded as negative in valence at all, at least prior to the point at which its damaging consequences become apparent. Depending on the circumstances, the present authors believe anger can be partly or wholly positive.

Finally, *hope* is, par excellence and much of the time, a case of a mixed-valence emotion. One of the defining attributes of hope is that we can never be confident of the outcome of our hopes (Lazarus, 1999b). If this uncertainty, and the anxiety associated with it, did not exist, the emotional state would not be hope but optimism. When we hope we are also usually anxious.

Because emotions are commonly combined in real life or experienced as mixed in valence, it becomes necessary to qualify what is said about their core-relational themes. These themes must be viewed as idealized statements about each emotion, not prescriptions about the way these emotions will actually be experienced in any given instance. The core-relational themes are prototypes of emotional stories or dramas rather than precise descriptions of a person's actual mental state.

In this light, the temptation is strong to want to rewrite the core-relational themes to include both positive and negative features. This is not a sound solution, however, because, given the complexity of emotions in everyday life, we could end up with a different relational meaning for nearly every instance of emotion. Doing this would defeat the need to seek general principles about the relational meanings underlying each emotion.

Instead, therefore, we must simply be wary about making automatic prescriptions about what is actually experienced in any given emotional encounter. What happens emotionally will often follow normatively from the core-relational theme, but it should not surprise us if it doesn't. From the standpoint of research, this means that we must always make a full (which means careful, in depth, and detailed) assessment of the emotional state of an individual in any adaptational encounter, whether it occurs within an organizational setting or in any other life context. Otherwise, we will assume erroneously that the emotional state is what we say it should be ideally—or even normatively—especially when it is a mixture of cognitive–motivational–relational contents.

We also need to realize that the concepts of appraisal and relational meaning imply that emotions are readily transformed into other emotions on the basis of a changed relational meaning that is constructed from the person–environment relationship. For example, shame may be managed by rejecting blame for a social failure and externalizing it. Instead of shame, the emotion is then apt to be anger at another person, object, or institution, which is deemed responsible for the debacle, or maybe shame mixed with anger.

If we treat the discrete emotions as if their psychosocial dynamics are entirely unrelated, we will overlook the ease with which a change in relational meaning transforms one into another. Furthermore, changes in this meaning are often self-generated; that is, they can be a result of a defensive reappraisal, which is focused on who is blamed for the failure in the case of shame and anger, ourselves or another, or credited with the success in the case of pride. But this gets us prematurely into the concept of coping, which is to be discussed in Subsection 4.

Superficially, the approach to the emotional life we have been presenting, which is centered on appraising a relational meaning in an adaptational encounter, appears to be totally subjective (i.e. it seems to be an example of a *phenomenological outlook*). However, it is not traditional phenomenology because its subjectivism is only partial. Persons who are making an appraisal are not just viewing encounters from the standpoint of what they wish but they are said to *negotiate* between two perspectives, a realistic one (A), and a wishful one (B), which we now define more precisely:

(A) As a consequence of our evolutionary endowment and ongoing struggles to survive and flourish, we try (and mostly succeed) to grasp the *objective realities* being faced in order to cope with them effectively.
(B) We also try to put the most *favorable spin* on what is happening so as not to lose our sanguinity or hope, though some people might prefer a negative spin in accordance with a consistently dour coping style.

The two perspectives have a parallel in the Freudian contrast between the reality principle and the pleasure principle, but to accept the parallel does not require that we necessarily adopt other features of psychoanalytic doctrine. The first perspective is not as simple as it might seem, however. Trying to grasp the objective realities presents many difficulties, the most important of which is deciding what is real, especially in social contexts that are complex and ambiguous, and concerning which different people construe what is happening in their own distinctive ways.

4. The role of coping and its efficacy

Coping has to do with how we manage our emotions (e.g. regulating the reaction or suppressing them) and influence the conditions and processes that bring them about (e.g. changing ourselves or the environment or reappraising the personal significance of what is happening). Organizations can influence the emotions and the coping process through their values and practices, both of which have to do with what might be referred to as their "organizational cultures".

These cultures contribute to emotions by influencing the relational meaning a working person constructs of daily events (Fireman, 1993) and the coping strategy that is selected. It does so by providing norms for the behavior considered acceptable or required (Hochschild, 1979; Rafaeli & Sutton, 1989; Van Maanen & Kunda, 1989), in addition to the norms provided by society at large and the subcultures within it. The culture can also vary with the kind of work a person does and the authority that person is granted within the company. Thus, the norms for the way managers should act and feel are apt to be different from those for ordinary workers.

In this connection, we might mention research on emotion work (e.g. Hochschild, 1979), and more recently on the relationship between social status and emotions (Gibson & Schroeder, 1999; Tiedens, in press; Tiedens, Ellsworth, & Mesquita, in press). This latter research is based on the idea that some emotions are more or less appropriate as experienced and displayed on the basis of our hierarchical position in the organization, and workers must cope with these institutional patterns accordingly. In other words, social position affects the kind and intensity of emotions and, in turn, emotions affect the perception of social status. This could influence the coping process, though not much research has been done on these complex connections.

Tiedens and her colleagues have studied the link between emotional patterns and social status and obtained provocative findings. Using various methodologies, they found that high-status people are likely to display anger, frustration, and pride, which these researchers came to regard as high-status emotions in what might have been a bit of tautological reasoning. Nevertheless, and lending credence to their reasoning, they found that people who displayed so-called high-status emotions were, indeed, perceived by others as having a higher social status than those who displayed so-called low-status emotions, such as sadness, guilt, and appreciation.

There may well be a connection between organizational culture and coping. This culture could facilitate coping in at least two ways: by (a) allowing or encouraging employees' "safe" expressions of stress and emotions in a non-evaluative or supportive environment (Fireman, 1993); and (b) having clear rules about what is acceptable and unacceptable behavior. On the other hand, organizational cultures could hinder effective coping in at least two ways: by (a) ignoring or rejecting the real emotions of their employees (Hochschild, 1979; Rafaeli & Sutton, 1987); and (b) legitimizing only rational problem solving (Sutton & Rafaeli, 1988). Practices that run counter to the individual's emotional and coping predilections can lead eventually to burnout (Morris & Feldman, 1996), spillover of the emotional state to other life areas (Wharton & Erickson, 1993), and personal alienation (Mumby & Putnam, 1992).

Emotion theorists, including those wedded to the concept of appraisal, have a tendency to understate or even overlook the place of coping in emotion. If such a role is acknowledged, coping is commonly treated as a separate process belonging to stress rather than emotion theory. However, coping should be regarded as an integral feature of the emotion process. It is misleading to treat it as solely a response to an emotion (i.e. as coming into play only after the emotion has been aroused).

Coping and the appraisals that underlie it influence which emotion will be displayed. For example, we are less likely to express our anger or we may reappraise the conditions for it if we fear retaliation from a powerful other, whether it is the person who provoked the anuer or a representative of management who disapproves. As a result, the anger may soften, become moot, or change to an altogether different emotion, such as guilt or anxiety. It might also be experienced but not expressed. This example indicates that coping mediates the emotional reaction to the emotion-provoking relationship and its subsequent emotions (Folkman & Lazarus, 1988a, b). In other words, coping enters the emotion process at the very outset of an adaptational encounter (i.e. at the initial arousal stage via the process of appraising).

Because stress is often involved in so-called positively toned emotions, coping can be important in these emotions too—in effect, in all emotions regardless of their affective tone. For example, even if, or perhaps because things are going very well for them, superstitious people may believe the "evil eye" will do them in or others will try to undermine their good fortune out of envy. They will be motivated to underplay happiness and pride to hide how good things really are (Bedeian, 1995; Natale, Campana, & Sora, 1988; Salovey & Rothman, 1991; Schoeck, 1969; Silver & Sabini, 1978). Because of a long history of experience with prejudice and discrimination, a diaspora Jewish businessmen's pattern is relevant. When asked how things are going, the standard response is to shrug their shoulders and say in mock deprecation of their good fortune "I make a living". In this way, they can defuse the threat of envy or jealousy on the part of important others.

One of the most important and challenging issues in the study of coping is how to evaluate its efficacy. In our estimation, the soundest basis for such an evaluation is the *person–environment fit*. This concept was pioneered at Michigan and applied to work stress by French, Caplan, & Van Harrison (1982). A good fit in an organizational setting means that job requirements match person characteristics; a poor fit means that the two components, job and personality, clash.

Early on, Lazarus & Folkman (1984; see also Lazarus, 1991b) criticized the analysis of the French group of person–environment fit as being too structural (i.e. French et al. treated fit as a stable property of the person and it is assessed for the job as a whole). We took the position that fit should be viewed in process terms; that is, it might be good with respect to one type of job function, time period, or some co-workers, but poor in other functions, time, and other co-workers (see also Chatman, 1989; and O'Reilly, Chatman, & Caldwell, 1991).

This is not to say that a good fit is always desirable. Given some organizational climates, a person might want to leave the organization rather than try to change himself or herself in order to fit in with organizational patterns that are ugly or immoral. From the advantage of hindsight, in the late 1930s and early 1940s we might have wished that more Germans would have rejected nationalistic and racist Nazi doctrines, which would shortly lead to unspeakable crimes against humanity and the ultimate destruction of the Third Reich and much of Europe. The same applies to the attitude toward slavery in the American South.

The most important personality variables to be considered in a person–environment fit include goals and goal hierarchies, beliefs about self and the environment, and personal resources. Job characteristics influential in this fit have to do with the many antecedent variables studied in much past research on work stress. They include, for example, any of the 57 environmental variables cited by Holt (1982) in his review of the field, which he subsumes under the broader categories of work overload, role ambiguity and conflict, poor labor–management relations, monotony, and lack of control over job demands and opportunities.

5. The importance of process as well as structure

The focus of much of psychology, as evidenced by traditional psychometrics, has been on what is stable over time rather than on change or flux. However, when we cope we are usually motivated to alter the sources of distress and dysfunction and/ or the way we deal with them, so change is especially important in emotion. Our lives are constantly changing as a result of changes in society, psychological development, illness, and aging. All this suggests that we should focus on process even more than structure.

Structure and process are two sides of the same coin. Emotions can be treated as relatively stable traits, as when we speak of angry persons or anxious persons, or as changeable states and processes, in which we observe flux in emotions in the same persons over time or across environmental conditions. Therefore, in an effort to understand what has been going wrong or right in a person's adaptational efforts, and when we speak of the arousal and regulation of our emotions, we must take into account *both* processes and structures (Lazarus, 1998a, b).

Process analysis calls for a very different approach to psychological, social, and physiological measurement than existed when most elders of our field began to study psychology. At that time and to some extent still, the reliability of a measure, such as intelligence or other personality characteristics, was said to depend on demonstrations of stability or consistency, which was obtained from repeated measurement. But we must seek alternatives to the traditional psychometric reliance on temporal or situational consistency, which refers to traits and is the opposite of process. Assessing person–environment fit or misfit in process terms requires longitudinal research designs so that *both* changing *and* stable features can be taken into account (e.g. Staw et al., 1986).

RECENT OUTLOOKS AND RESEARCH

Dissident voices still argue against the scientific adequacy of a cognitive–mediational approach to stress and the emotions, demonstrating, thereby, what might be considered residual behaviorism. The old-fashioned stimulus–response approach is totally circular in that its absence of concern with person variables makes it impossible to specify before the fact, and with any precision, what is stressful or not stressful and the degree and quality of that stress. This makes it difficult to predict accurately the qualitative and quantitative details of individualized reactions, which point to the simplistic and tautological nature of this doctrine.

There is certainly no shortage of modern research drawing on a cognitive–motivational–relational approach that takes individual differences into account, is process centered, adopts a modified subjectivism (as in the concept of appraisal we have advocated), and focuses on relational meaning. In Lazarus (1999a), which is a sequel to Lazarus & Folkman (1984), recent research was cited that drew on this kind of approach. The volume of such work is daunting but we might mention a few programmatic examples that seem relevant to organizational life, such as the *appraisal-centered research* by Tomaka and Blascovich and their colleagues (e.g. Tomaka, Blascovich, Kelsey, & Leitten, 1993 and Tomaka & Blascovich, 1994) on threat and challenge appraisals, a series of articles by Dewe (e.g. Dewe 1989, 1991, 1992) on work stress, and the cognitive and motivationally oriented writings and research of Locke and Taylor (1990).

With respect to *coping*, the volume of recent studies built around and supporting a cognitive–motivational–relational theoretical approach is also large (see e.g. Zeidner & Endler, 1996), although much of this research—probably too much—has been superficial and trivial (see e.g. Somerfield & Commentators, 1997 and Lazarus, 1998b, 1999a). Folkman's recent research (Folkman, 1997; Folkman, Moskowitz, Ozer, & Park, 1997) on stress and coping among caregivers of live-in partners dying of AIDS is impressive and supports the soundness of this kind of approach. Research by Tennen and Affleck (1996) is also exemplary in drawing on diverse, careful, and detailed methods in studying the daily process of coping and its role in chronic pain and depression.

Gottlieb's (1997) book on chronic stress and Eckenrode and Gore's (1990) book on work and family stress contain numerous examples of microanalytic research studies of the spillover of work stress into family life. In this research, demographically limited samples were employed, making the task of generalizing to other samples risky. Nevertheless, such research is useful in providing replicated portraits of the coping processes employed by husbands and wives when the husband is the sole family breadwinner. Westman and Etzion's (1995, 1999) research on the spillover of stress from work to family and vice versa employed husbands and wives, as well as school teachers and principals, adding substantially to what we know about this topic.

Much of the research cited above on appraising and coping is consistent with the epistemic and meta-theoretical principles laid out earlier in this chapter and in Lazarus (1999a). Unfortunately, too much research on stress and coping in general, and work stress in particular, fails to cast its analyses in terms of relational meaning. What is missing is an intimate sense of the ongoing emotional dramas that reflect how particular kinds of people struggle with the sources of stress in their lives. This intimate sense is exemplified in organizational settings in the research of Cohen-Charash (2000), Gibson (1993), Hochschild (1983), and Sutton & Rafaeli (1988).

In too much research, however, little attention is given to describing actual emotional encounters and the relational meanings working persons construct from them. Description is just as important to science as cause-and-effect analysis. From our point of view, this approach to science deprives us of the use of a powerful analytic tool—namely, the discrete emotions of individual persons as evidence about the nature of the adaptational struggle.

SOME DISCRETE EMOTIONS IN ORGANIZATIONAL LIFE

Below we have chosen a number of emotions that seem unequivocally relevant to organizational settings. They include anger, anxiety, guilt–shame, envy–jealousy, hope, happiness/joy, pride, love, and compassion. Other emotions are left out mainly because of space limitations, not because they play no role in organizational life. For each emotion that is examined, we first discuss its general psychosocial dynamics in everyday life and only then consider the conditions of organizational life that might contribute to it.

Anger

The core-relational theme for anger in the general case is a demeaning offense against me and mine. Its provocation is, in effect, a slight or injury to our identity. This is very similar to Aristotle's (1941) account of anger in "Rhetoric". As is the case with all emotions, anger is a joint product of a social provocation and diverse personality characteristics that increase vulnerability to feeling demeaned or belittled.

To treat frustration as *the* provocation to anger, as psychology has in the past (see Berkowitz, 1989), does not adequately explain anger because every other emotion that is regarded as negatively toned also involves frustration (Lazarus, 1991a). Therefore, the question of why the aroused emotion is anger and not anxiety, guilt, shame, envy, or jealousy is not answered when frustration is proposed as the sole or main cause of anger.

The goal that fuels anger (Lazarus, 1991a, 1999a) is preservation and enhancement of our personal or social identity. Pride and shame have a similar underlying goal, though these emotions have opposing significance for well-being. Pride involves support for our identity and, therefore, it is usually a positive experience whereas shame undermines such support; therefore, it is usually a negative experience. Whether collectively or individually, the presence of anger suggests that an action by another person or agency is construed as a demeaning offense.

If you wonder about the universality of this proposition, consider how often, in international politics, leaders as well as the populace as a whole act as if their country and, therefore, its individual citizens have been insulted. Nationalistic ire follows this collective appraisal (Smeller, 1963) and provokes countries to mount destructive wars that can seldom be truly won, especially if we consider long-term consequences.

Like every other emotion, anger and its main action consequence, aggression, is *sui generis* (i.e. it is a distinctive state of mind and body), the specifics of which must be understood differently than any other emotion. Given the frequently damaging social and personal consequences of overt aggression, if a person or society has the goal of controlling destructive anger, its cognitive and motivational underpinnings must be fully understood (see Toch, 1969, 1983 for an account of the writings of Seneca, the Roman philosopher and politician, whose interests centered on the social control of aggression).

With respect to organizational sources of anger, intense expressions of individual and collective anger in labor disputes, including riots and violence, have created social problems throughout history. Hiring practices, evaluation of another's work, layoffs, the insulting manner in which requests or orders can be given, failure on the part of someone in the same or a different department to follow a reasonable request or demand, and personality factors all contribute to the tendency to react with resentment and bitterness.

An important interpersonal condition that is likely to provoke anger in an organizational setting is the unwise use of managerial power. This could easily invite the perception of unfairness or lack of concern on the part of management for the well-being of subordinates. Lack of concern is not only apt to be damaging in the concrete sense of job security, career ambitions, and other harms and threats at work, yet it is readily viewed existentially by employees as demeaning.

Of the various discrete emotions, anger is the one that seems to receive the largest share of attention by organizational researchers. It has been studied in a number of contexts; for example, with respect to its role in negotiation (Alfred, Mallozzi, Matsui, & Raia, 1997) in supervisor–subordinate interactions (Glomb & Hulin, 1997), as a status-related emotion (Tiedens, 2000), and as an outcome of organizational practices that are mainly connected with unfair procedures and outcomes (Gibson, 1993; Pillutla & Murnighan, 1996; Weiss, Suckow, Cropanzano, 1999).

Data from Weiss et al. (1999) and Pillutla and Murnighan (1996) suggest that anger is the primary response to perceived unfairness, and that this perception is associated with negative, spiteful relationships. This too is quite consistent with the core-relational theme of anger, which emphasizes being slighted or demeaned in a social encounter. Unfairness communicates that the person lacks social significance, which is apt to be regarded as demeaning.

Allred et al. (1997) found that, in a negotiation, anger was negatively related to (a) compassion toward the other, (b) lack of future desire to work with the other person, and (c) impaired performance of the negotiating dyad. They also found that these effects were significantly stronger than the effects of mood, supporting the utility of studying discrete emotions in contrast with the general categories of positive and negative affectivity.

Whereas Glomb and Hulin's (1997) data showed that managers displaying anger were rated lower than those not displaying it, Tiedens (2000) found that displays of anger make the manager seem more competent. Gibson (1993) has provided detailed descriptions of the expression of anger at work, which reveal that most of the time (35%) anger was directed at supervisors, followed by peers (17%), and subordinates (11%). In that study, the main reason for anger was also perceived unfairness at both an interpersonal and organizational level. And most workers who experienced anger expressed that feeling directly to the person who provoked it, even when it was a supervisor. Taken together, these studies demonstrated the importance of anger and other discrete emotions in organizational life, as well as some of the dynamics of organizational anger.

Anxiety

This emotion, which has also been given considerable attention in the context of organizational life, stands in marked contrast to anger but must also be considered to be one of the important emotions. From a general standpoint, its core-relational theme is facing an uncertain threat, which has existential implications that go well beyond concrete and immediate threats by serving as a symbol of potential inability to survive and flourish.

When facing an opportunity (i.e. a highly anticipated state of affairs whose outcome is nevertheless uncertain and involves the need to use our resources to deal with unfamiliar situations) anxiety can be thought of in a positive light. For example, Lazarus and Launier (1978) and Lazarus and Folkman (1984) referred to this kind of anxiety as a challenge, which is liberating in contrast with a threat, which is constricting and can impair performance. In the organizational context, even opportunities can be associated with considerable anxiety, as in the concept of the fear of success, which first came to the attention of psychologists in connection with research on striving for achievement (Homer, 1972).

Anxiety is so central to our sense of well-being that psychologists have tended to regard it as *the* key emotion in adaptation (this was especially the case in the 1940s and 1950s) on which mental health and psychopathology were said to depend. Psychologists have since then come to realize that other emotions, such as anger, shame, guilt, envy, hope, and love, are also important in human adaptation and each contains its own special antecedents, qualities, and consequences, and can result from positive as well as negative events.

Although the existential aspects of anxiety have to do with life-and-death issues and who we are in the world, the consciously recognizable sources of anxiety are concrete and immediate in that they reflect limited goals at stake in our daily lives. This is especially true when threatened values and goals are important, but we have only limited personal resources to pit against them, which increases our existential sense of vulnerability.

Being evaluated is a ubiquitous and, in a sense, generic example of an environmental source of anxiety, the threat being a negative judgment that can have damaging social implications that often implies a person's general inadequacy. This evaluative threat can be provoked by a number of relational conditions that are not necessarily job related; for example, taking tests in school, having to perform in front of an audience and living up to others' expectations in a competitive or love relationship. Non-evaluative threats include a medical exam-ination for suspected disease and having to undergo risky surgery, the latter two conditions endangering our very existence and ability to function.

Although anger and anxiety are provoked by different environmental con-ditions and could even be considered emotional opposites with respect to the actions they generate (e.g. approach versus avoidance), they are also strikingly interdependent. A good analogy is an animal that is cornered and vacillates between the impulse to flee the danger or attack. If its aggressive display leads the predator to withdraw, the animal grows bolder; if it seems to enrage the predator, attack may be cast aside in favor of flight as long as there is an escape route.

Human anger, which is more to the point, follows a similar pattern. It is potentiated when we believe we can overcome an enemy, but inhibited when we believe we are too weak to avoid serious damage. In such a case, only anxiety or fright will occur, or the anxiety will be intermixed with anger. In both emotions, however, some of the same existential concerns about personal and social identity and life and death are at stake. The vacillation between anger and anxiety illus-trates their interdependence.

The contrast between anger and anxiety points up clearly the distinctiveness of discrete emotions. The importance of the basic contrast between anger and anxiety is well illustrated in the research of Laux and Weber (1991; see also Weber & Laux, 1993) who showed that coping differs greatly when the emotion is anger in contrast to anxiety. These researchers studied married couples who imagined angry or anxious marital encounters or actually experienced such transactions.

When couples were having an argument in which one or both personal iden-tities was assaulted, *anger* was most often expressed openly and would usually escalate with each partner attacking the other, presumably in an effort to repair the wound to their personal identity. Angry confrontations were characterized by Laux and Weber as "openly expressive and marked by defiance, that is, by fighting against inflicted harm and by correcting injustice" (Laux and Weber, 1991, p. 251).

On the other hand, in *anxious* encounters, which involved a shared threat to the well-being of the couple (e.g. when a job was in danger or a child was seriously ill), the couple's coping efforts were designed to bolster the relationship and produce cooperation. According to Laux and Weber, during anxiety the marital partners dealt with each other "by not expressing feelings, by re-appraising the situation and by rational action aimed at ... avoiding or escaping danger ... [in] coping with anxiety" (Laux and Weber, 1991, p. 251). Thus, the coping intentions of married couples in encounters involving anger and anxiety were distinctly different and flowed sensibly from the differences in the threats being faced, a pattern that seems eminently adaptive.

In the organizational context, anxiety is apt to be present whenever a worker faces judgments regarding his or her role in the organization, especially when that worker is faced with uncertainty about this role, and when organizational changes are anticipated. Kahn et al.'s (1964) research, which we cited at the outset, was focused heavily on role conflicts and ambiguity at work as primary sources of anxiety.

We suspect that in organizational settings in the Western world, where individual competition tends to be a strong feature, workers are likely to be more ashamed of their anxiety than anger, so their anxiety may be concealed more often than anger. Our hunch about this is partially confirmed by some research by Gibson (1993) who used the term fear rather than anxiety. Using a critical-incident methodology, he found that organizational fear usually revolves around felt threat and loss of control, especially as a result of one's own actions.

Although the largest source of fear was the supervisor (43%), the self was a second source (23%). Contrary to expressions of anger, which were generally overt and directed at the person who provoked the anger, expressions of fear were mostly suppressed (80% of research subjects). When fear was expressed, it was not to the agent of the fear but rather to close co-workers and family members. Apparently, workers did not express their fear to avoid appearing incompetent, hence vulnerable, which is why we view these data as partial confirmation of our hunch about the ego-syntonic nature of anger and the ego-alien nature of anxiety in Western societies. It seems to be the opposite in Japan.

Chronic or recurrent job insecurity also result in widespread anxiety in organizational settings (Astrachan, 1995). Consider, for example, the effects of awareness that a company is about to downsize, perhaps as a result of poor economic performance, pressures from investors for greater profit, or the merging of one company with another. These changes involve many threatening issues for most or all employees. For example, who is to be let go? Why are some workers being discharged but not others? What should the remaining workers think about their future job security? What is implied by this selection about our ability to succeed at a job? And what can be done to obtain another job?

Whether the threat of failure to be promoted or loss of job are collective or individual, anxiety remains one of the major emotional consequences of organizational life, sometimes suffused with anger, depending on what aspect of what is happening is being attended to. Managerial practices obviously have much to do with increasing or decreasing anxiety, but, as always, personality dispositions also contribute to the individual variation in the tendency to be made anxious.

Guilt and shame

From a general standpoint, these emotions have to do with social and personal standards of conduct that were internalized during a person's early development in contrast with mere compliance in which we manifest only lip service toward societal values (see Kelman, 1961; also Lewis & Haviland, 1993; Mascolo & Fischer, 1995). The negatively valenced core-relational theme for guilt is having transgressed a moral imperative. If there is a positively toned valence for guilt, it might be the self-righteous feeling of having our moral lapse remedied by performing acts of contrition. This process can be illustrated by referring to the Christian religious flagellants in the early Middle Ages who sought salvation by publicly whipping themselves which, we assume, produced physical pain but made them feel better emotionally.

With respect to shame, which is probably always negatively toned because of its terrible message that we have displayed a characterological defect, the core-relational theme is having failed to live up to an ego ideal, which might have no connection with moral values. Thus, we can even experience shame for not being an effective thief or con man.

Both guilt and shame are different, yet—like anger and anxiety—are also closely related in that both emotions represent a loss or threat of loss to our social and personal identity. They are of particular interest to social scientists because they serve as warning signals that make it possible to prevent potential guilt- or shame-provoking actions by means of anticipatory coping processes. The desire to avoid experiencing these emotions, and to remedy them when they occur, generates a strong wish to maintain self-control and the effort to avoid actions that might provoke guilt or shame (Fineman, 1993).

For example, when a worker does not contribute adequately to a work team, it is likely that there will be feelings of guilt or shame, aggravated perhaps by evidence of social or self-criticism, based on internalized standards of conduct. The manipulation of guilt and shame may also serve as managerial tools for controlling employees that can be used in situations of performance evaluations (Poulson, in press), just as some parents control their children by provoking these emotions.

The nature and significance of the personal failure on the input side, the internal subjective state experienced, and their behavioral manifestations on the response side distinguish guilt and shame. On the response side, a person who feels guilty usually seeks to expiate or atone for the moral failure by apologizing or somehow making restitution. The shamed person seeks to hide the character defect or shift the blame to someone else. How much emotional distress will be experienced depends on whether the guilt or shame is tied to a specific action or is regarded as a major character defect. The latter, which seems to be the rule in shame, is a far greater source of distress than the former, making shame one of the most distressing emotions people can experience.

In making decisions about subordinates, managerial personnel are under pressure to take on, accept, or at least display company values whether internalized or not, whereas their subordinates are apt to have quite different concerns. Values and norms that encourage guilt or shame may also be in conflict with each other, presenting a sort of catch-22, and these values may also conflict with a worker's personal values. The plight of shop foremen has long illustrated a classic form of organizational conflict. They are apt to be torn between their ways of thinking and feeling when they were ordinary workers and the need to represent management after being promoted to foreman status.

Envy and jealousy

Although laypersons frequently confuse the two emotions, psychologists recognize differences as well as similarities between them. Envy is a two-person emotional state in which one person hungers for what another has and feels unjustly deprived of it, which is basically the core-relational theme for this emotion. Jealousy, on the other hand, is a three-person emotion. One person resents another who is a rival for an expected or hoped-for reward from a third person in the triangle (see e.g. Lieblich, 1971; Rawls, 1971; Parrott & Smith, 1993; Salovey, 1991; Tellenbach, 1974; Titelman, 1981; White & Mullen, 1989). With the exception of Lieblich, the above sources deal mainly with the romantic and social contexts of jealousy.

Within an organization, promotion of a colleague for a positive performance can readily generate envy or jealousy. Envy occurs when the colleague gains; jealousy, when the colleague gains or threatens to gain at the jealous individual's expense. An underlying implication in jealousy, which is often hidden, is apt to be the self-deprecatory psychological message that another person's advancement indicates our limited potential for success.

Envy is common in organizations (Vecchio, 1995). For example, Duffy, Shaw, and Stark (1997) examined the outcomes of envy in groups. Respondents were 437 graduate students, placed into 143 groups ranging in size from 3 to 7, who participated in a semester-long research project. A path model revealed that envy was positively related to social loafing (when individuals do less of their share of work in a group) and negatively related to group cohesiveness and group potency (the ability of a group to perform well as assessed by group members). Although envy was not directly related to group performance, absenteeism, and satisfaction with the group, it mediated the relationship between a group's potency and social loafing, on the one hand, and impaired group performance, on the other. Given the increasing popularity of work groups in organizations, the influence of envy on employees, groups, and the organization as a whole may turn out to be substantial.

Envy also creates an unpleasant atmosphere in organizational life, as Cohen-Charash (2000) found in a study of the antecedents and consequences of envy. Respondents were employees from various organizations who represented a variety of work levels and professions. The litany of unpleasantness was substantial. Initial analyses revealed that the stronger the experienced envy, the greater was the incidence of negative reactions toward the envied person and the fewer positive reactions there were. Envious people displayed more actions intended to hurt the other, such as sabotage of the envied person's work and reputation, they were also less likely to help and cooperate with that person. In addition, the stronger the envy, the higher was the level of behavioral and cognitive actions intended to improve our competitive position, such as working harder; to this end, envious persons tried to form new coalitions and win the support of others. The envious person became more suspicious of other people at work and behaved unpleasantly in the presence of the envied person. Envy also affected a worker's emotions negatively, resulting in evidence of anxiety, depression, hostility, fatigue, and confusion.

With respect to research on *jealousy*, Miner (1990) has published a survey of 278 employees in 200 organizations and found ample evidence of this emotion. Thus, 77% of the respondents reported observing an encounter involving jealousy at work, 58% indicated they had themselves been involved in jealous encounters, and 29% indicated that they were the one who was jealous. Respondents indicated that they encountered jealousy at work approximately three times a month, either as witnesses or as directly involved themselves. Those reporting such an involvement indicated that these events occurred on an average of twice a month. Thus, situations of jealousy are common in organizations, yet have not been much studied.

Rawls (1971) has proposed that jealousy characterizes a person who is better off than others, but wants them to remain in an inferior position. Jealousy may lead such a person to deny others any benefit, even though they are not really needed and cannot be used by the jealous worker (Spielman, 1971). It could be said, in effect, that, whereas envious workers want to deprive others of their superior position, jealous workers want to protect their present institutional advantage (Cohen-Charash, 2000).

If there is a positive aspect to envy and jealousy, it could be the ability to see our deprivation or threat of loss as a challenge. Workers sometimes mobilize constructive efforts to improve their position. They may also work harder to gain what the competitor has or is threatening to take (Cohen-Charash, 2000).

Given the vast opportunities for envy and jealousy at work, both of these emotions play a major role in the workplace. Because organizations, as well as whole societies, are usually hierarchical in structure with respect to status and power, and competition and social comparison are widespread, the conditions for envy and jealousy are usually present in organizational life, with many negative consequences and a few positive ones too (Vecchio, 1995).

Hope

Because of its highly subjective nature, psychologists have shied away from the study of this emotion, though it is often a significant factor in adaptational struggles. Its role in the maintenance of morale and the feeling of well-being, even under adverse circumstances, is being increasingly recognized.

Speaking generally, the emotional reactions of hope and despair are polar opposites. Hope is a *vital coping resource* against despair (Lazarus, 1999b). As an emotion, its core-relational theme is to fear the worst but yearn for better. Hope also seems to depend on the belief that the hoped-for improvement is possible, either through our own efforts or external factors that we don't control, such as luck, fate, God, or a skillful and caring person. People differ greatly in their ability to sustain hope under unfavorable circumstances.

In an organization, especially when there is widespread uncertainty about our careers or other aspects of well-being, such as job security and social acceptance, the emotions of hope, anxiety, and despair are likely to be present, though they may not be acknowledged. Provocations for hope include opportunities for advancement, chronic or recurrent social disapproval or rejection, the threat of job loss, negative evaluations, and failure to advance. These sources of threat are probably exacerbated in an era of corporate downsizing, which means the abandonment of the old-fashioned expectation, now becoming only a forlorn hope, that working personnel could have a secure lifetime career in a major industry.

Although hope seems not to have been studied by organizational researchers, it should be because it is so important and ubiquitous in human affairs. Not only can organizations elicit hope by its managerial practices, but organizations and the people working in them can benefit when hope seems realistic or harmed when it seems unrealistic. For example, when an organization is downsizing, managerial encouragement of hope may lead workers to do what they can to increase the viability of their positions or to seek other job opportunities. Undoubtedly a myriad of personality and situational variables affect the ability or willingness of any individual to hope when in a threatening or opportunistic situation.

Happiness/Joy

From a general standpoint, happiness has two meanings: the first is a relatively detached assessment of our overall well-being, which might better be regarded as a mild, somewhat intellectualized satisfaction or dissatisfaction about how things are going in our lives. This should probably be referred to as *satisfaction about well-being* rather than happiness/joy because, as a generalized assessment of our lives, it is best regarded, at least in part, as a sentiment or disposition rather than an assessment based on the realities of our condition of life (Diener, 1984). The lack of a strong relationship between the objective conditions of life and their subjective evaluations has long posed a dilemma in the study of well-being. In any case, we are not inclined to treat this state of mind as an emotion.

When happiness is defined as an emotional state, however, we are dealing with the second meaning. Because this term expresses more intensity and verve than the ambiguous and seemingly more detached term, well-being, this mental state should be called *happiness/joy*.

There is very little agreement among psychologists and philosophers about the dynamics of either the sentiment of satisfaction about well-being or the emotion of happiness/joy. Aristotle defined the emotion very broadly as being able to use our physical and mental resources fully. Lazarus (1991a) recently suggested that happiness/joy is brought about by an extended process of striving and making progress, however fast or slow, toward a goal or goals. This way of looking at the basis of happiness/joy stands in contrast to actually attaining goals.

The reason for this stance is that success at getting what we think we want is apt to produce only short-lived gratification. This kind of success often leads, ironically, to disappointment because we tend to overvalue what we think we want. Even if what has been gained is greatly desired, the success soon fades into the past and people cannot live happily in the past without an encore. Thus, obtaining an advanced degree that we have been studying for over a period of years sets a person up for the next necessary step in life, say, getting a suitable job. Marriage too does not mean we live happily ever after, as our culture's simplistic expression has it, but rather that the couple has new opportunities and realities to deal with in living together, raising children, and establishing themselves economically, in addition to new pleasures and sources of joy.

In saying what we have above, we are making the claim that happiness/joy and satisfaction about our well-being, must be leavened by the realities of living. These states of mind can even be mixed with sadness because gaining one goal may interfere with gaining another goal that must be sacrificed, as when we achieve competitive success at the expense of family love or the social approval of our working peers.

A very interesting example of this principle in the organizational setting is the research of Weiss et al (1999). They found that happiness was experienced simultaneously with either pride *or* guilt when the gain depended on whether the procedure underlying it was biased against or for the person who received it. If the gain occurred in spite of an unfair bias *against* the person, it led to the coexistence of happiness and pride, the pride presumably stemming from the appraisal that we have overcome a major handicap. However, if the gain occurred because of an unfair bias *in favor of* the person, the result was the juxtaposition of happiness and guilt, the guilt presumably stemming from the appraisal that we had not earned it.

The insight that happiness/joy or satisfaction about our well-being are by-products of a continuing process of doing and striving implies that there is no sensible way to seek these states of mind as a life goal. Doing and striving are of primary importance rather than the outcomes of such striving. This seems to be a difficult lesson to learn because our culture's standard way of thinking about these mental states lacks the necessary depth and wisdom. What we have been saying can also help explain why there is so little correspondence between well-being and the realities of our lives.

In an organizational setting, some of the most important concrete issues at stake in happiness/joy or satisfaction over well-being are career advancement, income, praise, and pleasing social relationships at work. Our most important work-related goals may be in conflict, as when we must choose whether to invest our energies in achievement or affiliation (i.e. career advancement or the maintenance of warm, friendly interpersonal relationships). Most people vary in which of these goals is at the top of their goal hierarchy (see Vogel, Raymond, & Lazarus, 1959). Even in working life, interpersonal relationships provide many people with the main source of gratification. For others, the main source of gratification lies in the family, work being for them a demanding necessity that provides for the family well-being.

For the most part, organizational researchers have not examined happiness/joy as emotions, but have paid attention instead to job satisfaction and positive mood states (for exceptions see Gibson, 1993; Weiss et al., 1999), which have been regarded as a source of motivation (e.g. George, 1991; George & Brief, 1996). George (1991) reported that positive mood enhances prosocial behavior and improves performance. Positive mood was also found to facilitate memory, judgment, decision making, and creativity, although under certain conditions positive moods may hinder performance. This may happen, for example, when a person wants to maintain a good mood (for reviews on the influence of positive mood on performance see George & Brief, 1996; Isen & Baron, 1991). In any case, even the modest amount of research that has been conducted on this topic in the organizational setting points up the importance of happiness/joy at work.

Gibson (1993) found that in 38% of the encounters described in his study, joy was often credited to the work itself, followed by supervisors (25%) and peers (19%). In keeping with the issue of whether joy based on our work is expressed publicly, subjects failed to do so 81% of the time. Workers appear to put on a professional mask and make an effort to hide their joyful feelings because to do so was not considered safe or appropriate.

This coping strategy, therefore, could be based on the fear of dashed expectations. In other words, workers avoid admitting joy in the work performance to protect their reputation. Based on what respondents say, Gibson believes that the expression of joy is not considered professional. Additional relational meanings that could motivate the effort to conceal joy might be the fear of creating resentment and envy among fellow workers. However, under situations involving group success, workers were willing to express their joy freely.

Pride

Pride differs from happiness in that it stems from a favorable event that enhances our social and personal identity. From a general perspective, its core-relational theme is enhancement of our identity by taking credit for a valued object or achievement, either our own or that of someone or a group with whom we identify. Pride is clearly a major emotional opposite of shame. It contravenes the characterological putdown central to shame by enhancing our value as a person.

In a status-centered social world (i.e. when interpersonal competition is high), pride can be an important positive emotion in that we feel good about ourselves. But it can also create a sense of superiority over others, which is a mixed blessing because it can also lead to the denigration of out-groups, or much worse, regarding such groups as enemies (Allport, 1954). Because prideful attitudes are often defensive, signifying, perhaps, a weak or ambivalent self-esteem, we might speak of hubris rather than pride for this self-aggrandizing outlook.

Feelings of superiority create another interpersonal danger—namely, that of unseemly pride, which explains the widespread social distaste for boasting or bragging. Pride also has the historical distinction of being considered one of the seven deadly sins (Schimmel, 1992). Verbal expressions, such as "overweening pride" and the biblical warning that "Pride goeth before a fall" illustrate the negative side of our ambivalence about this emotion.

Although we sometimes conceive of pride as a favorable state of mind and associate putting our best foot forward aggressively with being successful, our culture ironically also venerates humility, which is an opposite of pride. This seeming contradiction is also found in other cultures. For example, the Japanese traditionally have been loath to express overt pleasure in the positive virtues of their family members, preferring to soft-pedal compliments about them by others.

These general considerations about pride apply to organizational settings where competition, status, and other social and financial rewards play such an important role. As noted on p. 58, some organizational researchers view pride as a high-status emotion (Tiedens, in press; Tiedens et al., in press), which when hurt (e.g. as a result of injustice) can cause people to reject benefits offered to them and behave spitefully (Pillutla & Murnighan, 1996). It is interesting that pride may be felt when outcomes are positive, regardless of the process. For example, it is felt when despite unfairness the person receives the desired outcome (Weiss et al., 1999). People who work in organizations want to feel proud of themselves and what they do, and when their pride is denigrated it can backfire on the organization itself.

Compassion

This emotion is based on the human potential for empathy. In general terms, the core-relational theme for compassion is being moved by another's suffering and wanting to help. Compassion probably enters organizational life most frequently in the context of hiring and firing employees and supervising and evaluating their work. It takes the form of conflict between the desire to be helpful and kind yet professional in doing their job.

Supervisors usually assume that in representing their organization they should treat people fairly and realistically on the basis of their actual work contribution. This responsibility becomes more poignant when a managerial decision must be negative. To act negatively toward an employee, even when it is justified, requires that supervisors set aside or distance themselves emotionally from the tendency to empathize with the plight of those for whom they are responsible. It may be that managers do not like to give negative feedback to employees (Murphy & Cleveland, 1995) because of the potentially negative effect of such feedback on a person's mood (Kruger, Lewinsohn, & Aiello, 1994).

Distancing can make us appear indifferent or hard-hearted. As a self-protective device, this coping process is commonly found in medical, nursing, and paramedic personnel who must constantly deal with people who are suffering from serious illness that can disable or kill. Not to be able to distance, however, is to be vulnerable to suffering excessively at another's legitimate distress.

Supervisors and managers in organizations vary greatly in the degree of empathy they feel toward subordinates. Some cannot stand the responsibility for making demands on others. They may experience too much empathy about the plight of those for whom they have managerial responsibility, and suffer excessive guilt in their jobs. Others regard themselves as tough-minded but fair, and some even relish the power they have over others. Still other supervisors may have to defend against organizational pressures, lest compassion lead to excessive personal distress.

Extremes of vicarious suffering on the part of supervisors and managers, or a lack of compassion, illustrate a person–job misfit, which could lead to failure as a supervisor or early job burnout. Organizational cultures differ greatly in this regard. One organization is perceived to be a harsh place to work, whereas another is considered nurturing, a difference that could conceivably affect the prospects of economic survival.

In the literature of organizational research, we found one study that examined compassion in the context of interpersonal negotiations (Allred et al., 1997). These researchers examined the effects of both compassion and anger on such negotiations. They expected compassionate displays to increase helping behavior and to decrease the incidence of punishment and retaliation. As might be anticipated, the effects of anger were conceived to be opposite. Indeed, the researchers found that the more compassionate one of the two negotiators felt toward the other, the greater was the willingness to cooperate with the other negotiator in the future, and the results of the negotiation for both were also better.

Love

In other writings (e.g. Lazarus & Lazarus, 1994), love was included among the emotions provoked by favorable life conditions, but you will see below that this can be misleading. From a general standpoint, the core-relational theme of love in our culture is to desire or participate in affection, usually but not necessarily reciprocated.

Love is, however, a complex and controversial emotion because, like anger, it has many different variants. Romantic love can be contrasted with companionate love (friendship) or parental love. An ongoing love can be in danger, shared or unrequited, homosexual or heterosexual, and modern society is hardly neutral about these variants. We must also distinguish between love that takes place at work and outside the organizational context. Thus, love in the family setting may conflict with work commitments. And vice versa, work can threaten love in family and other kinds of relationships.

Any time men and women are brought together in close functional relationships, as in organizational life, there is also the potential for sexual attraction, with or without love. Organizational managers probably view passionate love as potentially disruptive of the work missions of people. Love may also evoke the problems of sexual harassment, which constitutes a major institutional complication that generates considerable attention these days. We need only consider the confusion about what constitutes sexual harassment, and the high cost of lawsuits against organizations for the failure to deal with this effectively.

It is not evident that anyone really knows what to do about these complications of emotion. They may be quite messy for any organization. Unrequited love may lead to anger and jealousy, which also can have extremely destructive personal, social, and work consequences. One way or another, love can result in guilt, shame, jealousy, sadness, and so forth, which represent some of its emotional downsides. It can also result in much happiness/joy, which may facilitate or hinder work commitment (see earlier discussion of positive mood and work behavior). If we want to examine love in organizational life, these complexities and downsides must be taken into account in an organizational setting.

CONCLUSIONS

The most important lesson to be gained, from what we have been saying about emotions in organizational life, is that knowing the particular emotion that is aroused and its dynamics is useful, in that this knowledge could provide guidelines for managing the harmful and beneficial consequences of diverse emotions. As we have mentioned, such knowledge may be essential for diagnosing what is going on and managing it effectively, both at the individual and organizational level.

A cognitive–motivational–relational conceptualization of the discrete emotions and how they work provides a powerful analytic tool for correctly assessing person–environment relationships at work, which define what is important in ongoing adaptational struggles. To take advantage of this tool, we must ask about each adaptational encounter at work what might have brought an emotion about, how it is coped with, and what the consequences might be.

We must also evaluate the contribution of other aspects of the person's life, such as distinctive goal patterns, the inability to inhibit destructive impulses, and the problems of living outside the context of work, such as family or health crises, which could have major consequences for work in an organizational setting. If, for example, the emotional reaction was widely shared by other workers, this would suggest that the main culprit was some condition of the organizational environment. If, on the other hand, the number of workers reacting with a similar emotion was low, this would suggest that we are dealing with a personality problem, say, an angry or anxious person rather than being one that arose from the organizational environment.

As phrased above, however, this is not a very good way to make the point because emotions usually—we are tempted to say always—reflect the joint operation of *both* environmental (most often, interpersonal) conditions *and* personality characteristics. Emotions seldom reflect solely an environmental condition or a personality trait, but are best viewed as relational, especially when it is obvious that people differ greatly in their emotional reactions even in the same setting.

From our point of view, whether or not we understand exactly what is happening, it always represents a given person's cognitive–motivational–relational construction about those happenings. In other words, in their appraisals, people draw on both sources of information. The issue comes down to relational meaning, which provides us with the bottom line of the emotional process.

By having a viable theory about the arousal and regulation of each of the emotions, we can make reasonable suppositions about the sources of the emotions observed in organizational life. This kind of analysis is constantly employed in psychotherapy to help us understand what is happening to dysfunctional and emotionally distressed individuals (see Lazarus, 1989, 1991c). Its use in organizations and its potential for fruitful research and applications could produce major dividends. This cannot be gainsaid, if we wish to understand what is happening to individual persons or groups of people struggling to get along under the conditions of their working lives, and if we want to consider the implications for organizations in general and any individual organization in particular.

REFERENCES

Allport, G.W. (1954) *The Nature of Prejudice*. Reading, MA: Addison Wesley Longman.

Allred, K.G., Mallozzi, J.S., Matsui, F., & Raia, C.P. (1997) The influence of anger and compassion on negotiation performance. *Organizational Behavior and Human Decision Processes*, **70**, 175–187.

Aristotle (1941) Rhetoric. In R. McKeon (Ed.) *The Basic Works of Aristotle*. New York: Random House.

Ashforth, B.E. & Humphrey, R.H. (1993) Emotional labor in service roles: The influence of identity. *Academy of Management Review*, **18**, 88–115.

Astrachan, J.H. (1995) Organizational departures: The impact of separation anxiety as studied in a merger and acquisitions simulation. *Journal of Applied Behavioral Science*, **31**, 31–50.

Barrick, M.R. & Mount, M.K. (1991). The big five personality dimensions and job performance: A meta-analysis. *Personnel Psychology*, **44**, 1–26.

Bedeian, A.G. (1995) Workplace envy. *Organizational Dynamics*, **23**, 49–56.

Berkowitz, L. (1989). Frustration-aggression hypothesis: Examination and reformulation. *Psychological Bulletin*, **106**, 59–73.

Chatman, J.A. (1989). Improving interactional organizational research: A model of person-organization fit. *Academy of Management Review*, **14**, 333–349.

Cohen-Charash, Y. (2000) *Envy at Work: A Preliminary Examination*. (Manuscript in preparation).

Cooper, C.L. & Payne, R. (1980) *Current Concerns in Occupational Stress*. Chichester, UK: Wiley.

Cooper, C.L. & Payne, R. (1991) *Personality and Stress: Individual Differences in the Stress Process*. Chichester, UK: Wiley.

Davis-Blake, A. & Pfeffer, J. (1989) Just a mirage: The search for dispositional effects in organizational research. *Academy of Management Review*, **14**, 385–400.

Dewe, P.J. (1989) Examining the nature of work stress: Individual evaluations of stressful experiences and coping. *Human Relations*, **42**, 993–1013.

Dewe, P.J. (1991) Primary appraisal, secondary appraisal and coping: Their role in stressful work encounters. *Journal of Occupational Psychology*, **64**, 331–351.

Dewe, P.J. (1992) The appraisal process: Exploring the role of meaning, importance, control, and coping in work stress. *Anxiety, Stress, and Coping*, **5**, 95–109.

Diener, E. (1984) Subjective well-being. *Psychological Bulletin*, **95**, 542–575.

Duffy, M.K., Shaw, J.D., & Stark, E.M. (1997) *The Salieri syndrome: Consequences of envy in groups.* Paper presented at the Society for Industrial and Organizational Psychology, St Louis, MO, April.

Eckenrode, J. & Gore, S. (1990) (Eds) *Stress Between Work and Family.* New York: Plenum.

Fineman, S. (1993) Organizations as emotional areas. In S. Fineman (Ed.) *Emotion in Organizations*, pp. 9–35. London: Sage Publications.

Folkman, S. (1997) Introduction to the special section: Use of bereavement narratives to predict well-being in men whose partners had died of AIDS—Four theoretical perspectives. *Journal of Personality and Social Psychology*, **72**, 851–854.

Folkman, S. & Lazarus, R.S. (1988a) Coping as a mediator of emotion. *Journal of Personality and Social Psychology*, **54**, 466–475.

Folkman, S. & Lazarus, R.S. (1998b) Coping and emotion. *Social Science in Medicine*, **26**, 309–317.

Folkman, S., Moskowitz, J.T., Ozer, E.M., & Park, C.L. (1997). Positive meaningful events and coping in the context of HIV/AIDS. In B.H. Gottlieb (Ed.) *Coping with Chronic Stress*, pp. 293–314. New York: Plenum.

French, J.R.P., Jr, Caplan, R.B., & Van Harrison. (1982) *The Mechanisms of Job Stress and Strain.* Chichester, UK: Wiley.

George, J.M. (1990) Personality, affect, and behavior in groups. *Journal of Applied Psychology*, **75**, 107–116.

George, J.M. (1991). State or trait: Effects of positive mood on prosocial behaviors at work. *Journal of Applied Psychology*, **76**, 299–307.

George, J.M. (1995) Leader positive mood and group performance: The case of customer service, *Journal of Applied Social Psychology*, **25**, 778–794.

George, J.M. & Brief, A.P. (1992) Feeling good-doing good: A conceptual analysis of the mood at work-organizational spontaneity relationship. *Psychological Bulletin*, **112**, 310–329.

George, J.M. & Brief, A.P. (1996) Motivational agendas in the workplace: The effects of feelings on focus of attention and work motivation. In L.L. Cummings & B.M. Staw (Eds) *Research in Organizational Behavior*, pp. 75–109, Vol. 18. Greenwich, CT: JAI Press.

Gibson, D.E. (1993) *Behind the Mask: Emotional Episodes at Work.* Unpublished manuscript.

Gibson, D.E. & Schroeder, S.J. (1999) *Power and Affect: The Agent's View* (Manuscript in preparation).

Glomb, T.M. & Hulin, C.L. (1997) Anger and gender effects in observed supervisor-subordinate dyadic interactions. *Organizational Behavior and Human Decision Processes*, **72**, 281–307.

Gottlieb, B.H. (1997) (Ed.) *Coping with Chronic Stress.* New York: Plenum.

Hochschild, A.R. (1979) Emotion work, feeling rules, and social structure. *American Journal of Sociology*, **85**, 551–575.

Holt, R.R. (1982) Occupational stress. In L. Goldberger & S. Breznitz, (Eds), *Handbook of Stress: Theoretical and Clinical Aspects*, pp. 419–444. New York: The Free Press.

Horner, M.S. (1972) Toward an understanding of achievement-related conflicts in women. *Journal of Social Issues*, **28**, 157–175.

Hochschild, A.R. (1983) *The Managed Heart: Commercialization of Human Feeling*. Berkeley: University of California Press.

Isen, A.M. & Baron, R.A. (1991) Positive affects as a factor in organizational behavior. In L.L. Cummings & B.M. Staw (Eds), *Research in Organizational Behavior*, Vol. 13. pp. 1–53, Greenwich, CT: JAI Press.

Kahn, R.L., Wolfe, D.M., Quinn, R.P., Snoek, J.D., & Rosenthal, R.A. (1964) *Organizational Stress: Studies in Role Conflict and Ambiguity*. New York: Wiley.

Kelman, H.C. (1961) Processes of opinion change. *Public Opinion Quarterly*, **25**, 57–58.

Kluger, A.N., Lewinsohn, S., & Aiello, J.R. (1994) The influence of feedback on mood: Linear effects on pleasantness and curvilinear effects on arousal. *Organizational Behavior and Human Decision Processes*, **60**, 276–299.

Laux, L. & Weber, H. (1991) Presentations of self in coping with anger and anxiety: An intentional approach. *Anxiety Research*, **3**, 233–255.

Lazarus, R.S. (1966) *Psychological Stress and the Coping Process*. New York: McGraw-Hill.

Lazarus, R.S. (1989) Constructs of the mind in mental health and psychotherapy. In A. Freeman, K.M. Simon, L.E. Beutler, & H. Arkowitz (Eds) *Comprehensive Handbook of Cognitive Therapy*, pp. 99–121. New York: Plenum.

Lazarus, R.S. (1991a) *Emotion and Adaptation*. New York: Oxford University Press.

Lazarus, R.S. (1991b) Psychological stress in the workplace. In P.L. Perrewé (Ed.) Job stress. A special Issue of the *Journal of Social Behavior and Personality*, **6**, 1–13, Select Press, Corte Madera.

Lazarus, R.S. (1991c) Emotion theory and psychotherapy. In J.D. Safran & L.S. Greenberg (Eds) *Affective Change Events in Psychotherapy*, pp. 290–301. New York: Academic Press.

Lazarus, R.S. (1993) From psychological stress to the emotions: A history of changing outlooks. In *Annual Review of Psychology. 1993*, pp. 1–21. Palo Alto, CA: Annual Reviews.

Lazarus, R.S. (1995) Vexing research problems inherent in cognitive mediational theories of emotion—and some solutions. *Psychological Inquiry*, **6**, 183–264.

Lazarus, R.S. (1998a) Coping from the perspective of personality. *Zeitschrift für Differentielle und Diagnostische Psychologie*, **19**, 211–228.

Lazarus, R.S. (1998b) *Fifty Years of the Research and Theory of R.S. Lazarus: An Analysis of Historical and Perennial Issues*. Mahwah, NJ: Lawrence Erlbaum Associates.

Lazarus, R.S. (1999a) *Stress and Emotion: A New Synthesis*. New York: Springer-Verlag.

Lazarus, R.S. (1999b) Hope: An emotion and a vital coping resource against despair. *Social Research*, **66**, 1–26.

Lazarus, R.S. (2001) Relational meaning and discrete emotions. In K.R. Scherer, A. Schorr, & T. Johnstone (Eds) *Appraisal Processes in Emotion*. New York: Oxford University Press.

Lazarus, R.S. & Folkman, S. (1984) *Stress. Appraisal, and Coping*. New York: Springer-Verlag.

Lazarus, R.S. & Launier, R. (1978) Stress-related transactions between person and environment. In L.A. Pervin & M. Lewis (Eds) *Perspectives in Interactional Psychology*, pp. 287–327. New York: Plenum.

Lazarus, R.S. & Lazarus, B.N. (1994) *Passion and Reason: Making Sense of our Emotions*. New York: Oxford University Press.

Lewis, M. & Haviland, J.M. (1993) (Eds) *Handbook of Emotions*. New York: Guilford.

Lieblich, A. (1971). Antecedents of envy reaction. *Journal of Personality Assessment*, **35**, 92–98.

Locke, E.A. & Taylor, M.S. (1990) Stress, coping, and the meaning of work. In W. Nord & A. Brief (Eds), *The Meaning of Work*. New York: D. C. Heath.

Mascolo, M.F. & Fischer, K.W. (1995) Developmental transformations in appraisals for pride, shame, and guilt. In J.P. Tangney & K.W. Fischer (Eds) *Self-Conscious Emotions: The Psychology of Shame, Guilt, Embarrassment, and Pride*, pp. 64–113. New York: Guilford.

McClelland, D.C., Atkinson, J.W., Clark, R.A., & Lowell, E.L. (1953) *The Achievement Motive*. New York: Appleton-Century-Crofts.

Miner, F.C., Jr (1990) Jealousy on the job. *Personnel Journal*, **69**, 88–95.

Morris, J.A. & Feldman, D.C. (1996) The dimensions, antecedents, and consequences of emotional labor. *Academy of Management Review*, **21**, 986–1010.

Mumby, D.K. & Putnam, L.L. (1992) The politics of emotion: A feminist reading of bounded rationality. *Academy of Management Review*, **17**, 465–486.

Murphy, K.R. & Cleveland, J. (1995) *Understanding Performance Appraisal: Social, Organizational, and Goal-based Perspectives*. Thousand Oaks, CA: Sage.

Natale, S.M., Campana, C., & Sora, S.A. (1988) How envy affects management. *International Journal of Technology Management*, **3**, 543–556.

O'Reilly, C.S. 111, Chatman, J., & Caldwell, D.F. (1991) People and organizational culture: A profile comparison approach to assessing person-organizational fit. *Academy of Management Journal*, **34**, 487–516.

Parrott, W.G. & Smith, R.H. (1993) Distinguishing the experiences of envy and jealousy. *Journal of Personality and Social Psychology*, **64**, 906–920.

Pillutla, M.M. & Murnighan, J.K. (1996) Unfairness, anger, and spite: Emotional rejections of ultimatum offers. *Organizational Behavior and Human Decision Processes*, **68**, 208–224.

Poulson, C.F.I. (2000). Shame and work. In N.M. Ashkanasy, C.E.J. Härtel & W.J. Zerbe. (Eds) *Emotions in the Workplace: Research, Theory. and Practice*, pp. 250–271. Westport, CT: Quorum Books.

Rafaeli, A. & Sutton, R.l. (1987) Expession of emotion as part of the work role. *Academy of Management Review*, **12**, 23–37.

Rafaeli, A. & Sutton, R.l. (1989) The expression of emotion in organizational life. In L. Cummings, L. & B.M. Staw (Eds) Research in organizational behavior, pp. 1–42, Vol. 11. Greenwich, CT: JAI Press.

Rafaeli, A. & Sutton, R.l. (1991) Emotional contrast strategies as means of social influence: Lessons from criminal interrogators and bill collectors. *Academy of Management Journal*, **34**, 749–775.

Rawls, J. (1971) *A Theory of Justice*. Cambridge, MA: The Belknap Press of Harvard University Press.

Ruh, R.A., White, J.K., & Wood, R.R. (1975) Job involvement, values, personal background, participation in decision making, and job attitudes. *Academy of Management Journal*, **18**, 300–312.

Russell, J.A. (1980) A circumplex model of affect. *Journal of Personality and Social Psychology*, **39**, 1161–1178.

Salovey, P. (1991) Social comparison processes in envy and jealousy. In J. Suls & T.A. Wills (Eds) *Social Comparison: Contemporary Theory and Research*, pp. 261–285. Hillsdale, NJ: Lawrence Erlbaum Associates.

Salovey, P. & Rothman, A.J. (1991) Envy and jealousy: Self and society. In P. Salovey (Ed.) *The Psychology of Jealousy and Envy*, pp. 271–286. New York: Guilford.

Schimmel, S. (1992) *The Seven Deadly Sins: Jewish, Christian, and Classical Reflections on Human Nature*. New York: The Free Press.

Schlosberg, H.S. (1941) A scale for the judgment of facial expressions. *Journal of Experimental Psychology*, **29**, 497–510.

Schoeck, H. (1969) *Envy: A Theory of Social Behavior* (M. Glenny & B. Ross, Trans.). New York: Harcourt, Brace, & world.

Shaver, P., Schwartz, J., Kirson, D., & O'Connor, C. (1987) Emotion knowledge: Further exploration of a prototype approach. *Journal of Personality and Social Psychology*, **52**, 1061–1086.

Silver, M. & Sabini, J. (1978) The social construction of envy. *Journal for the Theory of Social Behavior*, **8**, 313–332.

Smelser, N.J. (1963). *Theory of Collective Behavior*. New York: The Free Press.

Somerfield, M.R. (1997) The utility of systems models of stress and coping for applied research: The case of cancer adaptation. *Journal of Health Psychology*, **2**, 133–183.

Spector, P.E., Fox, S., & Van Katwyk, P.T. (1999) The role of negative affectivity in employee reactions to job characteristics: Bias effect or substantive affect? *Journal of Occupational and Organizational Psychology*, **72**, 205–218.

Spielman, P.M. (1971) Envy and Jealousy: An attempt at clarification. *Psychoanalytical Quarterly*, **40**, 59–82.

Staw, B.M. & Barsade, S.G. (1993) Affect and managerial performance: A test of the sadder-but-wiser vs. happier-and-smarter hypothesis. *Administrative Science Quarterly*, **38**, 304–331.

Staw, B.M., Bell, N.E., & Clausen, J.A. (1986) A dispositional approach to job attitudes: A lifetime longitudinal test. *Administrative Science Quarterly*. **31**, 56–71.

Staw, B.M. & Ross, J. (1985) Stability in the midst of change: A dispositional approach to job attitudes. *Journal of Applied Psychology*, **70**, 469–480.

Sutton, R.l. (1991) Maintaining norms about expressed emotions: The case of bill collectors. *Administrative Science Quarterly*, **36**, 245–268.

Sutton, R.l. & Rafaeli, A. (1988) Untangling the relationship between displayed emotions and organizational sales: The case of convenience stores. *Academy of Management Journal*, **31**, 461–487.

Tellenbach, H. (1974) On the nature of jealousy. *Journal of Phenomenological Psychology*, **4**, 461–468.

Tennen, H. & Affleck, G. (1996) Daily processes in coping with chronic pain: Methods and analytic strategies. In M. Zeidner & N.S. Endler (Eds), *Handbook of Coping: Theory, Research, and Applications*, pp. 151–180. New York: Wiley.

Tiedens, L.Z. (2000) *Anger and Advancement Versus Status and Subjugation: The Effect of Negative Emotion Expressions on Social Status Conferral*. (Manuscript in preparation).

Tiedens, L.Z. (2000). Powerful emotions: The vicious cycle of social status positions and emotions. In N.M. Ashkanasy, C.E.J. Härtel, & W.J. Zerbe (Eds) *Emotions in the Workplace: Research, Theory, and Practice*, pp. 72–81. Westport, CT: Quorum Books.

Tiedens, L.Z., Ellsworth, P.C., & Mesquita, B. (2000). Stereotypes of status and sentiments: Emotional expectations for high and low status group members. *Personality and Social Psychology Bulletin*, **26**, 560–574.

Titelman, P. (1981) A pheomenological comparison between envy and jealousy. *Journal of Phenomenological Psychology*, **12**, 189–204.

Toch, H. (1969) *Violent Men*. Chicago: Aldine.

Toch, H. (1983) The management of hostile aggression: Seneca as applied social psychologist. *American Psychologist*, **38**, 1022–1025.

Tomaka, J. & Blascovich, J. (1994) Effects of justice beliefs on cognitive appraisal of subjective, physiological, and behavioral responses to potential stress. *Journal of Personality and Social Psychology*, **67**, 732–740.

Tomaka, J., Blascovich, J., Kelsey, R.M., & Leitten, C.L. (1993) Subjective, physiological, and behavioral effects of threat and challenge appraisal. *Journal of Personality and Social Psychology*, **65**, 248–260.

Van Maanen, J. & Kunda, G. (1989) "Real feelings": Emotional expression and organizational culture. In L. Cummings, L. & B.M. Staw (Eds) *Research in Organizational Behavior*, pp. 43–103, Vol. 11. Greenwich, CT: JAI Press.

Vecchio, R.P. (1995) It's not easy being green: Jealousy and envy in the workplace. *Research in Personnel and Human Resources Management*, **13**, 201–244.

Vogel, W., Raymond, S., & Lazarus, R.S. (1959) Intrinsic motivation and psychological stress. *Journal of Abnormal and Social Psychology*, **58**, 225–233.

Weber, H. & Laux, L. (1993) Presentation of emotion. In G. Heck, P.L. van Bonaiuto, I.J. Deary, & W. Nowak (Eds) *Personality Psychology in Europe*, Vol. 4, pp. 235–255. Tilburg, Netherlands: Tilburg University Press.

Weiss, H.M. & Cropanzano, R. (1996) Affective events theory: A theoretical discussion of the structure, causes and consequences of affective experiences at work. In L.L. Cummings & B.M. Staw (Eds) *Research in Organizational Behavior*, Vol. 18, pp. 1–74, Greenwich, CT: JAI Press.

Weiss, H.M., Suckow, K., & Cropanzano, R. (1999) Effects of justice conditions on discrete emotions. *Journal of Applied Psychology*, **84**, 786–794.

Westman, M. & Etzion, D. (1995) Crossover of stress, strain and resources from one spouse to another. *Journal of Organizational Behavior*, **16**, 169–181.

Westman, M. & Etzion, D. (1999) The crossover of strain from school principals to teachers and vice versa. *Journal of Occupational Health Psychology*, **4**, 269–278.

Wharton, A.S. & Erickson, R.J. (1993) Managing emotions on the job and at home: Understanding the consequences of multiple emotional roles. *Academy of Management Review*, **18**, 457–486.

White, G.L. & Mullen, P.E. (1989) *Jealousy: Theory, Research. and Clinical Strategies*. New York: Guilford.

Wright, J.C. & Mischel, W. (1987) A conditional approach to dispositional constructs: The local predictability of social behavior [Special Issue]. *Journal of Personality and Social Psychology*, **53**, 1159–1177.

Wundt, W. (1905) *Grundriss der Psychologie*, 7th rev. ed. Leipzig: Engelman.

Zeidner, M. & Endler, N.S. (1996) (Eds) *Handbook of Coping: Theory, Research, Applications*. New York: Wiley.

Part II

Measuring and assessing emotion at work

Chapter 4

Emotions in the workplace: biological correlates

M.G. King

Institute for Behavioural Research in Health, Curtin University of Technology, Perth, Western Australia

We may reinforce a man with food whenever "he turns red" (but) we cannot in this way condition him to blush.

(Skinner, 1938)

This chapter addresses the question of what, if any, are the biological correlates of the varied emotions which occur in the workplace? As a follow-up, the usefulness of psychobiological measures of workplace emotions in investigations is evaluated. In-depth discussions of "What is an emotion?" (James, 1884) can be found in Chapters 1–3 in this book. While avoiding the distraction of a linguistic analysis of workplace emotions, it must be noted from a psychobiological point of view that there is disturbing overlap in the connotation of similar terms such as sentiment, mood, hedonic tone, distress and eustress, affective state, and feeling tone. The reader is referred to Chapters 1–3 which deal with these definitions and boundary conditions. The starting point for the present chapter is that a person has a homeostatic feeling tone which can be indexed using a wide range of central and peripheral biological measures (see Table 4.1). This resting state is basically tonic and though it does fluctuate between normal limits over time (e.g. day/night and seasonal variations), it is not usually thought of as being elicited. In this context then, an emotion is seen here as phasic, a perturbation in the resting tone which is, by comparison to the resting tone, of relatively short duration. The emotion is more than likely to be a physiological reaction or behavioural response to a particular stimulus. In the context of biological measures, not only

Emotions at Work. Edited by Roy Payne and Cary Cooper.
© 2001 by John Wiley & Sons, Ltd.

Table 4.1   Biological correlates of emotions

Small-molecule neurotransmitters	Acetylcholine Dopamine Noradrenaline (norepinephrine) Serotonin
Hormones	Adrenaline (epinephrine) Cortisol
Immune system	Antibodies Cortisol Histamine Immunoglobulins (e.g. IgA) Macrophages Natural killer (NK) cells T and B cells
Neuroendocrines	Pro-opio-melanocortin fragments (POMC) Adrenocorticotropic hormone (ACTH) α-Melanocyte-stimulating hormone (αMSH) β-Endorphin Enkephalins Noradrenaline (norepinephrine)
Physiology/Functional neuroanatomy	Computerized tomography (CT) ElectroKardioGram (EKG) Electrodermal/Galvanic skin response (GSR) ("lie detector") Electroencephalogram (EEG) Magnetoencephalography (MEG) Magnetic resonance imaging of brain function (fMRI) Positron-emission tomography (PET) Single-photon-emission computed tomography (SPECT)

is the resting state able to be monitored in terms of the variables listed in Table 4.1, but so is its perturbation. This approach is elaborated further in "Working definitions" below.

We have chosen to examine biological *correlates* of emotions, as this avoids the theoretical stance entailed in orientations such as biological bases and physiological determinants of emotions.

WORKING DEFINITIONS

We cannot embark on such an enterprise without a minimalist working definition of emotions. On the one hand, the present book is concerned with the workplace and any definition should lend itself to workplace examples. At the same time, the present chapter is concerned with biological correlates and the definition must be at least compatible with the vocabulary of the neurosciences.

Emotions are conceived of as subjective events which have hedonic tone and motivational potential. First, let us consider the question of hedonic tone—the spectrum of human emotions which stretches from euphoria through to dysphoria. At the "positive" extreme, we find, for example, humour, orgasm, and satiety, while exemplars at the "negative" extreme are terror, pain, and depression.

Searching for common ground between "workplace emotions" and behavioural neuroscience would seem like an unrewarding activity. However, these disparate topics make use of work in a conceptually useful way.

WHAT IS WORK?

Like the bipolarity of emotions noted above, work also has two sides to it. To evaluate this, we begin with an acknowledgement of bipolarity of emotions in the workplace and then set about measuring these emotions biologically.

Consider Frolov (1962), the Soviet work physiologist, who argued that work is a privilege which not only leads to material gains but also dignifies the worker. Opposed to Frolov's positive view is the negative one that work is what most people don't want to do, but do it anyway to gain access to rewards and avoid punishments. When considering biological correlates of work, the positive/ negative stance is not helpful. What does help is the almost Skinnerian view that rewards and punishers modulate workplace behaviour (Skinner, 1938). But, whereas Skinner would have ended with such a conclusion, it is no more than a starting point in the case of biological correlates. It is the intention in the present chapter to open up the "black box" in order to appraise the usefulness of biological measures of workplace emotions.

Most readers are familiar with the Skinner Box. Basically, it is a controlled space in which an organism is able to obtain rewards (e.g. food/water) or prevent/ stop noxious stimuli. These are called primary reinforcers. The paradigm is analogous to workplaces where a worker is paid in kind. If the worker performs for a token (e.g. money), then the reinforcer is not said to be primary but secondary.

The definitions which fit most comfortably into the intersection of the two sets (workplace and psychobiology) comes from Rolls (1999, pp. 60–61) "... emotions are states elicited by rewards and punishers, including changes in rewards and punishments. A reward is anything for which an animal will work. A punisher is anything that an animal will work to escape or avoid."

In the human context, a reward is anything for which a person will work. A punisher is anything that a person will work to escape or avoid. Emotions, for the most part, are states elicited by rewards and punishers (which includes changes in rewards and punishments).

SOME MILESTONES IN THE PSYCHOBIOLOGY OF EMOTIONS

Charles Darwin

In 1872, Darwin published his second most famous work *The Expression of the Emotions in Man and Animals*. Prior to Darwin, emotion was thought of as an element of consciousness. He proposed that emotion could also be considered in terms of biology and, in particular, evolution. He studied facial expressions in blind children and in a range of other vertebrates. Facial expressions are not confined to humans, and the similarity of such expressions in chimpanzees as smiles and pouting are highly comparable. Darwin concluded that many of the ways in which we express emotions are genetically inherited patterns that originally had some survival value.

His second major innovation was to distinguish between emotion as subjective cognition, on the one hand, and, on the other, as an observable behaviour (e.g. facial expressions, reflex stances) which paved the way for subsequent approaches.

The question of genetically expressed rather than culturally acquired expressions has proved to be controversial. Cross-cultural studies identify six facial expressions which are readily correlated with human emotions: anger, disgust, fear, happy, sad, surprise. Other emotions (e.g. guilt, humour, and embarrassment) are not so readily recognizable.

William James

James (1884) proposed a bodily theory of emotion which is best known today for the dilemma of whether the bodily reaction causes the emotion or vice versa. To James the prototypic human emotions such as fear, grief, love and rage were based on bodily involvement "I saw the bear, I ran, I was afraid". Van Toller (1979) asks the pertinent question, "What if the person froze with fear?", a question James overlooked.

Carl Lange, a Danish physiologist, subsequently elaborated the theory in physiological terms. The James–Lange theory states that reflexes/responses precede emotions and the brain interprets these patterns of responding as emotions (i.e. the cognitive labelling of specific physiological responses). The response may involve heart-rate elevation, respiratory changes, perspiration, facial expressions, and reflex stances.

Cannon–Bard theory

W.B. Cannon (1927, 1929) disputed the James–Lange proposition, claiming that emotions were centrally felt (in the thalamus) and only then did actions follow.

Cannon's "wisdom of the body" assigned an important but secondary role to the part played by the autonomic nervous system (sympathetic and parasympathetic branches) in the expression of emotions. He proposed that brain structures such as the thalamus first asseses an emotion-provoking situation and simultaneously send signals to the autonomic nervous system and to the cerebral cortex which interprets the situation cognitively. Bard (1934) elaborated Cannon's proposal physiologically.

However, in a limited sense William James' controversial notion that the "mind" received information from the body about emotional states was not without support. With hindsight, we can say that emotions have proved more complex than either James or Cannon first imagined them to be. They were arguing over the primacy of central versus peripheral reactions, when today it is established that there is two-way traffic; both feedforward and feedback are involved in complex ways. Even the "cascade" of neural, endocrine, and immunological variables shown in Table 4.1 is being added to, since we now know that the various effector pathways also feed back to the brain. In the next section, we look at the interplay between central and peripheral factors, between afferents, efferents, and relevant brain structures during emotions.

The Papez circuit and limbic system

In 1937, the neuroanatomist James Papez argued that emotions were not initiated in any one brain centre (e.g. Cannon had argued incorrectly for the primacy of the thalamus).

He proposed that a brain circuit (now known as the Papez circuit) comprising four interconnecting centres was responsible for the central experience of emotions as well as for their peripheral effects. He identified these interacting centres as: the hypothalamus and associated mamillary bodies, the anterior thalamic nuclei, the cingulate gyrus, and hippocampus.

MacLean (1949) added to the Papez circuit. The additional structures were: parts of the prefrontal area, the hippocampal gyrus and subcortical areas (amygdala), medial thalamic nuclei, septal area, some basal nuclei, and a few brainstem formations. This elaborated circuit MacLean labelled the limbic system.

James Olds

Using stimulating microelectrodes in the brains of experimental animals, Olds and his co-worker, Milner, discovered so-called "pleasure centres" and "pain centres" which he proceeded to map anatomically. Implanted animals could self-administer or terminate a minute electric pulse by pressing a bar, a procedure subsequently referred to as electrical stimulation of the brain (ESB).

Depending upon where in the brain the electrode was implanted, the animal would either bar-press repeatedly to deliver a "pleasurable" stimulus (median forebrain bundle, MFB of the hypothalamus) or to terminate quickly a "painful" stimulus (periventricular nucleus, PVN). If the electrode was implanted in a "pleasure centre", rats made on average 2,000 presses per hour for up to 20 hours until they finally collapsed from exhaustion (see Olds and Forbes, 1981 for review).

Izard (1971) related the ESB of pleasure and pain centres with the facial expression of emotions, thus providing a physical pathway for the earlier proposals of Darwin.

ESB works across many species (e.g. rats, cats, monkeys) and is not confined to infrahumans as a few studies have reported emotional elicitation by ESB of pleasure centres in human patients (Campbell, 1973). They report "feeling wonderful", "happy", "drunk", and "pain free".

BRAIN OPIATES

In the 1960s, short fragments of a large polypeptide (pro-opio-melanocortin, POMC) were found to be active within the brain (enkephalins) initially in the hypothalamic–pituitary axis (HPA). When they were tested functionally, some of these sequences proved to be endogenous opiates (e.g. endorphins), which provided a chemical basis for the "pleasure centres" described by James Olds. It was thought initially that, because these "opiates" were endogenous to the brain, they would be non-addictive, thus providing a painkiller that was not addictive. However, subsequent research proved otherwise as the brain was found to become dependent on its own opiates.

In humans, brain opiates such as β-endorphin are sensitive to stress (Amir, Brown, and Amir, 1979). Evidence for other central neuropeptides in stress (e.g. Substance-P), however, is not so clear (Grossman, 1988; Schedlowski et al., 1995).

The psychopharmacological technique of "self-administration" of neuroactive substances, referred to as chemical stimulation of the brain (CSB), developed along parallel lines to that of ESB.

PSYCHONEUROENDOCRINOLOGY

CSB experiments on brain opiates were extended to other neuropeptides (e.g. adrenocorticotropic hormone, ACTH) and to small-molecule neurotransmitters (e.g. acetylcholine, dopamine). Guillerman and Schally won the Nobel Prize for Physiology and Medicine for their characterization of hybrid neuroendocrine cells. On the input side, these cells function as nerve cells receiving neurotransmitters across their synapses with other nerve cells. However, on the output where a nerve cell might synapse with other nerve cells, the neuroendocrine cells produce an endocrine which feeds hormones into the bloodstream. Using such cells between the hypothalamus and pituitary, for instance, brain cells can directly input into the endocrine system (see Table 4.1 for specific examples).

Emotional signals from the hypothalamus may act through these releasing and inhibiting factors to access the hormone system directly (King, 1985).

BRAIN IMAGING

During the 1950s, powerful "mind-reading" techniques, which imaged the working brain, were developing. Prior to that, the electroencephalogram, which measured generated electrical signals on the scalp, had been state of the art, but this technique was cumbersome and does not give repeated images over time. Since then, scanning and computerized tomography have developed a sophistication in output (positron-emission tomography, PET), single-photon-emission computed tomography (SPECT), and magnetoencephalography (MEG) that renders imaging the technique of choice. Of these imaging procedures, functional magnetic resonance imaging (fMRI) has proved to be the "royal road" for studying emotions and other mental processes.

The principles underlying traditional MRI techniques (Cohen and Bookheimer, 1994) also apply to fMRI. Subjects are placed in a static magnetic field which has the effect of aligning protons within the region of the body being scanned in one direction (vector). Then a radio-frequency pulse of specific duration and frequency is applied. This pulse has the effect of displacing the protons out of alignment and into another vector. Subsequently, the protons behave in different ways which include "relaxing" back to the fixed magnetic field and "dephasing" by losing some of their spin. Different types of images can be generated depending on which of these proton behaviours is processed electronically.

Like other bodily organs, the brain requires a reliable supply of oxygen in order to metabolize glucose to provide energy. fMRI is based on the observation that a local increase in neuronal activity is associated with increased metabolic rate. This is rapidly followed by increased blood flow to the activated region. Since oxygenated and deoxygenated haemoglobin have different magnetic properties, the ratio of oxygenated to deoxygenated haemoglobin is important and is reflected by the intensity of the detected signal. Greater amounts of oxygenated haemoglobin result in more intense signals. In other words, oxygenated haemoglobin functions as an endogenous contrast agent.

When a subject is engaged in a brain-activating emotional task, an increase in the metabolic rate occurs in the involved brain regions. The increase is thought to be accompanied by vasodilation and increased blood flow. The increase in oxygenated haemoglobin exceeds the tissues' metabolic demands, resulting in an increase in the oxygenated/deoxygenated haemoglobin ratio found in the local capillary beds. This results in less susceptibility to dephasing which gives increased signal strength.

fMRI enables researchers to characterize the functional neuroanatomy of emotional responses and to describe the detailed mechanisms underlying the complexity of emotions.

Compared with positron-emission tomography (PET), fMRI provides significant advantages in studying a spectrum of brain functions such as emotions, cognitive localization, and motoric outputs.

An important advantage of fMRI is that radioactive substances are not required. This gives greater safety in repeated scanning of the same subject. It also allows the method to be used in populations, such as children, who may be more at risk from radiation. Compared with PET, fMRI results in significantly better spatial and temporal resolution. The spatial resolution can be within a 2–3-mm range, while its temporal resolution lies in the single-second range (Kalin et al., 1997).

PSYCHONEUROIMMUNOLOGY

For many years, influential immunologists described the immune system as "stand-alone". As a defence system, its function was to defend the organism against minute enemies which could not be detected by the organism's other defences (e.g. the fight/flight reaction). However, in the mid-1970s two classic studies rekindled interest in two-way communication between the brain and the immune system. Ader and Cohen (1975) updated the findings of Métalnikov and Chorine (1926) who showed that behavioural-conditioning procedures can influence the immune system. From a psychosocial perspective, Bartrop, Luckhurst, Lazarus, Kiloh, and Penny (1977) reported clinical studies of immune breakdown as a consequence of bereavement in widowers.

Dialogue between the central nervous system (CNS) and the bodies' peripheral systems such as the immune system is complicated. Of particular relevance to the present chapter are a number of chemical messengers that have been shown to traffic between the CNS, the immune system, and the endocrine system (Exton, King, & Husband, 1999; King & Husband, 1996). Neurotransmitters such as norepinephrine (Table 4.1) and neuroendocrines such as ACTH/MSH (Table 4.1) are known to alter immune responses by binding to receptors on lymph cells (Blalock, Harbour-McMenamin, & Smith, 1985). Conversely, some soluble mediators of the immune system feed back to CNS structures, particularly the limbic system, influencing its neurotransmitter and neuropeptide activities. Via these pathways, emotions may impact on various components of immune defence. At a functional level, Wenner et al. (1996) recently reported that acute electrical stimulation of the lateral hypothalamus, a known "pleasure centre", increases natural-killer-cell (NK) activity in rats. Conversely, Kaname et al. (1999) used electrical stimulation of hypothalamic nuclei in cats to produce negative emotions (stimulation of the anteromedial nucleus produced restlessness, and ventromedial stimulation produced threat responses—see ESB above). Immuno-logical changes accompanied these emotional behaviours: (i) an increase in gran-ulocytes and a decrease in lymphocytes and (ii) decreased surface expression of the L-section of adhesion molecules in leukocytes. Recent clinical studies extended the pioneering study of Bartrop et al. (1977): correlational studies in cancer patients and asthmatics (Fawzy et al., 1990; Tulloch & King, 1997) showed strong links between illness and negative affect.

BRAIN STRUCTURES AND EMOTIONS

Since the present chapter assumes no sophistication in anatomy, physiology, and related disciplines, what follows is a "plain language" description (as much as is possible) of the relevant brain structures and their functional roles in emotions. For present purposes, we do not delve more deeply into functional neuroanatomy than we need to as there is a very real danger of alienating many readers, who do not need to know more than the broad facts. For the reader who does need more detail, Cohen and Bookheimer (1994) and Van Toller (1979) is recommended.

What follows is based largely on the traditional methods of functional neuroa-natomy, behavioural neuroscience, and psychopharmacology, and updated by the imaging techniques outlined above. Where possible, human studies have been referenced. However, until recently, more invasive techniques (e.g. surgical ablation of brain structures), had been the only approach possible, and, for ethical reasons, such studies were usually carried out on infrahuman subjects.

For those not familiar with anatomical terms, these can seem misleading in man. In a lower vertebrate (e.g. a lizard), the layout is relatively simple. The fore-, mid-, and hindbrain conveniently line up with other terms (anterior–posterior, front versus rear; dorsal–ventral, underneath versus on top).

Two factors complicate this in humans. First, humans stood upright which puts some of the nomenclature out (e.g. underneath versus on top). Second, humans developed a relatively enormous brain which gave rise to an evolutionary packa-ging problem, How to fit all that brain into one small skull? The solution was to wrap new layers of brain around the old. In overview, the human brain can be conveniently thought of as functioning on three separable but interacting strata.

1. The primitive brain (archipallium)

In evolutionary terms, this is the oldest part and is sometimes spoken of as the primitive/reptilian brain. It comprises the brainstem (medulla, pons, cerebellum, mesencephalon), the oldest basal nuclei (the globus pallidus), and the olfactory bulbs.

   Much of its connectivity is hard-wired and given over to day-to-day vegetative
activities, on the one hand, and self-defence, on the other.

2. The intermediate brain (paleopallium)

This is the old mammalian brain and comprises the structures of the limbic
system. Much of the connectivity is hard-wired but much is not.

3. The new mammalian brain (neopallium)

This is the latest evolutionary addition and is comprised of the cerebral hemi-
spheres (neocortex) and some subcortical groups. Higher cognitive activity occurs
here such as fine-grained analysis of the external world, but it is not without
support from the lower levels.

THE EMOTIONAL BRAIN (LIMBIC SYSTEM)

The second stratum is most heavily involved in emotions, albeit with inputs from
Level 1 (archipallium) and interconnections with Level 3 (neopallium). As mentioned above, the main brain structures in emotions are organized into the limbic
system which consists of some 53 regions with about 35 associated tracts. This
"emotional brain" continually samples all incoming sensory information. Directly
or indirectly, its outputs effect endocrine, visceral, motoric, and somatic motor
events and, recently, the immune system has been added to this list.
   Watts (1975) argues that the primary task for the limbic system is to monitor all
sensory inputs and categorize them as pleasant or unpleasant. This requires not
only constant surveillance but also ongoing checks against brain evaluations of
situations as either dangerous or benign. Then, at a behavioural level, the limbic-
system correlates commit the animal to approach/avoidance somatic movements
which are integrated with autonomic nervous system (ANS) activity, endocrine
arousal, and probably also with the immune involvement.
   The concept of two-way communication has become increasingly apparent,
with recent advances in our understanding of the linkages between the central
system, peripheral systems, and the information that peripheral systems feed back
to the central system.

SEPTUM

This area lies anteriorly to the thalamus and has been associated with different
kinds of euphoric sensations. A recent study found strong effects associated with
drug and sexual experience, and sexual orgasm with four centres being reported in

females and only one in men (Erdtmann-Vourliotis, Mayer, Riechert, & Holt, 1999). Although the reason for this is not yet clear, the observation that multiple orgasm is more common in females than in males seems pertinent.

CINGULATE GYRUS

This structure is located medially between the cingulate sulcus and the corpus callosum. The frontal part coordinates smell and visual images with pleasant memories of previous emotional experience. It also participates in the emotional reaction to pain and in the regulation of aggressive behaviour. Recent studies using fMRI (Maddock & Buonocore, 1997) have shown that in humans, the left posterior region is activated by threat-related words.

THALAMUS

Stimulation of the thalamus produces changes in emotional reactivity. Its importance is not due to the thalamus *per se*, but rather to its extensive network of connections with other limbic structures. These connect to the prefrontal areas and to the hypothalamus. The anterior nuclei also connect to the mamillary bodies and to the fornix, the hippocampus, and cingulate gyrus. This links them into the Papez circuit.

HYPOTHALAMUS

As the name suggests, the hypothalamus is located beneath the thalamus and some anatomists do not include this structure in the limbic system proper. Beginning with the now classic studies by Olds and Milner (1956), the lateral parts have been implicated with pleasure and rage. Wenner et al. (1996) recently corroborated the left-hemisphere (LH) pleasure centre and added the important new finding that its stimulation led to the subsequent rise in NK activity, thus implicating immune reactivity in LH stimulation (see Table 4.1 for the cascade of events).

VENTRAL TEGMENTUM

Located in the mesencephalon (midbrain), the main emotionally active centre in the ventral tegmental area (VTA) is a compact grouping of dopaminergic neurons (i.e. they release dopamine as a chemical messenger Table 4.1) whose axons lie in the nucleus accumbens. Stimulation of these neurons produces pleasurable sensations, including some which are akin to orgasm.

AMYGDALA

This almond-shaped nucleus lies buried within the tip of the temporal lobe and connects with the hippocampus and the thalamus.

The amygdala is essential for self-preservation and does this by recognizing threat and danger. Although the amygdala does not control the expression of emotion, it identifies occasions when emotions like fear, anger, and aggression are called for. In humans, damage to the amygdala may be associated with an impaired ability to recognize emotional faces and flattened emotions ensue especially with anger, rage, and fear (Heilman & Gilmore, 1998; Morris, Ohman, & Dolan, 1999). Kalin et al. (1997) report correlations between depth of depression and amygdaloid activity.

HIPPOCAMPUS

This structure, named for it resemblance to a seahorse, is strongly involved in memory, especially the consolidation of long-term memories. The importance of emotional memories as motivators should not be underestimated (Di Giusto, Cairncross, & King, 1971). Recent studies in humans using PET scanning (Henke, Weber, Kneifel, Wieser, & Buck, 1999) suggest that the hippocampal contribution may be limited to episodic memory, novelty detection, in-depth semantic processing of information, and to spatial memory, all of which impact on emotions.

BRAINSTEM

This region is clearly responsible for "lower" emotional reactions in infrahuman vertebrates such as reptiles and amphibians. However, the emotional baggage of evolution also carries into humans. These primitive structures remain active, not just as alerting mechanisms vital for survival; in other words, the ascending reticular-activating system and the hypothalamic–pituitary–adrenal (HPA) axis (Ziegler, Cass, & Herman, 1999), but in the maintenance of the sleep–wake cycle as a recent PET study has corroborated (Braun et al., 1997).

PREFRONTAL AREA

This area comprises the entire non-motor anterior region of the frontal lobes. Although it does not form part of the limbic system, it does have extensive two-way connections with the thalamus, amygdala, and other subcortical structures. These account for the important role it plays in the genesis and especially in the expression of affective states.

Dacosta's (1997) case review of severe chronic refractive schizophrenics updates favourably the practice of prefrontal lobotomy (leucotomy), which had fallen into disrepute during the 1960s for the treatment/management of difficult cases. Successful management of aggression was obtained, but the downside to lobotomy is that patients have generally flattened emotive states.

BRAIN PROFILES OF POSITIVE VERSUS NEGATIVE REACTIONS/EMOTIONS

Left/Right localization

Current brain models of emotion (e.g. Canli et al., 1998 propose that positive (approach related) emotions are lateralized towards the LH. In contrast, processing of negative (withdrawal related) emotions appear to be lateralized towards the right hemisphere (RH). However, it should be noted that laterality with respect to emotions is still a controversial topic.

Some investigators propose (e.g. Kalin et al., 1997) that non-specific arousal and alerting processes may also be associated with selective activation of the right posterior cortex, particularly the right temporoparietal regions.

In reference to more specific arousal, Kalin et al. report that the left anterior cortical regions are importantly involved in the processing of positive emotional states and associated behaviours, while the right frontal cortical regions appear to be involved in the processing of negative emotions such as fear and disgust.

In regard to PET studies of depression (Kalin et al., 1997), most, but not all studies, show that patients have decreased metabolism or blood flow in the left anterior regions. Using an image-analytic strategy that examined relations between specific depressive symptoms and patterns of regional blood flow in a large sample of depressed patients, individual differences in the reduction in cerebral blood flow in the left dorsolateral prefrontal cortex were associated with the symptoms of psychomotor retardation and depressed mood.

Cortical involvement

Kalin et al. (1997) also report contrasting effects over the cortex. The prefrontal cortex was not activated in processing positive emotions, but negative emotions induced bilateral activation in regions of the prefrontal cortex and in the parietal and occipital regions of cortex.

Teasdale et al. (1999) report that, in both elated and depressed moods, cerebral blood flow (CBF) was increased in the lateral orbitofrontal cortex. Midbrain CBF increased only in elated mood. By contrast, induced sadness increased regional CBF in ventral paralimbic regions (anterior insula, subgenual cingulate) and decreased regional CBF in dorsal neocortical and limbic regions (prefrontal, inferior parietal, dorsal anterior cingulate, posterior cingulate).

Visual induction

Positive visual stimulation (e.g. using film clips), eliciting happiness, activated the right and left insula, the right inferior frontal gyrus, left splenum and left pre-cuneus. In contrast to negative images, positive pictures activated the right and left medial frontal gyri, right precentral gyrus, and the left caudate.

Recall or imagination of personally saddening experiences increased CBF in the inferior orbitofrontal cortex. Sadness induced by recalling unhappy memories, while viewing unhappy facial expressions, has been found to increase CBF in the left prefrontal cortex, bilateral anterior cingulate, inferior prefrontal cortex, and hypothalamus. Negative visual stimuli activated the right medial and mid-frontal gyri, right anterior cingulate gyrus, and right thalamus. Presentation of film clips eliciting fear/disgust activated the left orbitofrontal cortex (Teasdale et al., 1999).

PERIPHERAL CORRELATES: PHYSIOLOGICAL, ENDOCRINOLOGICAL, AND IMMUNOLOGICAL

Thus far, we have focused on CNS correlates of emotions. However, two relevant points have been made above:

(i) effector systems are not only activated/inhibited by central outputs but
(ii) the peripheral systems also feed back information to the CNS.

Since the proposal of the James–Lange theory, argument has raged about Peripheral Nervous System (PNS) primacy in emotions. It now seems safe to conclude that, while the CNS generates emotional perception, it does so only in concert with the PNS, so that measuring peripheral-system variables makes pragmatic sense.

Watts (1975) argued that a primary task of the limbic system was to monitor all sensory inputs and categorize them as pleasant or unpleasant. This requires not only constant surveillance but ongoing checks against higher brain evaluations of situations as either dangerous or benign. Having done that, however, the task still remains to get the signal(s) out of the brain and into behaviour. Only there, can limbic messages commit the organism to reflex movements and motor approach/avoidance, which have to be integrated with ANS excitation/inhibition and an appropriate endocrine profile. (In addition to all this connectivity, we would now want to add immune involvement as well.) Finally, to complete the transaction, the whole apparatus must keep the CNS informed by feedback of relevant ongoing information.

For realistic reasons, most applied experimenters, with a focus on workplace applications, are more than likely to use peripheral measures. Although these do not tell the full story, the necessary biological sample(s) are characteristically easier to acquire and less intrusive (e.g. a "lie detector" test is easier, cheaper and far less disruptive to carry out than an fMRI scan). The GSR might not provide the ultimate sophistication in data, but, for most applications, fMRI would be an overkill.

MIXED EMOTIONS

Consistent with the strategy of this book, the present chapter makes a special effort to deal with a balanced spectrum of emotions. Influential theorists have attempted to redress the balance between reported studies of positive versus negative emotions. In 1960, Mowrer argued persuasively for "hope" and "fear" as the primary motivators. In the intervening decades, "fear" studies have proliferated, but for "hope" there is little.

The central focus of the present chapter is the topic of emotional stress in the workplace. Here there is a plethora of reviews, laboratory and field studies, and lesser reports, and, where these include emotions as is often the case, they usually focus on what popularly are known as unpleasant feelings or negative emotions. It is difficult to say why science knows so much more about the psychobiology of negative emotions than it does about the positives. The following may have some bearing on the matter:

(i) To begin with, the etymology of "stress" has not helped. The modern English word "stress" derives from the Old French *destresse*, which first gave us the Middle English *distresse* and then *stresse*. Only later did the quasi-scientific term *stress* come about (Selye, 1946). So, while there is common ground between stress and distress, there is no counterbalancing positive construct such as euphoria which has received comparable attention from researchers.

(ii) A more compelling reason for the imbalance is that granting bodies receive far more proposals on negative emotions. It beggars belief that researchers in the area prefer to work on negative rather than positive emotions. More likely, the researchers' predilection for negative emotions reflects the preferences of the money givers. Granting bodies find it more defensible to fund a study on depression rather than one on euphoria.

Hans Selye (1946), the pioneer of hormonal research on "stress", saw the need for greater balance, and, in Selye (1976), he revamped his "stress" system to include two major subcategories: *distress* and *eustress* (the latter derived from the Greek word *eu* for "good"). Belatedly, some stressors were seen as beneficial to the organism (e.g. moderate exercise, orgasm). Unfortunately, the term *eustress* has not proved popular, and, at best, has been replaced by "well-being" or, at worst, ignored.

PERIPHERAL PHYSIOLOGY

It is well documented that human's primitive "fight/flight" emotional reaction has a predictable physiology triggered by the sympathetic branch of the ANS (Van Toller, 1979): pupils dilate, hearing sharpens, muscles tense, heart and respiratory rates increase, and blood pressure rises as blood is diverted away from the extremities to the central vascular bed and the brain, in a genetically prescribed way that Darwin would have approved of. For the last 50 years, much of this activity could have been indexed by peripheral physiological measures such as EEG, EKG, and GSR, as shown in Table 4.1. The latter two could have been used readily in the workplace.

Influential phyiological theorists had argued that these predictable autonomic patterns were initially triggered by the CNS, but thereafter operated autonomously. However, experimental demonstrations of autonomic conditioning and biofeedback (Miller, 1969) began to challenge this "dogma" of autonomy. For example, Bolm-Audorff, Schwammle, Ehlenz, Koob and Kaffarnik (1986) report that the stress associated with public speaking causes cardiovascular changes, while predictable dysfunctional ventricular cardiovascular changes (Di Giusto, Di Giusto, & King, 1974; Punch, King, & Matyas, 1976) have been produced in normal humans undergoing fear conditioning.

ENDOCRINOLOGY

In concert with this defined physiological profile to distress and eustress, parallel hormonal patterns have also been measured. Selye (1946) first described a hormonal profile which he labelled the general adaptation syndrome (GAS), which was a non-specific reaction to stressors. Similar to the stance adopted by the ANS theorists, protagonists for the endocrine system argued for a long time, and in the face of mounting evidence to the contrary, that the endocrine system was an autonomous "stand-alone" system. Just as autonomic conditioning put paid to the ANS as autonomous, the same occurred with the endocrine system, when experiments began to accumulate which showed reliably that fear conditioning was capable of modifying the putative "stand-alone" hormonal system (Di Giusto, Cairncross, & King, 1971).

More recent studies on humans have confirmed that plasma concentrations of cortisol and catecholamine concentrations increase, along with some POMC-derived peptide hormones, during different stress situations such as taking examinations or public speaking (Bolm-Audorff et al., 1986; Dimsdale, Young, Moore, & Strauss, 1987; Johansson, Laakso, Karonen, & Peder, 1987; Meyerhoff, Oleshansky, & Mougey, 1988).

In keeping with an effort to balance our treatment of the bipolar dimension of hedonic tone, we now consider, as a counterfoil to fear, the hormonal correlates of sexual orgasm. (If you are still wondering what this has to do with workplace emotions consider the recent behaviour of Bill Clinton and Rupert Murdoch as trendsetters. If nothing else, the Lewinski affair highlights the volatility of emotions, how shared positive emotions can readily be transformed into negatives by the intrusion of social factors. However, if you seek answers you must look to other chapters.)

In contrast to decades of hormonal studies on human fear, only recently have human hormonal correlates during orgasm been successfully monitored (Krüger et al., 1998; Exton et al., 1999; Exton et al., in press). This group reports that sexual arousal and orgasm produce a distinct pattern of neuroendocrine alterations which varies but little between men and women. Although a broad spectrum of hormones was monitored, prolactin was the most responsive hormone in either sex. In addition, plasma noradrenaline was elevated significantly but in women only. The accepted gonadal hormones (estrogen, testosterone, and progesterone) were conspicuous by their unresponsiveness.

IMMUNOLOGY

As with the ANS and the endocrine system, the extent of autonomy afforded to the immune system has also been challenged in the last 30 years. In the case of the immune system, the breathing space afforded by the claim of autonomy has been put to good use. The immune system was the least understood of the peripheral systems, and, had the brain sciences muscled in during the 1920s, the basics of the immune system might not have been so easily mapped out. It seems with hindsight that each of the peripheral body systems needed a period of time during which it could explore itself, and the claim of "autonomy", though somewhat misguided, afforded that protection. But having said this, we must now acknowledge that the demand for the immune system to find its place among an integrated brain, endocrine, and peripheral physiological systems could not be staved off after the 1970s. History has shown that an earlier attempt by Métalnikov (1934), though heroic, was nonetheless premature; his message of integration was the same, but most immunologists were far from ready for it.

It is only since about the mid-1970s that the immune system was forced to join the orchestra with the brain as the conductor.

In the last decade, considerable interest has developed in the use of immune profiles. The measurement of IgA and cortisol in saliva have both proved useful. Gleeson et al. (1999) have used both salivary IgA levels and salivary cortisol to predict infection risk in elite swimmers. Both measures have also been used by

Kügler, Reintjes, Tewes, and Schedlowski (1996) to index the changes in emotional state of soccer coaches before, during, and after their teams competed.

Anderson (1996) observes that depression is an emotion/mood which has frequently been correlated with immune dysfunction, although the results of early studies tended to be varied. Discrepant findings may have arisen because lesser states of dysphoria, associated with the immune changes, are extremely subtle. A comprehensive review of the correlation by Weisse (1992) concluded that indices of immunocompetence were lower in populations experiencing depression. He also found strong evidence that the immune dysfunctions were related more to the dysphoric emotions than to situations or events. In a meta-analysis, Herbert and Cohen (1995) concluded that clinical depression was associated with several large changes in immunity. In addition to evaluating all published studies, the authors carried out separate analyses of studies that met the criteria of methodologically sound. Reliable immune alterations included lowered lymphocyte proliferative response and alterations in numbers of several white-blood-cell populations.

In summary, our main concern in this section on peripheral measures has been whether such measures can distinguish emotional from non-emotional responding (i.e. emotional from purely cognitive/conative activities). The answer seems to be in the affirmative. The harder ask, however, is whether peripheral measures— ANS physiology, endocrine, or immune—can distinguish between the emotions? But again the answer seems to be in the affirmative. Emotions all share some common bodily processes, but if we search across physiological, endocrinological, and immunological parameters a differentiating pattern can often be found for particular emotions. The strategy here is to move away from studies involving a single dependent variable and toward those involving several measures which range across the biological disciplines. Success in characterizing an emotion will lie in the particular mix of dependent variables, but the luxury of choice is now available to investigators.

CONCLUSION

It is becoming clear that the boundaries between the interacting systems shown in Table 4.1 can merge, as central neurotransmitters and neuropeptides are now known to change functions from neurohormone to lymphokine and back. Besedovsky and del Rey (1991) observe that neuroendocrines act not only as hormones but also as messengers within the immune system. The complete picture of the psychobiology of emotions is only now being sketched in and it also shows complicated pathways between central and peripheral factors.

Nonetheless, the potential for application of existing psychobiological measures (Table 4.1) far exceeds their current use. The way lies open for multidisciplinary research in workplace emotions, integrating the psychobiological measures discussed above with other more conventional measures.

Acknowledgement

The author thanks Justin Conti for his assistance.

REFERENCES

Ader, R. & Cohen, N. (1975) Behaviorally conditioned immunosuppression. *Psychosomatic Medicine*, **37**, 333–340.

Amir, S., Brown, Z.W., & Amir, Z. (1979) The role of endorphins in stress: Evidence and speculations. *Biobehavioral Reviews*, **4**, 77–86.

Anderson, J.L. (1996) The immune system and major depression. *Advances in Neuroimmunology*, **6**, 119–129.

Bard, P. (1934) The neurohumoral basis of emotional reactions. In C.A. Murchison (Ed.) *Handbook of General Experimental Psychology*. Worcester, MA: Clarke University Press.

Bartrop, R.W., Luckhurst, E., Lazarus, L., Kiloh, L.G., & Penny, R. (1977) Depressed lymphocyte function after bereavement. *Lancet*, **1**, 834–836.

Besedovsky, H.O. & del Rey, A. (1991) Physiological implications of the immune-neuro-endocrine network. In R. Ader, D. Felten, & N. Cohen (Eds) *Psychoneuroimmunology*, pp. 589–608. San Diego: Academic Press.

Blalock, J.E., Harbour-McMenamin, D., & Smith, E.M. (1985) Peptide hormones shared by the neuroendocrine and immunologic systems. *Journal of Immunology*, **135**, 858s–861s.

Bolm-Audorff, U., Schwammle, J., Ehlenz, K., Koob., H., & Kaffarnik, H. (1986) Hormonal and cardiovascular variations during a public lecture. *European Journal of Applied Physiology*, **54**, 669–674.

Braun, A.R., Balkin, T.J., Wesenstein, N.J., Carson, R.E., Varga, M., Baldwin, P., Selbie, S., Belenky, G., & Herscovitch, P. (1997) Regional cerebral blood flow throughout the sleep-wake cycle—an (H20)-O-15 PET study. *Brain*, **120** (part 7), 1173–1197.

Campbell, H.J. (1973) *The Pleasure Areas*. London: Eyre Methuen.

Canli, T., Desmond, E., Zhao, Z., Glover, G., & Gabrielli, J.D.E. (1998) Hemispheric symmetry for emotional stimuli detected with fMRI. *Neuroreport: An Interdisciplinary Journal for the Rapid Communication of Research in Neuroscience*, **9**(14), 3233–3239.

Cannon, W.B. (1927) The James-Lange theory of emotions: A critical examination and an alternative theory. *American Journal of Psychology*, **39**, 106–124.

Cannon, W.B. (1929) *Bodily Changes in Pain, Hunger, Fear and Rage*. New York: Appleton.

Cohen, M.S. & Bookheimer, S.Y. (1994) Localization of brain function using magnetic resonance imaging. *Trends in Neuroscience*, **17**, 268–277.

Darwin, C. (1872) *The Expression of Emotions in Man and Animals*. London: Murray.

Dacosta, D.A. (1997) The role of psychosurgery in the treatment of selected cases of refractory schizophrenia—a reappraisal. *Schizophrenia Research*, **28**(2–3), 223–230.

DiGiusto, E.L., Cairncross, K.D. & King, M.G. (1971) Hormonal influences on fear-motivated responses. *Psychological Bulletin*, **75**, 432–444.

Dimsdale, J.E., Young, D., Moore, R., & Strauss, H.W. (1987) Do plasma norepinephrine levels reflect behavioral stress? *Psychosomatic Medicine*, **49**, 375–382.

Erdtmann-Vourliotis, M., Mayer, P., Riechert, U., & Holt, V. (1999) Acute injection of drugs with low addictive potential (Delta(9)-tetrahydrocannabinol,3,4-methylenedioxymethamphetamine, lysergic acid diamide) causes much higher c-fos expression in the limbic brain areas than highly addictive drugs (cocaine and morphine). *Molecular Brain Research*, **71**(2), 313–324.

Exton, M.E., Bindert, A., Krüger, T., Scheller, F., Hartmann, U., & Schedlowski, M. (1999) Cardiovascular and endocrine alterations after masturbation-induced orgasm in women. *Psychosomatic Medicine*, **61**, 280–289.

Exton, M.E., King, M.G. & Husband, A.J. (1999) Behavioural conditioning of immunity. In M. Schedlowski & U. Tewes (Eds) *Psychoneuroimmunology: An Interdisciplinary Introduction*, pp. 453–471. New York: Kluwer Academic/Plenum.

Exton, N.G., Truong, T.C., Exton, M.S., Wigenfeld, S., Leygraf, N., Saller, B., Hartmann, U. & Schedlowski, M. (2000) Neuroendocrine response to film-induced sexual arousal in men and women. *Psychoneuroendocrinology.*, **25**(2), 187–199.

Fawzy, F.I., Kemeny, M.E., Fawzy, N.W., Elashoff, R., Morton, D., Cousins, N., & Fahey, J.L. (1990) A structured psychiatric intervention for cancer patients. II. Changes over time in immunological measures. *Archives of General Psychiatry*, **47**, 729–735.

Frolov, Y. (1962) *Work and the Brain*. Moscow: Foreign Languages Publishing House.

Grossman, A. (1988) Opoids and stress in man. *Journal of Endocrinology*, **119**, 377–381.

Gleeson, M., McDonald, W.A., Pyne, D.B., Cripps, A.W., Francis, J.L., Fricker, P.A., & Clancy, R.A. (1999) Salivary IgA levels and infection risk in elite swimmers. *Medicine and Science in Sports and Exercise*, **31**(1), 67–73.

Heilman, K.M. & Gilmore, R.L. (1998) Cortical influences in emotion. *Journal of Clinical Neurophysiology*, **15**(5), 409–423.

Henke, K., Weber, B., Kneifel, S., Wieser, H.G., & Buck, A. (1999) Human hippocampus associates information in memory. *Proceedings of the National Academy of Sciences (USA)*, **96**(10), 5884–5889.

Herbert, T.B. & Cohen, S. (1995) Depression and immunity: A meta-analytic review. *Psychological Bulletin*, **113**, 472–486.

Izard, C. (1971) *The Face of Emotions*. New York: Appleton-Century-Crofts.

James, W. (1884) What is an emotion? *Mind*, **19**, 188–205.

Johansson, G., Laakso, M.L., Karonen, S.L., & Peder, M. (1987) Examination stress affects plasma levels of TSH, and thyroid hormones differently in females and males. *Psychosomatic Medicine*, **49**, 390–396.

Kalin, N.H., Davidson, R.J., Irwin,W., Warner, G., Orendi, J.L., Sutton, S.K., Mock, B.J., Sorenson, J.A., Lowe, M., & Turski, P.A. (1997) Functional magnetic resonance imaging studies of emotional processing in normal and depressed patients: Effects of venlafaxine. *Journal of Clinical Psychiatry*, **58**(suppl. 16), 32–39.

Kaname, H., Mori, Y., Sumida, Y., Kojima, K., Kubo, C., & Tashiro, N. (1999) Relationship between uncomfortable emotional behaviors and both changes in the number of peripheral blood leucocytes and the surface expression of adhesion molecules. *NeuroImmunoModulation*, **6**(6), 460.

King, M.G. (1985) Brain neuropeptide-monoamine interactions in learning. In J.L. McGaugh (Ed.) *Contemporary Psychology: Biological Processes and Theoretical Issues*, pp. 37–43. Amsterdam: North-Holland.

King, M.G. & Husband, A.J. (1996) Konditionierung immunologischer Funktionen. In M. Schedlowski & U. Tewes (Eds) *Psychoneuroimmunologie*, pp. 537–560. Heidelburg: Spektrum.

Krüger, T., Exton, M.S., Pawlak, C., von zur Muhlen, A., Hartmann, U., & Schedlowski, M. (1998) Neuroendocrine and cardiovascular response to sexual arousal and orgasm in men. *Psychoneuroendocrinology*, **23**(4), 401–411.

Kügler, J., Reintjes, F., Tewes, U., & Schedlowski, M. (1996) Competition stress in soccer coaches increases salivary Immunoglobulin A and salivary cortisol concentrations. *Journal of Sports Medicine & Physical Fitness*, **36**, 117–120.

MacLean, P.D. (1949) Psychosomatic disease and the "visceral brain": Recent developments bearing on the Papez theory of emotion. *Psychosomatic Medicine*, **11**, 338–353.

Maddock, R.J. & Buonocore, M.H. (1997) Activation of left posterior cingulate gyrus by the auditory presentation of threat-related words: An fMRI study. *Psychiatry Research*, **75**(1), 1–14.

Métalnikov, S. (1934) *Role du système nerveux et des facteurs biologiques et psychiques dans l'immunité*, Monograph of the Pasteur Institute, Paris: Masson.

Métalnikov, S. & Chorine, V. (1926) Role of conditioned reflexes in immunity. *Annals of the Pasteur Institute (Paris)*, **40**, 893–900.

Meyerhoff, J.L., Oleshansky, M.A., & Mougey, E.H. (1988) Psychological stress increases plasma levels of prolactin, cortisol, and POMC-derived peptides in man. *Psychosomatic Medicine*, **50**, 295–303.

Miller, N.E. (1969) Learning of glandular and visceral responses. *Science*, **163**, 434–435.

Morris, J.S., Ohman, A., & Dolan, R.J. (1999) A subcortical pathway to the right amygdala mediating "unseen" fear. *Proceedings of the National Academy of Sciences (USA)*, **96**(4), 1680–1685.

Mowrer, O.H. (1960) *Learning Theory and Behavior*. New York: Wiley.

Oberbeck, R., Schürmeyer, Th., Jacobs, R., Benschop, R.J., Sommer, B., Schmidt, R.E., & Schedlowski, M. (1998) Effects of ß-adrenoceptor-blockade on stress-induced adrenocorticotrophin release in humans. *European Journal of Applied Physiology*, **77**, 523–526.

Olds, M.E. & Forbes, J.L. (1981) The central basis of motivation: Intra-cranial self-stimulation studies. *Annual Review of Psychology*, **32**, 523–574.

Punch, J.C., King, M.G., & Matyas, T.A. (1976) ECG T-wave amplitude, muscle tension and heart rate concomitants of conditioned suppression. *Physiological Psychology*, **4**, 294–302.

Rolls, E.T. (1999) *The Brain and Emotion*. New York: Oxford University Press.

Schedlowski, M., Flüge, T., Richter, S., Tewes, U., Schmidt, R.E., & Wagner, T.O.F. (1995) ß-endorphin, but not Substance-P, is increased by acute stress in humans. *Psychoneuroendocrinology*, **20**, 103–110.

Selye, H. (1946) The General Adaptation Syndrome and diseases of adaptation. *Journal of Clinical Endocrinology*, **6**, 117.

Selye, H. (1976) *Stress in Health and Disease*. London: Butterworths.

Skinner, B.F. (1938) *The Behavior of Organisms: An Experimental Analysis*. New York: Appleton Century-Crofts.

Teasdale, J.D., Howard, R.J., Cox, S.G., Ha, Y., Brammer, M.J., Williams, S.C.R., & Checkley, S.A. (1999) Functional MRI study of the cognitive generation of affect. *American Journal of Psychiatry*, **156**, 209–215.

Tulloch, B.J. & King, M.G. (1997) *Personality and Asthma: An Evaluation of Six Theories*. Paper presented at the Psychosomatic Medicine Conference, Cairns, Australia.

Van Toller, C. (1979) *The Nervous Body: An Introduction to the Autonomic Nervous System and Behaviour*. Chichester, UK: Wiley.

Watts, G.O. (1975) *Dynamic Neuroscience: Its Application to Brain Disorders.* New York: Harper & Row.

Weisse, C.S. (1992) Depression and immunocompetence: A review of the literature. *Psychological Bulletin,* **111**, 475–489.

Wenner, M., Kawamura, N., Miyazawa, H., Ago, Y., Ishikawa, T., & Yamamoto, H. (1996) Acute electrical stimulation of lateral hypothalamus increases natural killer cell activity in rats. *Journal of Neuroimmunology,* **67**(1), 67–70.

Ziegler, D.R., Cass, W.A. & Herman, J.P. (1999) Excitatory influence of the locus coeruleus in the hypothalamic-pituitary-adrenocortical axis responses to stress. *Journal of Neuroendrocrinology,* **11**(5), 361–369.

Chapter 5

Measuring emotions at work

Roy Payne
*School of Psychology, Curtin University of Technology, Perth,
Western Australia*

As the earlier chapters in this book demonstrate, it is not easy to separate emotion from other states such as moods or enduring emotional states arising from temperament (e.g. anxiety). Table 5.1 maps out a framework for distinguishing potential signifiers of emotions. It is a conceptual convenience to separate the signifiers because, within the person, all these variables are interrelated with each having an influence on every other. Pure emotions are conventionally associated with affect, of course, but their presence is also indicated through physiological changes which bring about symptomatic responses such as sweating, changes in facial expression, skin colour, etc. These are accompanied by changes in behaviour associated with the emotion, including changes in cognitive functioning which may in turn bring about a change in emotion.

All these different classes of signifiers can vary in duration as indicated in the table. Emotions are usually distinguished from moods by the fact that they are of shorter duration lasting minutes or hours, but as the table indicates the same sorts of feelings/emotions can last for days or weeks. When particular feelings are very common in a person's life they can be conceived as a trait such as anxiety or happiness. In an excellent review of the literature on subjective well-being (Diener, Suh, & Smith, 1999) conclude with this description of the happy person: "We would emphasize the happy person is blessed with a positive temperament, tends to look on the bright side of things, and does not ruminate excessively about bad events, and is living in an economically developed society, has social confidants, and possesses adequate resources for making progress towards valued goals" (Diener et al., 1999, p. 295). Whilst this clearly reflects a positive emotional state, measures of subjective well-being are regarded here as a characteristic of the person, rather than of an emotional state itself.

Emotions at Work. Edited by Roy Payne and Cary Cooper.
© 2001 by John Wiley & Sons, Ltd.

Table 5.1 Emotional signifiers by duration

	Short (min/hours)	Medium (days/weeks)	Long (months/years)
Cognitive signifiers	Memory/Mistakes	Concentration/ judgement	Field dependence, attributional style
Affective signifiers	Emotion/Moods	Anxiety, happiness	Trait anxiety, subjective well-being
Behavioural signifiers	Fight, flight, freeze	Sickness absence, drug taking, aggression	Hardiness, learned helplessness
Symptoms	Vomiting, sweating, headaches, sleep loss, etc.	Vomiting, sweating, headaches, sleep loss, etc.	Chronic illnesses, hypertension, CHD, depression
Physiological signifiers	Blood pressure, heart rate, catecholamines	Blood pressure, catecholamines, cortisol, salivary IgA	Blood pressure, cortisol, salivary IgA, cholesterol

A fairly recent development in the literature on emotions is the notion of emotional intelligence (Goleman, 1998) and Ayman Sawaf's chapter in this book (Chapter 14). Measures of this concept have been developed to assess the degree to which people have understanding and control of all their emotions. This might be conceived in Table 5.1 as an overall emotional disposition. Bar-on (1997) has produced such a measure which assesses the person's perceptions of their: emotional self-awareness, assertiveness, self-regard, self-actualization, independence, empathy, interpersonal relationships, social responsibility, problem solving, reality testing, flexibility, stress tolerance, impulse control, happiness, and optimism. Bar-on reports their use in selection and as tools in team development. This measure is not described more fully here because this chapter largely focuses on measures of affect which may be short or medium in duration. It does not describe measures of affect which are of long duration such as measures of trait anxiety/neuroticism or subjective well-being (Diener et al., 1999) except as they may have been used in studies which have measured emotions as conceived for this chapter, and controlled for them in some way.

Although Table 5.1 includes signifiers other than feelings, the chapter is mainly concerned with measures of feelings, though some questionnaire measures include questions that also ask about symptoms and cognitive functioning. Physiological signifiers are dealt with in the chapter by Maurice King (Chapter 4).

As is implied in Table 5.1, duration is important in determining the nature of a measure. A most thorough treatment of the importance of time and response scales in measures of emotions is that by Russell and Carroll (1999a). They

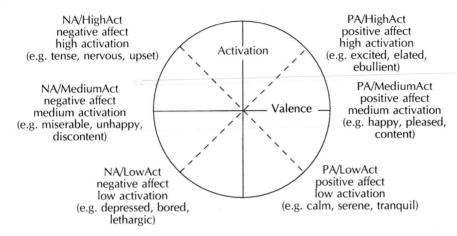

Figure 5.1 Six clusters of affect items defined by valence and activation (PA = positive affect, NA = negative affect)

review the extensive conceptual and empirical literature on two widely investigated aspects of affect: positive affect and negative affect. Some studies have shown measures of these concepts are independent of each other (Russell & Carroll, 1999a) and others have shown them to be bipolar opposites (Russell, 1989). In examining the evidence for these respective positions, Russell and Carroll show that the empirical relationship between positive and negative affect is influenced by (a) the content of the items selected to measure each construct, (b) the nature of the response scale, (c) whether the affect is short/momentary in duration or more extended in time. Figure 5.1 is taken from their article and categorizes adjectives that have been used to assess positive and negative affect. The model predicts that if items are used that are polar opposites (e.g. NA/HighAct versus PA/LowAct) then the measures will be strongly negatively correlated indicating a bipolar dimension. If the items are selected from parts of the two-dimensional space that are not polar opposites (NA/HighAct and PA/HighAct) then there will be little correlation between the measures suggesting independent unipolar measures. When Russell and Carroll analysed the item content of a number of different measures of positive and negative affect in this way, these predictions were upheld.

Russell and Carroll then proposed that the nature of the response scale could influence whether items were negatively correlated or were independent. They created 11 response scales which varied from strictly unipolar to strictly bipolar. The *strictly bipolar* scale for happiness versus sadness is:

Circle the number that best describes your present mood:

−7 −6 −5 −4 −3 −2 −1 0 1 2 3 4 5 6 7

Very sad   Neutral   Very happy

The strictly *unipolar* response scale:

If you feel happy tick here _____. If you ticked please indicate by how much:

1	2	3	4	5	6
Slightly		Moderately			Extremely

The point of this scale is that it measures happiness only, and that if sadness is measured in the same way then the two scales are likely to be independent of each other. An example of a scale which is *ambiguous* in its polarity is:

Circle the number that describes the degree to which you feel happy:

1	2	3	4
Not at all	A little	Quite a lot	Extremely

Again, when studies that have used different kinds of response formats are compared, the correlations between positive and negative affect vary in size in line with the response format. When the response format is ambiguous, but likely unipolar, the correlations were about 0.41. When the response format was ambiguous, but likely bipolar, the correlations varied from 0.64 to 0.86 across eight different studies.

Russell and Carroll also show how errors of measurement affect these relationship too, but what is more relevant to Table 5.1 is that they also consider the effect of the time period over which the respondent is asked to rate their mood or emotional state. It is obvious that if the person is asked to rate their immediate mood that they cannot be both happy and sad at the same time. In such measures, positive and negative affect are highly negatively correlated—they are bipolar. Russell and Carroll survey the evidence for bipolarity in measures which assess momentary mood and they conclude "Bipolarity has not been proved but it is a good bet—for momentary affect" (Russell & Carroll, 1999a, p. 19).

If the person is asked to rate their mood/emotional states over a more extended period, then most people in normal environments will have experienced both positive and negative experiences, even if neither were extreme. Scales constructed to do this such as Bradburn's (1969) and the Positive and Negative Affect Scales (PANAS; Watson, Clark, & Tellegan, 1988) have tended to produce measures of positive and negative affect which are independent of each other. The evidence for independence of these two dimensions is also assessed for studies where affect is extended over time. There are three main ways in which this has been studied. The first is *within-subjects* where the person provides reports/ratings of their mood over an extended period and the data are analysed for each person. The second is *aggregation by researcher* where the person provides ratings of their mood over time and the researcher aggregates them in some way (e.g. proportion of a given mood state, or average positive and negative affect). The third method is *aggregation by respondent* where the person is asked to give a global rating of their mood/ emotional state over an extended period of time such as "the last few weeks".

Russell and Carroll's main concern is with the bipolarity of affect, and having weighed the evidence from these sorts of studies, they find a number of flaws in the arguments that lie behind them. They conclude that even these studies do not provide strong support for the independence of positive and negative affect. Common sense, they suggest, would see them as opposites and for this reason most people might endorse this idea:

> (A) some people are frequently happy; others are frequently unhappy. (B) Some people are intense, others are even-tempered. Proposition A notes differences in means among individuals. Proposition B notes differences in variances (differences in intensity). If A and B are both true, as seems likely, then common sense is in harmony with the published evidence and with our analysis. This is not to say common sense is correct, but nothing so far challenges common sense (as we conceive it) on this matter.
>
> (Russell & Carroll, 1999a, p. 25)

This statement has relevance to the present chapter in that most studies do not measure both aspects of mood and also that it emphasizes the importance of examining carefully what any particular measure is asking the person to do. As Russell and Carroll have shown, minor differences in content, response format, or time focus can produce quite different sorts of relationships amongst measures of emotion/mood, and hence with other variables such as personality.

Whilst this is the central point to bear in mind about measures, their design is influenced by the models on which they are based. This is well illustrated by the 9 pages of response to Russell and Carroll offered by Watson and Tellegan (1999), which includes a hierarchical model of the structure of affect that can accommodate both bipolarity and independence. This in itself produces a 6-page response from Russell and Carroll (1999b). As the latter authors declare, "We cannot help feeling that the remaining disputes have more to do with words than with substance" (Russell & Carroll, 1999b, p. 611). The two papers do much to bring clarity to these issues. A major point for measurement that does emerge is: "In developing measuring devices, valence must be assessed in such a way that it is not confounded with high or low activation, and activation must be assessed in such a way that it is not confounded with valence" (Russell & Carroll, 1999b, p. 613).

MEHRABIAN'S COMPREHENSIVE FRAMEWORK FOR THE DESCRIPTION AND MEASUREMENT OF EMOTIONAL STATES

As Chapters 1–3 show, there are a number of frameworks for analysing/describing the range of emotional states. What is distinctive about Mehrabian's approach is that the framework is used to develop measures of a comprehensive range of emotional states. Mehrabian started from the work of Osgood, Suci, and Tannenbaun (1957) in their classic search for the basic dimensions of meaning. Their work produced three basic dimensions of meaning that they labelled evaluation, potency, and activity. Although these were conceived as dimensions of cognition, Mehrabian argued that they tapped the "lowest common denominators of cognitive operations—vague associations or emotions" (Mehrabian, 1995). Given the dimensions had been applied to a very wide range of stimuli, Mehrabian argued that they provided, "an alternative perspective on emotions as unverbalized and rudimentary forms of cognitive categorization that adults share with children and animals" (Mehrabian, 1995, p. 342).

Mehrabian and Russell (1974) propose that the emotional equivalent of evaluation is pleasure–displeasure, that of activity is arousal, and that of potency is dominance–submissiveness, or the feeling of being in control or out of control. They developed measures of each of these three dimensions. Six pairs of adjectives were rated on nine-point scales for each of the three emotional dimensions. State pleasure–displeasure was measured by adjectives such as: happy–unhappy, pleased–annoyed. The adjectives relating to state arousal included stimulated–relaxed and excited–calm. State dominance was assessed by adjectives such as controlling–controlled and influential–influenced. Right from the start, factor analyses of the measure produced three dimensions corresponding to each of the three states. Furthermore, Russell and Mehrabian (1977) investigated 42 other measures of emotion and showed their three dimensions accounted for most of the variance in them. Mehrabian (1995) provides the history of the development of the measure. The measure is different from other measures because it does not measure the emotion directly. It does not measure anger, anxiety, or guilt, for example. It measures where a person's emotions are located in the three- dimensional space. The following sample of emotional terms are taken from appendix A of the 1995 paper:

1. pleased, aroused, dominant: admired, excited, triumphant;
2. pleased, aroused, submissive: amazed, impressed, respectful;
3. pleased, unaroused, dominant: comfortable, relaxed, unperturbed;
4. pleased, unaroused, submissive: consoled, protected, sleepy;
5. displeased, aroused, dominant: angry, hostile, insolent;
6. displeased, aroused, submissive: bewildered, in pain, insecure;
7. displeased, unaroused, dominant: disdainful, indifferent, unconcerned;
8. displeased, unaroused, submissive: bored, fatigued, subdued.

The measure has been designed in both state and trait forms. How we label the states defined by their location in three-dimensional space is up to the reader/ researcher but it is easy enough to see that State 1 could comfortably be labelled "pride" and State 5 as "anger". The dichotomization of the dimensions helps illustrate the use of the approach, but, as they are all dimensions, then the range of different states it could accommodate is obviously very large and constrained only by the limitations of language. Guilt, for example, is a combination of displeasure, arousal, and submissiveness, and adjectives different than those in item 6 of the list above might get closer to its exact nature, but the three provided do not do a bad job: bewildered, in pain and insecure.

Mehrabian suggests the measures have a range of applications in both experimental and applied situations and some of the applied situations include the study of crowding and the atmosphere in a courtroom. These immediately suggest their use in different forms of organization and in different organizational cultures. They could also be usefully employed to investigate the emotional consequences of major organizational changes such as downsizing or the introduction of business process re-engineering.

MARSELLA'S FRAMEWORK OF MEASURES OF EMOTIONS IN WORKPLACE SETTINGS

Marsella (1994) has outlined the major issues concerning the measurement of emotions in workplaces. He very helpfully provides a list of major resources which include many measures of emotions as well as measures of other work-related concepts, including health and well-being. These are:

- *The Buros Mental Measurement Yearbook*;
- *The Encyclopedia of Clinical Assessment* (Woody, 1980);
- *The Measurement of Depression* (Marsella et al., 1987);
- *Measuring Mental Illness*, psychometric assessment for clinicians (Wetzler, 1989);
- *The Experience of Work*, a compendium of 249 measures and their use (Cook et al., 1981);
- *A Sourcebook of Tests and Measures of Human Behavior* (Andulis, 1977);
- *Personality Assessment via Questionnaire* (Angleitner and Wiggins, 1986);
- *Measures for Psychological Assessment*, a guide to 3,000 original sources and their application (Chun et al., 1975);
- *Measuring Health*, a guide to rating scales and questionnaires (McDowell and Newell, 1987).

Unfortunately, the article does not include references to some of these works, but from them he then lists examples of a whole range of measures, many of which are not strictly about emotional experience. They include measures of personality, measures of pathology, state-trait questionnaires covering anxiety, depression, anger, and pleasure. Measures of coping and mood are also listed as well as behavioural observation ratings. Biological measures include biochemical indicators from blood and urine, as well as psychophysiological measures such as blood pressure and heart rate. The section on occupational settings includes measures of job and organizational characteristics as well as measures of work related anxiety. Marsella also includes a three-dimensional framework for classifying measures of emotions. This appears as Figure 5.2. It is perhaps questionable to place

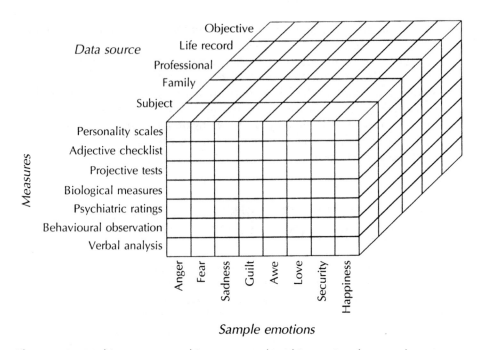

Figure 5.2   Multi-measure, multi-source, and multi-emotional research strategy

personality within the framework, as it is not an emotion, yet it is derived from experiences and dispositional influences which contain much emotional content, and undoubtedly influences the emotions experienced in different situations. Based on this framework, Marsella advises the use of (1) multiple measures such as mood checklists and biological indices; (2) more than one source of information (though this raises the question of what we do when these measures don't triangulate); and (3) the exploration of both positive and negative emotions. To understand the role of emotions in health and well-being, these need to be linked to indices of mortality, morbidity, social pathology, and health.

SOME MEASURES OF EMOTIONS IN ORGANIZATIONS

Having provided some frameworks for thinking about the variety of emotion-related states and how they might be measured, I now want to provide some examples of measures. This is not meant to be comprehensive but merely illustrative of measures that span a range of both positive and negative emotional states. One of the few measures of affective states that has been designed specifically to be used in organizations is Warr's (1990) job-related affective well-being.

WARR'S MEASURES OF JOB-RELATED AFFECTIVE WELL-BEING

Warr proposed two main dimensions of well-being which he labelled anxiety–contentment and depression–enthusiasm. Anxiety–contentment is assessed with six adjectives "tense, uneasy, worried" for the anxious end of the dimension, and "calm, contented, and relaxed" for the contented end of the dimension. The instructions to the respondent are: "Thinking of the past few weeks, how much of the time has your job made you feel each of the following?" The response scale is:

Never	Occasionally	Some of the time	Much of the time	Most of the time	All of the time
(1)	(2)	(3)	(4)	(5)	(6)

The anxiety items are reverse scored so a high score means high contentment. The adjectives assessing depression–enthusiasm are: "depressed, gloomy, miserable, cheerful, enthusiastic, and optimistic". Warr quotes an alpha coefficient of 0.76 for anxiety–contentment and 0.80 for depression–enthusiasm and a principal-components analysis of the scales showed them to be independent. These results are based on a large sample of workers in a range of UK organizations. Other researchers have since used the measures on good-sized samples and have argued that it would have been better to use common-factor analysis or confirmatory-factor analysis (Daniels, Brough, Guppy, Peters-Bean, & Weatherstone, 1997; Sevastos, 1996; Sevastos, Smith, & Cordery, 1992). In Warr (1994), the label of the anxiety dimension is changed to anxiety–comfort. A more radical alteration is Sevastos's claim, based on confirmatory-factor analysis, that the measures are best conceived as four unipolar scales rather than two bipolar dimensions (Sevastos, 1996). The four unipolar scales are anxiety, comfort (called relaxed by Sevastos), depression, and enthusiasm.

Warr's model also included a third dimension labelled tiredness–vigour to allow for the fact that tiredness can be associated with both positive and negative affective states. Hooper (1999) set out to evaluate the psychometric properties of the three-dimensional model. Hooper's data were collected from 275 white-collar workers in a large financial-services organization. The respondents were employed in a wide range of jobs within the organization. Hooper also used confirmatory-factor analysis and found that a six-factor unipolar model gave a better fit to the data than a three-factor bipolar model. Alpha coefficients for the six unipolar scales ranged from 0.73 to 0.94.

Whether the measures are treated as bipolar or unipolar, all the studies mentioned above provide evidence of the construct validity of the measures. All the affective measures correlate sensibly with measures of perceived work variables such as work pressure, job demands, role conflict, and role ambiguity. Hooper does, however, caution whether tiredness is a useful latent factor of well-being because it confounds physical and mental causes of tiredness. She does show, however, that vigour has useful discriminant validity as it helps to distinguish between "arousal" and "hedonic tone". The Payne, Wall, Borrill, & Carter (1999) study shows that both anxiety and depression correlate to 0.47 with negative affectivity, demonstrating the effect of disposition on reports of recent affect.

THE GENERAL HEALTH QUESTIONNAIRE

The General Health Questionnaire (GHQ) was developed by a British psychiatrist, David Goldberg (Goldberg, 1972; Goldberg, 1991). It has been extensively used in both work and community settings. Goldberg has developed a number of versions of the measure, which vary in length from 60 items, to 30 items to 12 items. These three versions measure recent psychological health/distress and the longer the measure the more reliable it is, though even GHQ-12 is highly reliable and very successful at identifying "cases" when compared to much more detailed psychiatric interviews. There is also a 28-item version which provides scores on four distinct, though not totally independent dimensions. They are: anxiety, depression, symptoms, and social functioning. In terms of the focus of this chapter on emotions, only the first two of these fall into this category. The other three versions of the GHQ are a mixture of items assessing emotions, cognitions, and behaviours, as well as symptoms such as sleep loss.

The instructions to the measures ask respondents to describe "their health *in general* over the *past month* and to concentrate on present and recent complaints, not those you have had in the distant past." There is a 4-point response scale which is scored 0–3. An example item is:

Have you recently felt constantly under strain?

| Not at all | No more than usual | Rather more than usual | Much more than usual |

It is clear from these instructions that the affective items in the GHQ fall into the medium-duration category in Table 5.1, and for practical purposes we have included these as measures of emotion. The scale is unipolar in Russell and Carroll's terms in that the emotional state is present only. It is also worth noting that there are no positive items in the GHQ, so the issue of the relationship between positive and negative affect is not present within the measure itself. Not surprisingly, scores on the affective scales of GHQ-28 or the total scales of GHQ-12, GHQ-30, and GHQ-60 are strongly correlated with measures of trait anxiety. In a study of long-term unemployed (Payne, 1988) found a correlation of 0.65 between GHQ-12 and neuroticism, as measured by the Eysenck Personality Inventory (Eysenck & Eysenck, 1975). Correlations with the anxiety and depression subscales of the GHQ-28 were 0.76 and 0.46, respectively, and similar correlations were obtained from a sample of employed people. In a sample of over

Table 5.2 A comparison of "caseness" as measured by GHQ-12

Source	Status	Sample size	Per cent cases
BHPS	Employed	5,001	17.8
BHPS	Unemployed	504	30.2
BHPS	Not in labour market	3,333	23.2
NHS	Employed	11,291	26.8

BHPS = British Household Panel Survey
NHS = National Health Service (all hospital employees)

9,000 people from all levels of hospital staff in the UK, Payne et al. (1999) found a correlation of 0.42 between GHQ-12 and a measure of negative affectivity.

It is worth noting that if a neurotic person reads the instructions carefully they should get very low scores on the GHQ because they normally feel these sorts of emotions. As already indicated, however, the measure detects "cases" very accurately, so most respondents clearly do not interpret the questions that way. This probably accounts for some of the failures to predict cases where anxious/neurotic people answer that the symptoms are "no worse than normal", and thus score very low, indicating low psychological distress.

One of the advantages of the measure is that it can be used to estimate "caseness" in populations. Goldberg has variously used a cut-off point for GHQ-12 of three or four symptoms as indicating "minor psychological distress". Table 5.2 shows some fairly recent data from the British Household Panel Survey and the dataset referred to in Payne et al. (1999) that is reported in Borrill et al. (1996). This study used a cut-off point of four or more symptoms. Both studies show that more than 20% of the workforce are suffering minor psychological distress at one point in time. For some subgroups in the Borrill et al. study the caseness was as high as 45% (e.g. female senior managers). In a study of a South Australian community reported in 1977 the rates for comparable white-collar workers and professionals were between 10–12% (Finley-Jones & Burville, 1977). The rates for unskilled workers were 19%.

Another measure which assesses a wider range of affective states is the Profile of Mood States (McNair, Lorr, & Droppleman, 1992).

PROFILE OF MOOD STATES (POMS)

POMS is a self-report measure of six affective states. The instructions ask the respondent to describe "How you have been feeling during the past week including today." In Table 5.1, therefore, it would be classified as recent state rather than present state. However, as with other measures, the timescale can be varied and for manual states shorter timescales have been successfully used such as: "today", "right now", and even "the past 3 minutes". There are 65 adjectives which have to be rated on the following response scale:

0 = not at all;
1 = a little;
2 = moderately;
3 = quite a bit;
4 = extremely.

The 65 adjectives represent the refinement of 100 different adjective scales by means of repeated factor analyses, and the adjectives were restricted to those that an average individual can easily understand. The factor structure reliably reveals six factors after oblique rotation. They are:

Scale	Example items	N items
Tension–anxiety	Tense, relaxed, panicky, anxious	9
Depression–dejection	Unhappy, sad, miserable, gloomy	15
Anger–hostility	Anger, bitter, furious, peeved	12
Vigour–activity	Lively, cheerful, active, vigorous	8
Fatigue–inertia	Listless, exhausted, sluggish	7
Confusion–bewilderment	Confused, forgetful, muddled	7

A total mood-disturbance score can be calculated.

The scales have been administered to hundreds of psychiatric outpatients, hundreds of college students, and 2,360 adult smokers. Kuder–Richardson reliabilities range from 0.95 to 0.87. In a sample of 100 outpatients in a psychiatric clinic, test–retest reliabilities varied from 0.65 for vigour to 0.74 for depression from initial assessment to pretherapy intake with the median gap being 20 days. After 6 weeks of treatment the test–retest reliabilities from assessment to therapy varied from 0.43 for vigour and 0.53 for anger. Thus, when mood is rated over the last week it is reasonably stable over time, but it is affected by psychotherapy showing the measure is sensitive to change.

Predictive validity studies have been carried out with brief psychotherapy patients, controlled outpatient drug trials, cancer patients, drug abusers, responses to emotion-inducing situations, and with sports athletes. The different scales in the measure behaved as predicted in all studies. Concurrent validity studies have related the scales to other measures such as the Beck Depression Inventory and the Manifest Anxiety Scale and the correlations with appropriate scales in POMS were moderately strong (0.51–0.8).

Women score higher than men on all scales, except anger where there is no gender difference. Men score higher on vigour. Other demographic variables have very small correlations with the scales (less than 0.2) though white men have higher scores on all scales except vigour, though correlations are only about 0.20. The scales do have some measure of correlation with social desirability. Correlations with the Crowne–Marlowe Social Desirability Scale were as follows on a sample of 150 outpatients: tension (-0.21); depression (-0.36); anger (-0.52); vigour (-0.33); fatigue (-0.18).

POMS is also useable in a short form which has only 30 items and again the internal reliability estimates for this form indicate it is a very good approximation to the full form. The POMS manual does not mention studies within organizations, but the instrument could clearly be used there in any of its different time-frame formats. The norms for the 2,360 adult smokers provide reasonable norms for comparisons with employed samples.

Mood adjective checklists have been utilized for decades, and Nowlis (1965, p. 104) provides an early review. A more recent version of measures derived from that early work can be found in Matthews, Jones, and Chaberlain, 1990.

THE UWIST MOOD ADJECTIVE CHECKLIST

The authors were employed in the Department of Applied Psychology at the University of Wales Institute of Science and Technology (UWIST) in Cardiff when they wrote the paper, and their definition of a mood is, "an emotion-like experience lasting for at least several minutes" (Matthews et al., 1990, p. 17). The items were selected from checklists of (Mackay, Cox, Burrows, & Lazzarini, 1978; Sjoberg, Svensson, & Perrson, 1979; Thayer, 1967). They were selected to measure the three hypothesized dimensions of: energetic arousal, tense arousal, and hedonic tone/pleasure–displeasure. The paper reports data from seven different studies, but the measure was applied consistently across them and they involved 388 people. There were roughly equal numbers of males and females largely drawn from a student population. The adjectives were presented randomly by computer and respondents were asked to rate the applicability of the adjective to "their present mood". The response scale had four points: "definitely", "slightly", "slightly not", and "definitely not." Scoring is from 4 to 1.

Using very-simple structure factor analysis they found three clear factors in the 46 items presented. Factor 1 was called hedonic tone and the best eight items which were eventually used to assess this were cheerful, contented, satisfied, happy, dissatisfied, sad, sorry. Factor 2 was labelled tense arousal and the highest loading eight items were anxious, jittery, tense, nervous, calm, restful, relaxed, composed. The third factor, named energetic arousal, finally contained eight items which are: active, energetic, alert, vigorous, unenterprising, sluggish, tired, and passive. The authors also created a general-arousal scale which assesses arousal irrespective of whether the arousal is pleasurable or unpleasurable. It is composed of 12 items: active, energetic, alert, sluggish, tired, passive, tense, jittery, nervous, calm, restful, and relaxed. All scales have a balance of positive and negative toned items. The alpha coefficients for the three main scales are all in the mid-80s and that for general arousal was 0.75. The scales are not independent as energetic arousal correlates to 0.43 with hedonic tone whilst tense arousal correlates to −0.37. The two arousal scales are independent of each other and hedonic tone is independent of general arousal.

The construct validity of the measure was explored by relating the scales to gender, social class, and education. Education was unrelated to mood. Older people were higher in both energetic and general arousal, though the age range is restricted in these samples and most people were between 18 and 40. Unemployed people were lower on hedonic tone. The evidence for gender differences in mood is equivocal, but some was consistent with the view that arousal is higher among women (Redgrove, 1976). Social class was not systematically related to mood, though it is related to psychological distress as measured by GHQ-12 with the lowest social classes scoring higher levels of distress (Finley-Jones & Burville, 1977). Systematic sampling of mood over time might well reveal such a class difference.

The mood measures were also related to the personality traits of extroversion and anxiety, as measured by Eysenck's Personality Questionnaire. As would be expected, tense arousal was related to neuroticism and extroversion was related to energetic arousal. Both were slightly related to hedonic tone, but the relationships disappeared when partial correlations were calculated. Matthews et al. (1990) also report a sensible pattern of correlations with another self-report measure of mood. They have also shown that the two arousal scales relate to physiological indicators of arousal such as the cardiac interbeat interval and skin conductance level. The authors also report eight studies of different stress situations and their effects on mood. The situations included the response to drugs, pain, muscle relaxation, sleep deprivation, and workload. Sleep deprivation and workload affected all three mood states with energetic arousal falling, tense arousal increasing, and hedonic tone decreasing. Energetic arousal was the only mood sensitive to drugs. The main claim the authors make for the measure, compared to previous checklists, is that three rather than two dimensions of mood can be measured reliably, and that the measure has satisfactory predictive and discriminant validity.

Whilst some measures attempt to assess a range of emotions/moods, others concentrate on single emotions such as anger, envy, jealousy, and happiness. Examples of these appear below.

ANGER

One of the best known measures of anger is the State-Trait Anger Expression Inventory, STAXI (Spielberger, 1996). This reference is to the manual which first appeared in 1979.

The STAXI consists of 44 items that form 6 scales and 2 subscales (the response format is a 4-point scale scored 1–4):

- *state anger* has ten items that measure intensity of angry feelings at a particular time;

- *trait anger* also has ten items that measure the disposition to experience anger;
- *anger-in* measures the frequency with which angry feelings are kept within the person (it has eight items);
- *anger-out* has eight items that assess the frequency with which the respondent expresses anger toward other people or objects;
- *anger control* is an eight-item scale measuring the frequency with which an individual attempts to control their angry feelings;
- *anger expression* uses the 24 items in the three previous scales to assess the frequency with which anger is expressed, regardless of the direction of the expression.

There are two subscales of the trait-anger scale:

- *angry temperament* is a four-item scale that measures the propensity to experience and express anger without specific provocation;
- *angry reaction* assesses the disposition to express anger when provoked or criticised (it has four items).

Only the state-anger scale is a measure of emotion/mood as considered here, and all the other scales are measures of temperament. The temperament scales have not been widely used in organizational studies, though Spielberger reports norms based on a sample of 1,868 military recruits which shows males to be higher than females on trait anger. However, both were lower than a sample of general medical and surgical patients (15.95 versus 18.21 with the female patients scoring much the same as the males). The military recruits don't appear to be particularly angry people. The measures could certainly be useful in comparative studies of organizational culture and maybe as selection tools. They would also be of interest in studies of organizational change as an individual difference variable in reactions to changes such as downsizing.

The state-anger scale would also be useful in such studies of course. The items for this measure appear below:

- I am mad;
- I feel angry;
- I am burned up;
- I feel irritated;
- I feel frustrated;
- I feel aggravated;
- I feel like I'm about to explode;
- I feel like banging on the table;
- I feel like yelling at somebody;
- I feel like swearing;
- I am furious;
- I feel like hitting someone;
- I feel like breaking things;

- I am annoyed;
- I am resentful.

The time frame is "right now" and the scale is: (1) not at all, (2) somewhat, (3) moderately so, (4) very much so. Once again, it would not be difficult to alter the instructions and the wording to measure recent anger over the last few weeks.

Concurrent validity studies have been carried out on samples of college students (280) and navy recruits (270). The manual fails to report the correlation between state anger and trait anger, but we would expect it to be moderate in size. Both state anger and trait anger correlate moderately with neuroticism ($r = 0.43$ and 0.50, respectively, for the male samples) as measured by the Eysenck Personality Questionnaire and with both state ($r = 0.63$) and trait anxiety ($r = 0.35$) as measured by the State–Trait Personality Inventory. State anger also correlates strongly with the Buss–Durkey Hostility Inventory (Buss & Durkee, 1957). The correlation varied from 0.66 to 0.73 for the males and females in the two samples.

The majority of the other studies referred to by Spielberger are in behavioural medicine and health psychology, and refer to results with the trait measures rather than state anger. Trait anger has been shown to be related to blood pressure and particularly in women who reported their work environment was hostile and tense (Julkunen & Korhonen, 1993). Trait anger has also been related to job satisfaction in an unpublished master's thesis (Miank, 1981).

ENVY

Most work organizations have, built into their structure and culture, differences by status and differences in the rewards associated with those status differences. Such systems are breeding grounds for envy. Surprisingly, it has not been a topic widely studied in organizational psychology. Smith, Parrott, Diener, Hoyle, & Kim (1999) have developed a measure of what they call "dispositional envy": the Dispositional Envy Scale (DES). Once again, the importance of the time frame in studying and measuring emotions is at issue. Strictly speaking, a disposition is not an emotion, but it can be construed as a person who experiences the emotion regularly. With this proviso, I believe it well worth describing their measure, as it could be quite easily amended to measure state envy or recent state envy by modification of the instructions, though Smith et al. have developed other measures to assess state envy and recent envy (*over the last 3 weeks*). Both of these measures have been related to the DES on a sample of undergraduates and results support the criterion-related validity of the instrument. The DES consists of the eight items listed below:

1. I feel envy every day;
2. the bitter truth is that I generally feel inferior to others;
3. feelings of envy constantly torment me;
4. it is so frustrating to see some people succeed so easily;

5. no matter what I do, envy always plagues me;
6. I am plagued by feelings of inadequacy;
7. it somehow doesn't seem fair that some people have all the talent;
8. frankly, the success of my neighbours makes me resent them.

The response scale is a −4 to +4 Likert scale running from *very strong disagreement* to *very strong agreement*, with 0 representing *neither agreement nor disagreement*.

These eight items are the survivors of an original pool of 54 items that were tested on two samples of undergraduates. The alpha coefficients for each sample were 0.86 ($N = 204$) and 0.83 ($N = 168$). Test–retest reliability over a 2-week period was 0.80.

Smith et al. have also related the DES to a range of well-established personality and satisfaction/happiness scales. The measure relates to these in ways that support its construct validity. People higher on envy are lower on self-esteem (correlations of −0.65 and −0.56). They are also more neurotic (correlations from 0.41 to 0.56), and more depressed (correlations from 0.36 to 0.51). Life satisfaction and happiness ratings are also negatively correlated with envy (correlations from −0.25 to −0.39). The authors have also shown that the DES predicts other measures of envy, even when social desirability has been controlled. As they also point out, the relationship between the DES and social desirability can be seen as an indication of its construct validity—being envious is not a highly regarded trait.

The authors do not report any studies of employed people, but it would be easy enough to alter items to fit the work context. Some suggestions appear below:

1. when I'm at work I feel envy every day;
2. the bitter truth is that I generally feel inferior to the people I work with;
3. feelings of envy constantly torment me when I'm at work;
4. it is so frustrating to see some of my work colleagues succeed so easily;
5. no matter what I do at work, envy always plagues me;
6. when I'm at work I'm troubled by feelings of inadequacy;
7. it somehow doesn't seem fair that some work colleagues seem to have all the talent;
8. frankly, the success of my work colleagues makes me resent them.

Envy is closely related to jealousy, but following Richard Lazarus and Yochi Cohen-Charash (Chapter 3) we shall treat it as a separate discrete emotion.

JEALOUSY

Smith et al. have shown that the DES relates moderately to the Interpersonal Jealousy Scale developed by Mathes and Severa (1981) though this measure concentrates on jealousy in romantic relationships. A detailed account of research on jealousy can be found in White and Mullen (1989), and most of their book is concerned with jealousy in romantic relationships, and the bulk of the work is by clinical psychologists. In an appendix to the book, White and Mullen describe seven measures of jealousy and several others that are less frequently used. Nearly all focus on intimate relationships and would be clearly relevant to couples who happen to work together too, but they would not tap into jealousy relating to other aspects of work relationships such as rewards and recognition. The measure that does include items that tap into this sort of jealousy is the Self-Report Jealousy Scale developed by Bringle and others (Bringle, 1981; Bringle & Williams, 1979). It is designed to measure dispositional jealousy and the 20 items cover sexual, social, family, and work domains. A nine-point scale is used and the end points are labelled "not very jealous" to "jealous". Factor analysis produces four factors consonant with the above four domains, though the factors are moderately correlated suggesting a generalized disposition as well as domain specific jealousy. The two items quoted for the work domain are:

• another person gets promotion for which you were qualified;
• someone else gets praise or credit for something you did.

Once again, it would be possible to rephrase these dispositional items so that they measured state jealousy or recent jealousy. No reference is made to work that has used the measure in organizational settings. The 28 pages of references in White and Mullen (1989) don't appear to have any that are not about intimate relationships, marriage, or other family relationships such as the ones between/amongst siblings. Although organizations contain many people who experience envy and jealousy, as a result of their treatment at work, there is little empirical work on either emotion. Their undesirable nature does, of course, make them sensitive topics, but their undesirability also makes them topics we should understand so that their presence can be minimized and their consequences defined and managed.

Another emotion that is prevalent in most relationships, including many work relationships, is guilt. Like envy and jealousy, however, it does not have a large empirical literature, in the workplace. It has been more developed in the clinical psychology literature, and there is potential for using the measures developed by clinicians in work settings.

INTERPERSONAL GUILT

O'Conner, Berry, Weiss, Bush, & Sampson (1997) have developed a measure of interpersonal guilt. They observe that guilt is very close to shame as an emotion, and that both emotions serve to maintain attachments to other individuals and broader social groups such as the family, school, workplace: "Guilt is a highly adaptive emotion when it serves to maintain the attachment and interdependencies that are essential for comfortable and productive lives" (O'Conner et al., 1997, p. 75). Interpersonal guilt occurs when people fear they have harmed others in the pursuit of their own goals. O'Connor et al. refer to several types of interpersonal guilt. The first is survivor guilt, which arises from the belief that we are experiencing good things that others are not experiencing, and that it may even be at the expense of those others.

Separation guilt is also the fear of hurting others because you have left them or become so different from them that you feel you are being disloyal. Omnipotent-responsibility guilt arises from an exaggerated sense of responsibility for the happiness and well-being of others. All three are often irrational and potentially capable of causing major psychological distress and disturbance. O'Conner et al. refer to other measures of guilt, but note that they have not focused on interpersonal guilt in particular and hence set out to design a measure that achieves that. In addition to these three types of guilt, they added a fourth which is conceptually different—self-hate guilt—which arises from failing to have met the expectations of demanding parents or other people who have importance for you (e.g. colleagues or bosses).

The Interpersonal Guilt Questionnaire (IGQ) comes in two versions. The IGQ-45 contains 45 items and the IGQ-67 contains 67 items. Examples for each subscale are:

- *Survivor guilt*—I conceal or minimize my success; it makes me uncomfortable to receive better treatment than the people I am with; I am uncomfortable talking about my achievements. As stated, the items are dispositional in terms of Figure 5.1. They could, however, be rephrased to be (a) measures of state or recent state and (b) focused on the workplace specifically (e.g. during the last few weeks, I have concealed or minimized my work achievements).
- *Separation guilt*—I feel that bad things may happen to my family if I do not stay in close contact with them; I prefer to do things the way my parents did them; I am very reluctant to express an opinion that is different from the opinions of my family or friends. Again, it would not be too difficult to rephrase these to fit into the work environment (e.g. during recent weeks, I have been reluctant to express an opinion that is different from my boss's/co-workers'/teammates' opinions).
- *Omnipotent-responsibility guilt*—it is very hard for me to cancel plans if I know the other person is looking forward to seeing me; I often find myself doing what someone else wants me to rather than doing what I most enjoy; I feel responsible at social gatherings for people who are not able to enter into conversations with others. Changing these to suit the work environment would produce items such as: during recent weeks at work, I have found myself doing what others want me to do rather than doing what I most enjoy.
- *Self-hate guilt*—if something bad happens to me, I feel I must have deserved it; if I fail at something I condemn myself and want to hurt myself; I always assume I am at fault when something goes wrong. This is much more a

dispositional concept than the others, and, although it would be possible to specify the above items were they only to be answered for the work context, it seems harder to argue that we would hate ourselves in such a limited part of our lifespace. That said, it might be that a particular leadership style such as that of the compulsive described by (Kets de Vries & Miller, 1984) could create such feelings.

Unfortunately, O'Conner et al. (1997) do not provide the response scale for these measures, but, given that the mean for the 22 items in the survivor guilt scales is 65 and the SD is 10, it looks as if it will be a five-point scale.

Using mixed-gender samples of people from a community organization ($n = 62$), therapists ($n = 35$), addicted clients ($n = 109$), and college students ($n = 111$), the authors report alpha coefficients for all scales that are acceptable but higher for the 67-item version where all scales are above 0.82. A Principal Component Analysis of the four scales separated the first three scales from the self-hate guilt scale and a composite interpersonal guilt score was created by adding the first three scales together.

To explore the construct validity of the scales, they were correlated with the Guilt Inventory (Kugler & Jones, 1992), Test of Self-Conscious Affect (TOSCA) (Tangney, Wagner, & Gramzow, 1992), and The Beck Depression Inventory (Beck, 1972). All scales correlated moderately strongly with the Beck ($r = 0.37$–0.52). All had similar size correlations with both state and trait guilt as measured by the Guilt Inventory. The same applied to the guilt and shame scales of the TOSCA. The scales did not correlate with the pride scale of the TOSCA. Given the moderately strong correlations with depression, it would seem wise to control for that in using these measures in organizations, but with reasonable modifications they appear to provide a sound basis for constructing work-related measures of guilt. They may be particularly relevant to the study of survivors and managers responsible for implementing downsizing policies in organizations. They might also cast light on the psychodynamics of managing people in stressful/dangerous occupations or ones that can be damaging to the clients (e.g. gambling, medicine).

CONCLUSIONS

In the process of searching for materials for this chapter I included the 13 emotions from Lazarus's list of discrete emotions (see p. 55, Chapter 3). They were each entered along with the keywords organization, work, and measure and the Psychlit and ABI Inform databases searched. The typical pattern of results for all but the main emotions relating to anxiety, depression, and happiness was a large number of hits for the emotion on its own, many fewer when combined with organization and hardly any when measure is added. As is evident from Chapter 3, there is a large and complex literature associated with anxiety, depression, and happiness/well-being. The largest part of all three is in the measurement of disposition, though there are also substantial literatures on immediate states as well as recent states. Emotions such as pride, hope, and shame as well as the ones mentioned above of envy, guilt, and jealousy present a very different picture. Such emotions are referred to in more qualitative approaches to studying organizations, but there remains great scope for increasing the provision of measures in these areas of emotion. We have learned much from the measurement of positive and negative affect, as described in the first part of this chapter, and it is hoped that such lessons can be applied to the development of a wider range of measures of emotions. And where we do wish to measure emotions qua emotions (i.e. very short-lasting feelings) there are technological developments such as bleepers and hand-held computers which will do much to facilitate data collection. There is much work to be done before we have the measure of emotion.

REFERENCES

Bar-on, R. (1997) *Development of The Bar-on EQ-i*, 105th Annual Convention of American Psychological Association, Chicago.

Beck, A.T. (1972) Measuring depression: The depression inventory. In T.A. Williams, M.M. Katz, & J.A. Shields (Eds) *Recent Advances in the Psychobiology of Depression*, pp. 299–302. Washington, DC: US Government Printing Office.

Borrill, C.S., Wall, T.D., West, M.A., Hardy, G.E., Shapiro, D.A., Carter, A., Golya, D.A., & Haynes, C.E. (1996) *Mental Health of the Workforce in NHS Trusts*. Sheffield: Institute of Work Psychology, University of Sheffield.

Bradburn, N.M. (1969) *The Structure of Psychological Well-being*. Chicago: Aldine.

Bringle, R.G. (1981) Conceptualizing jealousy as a disposition. *Alternative Lifestyles*, **4**, 274–290.

Bringle, R.G. & Williams, L.J. (1979) Parental-offspring similarity on jealousy and related personality dimensions. *Motivation and Motion*, **3**, 265–286.

Buss, A.H. & Durkee, A. (1957) An inventory for assessing different kinds of hostility. *Journal of Counselling Psychology*, **21**, 343–349.

Cook, J., Hepworth, S., Wall, T.D. & Warr, P.B. (1981) *The Experience of Work: A Compendium of 249 Measures and Their Use*. New York: Academic Press.

Daniels, K., Brough, P., Guppy, A., Peters-Bean, K., & Weatherstone, L. (1997) A note on a modification to Warr's measures of affective well-being at work. *Journal of Occupational and Organizational Psychology*, **70**, 129–138.

Diener, E., Suh, E.M., & Smith, H.L. (1999) Subjective well-being: Three decades of progress. *Psychological Bulletin*, **125**(2), 276.

Eysenck, H.J., & Eysenck, S.B.G. (1975) *Manual of the Esyenck Personality Questionnaire*. London: Hodder & Stoughton.

Finley-Jones, R.A. & Burville, P.W. (1977) The prevalence of minor psychiatric morbidity in the community. *Psychological Medicine*, **7**, 474–489.

Goldberg, D. (1972) *The Detection of Minor Psychiatric Illness by Questionnaire*. Oxford: Oxford University Press.

Goldberg, D.W.P. (1991) *A User's Guide to the General Health Questionnaire*. Windsor: NFER Nelson.

Goleman (1998) *Working with Emotional Intelligence*. New York: Bantam

Hooper, S. (1999) *Discriminant validity of Warr's (1990) tiredness-vigour dimension of job-related affective well-being.* Unpublished master's, Curtin University of Technology, Perth.

Julkunen, J., & Korhonen, H.J. (1993) *Anger Expression, Work Stress and Blood Pressure: An Interactional Approach.* Paper presented at the 7th European Health Psychology Society Conference, Brussels.

Kets de Vries, M. & Miller, D. (1984) *The Neurotic Organization.* San Francisco: Jossey-Bass.

Kugler, K.E. & Jones, W.H. (1992). On conceptualizing and assessing guilt. *Journal of Personality and Social Psychology*, **62**, 318–327.

Mackay, C.J., Cox, T., Burrows, B.C., & Lazzarini, A.J. (1978) An inventory for the measurement of self-reported stress and arousal. *British Journal of Social and Clinical Psychology*, **17**, 283–284.

Marsella, A.J. (1994) The measurement of emotional reactions to work: conceptual, methodological and research issues. *Work & Stress*, **8**(2), 153–176.

Marsella, A.J., Hirschfeld, R. & Katz, M. (1987) *The Measurement of Depression,* University of California Press.

Mathes, E.W. & Severa, N. (1981) Jealousy, romantic love, and liking: Theoretical considerations and preliminary scale development. *Psychological Reports*, **49**, 23–31.

Matthews, G., Jones, D.M., & Chamberlain, A.G. (1990) Refining the measurement of mood: The UWIST Mood Adjective Checklist. *British Journal of Psychology*, **81**, 17–42.

McDowell, K. & Newell, C. (1987) *Measuring Health: A Guide to Rating Scales and Questionnaires.* New York: Oxford University Press.

McNair, D.M., Lorr, M., & Droppleman, L.F. (1992) *Profile of Mood States.* San Diego: Educational and Industrial Testing Service.

Mehrabian, A. (1995) Framework for a comprehensive description and measurement of emotional states. *Genetic, Social and General Psychology Monographs*, 341–361.

Mehrabian, A. & Russell, J.A. (1974) *An Approach to Environmental Psychology.* Cambridge, MA: MIT Press.

Miank, D.C. (1981) The relationship of trait anxiety and trait anger to job satisfaction. Unpublished master's, University of S. Florida, Tampa.

O'Conner, L.E., Berry, J.W., Weiss, J., Bush, M., & Sampson, H. (1997) Interpersonal guilt: The development of a new measure. *Journal of Clinical Psychology*, **53**(1), 73–89.

Osgood, C.E., Suci, G.J., & Tannenbaun, P.H. (1957) *The Measurement of Meaning.* Urbana, IL: University of Illinois Press.

Payne, R. (1988) A longitudinal study of the psychological well-being of unemployed men and the mediating effect of neuroticism. *Human Relations*, **41**(2), 119–138.

Payne, R.L., Wall, T.D., Borrill, C., & Carter, A. (1999) Strain as a moderator of the relationship between work characteristics and work attitudes. *Journal of Occupational Health Psychology*, **4**(1), 3–14.

Redgrove, J. (1976) Sex differences in information processing: A theory and its consequences. *Journal of Occupational Psychology*, **49**, 29–37.

Russell, J.A. (1989) Measures of emotion. *Emotion: Theory, Research and Experience*, **4**, 83–111.

Russell, J.A. & Carroll, J.M. (1999a) On the bipolarity of positive and negative affect. *Psychological Bulletin*, **125**(1), 3–30.

Russell, J.A. & Carroll, J.M. (1999b) The phoenix of bipolarity: "Reply to Watson and Tellegan, 1999". *Psychological Bulletin*, **125**(5), 611–617.

Russell, J.A. & Mehrabian, A. (1977) Evidence for a three factor theory of emotions. *Journal of Research in Personality*, **11**, 273–294.

Sevastos, P. (1996) Job related affective well-being and its relationship to intrinsic satisfaction. Unpublished doctoral thesis, Curtin University of Technology, Perth.

Sevastos, P., Smith, L., & Cordery, J.L. (1992) Evidence on the reliability and construct validity of Warr's (1990) well-being and mental health measures. *Journal of Occupational and Organizational Psychology*, **65**(1), 33–49.

Sjoberg, L., Svensson, E., & Perrson, L.O. (1979) The measurement of mood. *Scandinavian Journal of Psychology*, **20**, 1–18.

Smith, R.H., Parrott, W.G., Diener, E.W., Hoyle, R.H., & Kim, S.H. (1999) Dispositional Envy. *Personality and Social Psychology Bulletin*, **25**(8), 1007–1020.

Spielberger, C.D. (1996) *State-Trait Anger Expression Inventory*. Tampa, FL: Psychological Assessment Resources Inc.

Tangney, J.P., Wagner, P., & Gramzow, R. (1992) Proneness to shame, proneness to guilt and psychopathology, *Journal of Abnormal Psychology*, **101**, pp. 469–478.

Thayer, R.F. (1967) Measurement of activation through self-report. *Psychological Reports*, **20**, 12–15.

Warr, P.B. (1990) The measurement of well-being and other aspects of mental health. *Journal of Occupational Psychology*, **63**, 193–210.

Warr, P.B. (1994) A conceptual framework for the study of work and mental health. *Work & Stress*, **8**(2), 84–97.

Watson, D., Clark, L.A., & Tellegan, A. (1988) Development and validation of brief measures of positive and negative affect: The PANAS scales. *Journal of Personality and Social Psychology*, **54**, 1063–1070.

Watson, D. & Tellegan, A. (1999) Issues in the dimensional structure of affect—effects of descriptors, measurement error, and response formats: Comment on "Russell and Carroll, 1999". *Psychological Bulletin*, **125**(5), 601–610.

Wetzler, S. (1989) *Measuring Mental Illness: Psychometric Assessment for Clinicians*. Washington, DC: American Psychiatric Association.

White, G.L. & Mullen, P.E. (1989) *Jealousy: Theory, Research and Clinical Strategies*, 1st ed. New York: Guilford Press.

Woody, R. (1980) *Encyclopedia of Clinical Assessment*. San Fransisco: Jossey-Bass.

Part III

Organizational influences on emotion

Chapter 6

Affect at work:
a historical perspective

Howard M. Weiss
Department of Psychological Sciences, Purdue University,
West Lafayette, IN, USA
Arthur P. Brief
Department of Psychology, Tulane University,
New Orleans, LA, USA

Our task was to write a history of research on affect in organizations. We accepted this task with excitement and trepidation. The excitement came from the opportunity to take a systematic look at the roots of a topic that has occupied our individual attention for many years. The trepidation came from the recognition that the task was rather daunting (Spector, 1996, estimated that by 1991 more than 12,400 studies had been published on job satisfaction), and by the recognition that, obviously, we are not trained historians.

In this, our own personal approach-avoidance conflict, the approach won out. Nonetheless, the enormity of the literature and its presence in multiple disciplines kept the avoidance component ever present and guided certain decisions about how to frame the historical analysis. To begin with, we have organized our analysis by period, and, within each period, focused our attention on the key studies. Anyone's determination of "key" studies will be subjective and ours is no exception. Our choices were based upon the citations of other papers of the time, discussions in well-known texts, our assessments after reading the literature as a whole, and, importantly, two lifetimes of study on the topic. We also discuss some general themes relevant to each time period.

Our second strategic decision was to focus primarily on the literature within industrial/organizational psychology and organizational behavior. Research

Emotions at Work. Edited by Roy Payne and Cary Cooper.
© 2001 by John Wiley & Sons, Ltd.

appropriate for this analysis, however, can also be found in the fields of sociology, vocational psychology (very much so), and human-factors engineering. Unfortunately, true exchange across fields has been rare and inclusion of these literatures would have produced three or more rather discrete histories. Also, it would have shifted our position from approach to avoidance.

Finally, one of the strategic decisions of the chapter was not of our choosing but was thrust upon us. We soon realized that any history of the study of work affect was going to be primarily a history of job satisfaction. The relationship between affect and satisfaction is complex. We have somewhat different opinions about whether affect is a constituent of satisfaction (Brief, 1998) or a cause of satisfaction (Weiss, in press). Nonetheless, we do agree that true affective experiences include more than satisfaction. They also include mood states and discrete emotions. Early on (see e.g. Hersey, 1932) and recently (e.g. Weiss and Cropanzano, 1996), the fullness of affect is acknowledged. Yet, even a cursory reading of the literature shows that for most of the century the study of work affect was the study of job satisfaction. Consequently, and sadly, much of our chapter on the history of the study of affect at work will be a history of job satisfaction. We believe that this point is itself instructive. We will revisit it later.

A BRIEF NOTE ON THE WORLD OF IDEAS

Scientific advances, as true for all other forms of human progress, are best understood by considering the contexts in which they were formulated. While the study of feeling in the workplace appeared to leap forward in the 1930s, that research was grounded in the world of ideas evident in the 1920s. Here, we briefly examine that world so as to comprehend better the origin, nature, and significance of those results, produced in the 1930s, that continue to frame investigations of workers' feelings, their satisfactions, moods, and emotions.

We, in part, identified the influential ideas evident in the 1920s by examining the citations of those who did path-breaking research on workers' feelings in the 1930s. Such a citation analysis limited us to consider, at least initially, only what the social sciences had to offer. While most of the research on work affect in the 1930s built upon the earlier works of psychologists, the contributions of sociologists, economists, anthropologists, and others also contributed to the intellectual and social scientific climate. Many such contributions could be noted. We will outline the ones, from a variety of disciplines, which we believe were most significant.

A particularly important idea is embodied in the writings of Emile Durkheim (1895), but was also advanced earlier by August Compte. This position is that social phenomena can be treated as objects of scientific analysis; that is, "social facts" can be approached in the same way as facts are treated in the natural sciences. In other words, Durkheim proposed that social phenomena could be considered objects in nature. Essentially, Durkheim issued a manifesto claiming that the study of social phenomena (i.e. sociology) is a positive science. More substantially, he (e.g. 1895, 1915) saw social facts as independent of psychological ones (i.e. the person). In essence, he focused attention, in an empirical way, at a unit of analysis above the individual.

Advocating ideas consistent with those of Durkheim was the British-born social anthropologist Radcliffe-Brown (e.g. 1922). He argued for the application of scientific methods to the study of a society and, in particular, to its "collective consciousness" (or common values). Analogously, Pareto (1935), the economist, in his *The Mind and Society* asserted that the study of society should be an "experimental science". These ideas in anthropology, economics, and sociology converged during the 1920s to emphasize something relatively new, the objective investigation of social entities. Organizations, of course, are one type of social entity, and so the scientific study of organizations was legitimized.

While Durkheim and the sociological position was focusing on the study of social structure and social phenomena, the science of individual behavior and mental phenomena was developing. In mainstream experimental psychology, the prevailing conceptual viewpoint was functionalism. Rebelling against the dry attempt to describe the structure of mental contents, the functionalists asked about the adaptive function of mental processes (Hergenhahn, 1992). Greatly influenced by Darwinian concepts of natural selection, functionalists like James, Cattell, and Thorndike broadened the focus of psychology in both its goals and methods. Greater attention was given to individual differences (a driving component of natural selection) as well as to the practical applications of psychology. Out of functional psychology, industrial psychology was born, but so too was developmental psychology, educational psychology, and consumer psychology.

Psychologists whose ideas evidenced a more direct concern for individual differences, during the period, included, for example, Münsterberg (1913) and Viteles (e.g. 1926), both noted for their contributions to industrial psychology. Münsterberg, who replaced William James as director of the psychology laboratory at Harvard, concerned himself with the application of scientific psychology to address "the best possible man" at work which translated into personnel selection, vocational guidance, and job placement to put the best person where s/he belonged. Likewise, Viteles's work emphasized individual differences, particularly in personnel selection, even up until the end of his career (Viteles, 1959).

Freudian and other psychodynamic ideas also provided an important context to the research on work affect. Very briefly, Freud's approach addressed motivational and emotional conflicts and their resolution, emphasizing the influences of experiences recalled from the past on the present, as well as interpretations of unconscious effects on conscious thoughts. Early "research" on work affect tried to apply psychodynamic ideas to the workplace. For example, Viteles (1926) advocated the use of clinical methods to examine issues of workers suffering from "emotional maladjustment", psychotic disturbances of personality affecting every phase of life.

Other psychological research was also important as a backdrop to the study of affect and work attitudes begun in the 1930s. The work of Floyd Allport (e.g.

1924), a social psychologist, was particularly influential and broad ranging. It addressed such matters as social attitudes and behaviors, emphasizing that the latter was something more than the behavior of individuals. In addition, with his brother Gordon, he worked on the classification and measurement of personality traits (Allport & Allport, 1928). Also impactful during the era were the ideas advanced by the psychologist Edward L. Thorndike (e.g. 1904, 1914; Thorndike, Cobb, Woodyard, & Staff, 1926). His writings too were far ranging, covering such topics as individual differences (particularly intelligence) and measurement. Another influential psychologist of the period, Thurstone (e.g. 1924a, b) worked in the areas of intelligence and measurement. Importantly, his psychometric concerns encompassed the measurements of attitudes (e.g. Thurstone, 1928; Thurstone & Chave, 1929).

Obviously, the ideas reviewed above were not the only ones that helped shape later studies of feelings in the workplace. Outside of the social sciences, for instance, Mary Parker Follett, a political philosopher, was advocating that "the potentialities of individuals remain potentialities until they are released by group life" (Follett, 1918, p. 6). Beyond the intellectual community of the early 20th century in America, events also were evident that must have affected the conduct of subsequent research on workers' feelings. These likely included, for example, the advancement of Taylor's (1903, 1911) scientific management, with its emphasis on labor efficiency; the recognition that Henry Ford received for his enlightened (often later characterized as paternalistic) labor practices; the spotlight the First World War placed on personnel problems; and, increasing labor unrest (Baritz, 1960).

What does all of the above imply for the research that was to come. In the 1920s, there appeared to be a (managerial) need to understand better the human element in organizational settings. But how should this need be met? Competing perspectives in both level of analysis and methods of analysis provided rich alternatives. These competing perspectives were both methodological and substantive. Alternatives in level of analysis contrasted the relative importance of the individual and, particularly, individual differences in personality (e.g. Münsterberg and Viteles) to the importance of social phenomena (e.g. Durkheim and Radcliff-Brown) as explanations for attitudes and behaviors. The alternative research strategies advanced could be characterized as qualitative (or clinical), entailing in-depth case analysis (e.g. Freud), qualitative versus quantitative (or correlational), entailing survey research methods (e.g. Thorndike and Thurstone). By crossing these methodological and substantive perspectives, we can identify four orientations toward the study of workers' feelings that might have emerged in the 1930s. In addition, research could have crossed the boundaries and combined methods and perspectives. As we will see, research in the 1930s did just that. However, as the research progressed beyond the 1930s, some orientations did not survive. "Why?" becomes a question of interest to be pursued.

In sum, the world of ideas in the 1920s that grounded the research on workers' feelings, that was to emerge in the 1930s, was influenced strongly by a belief that social facts could be approached in the same way as facts in the natural sciences.

Both qualitative and quantitative techniques, each potentially capable of yielding unique insights, were seen as consistent with this belief. Perhaps rooted in early ideological differences between psychology and sociology, belief in the dominance of the individual conflicted with belief in the power of social setting. This conflict was to become more than academic, for it surfaced in attempts to meet managers' perceived needs for scientific guidance in dealing with the human element.

THE 1930s: A PARADIGM DEVELOPS

We think it is fair to say that the study of affect at work became a clearly recognizable topic of scientific research in the 1930s, since it was during this time that the best known initial empirical studies on the topic were published. It is also fair to say that the research of the 1930s shaped the direction and style of inquiry for the next four decades. It was during this time that the predominant method of data collection took center stage (self-report questionnaires). It was during this time that the factual/correlational/inductive style of inquiry became the research approach of choice. It was during this time that affect at work became narrowly defined as job satisfaction. Finally, it was during this time that attention became focused on organizational conditions as causes of job satisfaction at the expense of individual differences and extraorganizational factors (family, religion, community, etc.).

There is a paradox in the research of this defining decade. On the one hand, within the body of literature published in the decade, there can be found a richness of conceptual and methodological thinking that does not characterize later research. Yet, in spite of this richness, the end of the decade saw a narrowing of perspectives and methods that came to define the field for many years thereafter in ways that limited scientific progress. We hope to show both the richness of the 1930s as well as the seeds of the predominant narrow style to come, by describing what we see as the key contributions of the era. This will be followed by a more general discussion of the themes of the decade.

We suspect that very few contemporary researchers are aware of *The Dissatisfied Worker* (Fisher and Hanna, 1931). Yet, while its core premise might seem strange, even objectionable today, it had great visibility in the 1930s. In addition, some of the ideas presented in the book have a very current ring to them.

The Dissatisfied Worker does not deal with dissatisfaction as we know it. Its main premise is that much vocational maladjustment at work is due to "nonadjustive emotional tendencies", psychopathologies in the worker if you will, rather than to objectionable factors inherent in the work situation. For Fisher and Hanna, much of what passes for dissatisfaction, or the symptoms of dissatisfaction, is really the consequence of chronic emotional disturbances, great and small. Mild maladjustments produce, for example, petty jealousies and lack of "cheerful cooperation". Major disturbances produce frequent job changes, tiredness, even hearing voices at work. Thus, what for others might be seen as consequences of stressful or dissatisfied work, are for Fisher and Hanna symptoms of psychopathologies.

The position expressed in the book can be extracted from any one of the many case studies reported. In one case, Fisher and Hanna described the reasons for the discharge of a worker in a department store. He "did not like supervision, (was) too slow, (showed) irregular attendance … All indications of dissatisfaction were regarded as suggesting a need for psychiatric attention" (Fisher & Hanna, 1931, p. 225).

Fisher and Hanna's position may seem, by our frame of reference, extreme, diversionary, and apologetic to management; but it has historical significance for three reasons. First, it had great visibility in the 1930s. Viteles (1932) devoted a whole chapter to the maladjusted worker in his early and influential text. The chapter relies heavily on the work of Fisher and Hanna. Apparently, in Viteles's view, emotional maladjustment as described by Fisher and Hanna was a major cause of labor problems of various types. He cites Fisher and Hanna to suggest that, "one half of the amount expended annually because of labor turnover is spent on the replacement of emotionally maladjusted workers" (Viteles, 1932, p. 589). References to Fisher and Hanna also can be found in Hersey (1932), Hoppock (1935), and other published works of the decade.

Second, Fisher and Hanna can be seen as expressing a dispositional approach to satisfaction. Discussions of "temperament" could be encountered frequently in the literature of the 1930s. Such discussions became less frequent in the decades that followed. Researchers in the 1930s would have no problem appreciating the idea, expressed by Fisher and Hanna, that underlying patterns of personality had great influence on the experience and expression of dissatisfaction.

Third, but lost to contemporary researchers, is the "misattribution" idea expressed by Fisher and Hanna. Early in their book, they suggested that people are often unaware of the source of their emotional unrest and consequently misattribute it to the nature of their work situation. In their view, because of underlying psychopathologies, people carry their dissatisfaction with them from situation to situation. "Now, since he does not usually know the reason for his dissatisfaction … it is not surprising that he very frequently attaches or attributes it to his work or work situation" (Fisher & Hanna, 1931, p. 5). In 1931, Fisher and Hanna were presenting a version of the "mood as information" idea recently expressed, for example, by Schwarz and Clore (1988).

Kornhauser and Sharp (1932), likely, is the first published study of job satisfaction to embody the paradigm that was to come. It (mostly) was a questionnaire study of multiple facets of job satisfaction, conducted in a single organization with correlational analyses of facet and overall satisfaction, and satisfaction–performance relationships.

The paper describes a study conducted at Kimberly Clark in 1930. Kornhauser and Sharp stated that their objective was to determine the major influences on individual "feelings and attitudes". While questionnaires were the primary source for data, these were supplemented by interviews. The study focused on what we would now call overall satisfaction and facet satisfactions (job security, super-vision, etc.).

In describing the way they put their questionnaire together, Kornhauser and Sharp asked, rhetorically, why they did not use a more rigorous approach to attitude measures, like that recently described by Thurstone (e.g. 1928). Their answer resonates. A Thurstone scale, they remarked, is excellent for "one re-stricted attitude". They, however, were interested in attitudes toward a range of issues, and it would simply be too time consuming and expensive to invest in such rigor.

Kornhauser and Sharp's concern with criterion relationships is also fascinating for its currency. Looking at the relationship between job satisfaction and per-formance, they concluded "efficiency ratings of employees showed no relationship to their attitudes" (Kornhauser & Sharp, 1932, p. 402), but they did report that satisfaction was correlated slightly with absenteeism.

The work of Kornhauser and Sharp had a clear "company" emphasis. It focused on what drove satisfaction among Kimberly Clark's workers, at the expense of attempting to build a general theory of job satisfaction. It also focused on the job-performance consequences of satisfaction. This orientation is surprising and ironic given certain earlier discussions by Kornhauser. For example, in 1930 he published a general "think piece" about the state of job satisfaction research (not much to talk about) and what needed to come. In that piece, Kornhauser expressed concern with industrial psychology becoming the "handmaiden of management". We, of course, are not doubting his sincerity. Nonetheless, it seems clear to us that the research reported by Kornhauser and Sharp did not stray very far from the needs of Kimberly Clark.

"No studies in the history of management have received so much publicity, been subject to so many different interpretations, and been as widely praised and as thoroughly criticized as those conducted at the Hawthorne plant of Western Electric, the equipment supply arm of AT&T" (Wren, 1994, p. 235). The series of studies (e.g. Mayo, 1933; Roethlisberger & Dickson, 1939), which began in 1927 with the now famous relay-assembly test-room study and six employees, ended with a massive interviewing program involving over 20,000 employees. For our purposes, the most salient conclusion drawn from this truly monumental effort is captured in the following quotation from Roethlisberger and Dickson (1939, p. 558):

> To each new concrete situation the adult brings his past "social conditioning". To the extent that this past social conditioning has prepared him to assimilate the new experience in the culturally accepted manner, he is said to be "adjusted". To the extent that his private and personal view of the situation is at variance with the cultural situation, the person is called "maladjusted".

This view led Hawthorne investigators (e.g. Mayo, 1931) to attack industrial psy-chologists as too focused on individual differences and not adequately appreciative of the import of the workplace's social organization and the individual's interactions with that organization. That is, emotional maladjustment in the workplace was not seen by the Hawthorne investigators as a problem solely attributable to the worker, but rather one resulting from a person–situation interaction. Over time, it seems, however, that the Hawthorne message came to be taken as the social organization was *the* dominant or even exclusive determinant of job satisfaction. This message had a lasting influence through the so-called "human relations" school of management thought. This school of thought, which was particularly influential during the 1930s, 1940s, and 1950s, was identified with the idea that a happy group is necessarily productive (Filley & House, 1969), an idea greatly influenced by Mayo's commentaries about the implications of the Hawthorne experience.

We have commented on the work of Rexford Hersey (Hersey, 1932) before (Brief, 1998; Weiss & Cropanzano, 1996) and will no doubt do so again. The creativity of his research, both in its ideas and methods, was remarkable in the 1930s. It would be no less so today.

For about a year, Hersey studied a small group of skilled workers in a railroad car and locomotive repair yard. Four times a day, in blocks of 10–13 weeks, the men were given what today would be called an emotion checklist. In addition to this affect measure, he collected extensive physiological and performance data. Then, without the aid of modern statistics or computers, Hersey attempted to examine, among other things, the variability of affect over time, the "life crises" that contributed to this affect, the cycles of affect hidden in the variability, and the relationship between daily emotional states and performance.

Many of Hersey's findings are remarkable for their prescience and currency. He demonstrated, for example, that individual daily affect level, while varying considerably over time, showed definite cycles, and that the period of the cycle was different for different workers. He observed a clear relationship between daily affect levels and daily performance levels, but also showed that the negative effects of negative emotional states were much more pronounced than were the positive effects of positive states. Hersey recognized the importance of "security", "satisfactory remuneration", "justice, equality, and independence", "an understanding and efficient supervisor", as well as other workplace factors as contributors to the worker's emotional adjustment. But, he also recognized the relevance of extra work influences on affect displayed at work:

> The fact that our emotions, and with them our interests, are thus so deeply tied up with our situations outside the plant may cause the influence and problems of the worker's home life to be a more important factor in his plant behavior than even his purely plant problems.
>
> (Hersey, 1932)

Such were some of Hersey's research conclusions of more than 60 years ago!

Hersey gave us a picture of what research on affect in organizations could have become, but never did become. He studied emotions, not attitudes. He made time a central element of his research, examining changes over time as real differences in affect level with real consequences, not just errors of measurement. He drew attention to the "crises", "events", "hassles" of life, both on and off the job. His work, unfortunately, never had the impact on affect research that it deserved.

In contrast to Hersey, Robert Hoppock's 1935 book entitled *Job Satisfaction* is remembered as one of the classic early studies of work attitudes. Katzell and Austin (1992) cite Hoppock (along with Kornhauser and Sharp, 1932) as one of the landmark studies in the developing interest in job satisfaction. Locke (1976, p. 1299) said that Hoppock "published the first intensive study of job satisfaction." Major texts in the field refer to Hoppock's historical significance (see e.g. Berry and Houston, 1993).

The influence of Hoppock's work, reinforcing both the developing survey approach to the study of satisfaction as well as the search for correlates among work factors, cannot be denied. Yet, in many ways, his intentions and methods were very different from what was to become typical practice in the area.

For one thing, Hoppock was more interested in the societal than the business implications of job dissatisfaction. He talked of riots, even revolution, as outcomes of subjecting people to intolerable working conditions, yet rarely discussed the implications for more narrow business objectives.

Consistent with his concern for the broader social implications of dissatisfaction, Hoppock's overall objectives were to first get, "some idea of the extent of dissatisfaction" in the general population, and then to discover some of the causes of that dissatisfaction. His method is also consistent with his social interests. Instead of the single organization survey, already seen in Kornhauser and Sharp (1932) and other studies, Hoppock attempted to gather data from all the workers in a single community (New Hope, Pennsylvania) and from broad samples of people in a single occupation (teachers). By today's standards, his "narrow" samples might be seen as providing very little information relevant to the broad questions he posed; for example, New Hope, his "typical" American town, had an unemployment rate of 6% in the middle of the depression! Nonetheless, Hoppock's sampling strategies stand in contrast to what was to come.

The diversity of methods and ideas about the "causes" of dissatisfaction are also of interest. In addition to the soon to be ubiquitous questionnaire, Hoppock reported a series of interviews with employed and unemployed workers. At one point, he mentioned that he asked a sample of research participants to take home a diary and record their daily satisfaction levels for 3 weeks. Unfortunately, almost no one returned the diaries. Apparently, Hoppock, like Hersey, believed that satisfaction was something that might vary meaningfully from day to day.

As Hoppock explored the "causes" of dissatisfaction, he focused his attention on the now well-discussed elements of the work environment (supervision, co-workers, opportunities for advancement, intrinsic job characteristics, occupational status, etc.). Yet, he also discussed the importance of non-work issues like religion and family expectations quite extensively. In addition, Hoppock followed in the tradition of Fisher and Hanna by exploring the relevance of "emotional maladjustment".

When we reread Hoppock's "influential" book, we are struck more by the differences with what was to follow than with the similarities. Its guiding theme was the social rather than managerial implications of satisfaction. Its methods were varied not narrow. Its operations embodied a real belief that dissatisfaction, as a construct, exists within a network of variables encompassing the self, work, family, and the larger social context.

These seminal studies illustrate the wide variety of ideas about affect in the workplace that were explored as the topic first began to generate research in the 1930s. The history of science tells us that early diversity is generally followed by a distillation and narrowing of concepts and methods. Furthermore, the narrowness that follows often does not center on the most productive or useful of the earlier concepts. So it was, we believe, with affect in the workplace. The ensuing decades saw a paradigm develop that carried over some of the ideas of the 1930s but lost others. What remained brought with it certain advantages, both methodological and conceptual, but the development of a paradigm also meant that many interesting methods and ideas were pushed into the background.

What was the paradigm that developed? To begin with, the new paradigm replaced the broad concept of affect with the narrower concept of job satisfaction. For the next 50 years, affect and job satisfaction erroneously became equivalent constructs. Certainly, job satisfaction, attitude, and affect are related constructs. Job satisfaction, the attitudes we hold about our jobs, can be seen as having an affective component (Brief, 1998) and/or affective causes (Weiss, in press). Nonetheless, affect itself is a rich concept encompassing moods and discrete emotions, and that richness was represented better in the work of the 1930s than it was in the five decades that followed. Hersey's (1932) measurement of daily moods and Fisher and Hanna's (1931) discussion of emotional maladjustment are illustrative of a richer conception of affect than was found in the organizational literature until very recently. After 1930, job satisfaction ruled the kingdom of work affect.

Along with the narrowing of the construct of interest came a narrowing of methods. In the 1930s, no single method could be seen as the method of choice. Studies reported data collection by interviews, observations, questionnaires, and mood checklists. By the end of the decade, the questionnaire clearly dominated the scene.

We can only speculate as to the reason for the narrowing of constructs and methods. Certainly, the developing technology of attitude measurement had something to do with it, as did the ease with which questionnaire studies of attitudes could be conducted. (Compare the effort levels of Hersey with those of Hoppock or Kornhauser and Sharp.) For whatever reasons, the end of the decade *saw the study of work affect become the study of job satisfaction by way of questionnaires.*

A third element of the new paradigm was a focus on raw descriptive relationships to the near exclusion of theory building. In 1932, Viteles described the style of investigation that was to characterize job-satisfaction research for the next three decades:

> It involves primarily an accumulation and interrelation of facts ... In accumulating
> these facts the investigator may start with a hypothesis but the objective must be not

that of finding facts which fit the hypothesis but of determining whether the hypothesis fits the facts ... He discards such convenient labels as purpose, urge, desire, appetite, and similar theoretical factors adopted on a priori grounds in the explanation of behavior in industry. He adopts ... the universal methods of science, those of collecting facts and formulating conclusions only on the basis of established correlations among observed facts.

(Viteles, 1932, pp. 568–569)

Just the facts; no theory allowed. And thus, a purely inductive approach, unburdened by a priori conceptual baggage (except, as always, the researcher's intuitive ideas), became the prescribed style of affect/satisfaction research. This style largely held sway until the late 1950s and early 1960s when there was an explosion of theoretical work on job satisfaction. Was this focus on facts a meta-analyst's dream? Perhaps, but it also was the blueprint for the collection of an enormous pot of disjointed, incoherent findings.

A fourth element of the emerging paradigm was a focus on work-environment causes of satisfaction, accompanied by a relative neglect of personal/dispositional or extra-work causes. As we read the seminal papers of the 1930s, we were struck by the frequency with which the importance of affective dispositional variables was acknowledged. Certainly, they played an important role in Fisher and Hanna (1931) and in Hoppock (1935); but even Kornhauser and Sharp (1932), the prototype of the new paradigm, measured dispositional variables and correlated them with job satisfaction (with some success.) We find this surprising because after the 1930s, with the exception of a few scattered papers, such personality variables were given very little attention until the late 1980s and early 1990s. The same can be said for the causal role of extra-work factors. Hoppock and Hersey, as examples, both examined the way family factors influence affect expressed on the job. However, as the research paradigm developed, the influence of working conditions became the dominant direction of inquiry; and personality and family generally were forgotten. Of course, this makes some sense if the overall objective was to study affect as part of a broader agenda of increasing organizational efficiency and, thus, serving management (Baritz, 1960). It makes less sense if understanding and theory building are primary objectives.

THE 1940s AND 1950s

The war years were ones in which industrial social scientists pitched in to help meet pressing human-resource needs critical to the nation (Baritz, 1960). This emphasis on immediate, practical results may explain why the 1940s produced little progress in the scientific study of workers' feelings. Strong's (1943) *Vocational Interests of Men and Women* provides an example of the limited progress that was made. Building on earlier scale development efforts (Strong, 1927), he demonstrated that future occupational satisfaction could be predicted (e.g. 10 years later) by the "match" between a person's vocational interests and those of people engaged in the occupation chosen by the person. Strong's program of research, while representing one of the earliest attempts to operationalize the notion of person–work environment fit (Dawis, 1992), remains outside of the mainstream of the social sciences; such is the case, according to Holland (1976), for vocational interest research generally. This may be so because the vocational interest literature is "rambling" and "formless" (Holland, 1976, p. 523) and seemingly independent of advances, for example, in personality and industrial/ organizational psychology.

The 1950s, unlike the preceding decade, produced considerable output that some might have considered progress. However, some of this output, in fact, was simply "old wine in new bottles", while others seemed promising but ultimately were not so. Weitz's (1952) research on dispositions and job satisfaction provides an example of rediscovery. He asserted "some individuals generally gripe more than others; in that case the number of dissatisfactions with the job should be placed in its proper background—namely, some 'gripe index' of the individual" (Weitz, 1952, p. 202). Weitz went on to report observing a very strong positive correlation between his individual difference measure, the "gripe index", and job dissatisfaction. What Weitz neglected to observe was that researchers in the 1930s, as we noted above, already had begun to map the individual difference—job-satisfaction territory—discovering several insights. Fisher and Hanna (1931, p. 27), for example, more than 20 years before Weitz (1952), noted, "In as much as his feeling and emotions are inherent aspects of himself, he carries them with him, so to speak, into every situation he enters." The absence of reference to early work on dispositions in Weitz' "rediscovery", whether due to lack of thoroughness or simple forgetting, is not unusual in the study of workers' feelings (or, more generally, in the social sciences). Ironically, some have observed that those advocating the so-called "dispositional approach" to job satisfaction (e.g. Staw & Ross, 1985) in the 1980s and 1990s had neglected Weitz (1952) (e.g. Judge, 1992). Weitz apparently could be faulted for the same thing.

An example of work that appeared promising but ultimately proved not to be so is that of Herzberg and his associates (Herzberg, Mausner, & Snyderman, 1959; Herzberg, Mausner, Peterson, & Capwell, 1957). In essence, they asserted that the factors which cause positive job attitudes (and which motivate workers) are different from the factors that generate negative job-related attitudes. Subsequent research and analyses cast very serious doubt on the veracity of this assertion (e.g. House & Wigdor, 1967; King, 1970), ultimately leading to the near disappearnace of Herzberg's ideas in mainstream discussions of satisfaciton or affect. However, an implication of it remains alive; that is, job satisfaction may not simply be the opposite of job dissatisfaction. Today, some organizational scientists (e.g. Brief, 1998), consistent with recent thinking in the social psychology of attitudes (e.g. Cacioppo & Berntson, 1994; Cacioppo, Gardner, & Berntson, 1997), construe job satisfaction as having positive and negative components. Furthermore, as has been pointed out by Weiss and Cropanzano (1996), Herzberg's attention to the driving force of work events, and his acknowledgment of real variability in affect levels over time, are ideas that have currency and deserve attention. Nonetheless, today Herzberg's ideas remain, for most, ideas of historical but not theoretical significance.

Another example of unfulfilled promises, at least with regard to understanding job satisfaction, is the theorizing of March and Simon (1958), evident in their now classic book *Organizations*. Unlike Herzberg's ideas (Herzberg et al., 1959) that were questioned empirically, March and Simon's failed to fulfill their promise because they were largely ignored. For example, they posited that the greater the predictability of instrumental relationships on the job, the higher the level of satisfaction. While the proposition has intuitive appeal, a precise test of it has yet to be conducted (Brief, 1998).

A final example of unfulfilled promises is represented by several investigations addressing the notion that job satisfaction is a function of the degree to which the job fulfills the individual's needs (e.g. Morse, 1953; Schaffer, 1953). Since the mid-1970s (e.g. Lawler, 1973), interest in such need-fulfillment approaches has declined dramatically (Pinder, 1998). This likely is attributable to vigorous criticisms of the approaches (e.g. Salancik and Pfeffer, 1977). These criticisms characterize need-fulfillment approaches, for instance, as conceptually vague, difficult to operationalize, and/or lacking adequate empirical support.

What did the 1950s produce of enduring value? The Technology Project of the Institute of Human Relations at Yale, for instance, yielded an emphasis on task characteristics as a determinant of affective reactions to a job (e.g. Walker & Guest, 1952). Hackman and Oldham's (1975) job-characteristic model can be traced directly back to this work (Brief & Aldag, 1978), as can other task-design approaches derived from Hackman and Oldham (e.g. Campion & Thayer, 1985; Campion & McClelland, 1991). The 1950s also gave us the beginnings of an emphasis on equity. Jacques (1956), for example, investigated the relationship between an "equitable work-payment structure", on the one hand, and a "sense of fairness of payment" and "satisfaction with personal earnings", on the other. (Also see Whyte, 1955.) As will be shown, these ideas took hold in the 1960s (e.g. Adams, 1965; Jacques, 1961; Patchen, 1961) and remain in play (e.g. Greenberg, 1987, 1990).

In the above paragraph, the word "emphasis" was used for a reason. The influence of the nature of the work performed and of just rewards on workers' affect were not discovered in the 1950s. Recall, for example, Hersey (1932) who concluded, "enjoyment in the activities called for by the nature of the work" is a prerequisite to the "relationship between man and job [being] satisfactory" (Hersey, 1932, p. 374) and that "justice", in part, entails reward in proportion to effort and efficiency through (a) appreciation (b) increased financial return (c) promotion (Hersey, 1932, p. 384). Thus, research in the 1950s appears to have helped create enthusiasm for the study of task characteristics and workplace justice that endures; but both of these, as factors affecting workers's feelings, were detected at least 20 years earlier. Such a lag between discovery and enthusiasm in the social-science community does not surprise us; what does is that so very few of the findings that emerged in the 1930s attracted attention in the 1940s and 1950s.

A null result and a smiling (sad) face were products of the 1950s that also have exhibited enduring influence. The null result, reported by Brayfield and Crockett (1955), was based upon their review of the job satisfaction–job performance literature. They found a negligible relationship between the two (as, we have noted, so did Kornhauser and Sharp some 20 plus years earlier). Subsequent reviews of the literature have yielded the same finding (e.g. Iaffaldano & Muchinsky, 1985; Vroom, 1964). The idea of a satisfied worker being a productive one is so intuitively appealing to many. The disconnection between satisfaction and performance, reported by Brayfield and Crockett, created a puzzle that has continued to intrigue organizational scientists. (Later we will discuss the more recent solutions offered to this problem.)

Now, on to smiling faces. In 1955, Kunin reported on a novel symbolic rating scale, the General Motors "Faces" scale, which he used to gauge job satisfaction. The scale was composed of a series of faces ranging from a scowling frown to a pleasing grin. The respondent indicated his/her attitude by checking the appropriate face on the scale. While the "Faces" scale has been used, at least to a limited extent, through the years, Brief and Roberson (1989) have urged that it be used more frequently, since it seems to capture the affective components of job satisfaction better than other more popular measures do.

In sum, the 1940s and 1950s, in comparison to the 1930s, cannot be characterized as particularly rich years for the study of worker affect. During the period, research was conducted that began to focus attention on task characteristics, workplace justice, and the satisfaction–performance puzzle. March and Simon's (1958) ideas about job satisfaction still are waiting to be attended to empirically; and the "Faces" scale still has not moved to center stage as a primary job-satisfaction measure of choice. What did not happen in the 1940s and 1950s leaves another task to be completed, formulating answers to "Why were so very few of the breakthroughs made in the 1930s not pursued aggressively in the following two decades?"

THE 1960s: THE "GOLDEN AGE"

The 1960s would appear to be a "golden age" in satisfaction research, at least in terms of the attention given to the topic. It is certainly true that affect remained satisfaction, that the questionnaire method still held sway, and that very little attention was given to "extra-work" issues like dispositions or family. However, it is also true that the 1960s saw the publication of key theoretical works on the topic of satisfaction (e.g. Porter, 1961; Katzell, 1964; Vroom, 1964; Locke, 1969) as well as the development of important theory-driven measures (Smith, Kendall and Hulin, 1969; Lofquist and Dawis, 1969). Also, in the 1960s, interest in the social implications of dissatisfaction re-emerged with the publication of *Work in America* (1969) and the accompanying concern with the quality of working life. Finally, the decade saw an explosion of interest in the use of employee surveys in applied settings. Clearly, job satisfaction was "hot", even if the construct itself still remained cognitively "cold".

If, as we suggest, the 1960s represented the first real attempt to develop systematic theories of job attitudes and theory-driven measures, then Vroom's (1964) *Work and Motivation* can be considered the prototype of that era. Although Fishbein and Ajzen (e.g. 1975) later used similar ideas to delineate a general theory of attitudes, Vroom's book, as the title suggests, was primarily a discussion of motivation; but he did not ignore job attitudes. Vroom presented a theory of motivation and job satisfaction firmly grounded in basic social and experimental psychology ideas. His expectancy theory could be traced from Lewin (1938) and Tolman (1932), through Atkinson's (1964) integration of McClelland's (e.g. 1961) theory of achievement motivation and Festinger's (1942) theory of level of aspiration. Vroom took great pains to characterize previous "job satisfaction theory" as *ad hoc*, and to rectify that with a theory.

Vroom's review of the extant research is both thorough and insightful. After describing the empirical research on causes and consequences of job satisfaction, he showed a clear awareness of the shortcomings of decades of research based upon Viteles's (1932) call for purely descriptive research. Vroom stated that (up to 1964) most of the research was atheoretical and focused on the practical objectives of correlating elements of the work environment with satisfaction. He argued that the choice of correlates had been driven primarily by nothing more than intuitive ideas about rewards and punishments. He observed that those correlations which were found were rarely impressive and concluded that this was "due to oversimplified theory which does not do justice to the complexity of the phenomenon" (Vroom, 1964, p. 160).

For Vroom, job satisfaction was an attitude, and attitude meant the valence of the attitude object, in this case the work role. Different properties of the work role could have different valences, and these different valences represented different facet satisfactions. Overall job satisfaction was the valence of the overall work role. It was, of course, a function of the work role's instrumentality for obtaining various second-level outcomes (pay, status, etc.) and the valences of those outcomes. Specifically, work-role valence (job satisfaction) was thought of as the result of the sum of the specific instrumentality × valence products.

It is not often recognized that Vroom saw his theory of satisfaction as an instantiation of the general fit model that already had been introduced in other forms by Strong (1943), Morse (1953), Schaffer (1953), and others. He explicitly argued that environmental outcomes work in combination with personality, described in need/motive terms. Vroom was, of course, interested in whether need/ motive fulfillment was best modeled by multiplicative or subtractive models, arguing for his multiplicative model. Nonetheless, it seems that he saw the core logic of expectancy theory as need/motive fulfillment or fit.

It is also important to recognize that, although Vroom's theory was known best for its motivational implications, it did a better job of predicting attitudes and preferences than it did predicting motivation and behavior (see Mitchell, 1974). While this result may be the consequence of methodological artifacts, it is the case, and, therefore, a bit disappointing that expectancy theory is not better known as a theory of job satisfaction.

Finally, we should note that a strength of Vroom's theory was its attempt to consider the association between satisfaction and performance in a systematic manner. For instance, Vroom stated:

> job satisfaction is closely affected by the amount of rewards that people derive from their jobs and level of performance is closely affected by the basis for attainment of rewards. Individuals are satisfied with their jobs to the extent to which their jobs provide them with what they desire, and they perform effectively in them to the extent that effective performance leads to the attainment of what they desire.
>
> (Vroom, 1964, p. 264)

Expectancy theory provided a way to think about how attitudes and behavior could be related to each other. In organizational research, this link was made more explicit by Porter and Lawler (1968). Vroom's review of the literature on the correlation between satisfaction and performance, along with the earlier review by Brayfield and Crockett, is often credited with destroying the overly simple idea that satisfaction causes performance. However, his rigorous explication of how the two constructs are theoretically embedded with motivation contributed as well.

In 1969, Locke asked the rhetorical "What is job satisfaction?" He answered it by presenting what has proven to be an enduring theoretical perspective in the tradition of fit or discrepancy positions. Throughout this paper, we have suggested that the concept of emotion was absent from most discussions of job satisfaction. In this regard, Locke is an exception. He is the only job-satisfaction theorist, until very recently, who made emotion a central construct. He defined satisfaction as an emotional event, and explicitly argued for the connection between evaluation and emotion (i.e. the latter is a product of the former). While his theory of emotional generation bears some resemblance to what today would be called "cognitive appraisal", ultimately his theory works better as a theory of evaluation not emotion. Nonetheless, it was an important theory of job satisfaction, stated with precision and insight.

For Locke, the key organizing concept for job satisfaction is an individual's "values". He defined values as, "that which one acts to gain and/or keep" (Locke, 1969, p. 315). Locke said that there are three key elements in the evaluation process: an individual's values; a perception of some aspect of the job; and a conscious or subconscious judgment of the relationship between our perception and our values. To this he added the concept of value importance. He saw value importance as moderating the relationship between percept–value discrepancy and job satisfaction.

Locke described his position as one emphasizing person–situation interaction, both the person (values) and environment (available outcomes) must be taken into account in predicting job satisfaction. He criticized those approaches that looked solely at the correlation between features of the environment and satisfaction, without taking individual differences in values into account. He did not describe, however, a dynamic interactionism in which people and environments act on each other over time. When all is said and done, Locke's position was very similar to the other discrepancy models of the 1960s; his value-discrepancy idea was not unlike other available alternatives and did not get at the core of emotional experiences in the workplace. Nevertheless, it was a rigorous explication of the value-discrepancy position and has had great influence on research on the causes of job satisfaction.

Adams (1963, 1965, but also see Homans, 1961 and Patchen, 1961) formalized notions about the relationship between perceived inequity and discomfort or tension, that had more loosely been dealt with in the job-satisfaction literature since the 1930s (e.g. Hersey, 1932). Essentially, his equity theory posited that a person's perceived ratio of inputs to outcomes, standing psychologically unequal to that person's perception of some other's input–outcome ratio, is associated with dissatisfaction and subsequent efforts to alleviate that dissatisfaction. As can be seen from the following decades, the attention Adam's theory received gave rise to a large and diverse literature concerned with organizational justice (e.g. Greenberg, 1987).

Through the 1960s, researchers at the University of Minnesota worked on the development of the theory of work adjustment (e.g. Lofquist & Dawis, 1969). It is a seminal work in the history of affect in organizations for at least three reasons. First, it is a systematic explication of the fit model that has steered vocational guidance as a discipline since its inception. Second, it is one of the few efforts in vocational psychology that have had an impact on mainstream organizational psychology. Third, it gave us the Minnesota Satisfaction Questionnaire (MSQ), one of the most popular facet-based measures of job satisfaction. The research that continued through the 1970s and beyond is summarized in Dawis and Lofquist (1984).

The most central concept of the theory of work adjustment is "mutual correspondence". "Correspondence can be described in terms of the individual fulfilling the requirements of the work environment and the work environment fulfilling the requirements of the individual" (Lofquist and Dawis, 1969, p. 45). The requirements of the work environment are primarily those of skill, and, consequently, one-half of the correspondence picture resolves to the typical logic of any employee-selection program. Success in this half is called "satisfactoriness", the extent to which the individual fulfills the requirements of the work environment.

The other half of the correspondence equation is the part that deals with satisfaction, and the key constructs are individual needs and the reinforcer system of the work environment. To summarize, work environments as a whole were described in terms of a discrete set of "reinforcers" and individual settings were described in terms of their "reinforcement value" on each of the reinforcers. Correspondingly, individuals were described using the same set of reinforcement categories, only for individuals these were labeled "needs". The overall correspondence of reinforcer levels (for the environment) and needs (for the individual) was asserted to predict satisfaction, as measured by the MSQ, which captures satisfaction along the same 20 dimensions as the environment was described.

Individual needs and environmental reinforcer patterns are the key components of the model and, therefore, deserve some discussion. The theory takes a sort of quasi-behavioristic approach to these concepts. At the microlevel, stimulus conditions vary in their ability to elicit approach responses. These are the reinforcement values of the stimulus conditions and, in the theory, they are described as properties of the environment. People are aware of their own consistencies in response, and this awareness is reflected in their preferences. Although ambiguously described, preferences are not in themselves causal of any attitudes or responses; they are simply the awareness of consistencies in responses driven by the reinforcer values of the environments. The theory does not address where the reinforcement power comes from (consistent with the behavioristic flavor). The preferences are the awareness of the underlying response tendencies. Finally, discrete preferences (and environmental reinforcer patterns) can be grouped together to form broader categories. At the individual level, these broader categories are called needs. Again, the correspondence of need and reinforcer values, described along the same dimensions, predicts satisfaction.

The theory of work adjustment has some practical value. In the vocational-guidance tradition, both environments and individuals can be assessed on similar dimensions, and, in some limited way, people can be advised about the correspondence between their stated preferences and the reinforcement values of occupations or organizations. This practical value notwithstanding, the theory appears to be limited as a conceptual framework for understanding work attitudes or affect. Environments are defined in terms of their ability to elicit approach/avoidance behaviors, and needs/preferences are simply people's awareness of the power these environments have over them. Since the needs have no external referent, the same construct is invoked on both sides of the fit equation.

This is, of course, a somewhat harsh evaluation, but one which we believe is justified. The theory appears to be an attempt at "psychologizing" an intuitive idea. That idea is simply this: people have preferences for certain environmental features and when environments provide those features satisfaction results. The usefulness of this position, as a scientific explanation of satisfaction or affect, remains open.

One of the most important pieces of work on job satisfaction conducted in the 1960s was the development of the Job Descriptive Index (JDI) (Smith et al., 1969). The JDI likely is the most enduring and influential measure of job satisfaction ever developed. Its status is, in no small measure, the consequence of the rigor with which it was developed. The JDI was not the kind of *ad hoc* measure so popular in previous decades. Like the MSQ, the JDI was a theory-driven measure. Unlike the MSQ, however, the development of the satisfaction measure was the central objective of the team at Cornell that developed it.

The basic framework which guided the development of the JDI was the classic discrepancy position popularized in the 1950s and 1960s. For Smith et al. (1969), satisfaction was a function of perceived characteristics in relation to a frame of reference. However, people can have different frames of reference at different times and this can bias their evaluations (or at least produce some inconsistencies). To help eliminate these inconsistencies, Smith et al. felt that a descriptive measure, which asked respondents to describe the environment in terms of characteristics demonstrated to be associated with satisfaction, would be a less biased procedure than asking for evaluations directly. Hence the development of the famous descriptive items of the JDI (e.g. referring to co-workers as "boring", "responsible", and "intelligent").

Smith et al. also recognized the limitations of the descriptive method. They understood that there is a big inferential leap from asking a person whether his or her work environment is "hot" to inferring that the person is dissatisfied. Therefore, their original method involved a triadic scoring procedure in which people were asked to use the JDI items to describe their current jobs, the jobs they would most like to have, and the jobs they would least like to have. They then tried to score the distance between current, best, and worst jobs. As often happens, the simple description of current job showed better discriminant and convergent validity than did the more complicated methods. Thus, the descriptive, facet-based JDI was born.

As we have said, the 1960s was a time of historically important theoretical and measurement activity. Equity theory was formalized. Discrepancy theories of satisfaction reached their pinnacle and remained the predominant explanatory model through the 1980s. The two key measures of job satisfaction, the MSQ and the JDI, were developed at the then two most important centers for research on satisfaction, the University of Minnesota and Cornell University, respectively.

The 1960s was also a time in which society stopped looking exclusively at the practical implications of job satisfaction and started looking at the social implications of satisfaction. *Work in America* (1969) laid out those social concerns, and job satisfaction became a part of the social-indicators movement. The vast majority of organizational scholars, however, continued to focus exclusively on job satisfaction as a potentially important determinant of *organizational* outcomes.

THE 1970s

While the 1960s can be seen as a decade of broad theoretical and measurement activity, the 1970s can be seen as a period of quiescence and consolidation. Only one major theoretical presentation equivalent in impact to Herzberg (e.g. Herzberg et al., 1959) in the 1950s or Vroom (1964) or Locke (1969) in the 1960s was presented, Salancik and Pfeffer's (1977) ideas about the influence of social information. No new measurement system to rival the MSQ or the JDI was developed. Instead, affect research, still equivalent to job-satisfaction research, focused its attention on building an empirical structure based on the fit/ discrepancy foundations of previous decades.

Four activities of the 1970s are worth noting. To begin with, the decade saw the publication of a number of important reviews of satisfaction (and motivation) research that helped to organize thinking and direct future research. In 1973, Lawler's book, *Motivation in Work Organizations*, was published. In this work, Lawler summarized the general way in which expectancy theory integrates satisfaction and motivation, following the lead of earlier works by Vroom (1964) and Porter and Lawler (1968). He also provided an extensive review of the extant theories of job satisfaction, popularizing the term "discrepancy theories" to classify those theories that explain satisfaction as the result of the difference between the perceptions of outcomes received or environmental conditions and various standards.

Mitchell's (1974) review of expectancy-theory research also was an important contribution. Although focusing primarily on motivation, expectancy-theory research on satisfaction was not neglected. More than any other review of the topic, Mitchell's paper served to underscore the conceptual and methodological precision required of rigorous research on expectancy theory, precision that had, to that point, been elusive. Unfortunately, rather than stimulating better research, the paper seems to have depressed the field's enthusiasm for expectancy theory by upgrading the standards for acceptable empirical work.

Finally, Locke's chapter in the *Handbook of Industrial and Organizational Psychology* (Dunnette, 1976) was a "tour de force" review devoted entirely to job satisfaction. Given that Locke's (1969) own position had been articulated earlier, the chapter broke no new conceptual ground; nevertheless, the thoroughness of the review allows it to still serve as an important reference after almost 25 years.

The 1970s saw more focus on the motivational and attitudinal effects of specific, narrow elements of the work environment. Particularly important were Lawler's work on pay and Hackman and Oldham's work on task design. Lawler's (1971) book on the motivational aspects of pay integrated expectancy theory, equity theory, and discrepancy theory, thereby producing a coherent position with both theoretical and practical implications. Yet, this integration attracted very little empirical attention.

Hackman and Oldham (1975) developed an important theory and accompanying measurement system, focusing on the motivational and attitudinal effects of task characteristics. Their work, as noted previously, was based upon earlier work by Turner and Lawrence (1965). Extensive reviews and critiques exist elsewhere (see Roberts and Glick, 1981 and more recently Brief, 1998). Here we only wish to say that the Hackman and Oldham model attempted to provide some theoretical coherence to a tradition of job redesign/job enrichment that had been thriving through the 1960s, and that it stimulated an enormous amount of empirical research in the 1970s and 1980s.

Earlier we said that, unlike the 1960s, the 1970s was not a decade of active development of broad theories of job affect generally, or satisfaction specifically. One notable exception to this is embodied in two seminal papers by Salancik and Pfeffer (1977, 1978). In these papers, Salancik and Pfeffer gave birth to what has become known as the Social Information Processing (SIP) theory of job satisfaction.

In these papers, Salancik and Pfeffer argued that jobs (broadly conceived) are ambiguous stimuli and subject to multiple interpretations. Various attitudinally relevant expressions of co-workers can serve as cues that influence workers' judgments about these ambiguous job stimuli. The social environment has both direct and indirect influences on judgments about work. It has direct influences on overall attitudes and indirect influences on the perceptions and standards that feed into the attitude judgments.

With these ideas, Salancik and Pfeffer were responding to Hackman and Oldham's model, in particular, and more broadly to all positions that argued that satisfaction is exclusively the result of comparisons between standards and objective job characteristics. Of course, both the general discrepancy theories of job satisfaction and the Hackman and Oldham model argue that perceptions of the work environment are a proximal cause of satisfaction judgments. Consequently, if social information is seen as one influence on these perceptions, there is no real conflict among the positions.

However, Salancik and Pfeffer did make two statements that can be seen as being in conflict with these more traditional positions. First, they suggested that attitudes could directly be influenced by social information, unmediated by perceptions of work environment. That is, a person's satisfaction can be directly influenced by the expressed attitudes of his/her co-workers and later his/her perceptions will come around to be consistent with his/her attitudes. Second, they suggested that job satisfaction should not be considered a relatively stable, environmentally driven judgment. Rather, they implied that satisfaction might better be considered a judgment made "on demand" and subject to transient influences. This position has long been controversial, but is consistent with much current social psychological thinking on attitudes (e.g. Wilson and Hodges, 1992).

In sum, the 1970s was a period in which incremental gains in understanding worker affect were made, as characterized by the contributions of Lawler, Mitchell, Locke, and Hackman and Oldham. Only Salancik and and Pfeffer provided a truly divergent prospective by more fully recognizing the import of the worker's social milieu in the organization. In a significant way, this recognition builds on the contributions of Mayo and his colleagues (e.g. Mayo, 1933), who long ago emphasized the role of social organization in explaining the affective reactions of workers to their jobs.

THE 1980s

The 1980s were a transitional period in the history of the study of work affect. While much research was conducted in the conceptual and methodological traditions that emerged in the 1960s and 1970s, the end of the decade saw a reawakening of interest in broader aspects of affect. This reawakening was seen in research on the work consequences of mood states, research inspired by a similar reawakening in social psychology. It also was seen in the rediscovery of dispositional influences on job satisfaction, dispositions that now were distinctly affective in tone. The new interest in affect was to continue into the 1990s. For understanding affect in the workplace, the 1980s was a fertile period. Some seeds, planted much earlier, began to germinate; and the seeds of ideas new, at least, to the job-satisfaction literature were sown.

Recall that in the 1930s, Hersey (1932) explicitly recognized the contribution of justice in the plant environment to worker adjustment. To him, justice pertained to safeguards against unfair treatment, punishment in proportion to negligence and inefficiency, reward in proportion to effort and efficiency, and education, not dictation. Also recall that in the 1960s Adam's (e.g. 1965) equity theory, addressing the fairness of outcomes, was introduced and subsequently applied to understanding, for example, satisfaction with pay. In the 1980s, Folger and Greenberg (1985), building on the path-breaking work of Thibaut and Walker (1975) in social psychology, focused the attention of organizational scholars on "procedural justice" (see also e.g. Bies, 1987 and Greenberg, 1987). Procedural justice is concerned with the methods, mechanisms, and processes used to determine outcomes; it has repeatedly been found to influence such variables as job satisfaction, particularly when outcomes (e.g. rewards) are low (Brockner & Wiesenfeld, 1996). Folger and Greenberg, in drawing attention to the importance of procedural justice in the workplace, did go back to the contribution of Adams in the 1960s, but not to those of Hersey and other organizational researchers in the 1930s.

In the mid-1980s, Staw and his colleagues (Staw & Ross, 1985; Staw, Bell, & Clausen, 1986) produced two of the most important papers of the last 20 years when they reintroduced the so-called "dispositional approach" to job satisfaction. They, as well as other aligned investigators (e.g. Arvey, Bouchard, Segal, & Abraham, 1989; Brief, Burke, Atieh, Robinson, & Webster, 1988; Schmitt & Pulakos, 1985), however, again did not look back to the 1930s, for instance, to Fisher and Hanna's (1931) treatment of temperament. In the 1930s, various dimensions of personality were shown to be predictive of workers' feelings, and, in the 1980s, these relationships were "discovered" once again (see the preceding section on the 1940s and 1950s, particularly that regarding Weitz, 1952). The cost of all of this rediscovery is the failed potential to accumulate and build knowledge over time; if an idea always is seen as "new", then the research community does not digest it adequately and, thus, does not absorb it into its body of knowledge. Without such absorption, the idea not only is forgotten, it fails to become a theoretical building block.

In the 1930s, researchers did not necessarily assume that affect at work and job satisfaction were conceptual equivalents. As we showed, however, by the 1970s the latter came to be defined in terms of the former. In a significant but under-attended-to paper, Organ and Near (1985) questioned the view of satisfaction exclusively as affect. More specifically, they, drawing on what was known about measures of subjective well-being (e.g. McKennel, 1978), speculated that standard measures of job satisfaction are more cognitively rather than affectively laden. Brief and Roberson (1989), influenced by Organ and Near as well as by the literature on the social psychology of attitude organization (e.g. Bagozzi & Burnkrant, 1979), empirically explored the affective and cognitive content of three often used measures of job satisfaction. They concluded that only the Faces scale (Kunin, 1955) captured worker affect relatively well. Thus, Brief and Roberson unmasked a paradox of some consequence. Researchers were conceptualizing job satisfaction as an affective reaction, but their measures of the attitude often captured little affect.

Built, in part, on earlier works in the person–environment fit tradition (e.g. Holland, 1976), Schneider (1987) advanced a creative framework asserting that attraction to an organization, selection by it, and attrition from it yield particular kinds of persons in an organization. He explicitly asserted that his model implies, "people in a setting *will* have the same job attitudes" (Schneider, 1987, p. 450). The potential import of such sharing for understanding differences among organizations would seem hard to overstate; yet, Schneider's idea, with few exceptions (e.g. George, 1996), remains unexplored (see Schneider, Goldstein, and Smith, 1995).

Attention in the 1980s was also drawn to several consequences of workers' feelings and attitudes. Ultimately receiving the most attention by far were organizational citizenship behaviors (OCBs) (e.g. Bateman & Organ, 1983; Organ, 1988; see also Brief & Motowidlo, 1986). OCBs, akin to a set of spontaneous and innovative organizational behaviors identified by Katz (1964) (i.e. helping co-workers, protecting the organization, making constructive suggestions, developing ourselves, and spreading goodwill), have been found to be correlated consistently with job satisfaction (Organ & Ryan, 1995). And, if we construe OCBs as a kind of job performance (see Borman & Motowidlo, 1993), then these results may be taken as a clue to solving the satisfaction–performance puzzle (Brief, 1998).

Baron (1984) and others (e.g. Carnevale & Isen, 1986) produced results indicating that positive affect encourages the adoption of constructive approaches to conflict resolution (e.g. collaboration), while discouraging less desirable means of dealing with disagreements (e.g. avoidance and direct competition). The less hostile social climate created by positive worker affect ought to be associated with "smoother organizational functioning" (Schneider, 1984, p. 198). Regrettably, it does not seem that interest in collaboration in organizations, as a consequence of workers' feelings, ever became widespread among organizational scientists. Also appearing not to have attracted widespread interest are a series of findings produced by James and his colleagues (James & James, 1980; James & Tetrick, 1986). They showed that a likely consequence of job satisfaction is how workers perceived the characteristics of their jobs. Logic would dictate that the more workers perceive their jobs in favorable terms, the more satisfied they are with them. While James and others' results support this logic, they also show that being satisfied appears to produce more positive job perceptions. As suggested, the methodological and other implications of a "satisfaction causes perception" argument, to date, have not received adequate consideration; thus, the potential value of James and his colleagues' results are yet to be assessed fully.

In sum, the 1980s were an exciting time for the study of workers' feeling. The importance of justice and disposition to satisfaction received renewed, vigorous attention that continues today. The affective and cognitive components of job attitudes were recognized explicitly for the first time in the 1980s. As will be seen in the next section, the component structure of job satisfaction has not continued to be pursued *per se*, but the future did yield a concern for the contribution of affect to satisfaction (Weiss & Cropanzano, 1996). The future, stimulated by Schneider's (1987) attraction–selection model, also brought the recognition that affect can be shared and that shared affect has important organizational consequences. Among these consequences are two that were attended to in the 1980s, OCBs and collaboration, but not at the organizational level of analysis, where we suspect shared affect exerts its most potent influence. Lastly, the 1980s gave us a reason to consider how job satisfaction and affect might influence how people perceive their work environments. In total, the decade can be characterized as one in which some earlier promises began to be fulfilled and new ones made. In the 1990s and beyond, we address how well these new promises were fulfilled and whether the conceptual and methodological richness of the 1930s was ever recaptured.

1990s

In previous decades, we were able to rely on the filter of time to help us decide what to discuss. Unfortunately, that filter is not yet in place, as we look back over the 1990s. Nonetheless, we will examine the work of the decade and summarize what we believe were some of its key trends and ideas.

In many ways, the 1990s were characterized by extensions and elaborations of trends that began in the 1980s. For example, the 1980s provided a rebirth of interest in a broader conceptualization of affect than job satisfaction, and the 1990s witnessed the development of a general theory of affect at work (Weiss and Cropanzano, 1996), the application of the concept of "emotional intelligence" to work experiences (e.g. Goleman, 1998) and increased attention to the role of mood (Isen and Baron, 1991). As another example, the 1980s provided a rebirth of interest in dispositions, and the 1990s followed up with general theories of dispositional effects (Judge, Locke and Durham, 1997).

At the same time that we saw increased attention to the new issues of the 1980s, we also saw new ways of looking at age-old problems. Fit, the overriding theoretical framework for most theories of job satisfaction, generated new conceptual and empirical efforts, as did the ubiquitous problem of the relationship between satisfaction and performance. Let us begin with the age-old problems.

We, along with many others, have pointed to the near obsession that researchers have had with finding a relationship between satisfaction and performance.

Later, we will comment on the sources of this obsession. Here, we note only that the fever still raged in the 1990s. However, unlike previous decades in which pure empiricism reigned, this decade produced more thoughtful, if not more successful, attempts at examining the relationship.

A number of papers were published examining the affect–performance relationship at the unit level, as opposed to the traditional individual level (e.g. George, 1990; Ostroff, 1992; Ryan, Schmit, & Johnson, 1996). The logic of all three studies is similar. Recognizing that affect–performance relationships at the individual level have not been impressive, these authors argued that group-level analyses of the same variables may find more substantial correlations. Why? The general argument is that performance at the individual level is too narrow and does not include criteria that will show up at the unit level. So, for example, certain social acts of an individual, like collaborating and helping co-workers, understandably manifest their effects at the unit level of analysis, but not necessarily in terms of an individual's task performance; that is, people are thought of as being able to contribute to the whole in ways beyond reliably performing the tasks assigned to them (e.g. Katz, 1964). Thus, unit affect–unit performance relationships should capture this wider criterion space better than individual satisfaction–individual performance does.

The studies in this area have taken a similar methodological approach. Individual-level measures of affect/satisfaction have been aggregated to unit levels (usually averaging of unit member responses after appropriate examination of unit homogeneity) and correlated with unit-level performance indices. Thus, the affect measures are aggregations of individual responses, while the performance measures are generally existing unit-level operations.

Results from these aggregation efforts have been mixed. Ostroff (1992) looked at aggregated levels of teacher satisfaction as a correlate of school performance across approximately 300 schools. School-level performance measures included such things as student reading scores, student dropout rates, etc. Ignoring indices of teacher turnover intentions, correlations were in the 0.20–0.30 range. These are somewhat, if not dramatically, better than what is normally found at the individual level and, thus, show some promise.

Ryan et al. (1996) published a similar study looking at satisfaction predictions of unit performance across branches of a financial institution, measured over 2 years. Their findings were somewhat different than Ostroff's. When aggregated satisfaction was correlated with branch performance, correlations were lower, and at a level typical of what is found at the individual level. When branch-level customer satisfaction was correlated with aggregated levels of employee satisfaction, the correlation was higher, but structural equation modeling suggested that the direction of causality was from customer to employee.

George (1990) examined the "group affective tone" in units of a retail sales organization, and correlated this with group indices of helping and cooperation. Group affective tone was measured by aggregating individual-level responses to state measures of positive and negative affect. Results indicated that negative affective tone was a strong predictor of helping at the group level. Positive affective tone showed a smaller relationship. George's work is interesting because it focused on true affective states, rather than satisfaction, and because the choice of dependent variables, such as helping, was based on sound basic research on the behavioral effects of mood states. Surprisingly, however, the finding of stronger effects of negative affect than positive affect on the helping behavior is not consistent with the findings of the basic research on the topic (Weiss & Cropanzano, 1996).

An alternative approach to "aggregation" was offered by Fisher and Locke (1992). Their aggregation was not across people but rather across behaviors. Working from the position offered initally by Fishbein and Ajzen (1974), Fisher and Locke argued that attitudes–behavior relationships most likely will be found when there is a "correspondence in the levels of aggregation" of the attitude and the behavioral dependent variable. Job satisfaction, a general attitude towards our jobs, will most efficiently predict a composite of a broad set of job behaviors. Unfortunately, they argued, most research has examined the relationship between satisfaction and narrower behaviors, a strategy that produces an aggregation mismatch, and, therefore, is doomed to failure. Fisher and Locke presented preliminary data supporting their position but there has been little follow-up.

Fit has been an implicit concept in most theories of job satisfaction presented over the decade. While we will have more to say about this later, here we want to note that the topic received some much needed theoretical examination in the 1990s. Interesting conceptual pieces on fit were published by Edwards (1991), Schneider, Kristof-Brown, Goldstein, and Smith (1997), and Kristof (1996). In addition, a review of the continuing research on the theory of work adjustment, with emphases on the fit components, was published by Dawis (1992). All of these works provide useful summaries of the broad array of research on the concept of fit. While the works acknowledge that the relevance of the concept is not limited to the problem of job satisfaction, they also point to satisfaction being its most popular application.

As we indicated earlier, Staw and his colleagues (e.g. Staw and Ross, 1985) rekindled interest in affective disposition. That interest continued through the 1990s. While much of that research is well situated within the correlational tradition of job satisfaction, some of it had more theoretical flavor.

Brief (1998), in part building on the work of Staw and his colleagues, posited an integrated model of job satisfaction which recognizes the influences of both personality (e.g. neuroticism) and objective job circumstances on the affective and cognitive components of job satisfaction. In the model, these influences are depicted as being mediated by how workers interpret their job circumstances. While the model awaits evaluation in the work domain, a version of it has been tested successfully in the health domain (Brief, Butcher, George, & Link, 1993).

In two papers published late in the decade, Judge et al. (1997) and Judge, Locke, Durham, and Kluger (1998) presented and tested their core evaluations approach to disposition–satisfaction relationships. They argued that traits which are broad in scope, fundamental as opposed to basic, and evaluative as opposed to descriptive in character will predict job satisfaction better than will traits not so characterized. Fitting this description are what they called "core evaluations", which appear to be broad evaluative and belief statements about the self, other people, and the world in general.

Their position is interesting for two reasons. First, it specifically suggests that these core evaluations frame situational appraisal. In this way, Judge et al. provide a process link between disposition and the appraisals that drive affective reactions. Second, the trait-classification scheme (fundamentality, evaluation, scope) attempts to provide some systematic order for the plethora of traits available for study.

That being said, much more needs to be accomplished before the theory can be fully evaluated. To begin with, the operational definitions of fundamentality, scope, and evaluation need to be better explicated. "Fundamental traits are those that are more basic than others" is more a statement of the synonymous nature of two words (fundamental and basic) than a useful definition of a construct. Evaluative traits are said to better predict other evaluations, but no real explanation is offered for this proposition.

Furthermore, the one test of the theory (Judge et al., 1998) appears to be a simple examination of the relationship between well-known traits (neurotocism, self-esteem) and job satisfaction. While the authors bring these dispositions together under their core-evaluations framework, that framework appears to provide little added information over and above the trait–satisfaction relationships that have already been demonstrated for these dispositions. More work needs to be done on those interesting and original elements of Judge et al.'s theory. These are the classification system for traits, the links between trait characteristics and outcome predictions, and the concept of core evaluations.

In 1996, Weiss and Cropanzano presented Affective Events Theory (AET). Less a theory than a framework for studying emotions in the workplace, AET's emphasis is on systematically distinguishing affect from satisfaction and then providing a discussion of the way affect is experienced at work. It discusses both the causes of affective experiences, borrowing heavily from the basic literature on moods and emotions, and the consequences, including both performance and satisfaction.

AET only now is beginning to generate empirical research, and so its heuristic ability cannot yet be evaluated. Nonetheless, some of its key theoretical elements appear worthy of presentation. First, of course, is the distinction AET makes between satisfaction and affect. AET defines satisfaction, not as an affective reaction to our jobs, but as an evaluative judgment we make about our jobs. This evaluative judgment is the consequence of affective experiences at work and beliefs about our jobs. Affect and beliefs jointly influence the evaluation that is job satisfaction.

Second, AET places great emphasis on the causal role of events in influencing affect, performance, and attitudes. As we have seen, most theories of satisfaction focus on the way people judge the features of the work environment (the pay, the career opportunities, etc.). In contrast, AET suggests that things happen to people at work, these events often have emotional consequences, and these emotional states influence both attitudes and behaviors.

Third, the influence of affective states is immediate (i.e. affect influences performance when the person is in the affective state). Since affective states can and do vary over time, the relationship between affect and performance must be studied as it unfolds over time.

Finally, AET makes the distinction between affect-driven and judgment-driven behaviors. Some behaviors are the immediate consequences of current affective states. These behaviors are not influenced by our overall evaluations of our jobs. Other behaviors are mediated by these judgments. AET discusses which types of work behaviors are likely to be affect driven and which types are likely to be judgment driven.

As we said, AET is too recently presented to evaluate in its entirety. Research has demonstrated that satisfaction is a function of both beliefs and affective experiences (Weiss, Nicholas, & Daus, 1999), but, beyond that, the usefulness of the theory remains to be evaluated.

DISCUSSION

We now have finished documenting the historical trends in the study of work affect and would, of course, be remiss if we did not provide some general discussion of themes and conclusions. Many of the central themes apparent in the history have been made during the historical presentation itself. Nonetheless, a number of issues are so important that they require repetition and elaboration.

As we pointed out at the very beginning of the chapter, until very recently the history of affect in organizations has been a history of job satisfaction. At the dawn of this history, affect was not so narrowly conceived. Fisher and Hanna (1931), Viteles (1932), and Hoppock (1935), among others, discussed "emotional maladjustment", and Hersey (1932) measured what would now be called mood states as early as the 1920s. Yet, it is clear that affect quickly evolved to job satisfaction. Many researchers might take exception with our observation, arguing that satisfaction is an affective response. To this we respond that, while the nature of the connection between the constructs of satisfaction (or any attitude) and affect itself is a point of argument (see Brief, 1998; Eagly & Chaiken, 1993; Weiss, in press), it is clear that there is much more to affect than satisfaction. People can and do feel angry at work, or happy, or guilty, or sad. These discrete emotional states have distinct causes and consequences not captured at all by satisfaction. People also experience mood states that can fluctuate dramatically during the course of a single day (Weiss et al., 1999). These also are not captured by the construct of job satisfaction.

One might argue that the study of affect remained active in the form of stress research; and, certainly, work stress has remained an active and productive research topic. However, work-stress research rarely has focused on the experience of affect. When stress and affect do come together, it is primarily in the form of examination of simple associations (Does stress cause job dissatisfaction?), typically not with any real attempt at process integration. This might change dramatically over the next few years as a consequence of developments in each literature. On the stress side, it is increasingly clear that the constructs of stress and emotion are becoming more entwined. Witness the change in title of the latest edition of this book or see Lazarus's (1991) arguments. Simultaneously, we finally are witnessing the (re?) emergence of interest in affect apart from satisfaction. George's writings in the 1980s and 1990s on the effects of mood in work settings, Weiss and Cropanzano's AET, and other papers document this resurgence. We are even seeing a more thorough examination of the relationship between emotion and satisfaction (Weiss et al., 1999). This all represents a new understanding of the importance of the broader meaning of affect.

Even considering the history of job satisfaction alone, we are struck by the narrowness and simplicity of theoretical work on the topic. Certainly, one might be tempted to argue that theory became more substantial in the 50-year period beginning in the 1930s and ending in the 1980s. One might contrast Vroom's expectancy theory or Locke's value discrepancy position with more empirically driven correlational efforts of earlier decades, and use that as evidence of theoretical progress.

We don't see it that way. In our opinion, the theories of the 1960s era (with the possible exception of Herzberg) should be seen as variants of the general "fit" model that guided the earliest thinking on job satisfaction and had its roots in the vocational guidance literature of the early part of the century. The essential structure of any fit model is that the individual comes to the work situation with various goals, needs, values, desires, etc., and the work situation can be characterized in terms of whether it is facilitative or is antagonistic to meeting these goals, needs, desires, values, etc. (Schneider et al., 1997). Facilitative situations produce satisfaction, antagonistic situations produce dissatisfaction. This is the "theory" of satisfaction which explicitly guided vocational guidance at the beginning of the century and continues in this work today. This is the "theory" which was implicit in the research of Hoppock and Kornhauser. This is the unstated "theory" that lurked behind the pure correlational studies of the 1940s and 1950s.

This is also the "theory" that ties together all the "discrepancy models" (Lawler, 1973) of the 1950s and 1960s. Discrepancy is the flip side of fit. The differences between Vroom and Locke and Katzell are over how to characterize the individual differences in persons and environments and how to model the connections. The underlying logic is the same.

The general concept of fit explicit in such theories as the theory of work adjustment, and implicit in such works as those of Locke and Vroom, certainly has an intuitive appeal. Yet, how are we to evaluate its actual usefulness? Two general strategies seem appropriate, and by both "fit" appears not to deserve its explanatory monopoly.

One strategy is to ask whether "fit" describes the actual psychological processes by which people generate satisfaction judgments; that is, do people examine their environmental outcomes and consciously or unconsciously engage in the specified comparisons? Interestingly enough, as far as we know, there is no research which directly examines this question. No tradition of direct process research exists in the domain of job satisfaction. Nonetheless, indirect evidence tells us that this is probably not what's happening. To begin with, much research shows that people often construct their attitudinal responses when called upon, and these constructions are influenced by many contextual factors. The attitudinal construction process does not seem to be well described by the arithmetic of fit. Research also tells us that the immediate history of affective experiences influences later judgments of satisfaction, that frequent small events are more influential in judgments of satisfaction than are infrequent large events, and that negative information may carry more weight than positive information does in attitude formation. Again, the arithmetic of fit doesn't fit.

Some might argue that this process criterion is too severe, that few theories are subjected to a requirement that they provide direct process evidence. Rather, they might suggest the validity of the theory is supported by the indirect evidence provided by the ability of the components of the theory to predict conceptual criteria. Such predictive efficiency, established experimentally or non-experimentally, builds confidence that the theory models the underlying process. Here, one might argue "fit" does reasonably well. While literature reviews of "fit" models of satisfaction are rare, those that do exist are generally supportive (Edwards, 1991).

But what should be our standards with this strategy? Sheer predictive power would be inappropriate for explanation. Understanding the why and the how of the process is the aim of scientific theory, not merely prediction (e.g. Brief & Dukerich, 1991; Outhwaite, 1990). Moreover, with fit, the precision is never impressive (again, see Edwards, 1991 or Dawis, 1992). Add to this the observation that most fit studies are plagued by the inflationary biases of self-report data and the results become even less convincing. Overall, it appears that the fit model has little supportive process evidence and predicts satisfaction at too weak a level to generate confidence that it is capturing process. It is time to bring new perspectives to theories of job satisfaction.

Job satisfaction simultaneously is considered an attitude and an emotional reaction. It is surprising, therefore, that theories of job satisfaction have paid so little attention to either basic theories in attitude formation or basic theories in emotion. There is little evidence that the satisfaction researchers of any era paid any attention to the attitude researchers of the same era. The satisfaction literature of the 1930s and 1940s makes reference to advances in attitude measurement but rarely incorporates them. The satisfaction literature of the 1950s makes little mention of the Yale School of attitudes (e.g. Hovland, Janis, & Kelley, 1953), the literature of the 1960s does not seriously entertain the relevance of dissonance concepts other than invoking Adam's (1965) applications of it, the literature of the 1970s and 1980s does not discuss the cognitive-response position (e.g. Greenwald, 1968), and the literature of the 1980s or 1990s rarely mentions dual-process models of attitude change (e.g. Petty & Cacioppo, 1986) or any of a number of other topics on attitudes (e.g. strength).

Of course, in any decade, we will find a smattering of studies that try to interpret some basic idea in the attitude literature. However, our focus is not on these isolated studies. Our focus is on the key studies, the major themes, the central approaches of the various periods. When this is the focus, we remain convinced that the literature is conspicuous in its lack of attention to the basic psychology of its key construct. The same can be said with regard to emotion and satisfaction.

In addition, we are struck by the disproportionate amount of energy devoted to the never-ending search for a relationship between performance and satisfaction. When Kornhauser and Sharp first examined the relationship in 1932, they found none. Review after review after review finds only a negligible relationship. Seven decades of research have offered no compelling theoretical reasons for a relationship to exist, at least at the individual level of analysis. Yet, the relationship remains a focus of attention. Why? In some of the research from the 1930s we reviewed, it was noted that a managerial bias was evident, and performance, as a consequence of satisfaction, certainly would be something to attract the interests of managers. This bias, which was transformed into an almost exclusive focus of research on what is thought to be of concern to management (Baritz, 1960), is alive and well today among organizational researchers (Brief, 2000). Thus persists the search for a meaningful satisfaction–performance relationship.

As already noted, several qualities of the research of the 1930s did *not* persist over the decades and probably should have. In closing, two of these, one substantive the other methodological, are revisited, for we judge their resurrections especially promising. The substantive issue concerns the near disappearance of the worker's social milieu outside of the workplace, particularly his/her family and friends. A common theme in the 1930s was what happened at home affected adjustment at work. For example, financial and marital problems were shown to produce disturbances in the workplace. Today, with few exceptions (e.g. Edwards & Rothbard, 1999; George & Brief, 1996), organizational researchers fail to recognize that workers are people too, with parents, spouses, children, lovers, and friends—all of whom could affect directly how a person feels at work and/or could condition how the person affectively responds to his/her job. Regarding the latter, for instance, it may be the case that a worker providing the only financial support for her three children reacts differently to the features of her job than the worker who supports only herself (e.g. Doran, Stone, Brief, & George, 1991; George & Brief, 1990). Again, the relative neglect of the worker's social milieu outside of the workplace may be due to a managerial bias, for management's control of the worker generally stops at the workplace door.

The methodological issue we want to emphasize in closing is the now near void of qualitative approaches to the study of worker affect. The few exceptions in the literature of qualitative research addressing affect typically have been concerned with the display of prescribed emotions in the workplace (e.g. Rafaeli, 1989; Rafaeli & Sutton, 1991), not with the focus of this chapter—the experience of affect. Qualitative research, in the form of grounded theory building (e.g. Glaser & Strauss, 1967), is needed sorely to help formulate, at least tentatively, answers to many of the currently neglected theoretical questions noted throughout this chapter (also see Brief, 1998). Hersey's (1932) research provides a terrific model for these needed efforts to understand better, for example, how workplace attributes may vary in their affect intensity, producing potential differences across individuals, and how emotions experienced in the workplace may focus cognitive attention and, subsequently, influence behavior.

More than 60 years have passed since Hersey's (1932) classic study of workers' emotions in shop and home. Following this remarkable contribution, and those of the other investigations from the 1930s we highlighted, progress was made, but it has been slow and episodic. Perhaps what appear to be significant advances made in the 1990s signal the beginning of a period of more rapid and steady progress towards a fuller appreciation of the origins and functions of moods and emotions in the workplace. If our historical analysis, in any way, helps fuel this progress, the principal aim of this chapter will have been realized.

REFERENCES

Adams, J.S. (1963) Toward and understanding of inequity. *Journal of Abnormal Psychology*, **67**, 422–436.

Adams, J.S. (1965) Inequity in social exchange. In L. Berkowitz (Ed.) *Advances in Experimental Social Psychology*, Vol. 2, pp. 267–299. New York: Academic Press.

Aldag, R.J. & Brief, A.P. (1979) *Task Design and Employee Motivation*. Glenview, IL: Scott, Foreman.

Allport, F.L. (1924). *Social Psychology*, Vol. 19. Boston: Houghton Mifflin.

Allport, G.W. & Allport, F.H. (1928) A test for ascendance-submission. *Journal of Abnormal and Social Psychology*, **23**, 118–136.

Arvey, R.D., Bouchard, T.J., Jr, Segal, N.L., & Abraham, L.M. (1989) Job satisfaction. Environmental and genetic components. *Journal of Applied Psychology*, **74**, 187–192.

Atkinson, J.W. (1964) *An Introduction to Motivation*. Princeton, NJ: D. Van Nostrand Company.

Bagozzi, R.P. & Burnkrant, R.E. (1979) Attitude organization and the attitude-behavior relationship. *Journal of Personality and Social Psychology*, **37**, 913–929.

Baritz, L. (1960) *The Servants of Power: A History of the Use of Social Sciences in American Industry*. Middletown, CT: Wesleyan University Press.

Baron, R.A. (1984) Reducing organizational conflict. An incompatible respond approach. *Journal of Applied Psychology*, **69**, 272–279.

Bateman, T.S. & Organ, D.W. (1983) Job satisfaction and the good soldier. The relationship between affect and employee "citizenship". *Academy of Management Journal*, **26**, 587–595.

Berry, L.M. & Houston, J.P. (1993) *Psychology at Work: An Introduction to Industrial and Organizational Psychology*. Madison, WI: Brown & Benchmark.

Bies, R.J. (1987) The predicament of injustice: The management of moral outrage. In B.M. Staw & L.L. Cummings (Eds) *Research in Organizational Behavior*, Vol. 9, pp. 289–319. Greenwich, CT: JAI.

Borman, W.C. & Motowidlo, S.J. (1993) Expanding the criterion domain to include elements of contextual performance. In N. Schmitt & W.C. Borman (Eds) *Personnel Selection in Organizations*, pp. 71–78. San Francisco: Jossey-Bass.

Brayfield, A.H. & Crockett, W.H. (1955) Employee attitudes and employee performance. *Psychological Bulletin*, **52**, 396–424.

Brief, A.P. (1998) *Attitudes In and Around Organizations*. Thousand Oaks, CA: Sage Publications.

Brief, A.P. (2000) Still servants of power. *Journal of Management Inquiry*, **9**, 342–351.

Brief, A.P. & Aldag, R.J. (1978) The Job Characteristic Inventory: An examination. *Academy of Management Journal*, **21**(4), 659–670.

Brief, A.P., Burke, M.J., Atieh, J.M., Robinson, B., & Webster, J. (1988) Should negative affectivity remain an unmeasured variable in the study of job stress? *Journal of Applied Psychology*, **73**, 199–207.

Brief, A.P., Butcher, A.H., George, J.M., & Link, K.E. (1993) Integrating bottom-up and top-down theories of subjective well-being: The case of health. *Journal of Personality and Social Psychology*, **64**, 646–653.

Brief, A.P. & Dukerich, J.M. (1991) Theory in organizational behavior: Can it be useful? *Research in Organization Behavior*, **13**, 327–352.

Brief, A.P. & Motowidlo, S.J. (1986) Prosocial organizational behaviors. *Academy of Management Review*, **11**, 710–725.

Brief, A.P. & Roberson, L. (1989) Job attitude organization: An exploratory study. *Journal of Applied Social Psychology*, **19**, 717–727.

Brockner, J. & Wiesenfeld, B. (1996) The interactive impact of procedural fairness and outcomes favorability: The effects of what you do depend on how you do it. *Psychological Bulletin*, **120**, 189–208.

Cacioppo, J.T. & Berntson, G.G. (1994) Relationship between attitudes and evaluative space: A critical review, with emphasis on the separability of positive and negative substrates. *Psychological Bulletin*, **115**, 401–423.

Cacioppo, J.T., Gardner, W.L., & Bernston, G.G. (1997) Beyond bipolar conceptualizations and measures: The case of attitudes and evaluative space. *Personality and Social Psychology Review*, **1**, 3–25.

Campion, M.A. & McClelland, C.L. (1991) Interdisciplinary examination of the costs and benefits of enlarged jobs: A job design quasi-experiment. *Journal of Applied Psychology*, **76**, 186–198.

Campion, M.A. & Thayer, P.W. (1985) Development and field evaluation of an interdisciplinary measure of job design. *Journal of Applied Psychology*, **70**, 29–43.

Carnevale, P.J.D. & Isen, A.M. (1986) The influence of positive affect and visual access on the discovery of integrative solutions in bilateral negotiations. *Organizational Behavior and Human Decision Processes*, **37**, 1–13.

Dawis, R.V. & Lofquist, L.H. (1984) *A Psychological Theory of Work Adjustment*. Minneapolis, MN: University of Minnesota Press.

Dawis, R.V. (1992) Person-environment fit and job satisfaction. In C.J. Cranny, P.C. Smith, & E.F. Stone (Eds) *Job Satisfaction*, pp. 69–88. New York: Lexington Books.

Doran, L.I., Stone, V.K., Brief, A.P., & George, J.M. (1991) Behavioral intentions as predictors of job attitudes: The role of economic choice. *Journal of Applied Psychology*, **76**, 40–45.

Dunnette, M.D. (1976) *Handbook of Industrial and Organizational Psychology*. Chicago: Rand McNally.

Durkheim, D.E. (1895) *Les règles de la méthode sociologique [The Rules of Sociological Method]*. Paris: Felix Alcan.

Durkheim, D.E. (1915) *The Elementary Forms of Religious Life: A Study in Religious Sociology* (J. W. Swain, Trans.). New York: Macmillan (Original work published 1912.)

Eagly, A.H. & Chaiken, S. (1993) *The Psychology of Attitudes*. Fort Worth, TX: Harcourt Brace Jovanovich.

Edwards, J.R. (1991) Person-job fit: A conceptual integration, literature review, and methodological critique. *International Review of Industrial/Organizational Psychology*, **6**, 283–357.

Edwards, J.R. & Rothbard, N.P. (1999) Work and family stress and well-being: An examination of person-environment fit in the work and family domains. *Organizational Behavior & Human Decision Processes*, **77**(2), 85–129.

Festinger, L. (1942) A theoretical interpretation of shifts in level of aspiration. *Psychological Review*, **49**, 235–250.

Filley, A.C. & House, R.J. (1969) *Managerial Process and Organizational Behavior*. Glenview, IL: Scott, Foreman.

Fishbein, M. & Ajzen, I. (1974) Attitudes toward objects as predictors of a single and multiple behavioral criteria. *Psychological Review*, **81**(59–74).

Fishbein, M. & Ajzen, I. (1975) *Belief, Attitude, Intention, and Behavior. An Introduction to Theory and Research*. Reading, MA: Addison-Wesley.

Fisher, C.D. & Locke, E.A. (1992) The new look in job satisfaction research and theory. In P.C.S.C.J. Cranny & E.F. Stone (Eds) *Job Satisfaction: How People Feel about Their Jobs and How It Affects Their Performance*, Vol. 1, pp. 165–194. New York: Lexington.

Fisher, V.E. & Hanna, J.V. (1931) *The Dissatisfied Worker*. New York: Macmillan.

Folger, R. & Greenberg, J. (1985) Procedural justice: An interpretive analysis of personal systems. In K.M. Rowland & G.R. Ferris (Eds) *Research in Personnel and Human Resources Management*, Vol. 3, pp. 141–183. Greenwich, CT: JAI.

Follet, M.P. (1918) *The New State: Group Organization the Solution of Popular Government*. New York: Longmans, Green.

Freud, S. (1922) *A General Introduction to Psychoanalysis* (J. Riviere, Trans.). London: Allen & Unwin. (Original work published in 1920.)

George, J.M. (1990) Personality, affect and behavior in groups. *Journal of Applied Psychology*, **75**, 107–116.

George, J.M. (1996) Group affective tone. In M. West (Ed.), *Handbook of Work Group Psychology*. Chichester, UK: Wiley.

George, J.M. & Brief, A.P. (1990) The economic instrumentality of work: An examination of the moderating effects of financial requirements and sex on the pay-life satisfaction relationship. *Journal of Vocational Behavior*, **37**, 357–368.

George, J.M. & Brief, A.P. (1996) Motivational agendas in the work place: The effects of feelings on focus of attention and work motivation. In B.M.S.L.L. Cummings (Ed.) *Research in Organizational Behavior*, Vol. 18, pp. 75–109. Greenwick, CT: JAI.

Glaser, B. & Strauss, A. (1967) *The Discovery of Grounded Theory*. Chicago: Aldine.

Goleman, D.P. (1998) *Working with Emotional Intelligence*. New York: Bantam Books.

Greenberg, J. (1987) A taxonomy of organizational justice theories. *Academy of Management Review*, **12**, 9–22.

Greenberg, J. (1990) Organizational justice: Yesterday, today, and tomorrow. *Journal of Management*, **16**, 399–432.

Greenwald, A.G. (1968) Cognitive learning, cognitive response to persuasion and attitude change. In A.G. Greenwald, T.C. Brock, & T.M. Ostrom (Eds) *Psychological Foundations of Attitudes*. New York: Academic Press.

Hackman, J.R. & Oldham, G.R. (1975) Development of the job diagnostic survey. *Journal of Applied Psychology*, **60**, 159–170.

Hergenhahn, B.R. (1992) *An Introduction to the History of Psychology, 2nd ed.* Belmont, CA: Wadsworth.

Hersey, R.B. (1932) Workers' Emotions in Shop and Home: A Study of Individual Workers from the Psychological and Physiological Standpoint. Philadelphia: University of Pennsylvania Press.

Herzberg, F., Mausner, B., Peterson, R.O., & Capwell, D.F. (1957) *A Review of Research and Opinion*. Pittsburgh: Psychological Service of Pittsburgh.

Herzberg, F., Mausner, B., & Snyderman, B. (1959) *The Motivation to Work*. New York: Wiley.

Holland, J.L. (1976) Vocational preferences. In M.D. Dunnette (Ed.) *Handbook of Industrial and Organizational Psychology*, pp. 521–570. Chicago: Rand McNally College Publishing Company.

Homans, G.C. (1961) *Social Behavior: Its Elementary Forms*. New York: Harcourt, Brace, & World.

Hoppock, R. (1935) *Job Satisfaction*. New York: Harper.

House, R.J. & Wigdor, L.A. (1967) Herzberg's dual-factor theory of job satisfaction: A review of the evidence and a criticism. *Personnel Psychology*, **20**, 369–389.

Hovland, C.I., Janis, I.L., & Kelley, H.H. (1953) *Communication and Persuasion; Psychological Studies of Opinion Change*. New Haven, CT: Yale University Press.

Iaffaldano, M.T. & Muchinsky, P.M. (1985) Job satisfaction and job performance: A meta-analysis. *Psychological Bulletin*, **97**, 251–273.

Isen, A.M. & Baron, R.E. (1991) Positive affect as a factor in organizational behaviour. In B.M. Staw and L.L. Cummings (Eds) *Research Organizational Behavior*. Greenwich, CT: JAI Press.

Jacques, E. (1956) *Measurement of Responsibility*. London: Tavistock.

Jacques, E. (1961) *Equitable Payment*. New York: Wiley.

James, L.R. & James, A.P. (1980) Perceived job characteristics and job satisfaction: An examination of reciprocal causation: *Personnel Psychology*, **33**, 97–135.

James, L.R. & Tetrick, L.E. (1986) Confirmatory analytic test of three causal models relating job perceptions to job satisfaction. *Journal of Applied Psychology*, **71**, 77–82.

Judge, T.A. (1992) The dispositional perspective in human resource research. In G. Ferris & K. Rowland (Eds) *Research in Personnel and Human Resource Management*, pp. 31–72. Greenwich, CT: JAI Press.

Judge, T.A., Locke, E.A., & Durham, C.C. (1997) The dispositional causes of job satisfaction: A core evaluations approach. In L.L.C.B.M. Staw (Ed.) *Research in Organizational Behavior*. Greenwich, CT: JAI.

Judge, T.A., Locke, E.A., Durham, C.C., & Kluger, A.N. (1998) Dispositional effects on job and life satisfaction: The role of core evaluations. *Journal of Applied Psychology*, **83**(1), 17–34.

Katz, D. (1964) The motivational basis of organizational behavior. *Behavioral Science*, **9**, 131–146.

Katzell, R.A. (1964) Personal values, job satisfaction and job behavior. In H. Borow (Ed.) *Man in a World of Work*. Boston: Houghton-Mifflin.

Katzell, R.A. & Austin, J.T. (1992) From then to now: The development of industrial and organizational psychology in the United States. *Journal of Applied Psychology*, **77**(6), 803–835.

King, W. (1970) Clarification and evaluation of the two-factor theory of job satisfaction. *Psychological Bulletin*, **74**, 18–31.

Kornhauser, A.W. (1930) The study of work feelings. *Personnel Journal*, **9**, 348–351.

Kornhauser, A.W. & Sharp, A.A. (1932) Employee attitudes; suggestions from a study in a factory. *Personnel Journal*, **10**, 393–404.

Kristof, A.L. (1996) Person-organization fit: An integrative review of its conceptualizations, measurement, and implications. *Personnel Psychology*, **49**, 1–49.

Kunin, T. (1955) The construction of a new type of attitude measure. *Personnel Psychology*, **8**, 65–78.

Lawler, E.E. (1971) *Pay and Organizational Effectiveness: A Psychological View*. New York: McGraw-Hill.

Lawler, E.E. (1973) *Motivation in Work Organizations*. Monterey, CA: Brooks/Cole Publishing Company.

Lazarus, R.S. (1991) *Emotion and Adaptation*. New York: Oxford University Press.

Lewin, K. (1938) The conceptual representation and measurement of psychological forces. *Duke University. Contributions to Psychological Theory*, **4**, 247.

Locke, E.A. (1969) What is job satisfaction? *Organizational Behavior & Human Decision Processes*, **4**(4), 309–336.

Locke, E.A. (1976) The nature and causes of job satisfaction. In M.D. Dunette (Ed.) *Handbook of Industrial and Organizational Psychology*, pp. 1297–1349. Chicago: Rand McNally.

Lofquist, L.H. & Dawis, R.V. (1969) *Adjustment to Work*. New York: Appleton-Century-Crofts.

March, J.G. & Simon, H.A. (1958) *Organizations*. New York: Wiley.

Mayo, E. (1931) Economic stability and the standard of living. *Harvard Business School Alumni Bulletin*, **7**, 293.

Mayo, E. (1933) *The Human Problem of an Industrial Civilization*. New York: Macmillian.

McClelland, D.C. (1961) *The Achieving Society*. Princeton, NJ: D. Van Nostrand.

McKennell, A.C. (1978) Cognition and affect in perception of well-being. *Social Indicators Research*, **5**, 389–426.

Mitchell, T.R. (1974) Expectancy models of job satisfaction, occupational preference and effort: A theoretical, methodological, and empirical appraisal. *Psychological Bulletin*, **81**(12), 1053–1077.

Morse, N.C. (1953) *Satisfactions in the White-collar Job*. Ann Arbor, MI: Survey Research Center, Institute for Social Research, University of Michigan.

Münsterberg, H. (1913) *Psychology and Industrial Efficiency*. New York: Houghton Mifflin.

Organ, D.W. (1988) *Organizational Citizenship Behavior: The Good Soldier Syndrome*. Lexington, MA: Lexington Books.

Organ, D.W. & Near, J.P. (1985) Cognitive vs. affective measures of job satisfaction. *International Journal of Psychology*, **20**, 241–254.

Organ, D.W. & Ryan, K. (1995) A meta-analytic review of attitudinal and dispositional predictors of organizational citizenship behavior. *Personnel Psychology*, **48**, 775–802.

Ostroff, C. (1992) The relationship between satisfaction, attitudes, and performance: An organizational level analysis. *Journal of Applied Psychology*, **77**, 963–974.

Outhwaite, W. (1990) Realism, naturalism and social behaviour. *Journal for the Theory of Social Behaviour*, **20**(4), 365–377.

Pareto, V. (1935) *The Mind and Society, 4 vols.* New York: Harcourt, Brace.

Patchen, M. (1961) *The Choice of Wage Comparisons.* Englewood Cliffs, NJ: Prentice Hall.

Petty, R.E. & Caccioppo, J.T. (1986) *Communication and Persuasion: Central and Peripheral Routes to Attitude Change.* New York: Springer-Verlag.

Pinder, C.C. (1998) *Work Motivation in Organizational Behavior.* Upper Saddle River, NJ: Prentice Hall.

Porter, L.W. (1961) A study of perceived need satisfactions in bottom and middle management jobs. *Journal of Applied Psychology*, **45**, 1–10.

Porter, L.W. & Lawler, E.E. (1968) *Managerial Attitudes and Performance.* Homewood, IL: Dorsey.

Radcliffe-Brown, A.R. (1922) *The Andaman Islanders: A Study in Social Anthropology,* Anthony Wilkin Studentship Research No. 1906. Cambridge: The University Press.

Rafaeli, A. (1989) When cashiers meet customers: An analysis of the role of supermarket cashiers. *Academy of Management Journal*, **32**(2), 245–273.

Rafaeli, A. & Sutton, R.I. (1991) Emotional contrast strategies as means of social influence: Lessons from criminal interrogators and bill collectors. *Academy of Management Journal*, **34**, 749–775.

Roberts, K.H. & Glick, W. (1981) The job characteristics approach to job design: A critical review. *Journal of Applied Psychology*, **66**, 193–217.

Roethlisberger, F.J. & Dickson, W.J. (1939) *Management and the Worker.* Cambridge, MA: Harvard University.

Ryan, A.M., Schmit, M.J., & Johnson, R. (1996) Attitudes and effectiveness: Examining relations at an organizational level. *Personnel Psychology*, **49**, 853–882.

Salancik, G.R. & Pfeffer, J. (1977) An examination of need-satisfaction models of job attitudes. *Administrative Science Quarterly*, **22**, 427–456.

Salancik, G.R. & Pfeffer, J. (1978) A social information processing approach to job attitudes and task design. *Administrative Science Quarterly*, **23**, 224–253.

Schaffer, R.H. (1953) Job satisfaction as related to need satisfaction in work. *Psychological Monographs*, **67** (14, Whole No. 364).

Schmitt, N. & Pulakos, E.D. (1985) Predicting job satisfaction from life satisfaction: Is there a general satisfaction factor? *International Journal of Psychology*, **20**, 155–168.

Schneider, B. (1984) Industrial and organizational psychology perspective. In A.P. Brief (Ed.) *Productivity Research in the Behavioral and Social Sciences.* New York: Praeger.

Schneider, B. (1987) The people make the place. *Personnel Psychology*, **40**, 437–453.

Schneider, B., Goldstein, H.B., & Smith, D.B. (1995) The ASA framework: An update. *Personnel Psychology*, **48**, 747–773.

Schneider, B., Kristof-Brown, A., Goldstein, H.W., & Smith, D.B. (1997) What is this thing called fit? In N. Anderson & P. Herriot (Eds) *International Handbook of Selection and Assessment.* London: Wiley.

Schwarz, N. & Clore, G.L. (1988) Mood, misattribution, and judgments of well-being: Informative and directive functions of affective states. *Journal of Personality and Social Psychology*, **45**, 513–523.

Smith, P.C., Kendall, L.M., & Hulin, C.L. (1969) *The Measurement of Satisfaction in Work and Retirement: A Strategy for the Study of Attitudes.* Chicago: Rand McNally.

Spector, P.E. (1996) *Industrial and Organizational Psychology: Research and Practice.* New York: Wiley.

Staw, B.M. & Ross, J.V. (1985) Stability in the midst of change: A dispositional approach. *Journal of Applied Psychology*, **70**, 469–480.

Staw, B.M., Bell, N.E., & Clausen, J.A. (1986) The depositional approach to job attitudes: A lifetime longitudinal test. *Administrative Science Quarterly*, **31**, 56–77.

Strong, E.K. (1927) *Vocational Interest Blank.* Palo Alto, CA: Stanford University Press.

Strong, E.K. (1943) *Vocational Interests of Men and Women.* Palo Alto, CA: Stanford University Press.

Taylor, F.W. (1903) *Shop Management.* New York: Harper.

Taylor, F.W. (1911) *The Principles of Scientific Management.* New York: Harper.

Thibaut, J.W. & Walker, L. (1975) *Procedural Justice: A Psychological Perspective.* Hillsdale, NJ: Lawrence Erlbaum Associates.

Thorndike, E.L. (1904) *Introduction to the Theory of Mental and Social Measurement.* New York: Science Press.

Thorndike, E.L. (1914) *Educational Psychology*, Vol. 3, *Mental Work and Fatigue, and Individual Differences and Their Causes.* New York: Teachers College, Columbia University.

Thorndike, E.L., Cobb, M.V., Woodyard, E., & staff (1926) *The Measurement of Intelligence.* New York: Teachers College, Columbia University.

Thurstone, L.L. (1924a) *The Fundamentals of Statistics.* New York: Macmillan.

Thurstone, L.L. (1924b) *The Nature of Intelligence.* New York: Harcourt, Brace.

Thurstone, L.L. (1928) Attitudes can be measured. *American Journal of Sociology*, **33**, 529–554.

Thurstone, L.L. & Chave, E.J. (1929) *The Measurement of Attitude.* Chicago: University of Chicago Press.

Tolman, E.C. (1932) *Purposive Behavior in Animals and Men.* New York: Century.

Turner, A.N. & Lawrence, P.R. (1965) *Industrial Jobs and the Worker.* Boston: Harvard University Graduate School of Business Administration.

Viteles, M.S. (1926) Psychology in industry. *Psychological Bulletin*, **23**, 631–680.

Viteles, M.S. (1932) *Industrial Psychology.* New York: Norton.

Viteles, M.S. (1959) Fundamentalism in industrial psychology. *Occupational Psychology*, **33**, 98–110.

Vroom, V.H. (1964) *Work and Motivation.* New York: Wiley.

Walker, C.R. & Guest, R.H. (1952) *The Man on the Assembly Line.* Cambridge, MA: Harvard University Press.

Weiss, H.M. (in press) Deconstructing job satisfaction. *Human Resource Management Review.*

Weiss, H.M. & Cropanzano, R. (1996) Affective Events Theory: A theoretical discussion of the structure, causes and consequences of affective experiences at work. In B.M. Staw & L.L. Cummings (Eds) *Research in Organizational Behavior: An Annual Series of Analytical Essays and Critical Reviews*, Vol. 18, pp. 1–74. Greenwich, CT JAI:

Weiss, H.M., Nicholas, J.P., & Daus, C.S. (1999) An examination of the joint effects of affective experiences and job beliefs on job satisfaction and variations in affective experiences over time. *Organizational Behavior & Human Decision Processes*, **78**(1), 1–24.

Weitz, J. (1952) A neglected concept in the study of job satisfaction. *Personnel Psychology*, **5**, 201–205.

Whyte, W. F. (1955) *Money and Motivation*. New York: Harper & Row.

Wilson, T.D. & Hodges, S.D. (1992) Attitudes as temporary constructions. In L.L.T.A. Martin (Ed.) *The Construction of Social Judgments*, pp. 37–65. Hillsdale, NJ: Lawrence Erlbaum Associates.

Wren, D.A. (1994) *The Evolution of Management Thought*. New York: Wiley.

Chapter 7

Culture as a source, expression, and reinforcer of emotions in organizations

Janice M. Beyer
*Harkins and Company Centennial Chair in Business
Administration, Department of Management,
University of Texas at Austin*
David Niño
Administrative Sciences, University of Houston—Clear Lake*

The field of organizational studies has been late in including emotions as part of its purview. For example, a reader who looked in the subject indices of the two classic handbooks on organizations (March, 1965; Nystrom & Starbuck, 1981) would not find a single entry for affect, for emotions, or for feelings. Until the late 1980s, the field seemingly remained under the thrall of the rational image of organizations advanced with Weber's (1947) concepts of legal-rational authority and bureaucracy. Barley and Kunda (1992), suggested that it was the rediscovery of the importance of culture that turned some organizational scientists and managers away from rationalism and toward a more humanistic view of organizations that could take account of the emotional side of organizational life. They postulated that one of the appeals of culture was that the emotional commitment it engendered would foster financial gain (Barley & Kunda, 1992, p. 383).

* David Niño would like to acknowledge the support of the Red McCombs School of Business at the University of Texas at Austin, where he was a doctoral student while co-authoring this chapter.

Emotions at Work. Edited by Roy Payne and Cary Cooper.
© 2001 by John Wiley & Sons, Ltd.

Taking a different perspective on the issue in their book on culture, Trice and Beyer (1993) emphasized the emotional side of all cultures by specifying "emotionally charged" as one of the six characteristics of culture, and by centering their analysis of culture on its role in managing uncertainties. They theorize that human cultures are repositories of those beliefs and practices that help people to face and deal with the chaos and uncertainties that are an inevitable part of life in all human societies. To support this contention, they argue that humans are less specifically regulated by genetic programming than other species, and thus require the guidance of cultures "to collectively survive, adapt, and achieve" (Trice and Beyer, 1993, p. 3). They also quote Geertz's trenchant observation:

> We are, in sum, incomplete or unfinished animals who complete ourselves through culture—and not through culture in general, but through highly particular forms of it. (Geertz, 1970 61).

> [To be human] is not just to talk; it is to utter the appropriate words and phrases in the appropriate social situations in the appropriate tone of voice ... It is not just to eat; it is to prefer certain foods cooked in certain ways, and to follow a rigid table etiquette in consuming them; *it is not even just to feel, but to feel certain quite distinctive emotions—patience, detachment, resignation, respect* [italics added].
> (Geertz, 1970, p. 64)

In their subsequent discussion of the emotionally charged nature of cultures, Trice and Beyer point out that it is because cultures help people to manage the anxieties associated with uncertainty that cultures are infused with emotion as well as meaning. They argue that people cling to and cherish established cultural beliefs and practices because they seem to make the future more predictable by making it conform to the past. Thus, allegiances to cultural ideologies and the cultural forms[1] used to express those ideologies spring more from people's emotional needs than from rational consideration. Also, when cultural ideologies are questioned or threatened, their adherents react emotionally; cultural practices remain "objects of passionate adoration long after they have outlived their usefulness. Men fight and die for them" (Ferguson, 1936, p. 29).

From Trice and Beyer's (1993) perspective on culture, it is relatively easy to see that cultures play multiple roles *vis à vis* emotions. Most widely recognized in the organizational culture literature to date is that cultures manage emotions, as the quote from Geertz above suggests, by guiding both their experience and expression both externally and internally. From their cultures members learn not only how they should express their emotions, but also which emotions they should experience—how it is appropriate to feel and not feel in a given situation. To do this, cultures must serve as repositories (1) of appropriate emotions that members are expected to draw on as needed and (2) of the scripts, symbols, language, stories, and other cultural forms through which these emotions can be appro-

---

[1] Trice and Beyer (1993, p. 77) define cultural forms as observable entities used by members of a culture to express, affirm, and communicate the substance of their culture to one another. They discuss a variety of cultural forms they classify in four categories: symbols, language, narratives, and practices.

priately expressed, celebrated, and reinforced. In this way, cultures guide or channel emotions into acceptable manifestations.

In addition, cultures provide individual members with social identities that bind them emotionally to other members of the culture. Unfortunately, the "stronger and more emotionally charged" identification with the culture is, "the more likely its adherents will come to have intolerant and emotionally charged reactions to people who hold other ideas" (Trice & Beyer, 1993, p. 11). Because members of a given culture tend to see the ideas of outsiders as threats to the valued culture and the identities they derive from it, they are prone to ethnocentrism. They defend their cultural identities by considering members of other cultural groups inferior and sometimes even their enemies.

To explore these issues we will discuss five ways in which cultures shape emotions—namely, how cultures:

- manage the anxieties posed by uncertainties;
- provide ways to express emotions;
- encourage and discourage the experience of emotions;
- engender identification and commitment; and
- produce ethnocentrism.

To help us to illustrate these features of cultures, we will begin our discussion by summarizing a recent dramatic and tragic episode in one organization's history. Before beginning that story, we want to clarify what we mean by emotions, since they have been defined in a variety of ways. In this chapter, when we refer to emotions we mean strong generalized feelings with both psychical and physical manifestations (Guralnik & Friend, 1966). At the end of the story, we will analyze what happened from these five perspectives, and, in the process, add additional illustrations from other accounts in the organizational literature.

A CULTURAL TRADITION "TURNED TRAGIC"[2]

For months, crews of students at Texas A&M University had labored cutting thousands of large trees, trimming them to specified lengths, and hauling them to the site. Now, in the wee hours of the morning, 70 or more students were climbing around the 59-foot stack of logs they had built, fastening new logs to the center pole and to each other (Copelin, 1999b). It was 18 November, and the big event for which they were preparing—the traditional annual bonfire before the football game with arch rival University of Texas—was only a week away, and there were still additional levels to be built on top of what they had already done. Around 2:30 a.m. some of the students working on the stack felt movement under them, and, before anyone realized what was happening, the whole stack began to

---

[2] Beach, 1999.

collapse. As it fell, a million pounds of huge logs came crashing down, hitting and burying many of the student workers.

Word of the tragedy spread quickly and students as well as emergency workers rushed to the scene to help in the rescue effort. But because of the size of the stack, the weight of the logs, and the precarious positions of the fallen logs on each other, it took many hours before all of the fallen were rescued. It took weeks before the full extent of the tragedy was known—that 11 students and one recent graduate had been killed and another 27 injured, some of them very seriously.

What was expected to be the emotional high point of the school year suddenly became a time of grief for everyone on the campus and for A&M alumni everywhere. Outsiders wondered why so many students would be working in the middle of the night on such a potentially dangerous task. Those connected with A&M, even the parents of the injured and dead students, did not raise that question. They knew the many meanings that the Bonfire had to those who participated in this annual tradition. As an article written the same day as the tragedy explained:

> It's a monument to Aggie spirit, steeped in legend that passes from Aggie to Aggie from the moment they step onto campus—even earlier. It's the biggest and most visible of all traditions at the university where the word [tradition] is heard often. And it's a symbol of fierce pride in a campus that started as an all-male military institution and grew into the second largest public university in the state, a co-ed school respected nationally for its engineering and veterinary medicine programs.
>
> (LeBlanc, 1999, p. A7)

Alumni who were interviewed explained further:

> It's special that A&M students can come together and focus all their energy to build something that doesn't even seem like it should be able to be built.
>
> It's really come to symbolize the university. People are always looking forward to the start of Bonfire. They're talking up how much fun they're going to have there.
>
> (LeBlanc, 1999, p. A7)

An article in *Newsweek* magazine (Pierce, 1999, p. 44) referred to the Bonfire as "the pride of the Aggies," and "a symbol of solidarity against their rivals at the University of Texas." As another account explained:

> The night that it burns is the biggest party night of the year in College Station, not just for students, but for residents and even high school kids. Bonfire has become a tourist attraction, bringing former students and their families back to the campus by the thousands; attendance estimates in recent years range up to 70,000 ... Aggies say that Bonfire is the largest student- organized project in the nation. Total participation is around five thousand students.
>
> (Burka, 2000, p. 147)

MANAGING EMOTIONS

To manage feelings about the tragedy, and to give the deaths meaning, many symbolic events occurred on the College Station campus of A&M. There were organized prayer vigils and many informal gatherings of weeping students. To mark the first 24 hours after the tragedy, buglers from the school band played taps. At the beginning of the football game the following week, four jets from an Air Force reserve squadron, piloted by A&M alumni, flew over the football field in a "missing man" formation. Then 12 white doves, symbolizing those killed in the tragedy, were released and circled the football field (Davenport, 1999, p. A1).

The University of Texas responded to the tragedy with its own symbolic acts, which included canceling its pre-game rally, darkening the university tower, and holding a memorial service (dubbed the Unity Gathering) that included playing the A&M alma mater song on the carillon from the UT tower (Shah, 1999, p. A1). Other UT ceremonies and rituals traditionally connected with the UT–A&M game were toned down because of the tragedy. A&M, in turn, responded by omitting one of the most anti-UT yells—"Beat the hell out of t.u."—during the yell practice that replaced the Bonfire burning (Copelin, 1999a, p. A–11).

An A&M student who wrote about campus reactions to the collapse pointed out that, while not all students participated in building the bonfire, almost all attended the burning each year. In trying to explain its meaning, she quoted a campus slogan written on a framed print that hangs in her room:

> Aggieland—From the inside looking out, you cannot explain it; from the outside looking in, you cannot understand it.
>
> (Hight, 1999, p. A5)

The Bonfire also arouses some less constructive emotions. A UT student who was interviewed commented that he had experienced a "vicious rivalry"—one that ignited a "competitive passion" between him and a friend who attended A&M. He also commented that, in reality, the rivalry was mean spirited, but had been only temporarily transformed from tradition into tragedy. Three times in the past, UT students had tried to firebomb the structure, with no serious results. One reporter commented:

> the catastrophe at A&M seemed to raise old questions about college traditions and big-time athletic programs—and whether the passion that fuels them is out of control.
>
> (Pierce, 1999, p. 44)

THE AFTERMATH OF THE TRAGEDY

The responses to the tragedy, associated with the Bonfire building in 1999, provide an especially rich illustration of how cultures store, sustain, celebrate, channel, and enhance emotions. As the texts already cited show, both bystanders and participants recognized that the importance of this event resided in the meanings it symbolized and expressed. But outsiders to the A&M culture were still puzzled and even horrified that something like this could happen at a university known for its engineering expertise.

Within days of the tragedy A&M President Ray Bowen conceded that the Bonfire tradition might end, depending on the results of a subsequent investigation into its causes. This possibility, based in the usual "rational" response to a serious accident, was greeted by surprising reactions from the parents of the victims of the tragedy. The engineer father of one of the men killed remarked that it was "a wonderful tradition" and that his son would have wanted the Bonfire to continue. A mother of another said it would be "an additional tragedy" to end the Bonfire tradition. Still another said, "We absolutely want it to continue." She was surprised that her friends thought it was a stupid thing to happen and defended the building of the Bonfire, saying, "But it's through those traditions that camaraderie is built. That is the way *those kids are connected for the rest of their lives* [italics added]" (Haurwitz, 1999b, pp. B1, B3). Many other parents, alumni, and students sent e-mails to A&M President Bowen, some advocating an end to the tradition, a larger number responding with messages favoring its continuance. Since then, some alumni have threatened to cut off donations to the university if Bonfire is not continued. An analysis published 6 months after the tragedy concluded: "The overwhelming belief on campus is that to cut back or abandon Bonfire is to commit the ultimate negative act—*to surrender to death* [italics added]" (Burka, 2000, p. 149).

Less than a month after the accident, President Bowen said he thought that the tradition would continue "assuming it can be done safely" (Haurwitz, 1999a, p. B3). By the following spring, it was reported, he "had made up his mind about one thing: If there is to be a bonfire, it will be a student-run event" (Burka, 2000, p. 149).

What does it mean that the parents of the dead students, other students, many vocal alumni, and some of the faculty and administrators involved apparently still feel—despite the recent tragic collapse—that both the enormous efforts and risks involved in Bonfire should continue? Considering that the results were burnt up in one night of revelry, the Bonfire's main value cannot be in the structure itself, but rather in the symbolic meaning that has been invested in it over time.

THE ELABORATION OF A CULTURAL TRADITION

When it began, in 1909, the A&M Bonfire consisted of a rather modest pile of lumber and trash. The first all-log bonfire was built in a tepee design in 1942. Since then the bonfire's construction has been elaborated to yield taller and more complex structures. In 1967 the tepee-shaped stack reached 90 feet, and then, in 1969, a record 105 feet. At that point, administrators, fearing that sparks flying so high in the air could create a fire hazard for nearby buildings, imposed a 55 feet limit. The basic design was also changed in 1978 to what has come to be called a wedding cake design (i.e. stacked layers of logs standing vertically and bound together around a center pole with cables). The 1999 Bonfire had been constructed in that design (Burka, 2000, p. 123) and had already exceeded the 55-foot limit when it collapsed.

The amount of effort that has gone into its construction in recent years is staggering: 6,000–8,000 students cut and assemble, with the help of cranes donated by alumni, approximately 7,000 huge logs according to a student-kept plan and under supervision of small numbers of students who are juniors and seniors. Some 45 different crews work around the clock in double shifts, beginning early in the fall semester. Building Bonfire "destroys thousands of trees every year, inflicts dozens of serious injuries, occupies upward of 100,000 man- hours, [and] puts some students in academic jeopardy" (Burka, 2000, p. 120). Probably as a result of these excesses, a group called Aggies Against Bonfire was formed in the late 1980s, but has since been "replaced by Aggie Replant, an organization that plants trees in the spring to make up for those that were cut down in the fall" (Burka, 2000, p. 149).

If the chief cultural value of Bonfire is that students learn and experience teamwork to perform a difficult and challenging task, there are clearly other possibilities for achieving the same objective. For example, the same amount of effort could build one or more new homes for the poor or homeless. Clearly other values and meanings were also being expressed through Bonfire. The students and alumni who supported them were devoting their time and effort to a symbolic degradation of their rival university—the University of Texas (UT). Since at least the 1940s, the Bonfire tradition has included placing a wooden outdoor toilet on its top to symbolize the identity of the traditional rival—the University of Texas at Austin. Presumably burning this symbol was an outlet for the hostile feelings of the Aggies toward UT.

But other, more serious purposes are stated in defense of this ritual. One of the core beliefs at A&M is that its mission should include "other education" through which students learn from participating in activities outside the classroom (Burka, 2000 p. 146). The faculty advisor to the students building the 1999 bonfire, Rusty Thompson, who was not present when the collapse occurred, made it clear that part of the tradition of Bonfire was to give the students minimal faculty or staff supervision. "It's student-run and staff advised—not by accident, but on purpose," another A&M administrator explained (Ward, 2000b, p. A1). The student-body president, Will Hurd, 22, reported that he came to A&M rather than Stanford, where he had been offered a scholarship, because of the opportunities A&M's "other education" offered him "to develop as a whole person" (Burka, 2000, p. 146).

A couple days after the tragedy, Thompson argued that it should continue because, as he put it, "Those students *who gave up their lives*" would "want to hear the Aggie yell [italics added]" (Spencer, 1999, p. B7). The italicized phrase is one often used to refer to soldiers who die in battle,[3] presumably defending the

---

[3] The phrase is also used to refer to police or firefighters who die in the line of duty because they are also seen as defenders of human welfare and order in society.

welfare and rights of their societies. Its borrowing for this occasion indicates how "sacred" the Bonfire has become within the A&M culture.

Later, in a Special Bonfire Memorial Issue of the *Texas Aggie* magazine, Thompson referred to junior-level students[4] who supervised the construction as "true professionals in every sense of the word" (Pirtle, 1999, p. 3). However, as time passed, various faculty members, especially those on the engineering faculty, came forward to report that they had voiced concerns to the university administration in the past about the safety of the bonfire construction and about the drinking of alcoholic beverages by the crews, but that their concerns had been ignored. A former A&M president had raised the issue with the university's Regents in 1990, a faculty and staff committee had recommended its size be reduced to 44 feet, but nothing had been done to implement this recommendation, apparently because of fears of negative reactions by students (Gamboa, 2000a, p. B1, B2). There was also one prior partial collapse of the Bonfire in 1994, but no one had been injured or killed.

UNANSWERED QUESTIONS

Soon after the collapse, the University hired four consulting firms and allocated 1 million dollars to investigate the tragedy and try to uncover its cause, including one group to investigate how well the 1999 log stack corresponded to those used in previous years and a second to collect reports of participants and relate them to the Aggie culture. In mid-February of 2000, two of the firms requested additional funds and time to complete their investigations (Gamboa, 2000b, p. B7).

While these investigations were proceeding, various troubling reports surfaced. One said that some rescuers and participants observed many beer cans and other containers of alcohol around the construction site the night of the accident (Ward & Gamboa, 2000a, p. B1). Autopsies of the dead students revealed that two of them had high alcohol levels in their blood. Despite this information, A&M officials steadfastly insisted that they did not believe that the drinking of alcohol "could have been a cause of the collapse." (Ward & Gamboa, 2000a, p. B1). Other reports revealed that a cable meant to bind the bottom logs together had not been used (*Austin American Statesman*, 19 February 2000a, p. B1), and that the log pile had been leaning before it fell (Ward, 2000a).

Official planning for the 2000 Bonfire was postponed until A&M's President and administration received the inquiry team's official report, which cost an estimated $1.8 million. On 2 May 2000, the inquiry team revealed its conclusions about the causes of the Bonfire collapse in a large and televised public meeting in Reed Arena (Ward & Gamboa, 2000b). Their findings disclosed both physical and organizational reasons for the failure. The most significant physical failures were

---

[4] Called Redpots for the headgear they wore. All of the students were assigned a status in a hierarchy according largely to their years in school and experience with Bonfire, with each level wearing a different color of hat.

attributed to excessive internal stresses resulting from how the second tier logs were wedged against the first tier, and to the lack of strength in the wires connecting the logs. The 1999 Bonfire used wires instead of the stronger exterior restraining cables used in previous years. These physical failures were reportedly driven by organizational failures. For example, the inquiry reported that Bonfire was built each year without thoroughly documented designs and construction methods. Compounding this problem was the finding that largely unsupervised student builders lacked the knowledge and skills needed to build a complex Bonfire structure.

The report also identified the University's culture as a contributing organizational factor. Despite problems and warning signs that had been publicly reported in the past, the decision-making culture surrounding the Bonfire was biased toward building it in ways that were believed to replicate tradition. However, as one investigator pointed out, the "bonfire never was built the same way twice" (Ward & Gamboa, 2000b, p. A12). For example, an earlier report indicated that where 15-foot logs had been used in the past as the first level of the stack, the 1999 Bonfire used 18-foot logs (Copelin, 1999b). In the absence of well-documented blueprints, student builders apparently took liberties in making what they likely considered to be small design changes over the years, ultimately resulting in a seriously flawed structure. Finally, the report found that a lack of proactive management kept the A&M administration from reassessing Bonfire when problems arose. As one commentator wrote, "At any other university, this [reassessment] process would be routine. At Texas A&M it is charged with emotion" (Burka, 2000, p. 118). There was ample evidence of the strong emotions of students at the hearing. They booed for example, when they heard statements critical of the tradition. Many showed up wearing T-shirts bearing such slogans as:

A fire that burns in your heart will never die;
Keep the fire burning;
Texas A&M. Where Bonfire is more than a tradition. It's life.
                                                              (Greenberger, 2000, p. A11)

After hearing the results of the inquiry, President Bowen stated that while his "heart" wanted to continue the Bonfire, his "brain" recognized the possibility of ending the tradition (Ward & Gamboa, 2000b, p. A12). He promised a decision within 6 weeks and emphasized that his heart would not be making that decision. Ending the tradition will obviously not be easy. Students and alumni are so adamant to continue the tradition that they have stated they would build Bonfire off campus, if necessary. As the 2 May 2000 issue of the student newspaper reported, some students have already started organizing for a November 2000 Bonfire (Ward and Gamboa, 2000b). Well before the results were announced, many alumni and students maintained that they would fight for the continuance of Bonfire no matter what the outcome of that report was (Copelin, 2000, p. A1).

It seems clear that the Texas A&M students and alumni are reluctant, perhaps unwilling, to fully recognize or accept a cause that would undermine the cultural rationales for why and how the Bonfire tradition has been carried out, despite increasing evidence showing that the 1999 Bonfire structure departed in important ways from earlier ones. Such a departure was likely the product of decisions made by A&M student builders, whom, the student culture asserts, are professional enough to be trusted to handle such a grave responsibility. This core cultural tenet and thus the whole student culture have been thrown into question by having their decisions implicated as a cause of the tragedy.

As the evidence mounted, the misgivings of other groups led them to take actions opposing or threatening continuance of the tradition. The first development was that a panel of A&M professors announced it wanted the university to discontinue or at least drastically change the annual bonfire (*Austin American Statesman*, 1 June 2000b, p. B1). The chair of that panel, Jonathan Smith, told the local College Station newspaper: "I can't see that the event as we've known it can continue. ... I think there are insurmountable problems" (*Austin American Statesman*, 1 June 2000b, p. B1). Two weeks later, the Texas Board of Professional Engineers launched its own inquiry into the causes of the 1999 collapse. At that time the Board's executive director stated that if A&M chose to continue Bonfire, "appropriate personnel, including professional engineers, have to be involved" (Haurwitz, 2000, p. B1).

President Bowen finally announced his decision on the future of Bonfire on 16 June 2000, more than 7 months after the 1999 collapse. He "ordered a two-year moratorium to plan a dramatically restructured event" in which Bonfire would be overseen, and, in some phases, executed by professionals instead of students. "I will do what is right," Bowen said, "Even though my decision could be judged as 'tough' on the students" (Copelin and Adame, 2000, p. A1). Bowen himself had been an A&M student as an undergraduate and had participated in Bonfire.

Nonetheless, Bowen's decision dictated many changes with cultural implications:

(1) no Bonfire in 2000 or 2001;
(2) planning for 2002 will begin in 2001, but over a shorter interval, and will include university officials and professionals as well as students;
(3) future Bonfires will be single-story tepee-shaped structures;
(4) plans for future Bonfires must be approved by the University;
(5) design, construction, and safety plans will be prepared by licensed professionals;
(6) the process of choosing student leaders will be more inclusive;
(7) the construction site will have limited access and be monitored by video (Copelin & Adame, 2000, p. A1).

Both the A&M student-body president and the president of the Association of Former Students supported Bowen's decision. Student reactions were mixed. "When Bowen said 'Bonfire is not the defining activity of the former all-male, all-military school', many scoffed" (Copelin and Adame, 2000, A1), and some students hissed when Bowen said students would not be allowed to cut logs for future Bonfires. Others seemed glad the tragedy they had observed had finally been put to rest. A local restaurant owner predicted bonfires will be built on private land. A biology professor predicted enthusiasm for Bonfire will wane, and that stricter supervision will undermine the future of Bonfire by lessening its attraction to students. This prediction recognized the cultural inconsistency professional supervision over this event will introduce.

DISCUSSION: HOW CULTURES EXPRESS AND ENGENDER EMOTIONS

The central premise of this chapter is that, as Trice and Beyer (1993) pointed out, cultures are emotionally charged—that all cultures are, to various extents, imbued with emotions. Much of the heavily cited theoretical literature on organizational cultures has tended to emphasize the cognitive aspects of culture (e.g. Denison, 1990; Hofstede, 1980; Sackmann, 1991; Martin, 1992; Schein, 1985, 1992; Schneider, 1990)[5], and, like the other literature on organizations, has tended to de-emphasize, marginalize, or ignore its emotional bases and consequences (Martin, Knopoff, & Beckman, 1998). But, as the leading anthropologists cited earlier have long recognized, cultures clearly concern matters that engage people's emotions. The substance of their cultures—what people collectively believe, value, and expect—is, in turn, colored and shaped by their emotions. Furthermore, people express and reinforce those emotions considered appropriate through a variety of cultural forms. Thus, it is not surprising that in ethnographic and other qualitative studies of people functioning in real organizations, the emotional nature of culture asserts itself, as will be evident from some of the illustrations used in the discussion that follows.

Thus, while they can be separated conceptually, in the realities of social life, cultures and emotions are inextricably and closely linked. One purpose of this chapter has been to document this close linkage. We will now use the tragedy at Texas A&M and other concrete examples from the literature on organizations to make evident the five ways, identified on p. 75, that cultures embody and foster emotions.

Managing the anxieties of uncertainty

Clearly, the Bonfire tragedy at Texas A&M University was only one manifestation of an undergraduate student culture that had developed over many years. This tradition, like the rest of that culture, managed the anxieties associated with

---

[5] Among these volumes, only the Schein books treat emotions in more than brief mentions.

uncertainty by serving as part of a rite of passage for A&M students. The central cultural consequences of rites of passage are to reassure both the society and the young persons undergoing the rites that they are ready and able to assume the responsibilities of adulthood. The socialization of the young is always fraught with uncertainty, and following prescribed rites and rituals along the way helps to reassure parents, society, and the young that the process will be successful.

In modern US society, higher education serves as more or less potent rites of passage for its students. Such rites include three stages: a rite of separation, which symbolizes and facilitates the neophyte's letting go or moving away from an old identity; a rite of transition, which usually involves humiliations and other ordeals that test the neophyte's fitness for the new status; and a rite of incorporation, which marks the re-entry of the neophyte into the larger social group with a new status (Van Gennep, [1909] 1960; Trice & Beyer, 1993). Many college and university students are separated from the family home during this passage and thus stimulated to shed their childhood identity. The ordeals associated with college work test college students to determine if they are mature and skilled enough to assume approved of roles in adult society. In the US, with its utilitarian view of higher education, the rite of incorporation occurs when students graduate and move into gainful employment—they have then successfully achieved adult status.

The stated, manifest reasons for the Bonfire tradition at A&M are to learn teamwork and leadership—two skills considered important to successful careers in current US society. Two latent reasons that the Bonfire tradition at A&M is such a potent part of the undergraduate students' rites of passage are that (1) the extensive labor that goes into building the stack of logs symbolizes, in a much more concrete way than grades and academic learning can, the difficult ordeals that students undergo and have to surmount, and (2) the continuity of the tradition tends to reassure everyone involved that the world has not changed very much—that the same things still matter in becoming a successful adult. In general, the predictability and repetitiveness of rituals contribute importantly to people's emotional well-being.

The ordeals incorporated into higher education—exams, theses, and the like—as a rite of passage are usually initiated and preserved by the faculty. In the case of A&M's bonfire, however, the ordeal was originated and perpetuated by student groups and strongly supported by former students—the alumni. In a sense, then, Bonfire is an important tradition not to a university's overall culture, but only to its student subculture. The faculty subculture might be best described as tolerant of the tradition. Various faculty members have criticized aspects of Bonfire over the years. The subcultures of the university administration seem to see their roles as serving the students and retaining the support of the alumni. Thus, neither the faculty nor the administration are really members of the student culture we have described.

It has been observed that various occupations that do not require college degrees but involve life-threatening work develop their own distinctive rites of passage that help to prepare recruits for the uncertainties and associated emotional demands of their work. Examples are the military, firefighters, police, high-steel ironworkers, and miners (Trice and Beyer, 1993; Trice, 1993). The rite of passage undergone by smokejumpers—firefighters who parachute into forest fires—involves keeping recruits up the whole night before their first jump. They believe that the exhausted recruits will be less likely to hesitate before jumping than if they were clear-headed and thinking about the implications of what they were doing (McCarl, 1976). Novice high-steel ironworkers are harassed during their rites of passage with verbal insults and physical sparring. In this way their trustworthiness, competence, and emotional self-control under pressure are tested (Haas, 1977). Similarly, psychological studies of combat pilots and bomb disposal crews found that both gained confidence during demanding training because it helped them to overcome their fears and be less afraid in the face of the mortal danger they regularly encountered in their work (Rachman, 1990).

While not life-threatening to members, the prospect or reality of organizational death also creates a whole range of other uncertainties for members of the organizations involved. Harris and Sutton (1986) studied what happened among employees of eight organizations that went out of business or otherwise ceased to exist. They found that members of these organizations held parting ceremonies in which they (1) managed uncertainties by exchanging information about job prospects, names and addresses of one another, and promised to keep in touch; and (2) exchanged emotional support by collectively expressing their anger and sadness, taking photographs, and celebrating the positive memories of the past by sharing stories of the "old place" (Harris and Sutton, 1986, p. 15).

Other research revealed that more mundane uncertainties are also expressed and managed in organizations through stories. Research revealed that stories conveyed messages about such common emotional concerns as how to behave with higher status persons, the possibilities of termination, and how an organization can successfully deal with environmental uncertainties (Martin, Feldman, Hatch, & Sitkin, 1983). Another cultural form that organizations use to cope with uncertainty is the meeting. Schwartzman (1986) observed that meetings become more frequent when organizations are dealing with high internal and external uncertainties, and that, in such circumstances, the meeting itself becomes a symbol for the feeling of taking collective action and thus ensuring survival.

Providing ways to express emotions

As some of the above examples show, one way for people to deal with uncertainty is by expressing their positive and negative emotions to and with each other. Cultures, and especially cultural rites, provide avenues for them to do this. A central purpose of the whole Bonfire tradition was to express and heighten positive emotions connected with belonging to the A&M student culture. Both participants and the audience who watched the building and burning of the huge stack of logs were stimulated by the event to exhibit excitement, elation, and strong attachment to one another and to their university. Perhaps even more than the football game that it preceded, the Bonfire traditionally served as a rite of integration that encouraged the expression of common feelings that bind A&M students and alumni to each other and to their university.

When the 1999 Bonfire stack collapsed with loss of multiple lives, and injuries, ways were quickly found by the students and staff at A&M to modify traditional practices into ceremonies expressing collective grief. Immediately after the collapse, students spontaneously gathered in groups to grieve and comfort one another at the site. Many brought flowers. Traditional pre-game ceremonies were replaced by memorial services and prayer vigils at churches and funeral homes in College Station.

Given the enormity of the tragedy, the students and staff at the UT also felt a need to express grief and to avoid expressing inappropriate emotions. They did so by a series of actions, some of which were already mentioned: canceling the pre-game rally in Austin, darkening the university tower, playing the A&M school song on the carillon, and holding a memorial service dubbed the Unity Gathering. To ceremonially express the feelings of A&M's many alumni, a vigil was also held at the Texas Capitol building in Austin (Beach, 1999).

Perhaps the most prominent stream of organizational research dealing with the expression of emotions focuses on what is called emotional labor. This concept is used to refer to situations in which employees are expected to actively display "socially desired emotions" in the course of their work (Hochschild, 1983). Many service occupations present situations in which emotional labor is expected. Examples include flight attendants, funeral directors, theme-park workers, and waiters in restaurants, all of whom are expected to enact positive emotions in response to whatever clients and customers might do (Ashforth & Humphrey, 1993). For example, at Disneyland, all employees are trained to exhibit helpful and cheerful dispositions—to perform a role as if "onstage" (Van Maanen, 1991). The customary ways these emotions are expressed become cultural rituals of the occupation. What is interesting about emotional labor is that it is exhibited emotion, but not necessarily felt emotion. In fact, in many of these occupations, occupants have to cope with their negative feelings toward customers and other stresses "backstage". However, these types of organizations often go through considerable effort to help ensure that employees will be inclined to experience "appropriate" feelings that match those that they are expected to display (Sutton, 1991).

An example of negative felt emotions vented through cultural ceremonies is provided by public meetings of creditors during organizational bankruptcies. Such meetings help all those involved to express emotions. In particular, they give creditors an opportunity to engage in denigration via confrontation. In one such meeting observed by researchers (Sutton & Callahan, 1987), creditors voiced nasty insults toward the company and its officers. For example, one creditor told the president of the bankrupt firm to stop making excuses for his incompetence. In some cases, the CEO of the bankrupt company accepted responsibility for some of the problems leading to the bankruptcy and apologized to the creditors. Trice and Beyer (1993) called such ceremonies rites of degradation and argued that their manifest purpose was to dissolve or greatly reduce the power of those degraded. Clearly, they also provide an occasion for the public venting of negative emotions.

An occupation in which members' emotional labor involves exhibiting negative emotions is that of the bill collector. Occupants are selected, socialized, and rewarded for conveying urgency by threatening debtors and expressing irritation and anger (Sutton, 1991). Their employers expect that in this way they will be able to control debtors' behavior—presumably to get them to pay the offending bills. However, bill collectors do not always feel the emotions they display; occasionally they feel sympathy for debtors who suffer financial problems that are not their fault.

Encouraging and discouraging the experience of emotions

As the Bonfire rite exemplifies, cultural forms not only express emotions—the very process of expressing emotions usually also heightens the experiencing of those emotions. In the process, Bonfire discouraged both the expression and experiencing of other emotions. The traditional Bonfire burning encouraged students and others who attended to have fun and to experience positive feelings toward A&M and negative feelings toward UT. Participants would find it difficult to feel emotionally neutral or negative toward either A&M or UT, given the strong feelings being loudly expressed around them. The vast majority probably shared these feelings. After the Bonfire collapse, however, cultural norms developed that discouraged the expression, and thus the feeling of some of these emotions. The usual feelings of fun, camaraderie, and ridiculing of UT were no longer appropriate. Some anti-UT yells were suppressed. It was appropriate instead for members of the culture to express and experience a whole different set of emotions. In the ceremonies that were substituted for the Bonfire burning, all of the symbols and the rhetoric encouraged shared feelings of grief. At UT, students and staff also recognized that the tragedy at A&M had to be marked by appropriate ceremonies that would allow the members of that community to express and share the grief of their traditional rivals because, in a sense, the two universities communities were bound together through their traditional rivalry and the emotion it engendered.

Members of occupations whose work involves coping with painful emotions develop various cultural rituals, norms, and taboos that encourage or discourage the experience and expression of their feelings. One telling example is work that entails watching the process of dying, which usually and universally evokes strong feelings of sadness and regret. In one hospice, the nurses coped with this difficult situation by adopting a value system that said that they were helping people have a good death and that they should simply "deal with it" (McNamara, Waddell, and Colvin, 1995). Notably, they also shared stories that recounted when they were able to help, that justified the value of their work, and that turned instances of the failure to help into dark humor. They also practiced a taboo that involved never admitting the emotional pain they experienced from doing their work. All nurses were not comfortable with this "conspiracy of silence", however (McNamara et al., 1995, p. 233). In another hospice, workers developed a norm that dealt with the feelings stemming from their failure to help patients have a good death with expressions of anger, sometimes vented against patients, often vented against themselves (Kotarba & Hurt, 1995).

Especially in dangerous occupations in which feeling fearful is frequently a "natural" emotional reaction, but probably not a functional one, workers learn various implicit taboos to insulate them to a degree from experiencing emotions that might interfere with the performance of their job and their general well-being. For example, high-steel ironworkers have an unspoken taboo that prohibits talking about wet or windy weather and other circumstances that increase the dangers of their jobs (Trice & Beyer, 1993). Prostitutes have a taboo about kissing their clients to avoid emotional involvement with them (Prus & Irini, 1980). Other occupations also create taboos that militate against the expression and feeling of inappropriate emotions. For example, medical students must learn to manage the feelings that may arise from contact with the human bodies of their patients in all kinds of situations without resorting to any overt discussion of managing their emotions (Smith & Kleinman, 1989; Trice, 1993).

Another occupation in which members are concerned to discourage both the experience and expression of emotions is that of the funeral director. From the funeral director's point of view, acutely expressive behavior can interrupt the pacing of funeral events, upset the "dignity" of the scene, and thereby "hamper his work" (Barley, 1983, p. 402). To manage potentially disruptive emotions, funeral directors employ various props to express messages that put loved ones and those attending funeral events at ease because they are familiar rather than strange or unfamiliar. Funeral directors manage the removal of the body from a home so as to return the premises to its "natural" state as quickly as possible, and pose the features of the deceased to resemble that of a person at sleep. For similar reasons, the furniture in the funeral parlor is chosen to resemble a living room.

Felt emotions must be managed in many other work situations. In order for both parties in all sorts of service encounters to feel comfortable enough to share requisite amounts of information, the two sets of participants must arrive at an appropriate level of psychological involvement with one another. Such encounters can be conceptualized as emotional exchanges that involve many cultural elements: language, gestures, ritualized behaviors, physical settings, symbols, and displayed emotion that together comprise rites of integration. To create high levels of involvement in some situations would clearly be inappropriate and dysfunctional (e.g. in convenience stores and fast-food restaurants). In other types of service encounters, low levels of involvement would be counter-productive and likely to create client dissatisfaction (e.g. in exchanges between doctors, therapists, or lawyers and their clients, Siehl, Bowen, & Pearson, 1992).

Engendering identification and commitment

The strongest emotions that cultures engender seem to be those of belonging to social groups. As mentioned earlier, people sometimes give their lives for the cultures to which they belong. The very process of belonging encourages identification with the group, and the behaviors that enact that belonging encourage commitment to the group. By working in building the Bonfire stack, and even by attending the burning and cheering for their team, A&M students were strengthening their identification with and commitment to that institution and to each other. As Salancik (1977) explained, four characteristics of acts enhance commitment: explicitness, revocability, volition, and publicity. Actions connected with Bonfire are clearly explicit, volitional, and public. While they are revocable, A&M is known for the loyalty of its alumni, who participated in various ways in the Bonfire building[6] and the ceremonies that followed its tragic collapse in 1999. They still felt part of something larger than themselves—part of a meaningful collectivity. Also, as mentioned earlier, the building and burning of the Bonfire customarily served as a rite of integration, which also strengthened bonds among the students and thus with A&M.

Cultural ceremonies held by other social groups and organizations also serve to create identification and reinforce members' commitment through participation as actors or audience in the rite. Trice (1993) pointed out that rodeos serve to renew commitment to ranch life. Van Maanen (1973) analyzed how the humiliations and ordeals collectively experienced during police training help to create commitment to the peer group in the occupation. Similarly, McCarl (1976) showed how the elaborate rites of passage undergone by smokejumpers bind them to each other and to that occupation.

A powerful example of just how emotionally identified members may become with their employing organization was provided by the responses of employees to the breakup of the Bell System as a result of a court decision. In general, this US company was known for its exemplary human relations (Moore, 1982) and was so supportive to its employees that it was popularly called Ma Bell. As a result, most employees felt a strong sense of belonging and anticipated working for the Bell system until they retired. The long tenure of many Bell employees undoubtedly contributed to the strength of both the Ma Bell culture and the employees' identification with it. In questionnaires collected at the time of the divestiture, AT&T employees expressed the following types of emotions:

> angry, sad, a little scared about my future ... I felt like I had gone through a divorce that neither my wife or children wanted ... I felt sad and somewhat resentful ... a sense of loss.
>
> (Tunstall, 1985, pp. 56–57)

---

[6] Indeed, one of those killed in the collapse was a recent graduate. Other alumni lent their cranes and other equipment needed for the construction of the Bonfire stack. As already mentioned, the pilots who flew jets as part of the commemoration ceremonies at the 1999 football game were also alumni.

Commitment and identification do not rely on behaviors alone. Affective and cognitive processes, various kinds of repeated social interactions, and symbols associated with group status help to attach members to social identities they derive from membership in social groups (Beyer, Hannah, & Milton, 2000). In Weick's analysis (1993) of the notorious Mann Gulch disaster, he explained that one of the factors contributing to the death of the smoke jumpers was that they failed to drop their heavy tools as they fled from the fire about to engulf them. In their panic, hanging on to their tools probably made them feel more resourceful and less helpless. Their tools marked who they were and what they knew—in effect, their tools represented their occupational identity. Tragically, carrying them also slowed down their flight from the flames racing toward them and thus contributed to their death.

In his ethnographic study of a high technology company, Kunda (1992, p. 170) found that some members identified strongly with the company, embracing the role prescribed for them by the corporate culture. An example of an employee expressing such role embracement follows:

> You know, I like Tech. I don't think of leaving. People might say that the culture swallowed me, but there really is a feeling of loyalty I have. We have a lot of that in the culture. We like working for Tech. It is a positive company. You really get involved. I get a real charge when Tech gets a good press. Or when people from another company I knew were dumping on Tech, I was offended.
> (Kunda, 1992, p. 170)

Other employees identified less strongly and maintained some emotional distance from role prescriptions through denial, depersonalization, or dramatization. Respective examples of quotes illustrating each follow:

> Loyalty—they make a big deal about that—is old school. What is important is work. Some people feel a sense of belonging, but in my case it's not strong. It's a nice company, but it isn't my mother.
> (Kunda, 1992, p. 182)

> I've learned here that you can do your own job, but you have to let the waves flow over you; ignore them or you'll go crazy.
> (Kunda, 1992, p. 184)

> Techies. We're all Techies. The whole goddam industry. It's a type of individual who is aggressive and involved, looks loyal, puts in a lot of time, but underneath the surface is self- serving and owes allegiance only to himself.
> (Kunda, 1992a, p. 185)

With this analysis and many more, Kunda paints a nuanced picture of both the normative control that the corporate culture of this high tech firm achieves and the limits to that control. His work reminds us that, as discussed early, not every student, staff member, or alumnus from Texas A&M embraces the culture or sees Bonfire as a sacred symbol of that culture.

Producing ethnocentrism

The dark side of identification and commitment is that it may give rise to feelings of group superiority, which all to frequently produce feelings of hostility toward other groups. One of the underlying themes of the A&M–UT rivalry, like that of most traditional school rivalries, is that members of each school claim superiority over members of the other. In the bonfire ritual at A&M, striving for superiority is perhaps best represented by the students' persistent efforts to make the bonfire bigger and more impressive each year. It began as a large heap of trash in 1909 and grew until it reached 125 feet in 1969, whereupon the A&M administration decreed that in the future, the Bonfire should not exceed 55 feet. The builders of the 1999 bonfire clearly and disastrously disregarded this limitation.

In addition, the cultural events celebrating the A&M–UT rivalry encouraged strong feelings of hostility in each community toward the other school. These feelings were directly expressed through the traditional yells used at the Bonfire and the subsequent football game. The combination of strong feelings of superiority and hostility that mark ethnocentrism was perhaps mostly clearly symbolized by the outhouse labeled u.t. that was traditionally placed on top of the A&M Bonfire.

While ethnocentrism reinforces members' identification with their group, it paradoxically depends on the existence of some sort of connection with the supposedly inferior groups. In the case of the A&M–UT rivalry, each school depended on the rivalry and its enactment in the events surrounding the annual football game to help to define what it meant to be a member of that university community. The associated cultural forms, such as Bonfire, traditionally used by each, accentuated the boundaries between the two cultures and thus symbolized what members of each community were *not* as well as who they were and what values they endorsed. In 1999, however, after the tragic collapse on the Bonfire stack, a Unity Gathering was held at UT and attended by representatives of both university communities. It clearly served as a rite of conflict reduction, temporarily reducing the hostilities and aggression that typically were expressed by each side toward the other during the week preceding the annual football game. The fact that specific efforts were directed at discouraging expressions of hostility after the bonfire collapse shows how strongly these feelings of hostility normally were.

Of course, ethocentrism arises in other organizational settings. Evidence of it was uncovered by Kunda (1992) in his ethnography of a large US high-technology firm. He found that some engineers contrasted that firm favorably with other places they had worked: "other places, they milk your knowledge and then they kill you" (Kunda, 1992, p. 174); "In comparison, here the pressure is fairly low. ... Things were crazy there. I burnt out. Had to see a psychiatrist. I really needed help." (Kunda, 1992, p. 175). Also, some employees expressed little tolerance for those who did not fit into the culture. One described a fellow worker as "a wimp" because he could not handle the ambiguity and "doesn't go out and get it done." (Kunda, 1992, p. 173).

As these and earlier quotes from Kunda's work show, when people identify with their work, they tend to define themselves in relation to the organizations and cultures to which they belong. So, if their organizations are doing well, they assume an elite status and embrace that status as a part of their own identity. As Collins and Porras (1994, pp. 121–127) put it, they assume an almost evangelic feeling of pride. Their pride and associated ethnocentrism is evidenced by their calling themselves by company-related names, such as "Nordies" (Nordstrom), "Motorolans" (Motorola), "IBMers" (IBM), and "Proctorized" (Proctor and Gamble).

Conversely, when their organizations or cultures are criticized, members experience criticism as a threat to their own sense of self. Elsbach and Kramer (1996) documented how members of the eight top-twenty business schools responded ethnocentrically to annual results of *Business Week* rankings. When some schools fell in ranking relative to others, their members responded defensively, often by highlighting positive and distinctive cultural attributes of their schools. They argued that outsiders evaluating them could not appreciate their schools' unique values, such as strong research orientations and friendly environments, or their unique practices, such as innovative academic programs and active alumni-support networks. In effect, members emphasized the distinctiveness of their cultures to bolster their claim to a place in the elite group of top-ranked schools.

The strong identification with an occupational subculture can also lead to ethnocentric feelings of group superiority that justify protecting group members from sanctions. Van Maanen (1973) related a story that showed how one policeman protected another from the discovery that he was having a dalliance with a girlfriend when he should have been on duty to respond to an emergency. Occupational ethnocentrism connected with subcultures in workplaces can also contribute to conflict between management and members of an occupation or between members of different occupations (Trice, 1993). Each occupation feels that it should control how its members do their work because outsiders do not fully understand it. For example, technical workers identify themselves by such terms as "hardware", "software", and "engineering," which represent to them distinct and non-overlapping areas of expertise that make cooperation difficult (Gregory, 1983). Various cultural rituals that may seldom produce consequences of practical importance help to reinforce feelings of occupational superiority (Trice, 1993). Lawyers search extensively for cases and arguments that are unlikely to be relevant to a court decision. Newsreporters have rituals that guard against deadline pressures, libel suits, and the wrath of superiors. Nurses and doctors in operating rooms engage in towel folding and handwashing rituals. Professors perform elaborate rituals in evaluating one another for promotion to tenure. In addition, members of subcultures generate jargon and specialized language that marks insiders and tends to exclude outsiders from their subcultures.

SUMMARY AND CONCLUSIONS

Although emotions have been relatively neglected in much of the theorizing about cultures in organizations, many qualitative studies of organizational life reveal that cultures and emotions are closely intertwined. Observing the details of organizational life reveals that people's emotions are shaped by cultural beliefs and practices. The most basic reason that cultural beliefs are emotionally charged is that they give people some sense of a degree of predictability and continuity in facing the anxieties stemming from the many uncertainties of modern life. In addition, culture guides or channels emotions into acceptable manifestations. Cultures provide accepted ways to express emotions, actually stimulating people to feel what are considered appropriate emotions, and helping them to avoid feeling inappropriate emotions. Finally, cultures help to bind people emotionally to each other in ways that can give rise to feelings of exclusiveness and superiority.

The dramatic events surrounding a recent tragedy involving a highly valued cultural tradition at a respected US university illustrate all of these ways in which cultures and emotions are intertwined. They showed how strong and complex the felt and expressed emotions associated with a cherished tradition can be. Other examples drawn from research on organizations show that cultures and emotions are strongly linked in many other kinds of organizations. In particular, they illustrate how cultural practices both enable the expression of desired emotions and help to prevent expression of undesirable ones. This linkage is especially vivid in occupational settings where emotion management is important. In these settings, people have created and preserved rituals, norms, and taboos that discourage and temper emotions likely to undermine effective performance from not only being expressed, but also from being experienced.

The role of culture as a sort of glue that binds people together has been better recognized. Cultures are often cited as powerful sources of identification and commitment. As our examples illustrate, these feelings of belonging are among the strongest emotions engendered by culture. A related consequence of this strong identification is less often discussed—that belonging to cultures can lead to collective feelings of group superiority. As people celebrate what they share, they also emphasize what makes them distinctive from others, and these processes can lead to feelings of distrust and hostility toward others, especially when people feel their cultures are threatened.

The cultures that people create and pass on to their followers give meaning to everyday organizational life. By reducing the anxieties associated with an uncertain future, cultures provide a shared sense of comfort and predictability in the present. They also give people reasons to celebrate and want to preserve a shared past. People cling to their cultural beliefs and invest powerful emotions in them. Managing cultures thus inevitably entails managing emotions, and managing emotions requires considering the cultural beliefs and practices that people hold dear.

REFERENCES

Ashforth, B.E., & Humphrey, R.H. (1993) Emotional labor in service roles: The influence of identity. *Academy of Management Review*, **18**, 88–115.

Austin American Statesman (2000a) A&M's bonfire stack lacked binding cable. 19 February 2000, p. B1.

Austin American Statesman (2000b) Faculty group want A&M to cancel Bonfire. 1 June 2000, p. B1.

Barley, S.R. (1983) Semiotics and the study of occupational and organizational cultures. *Administrative Science Quarterly*, **28**, 393–413.

Barley, S.R. & Kunda, G. (1992) Design and devotion: Surges of rational and normative ideologies of control in managerial discourse. *Administrative Science Quarterly*, **37**, 363–399.

Beach, P. (1999) A&M tradition turns tragic: Bonfire collapse kills 11; rescuers still searching. *Austin American Statesman*, 19 November 1999, pp. A1, A9.

Beyer, J.M., Hannah, D.R., & Milton, L.P. (2000) Ties that bind: Culture and attachments in organizations. In N. Ashkanasy, C. Widerom, M. Peterson (Eds) *Handbook of Organizational Culture and Climate*. Thousand Oaks, CA: Sage Publications.

Burka, P. (2000) The Aggie Bonfire tragedy. *Texas Monthly*, 117–123, 145–149.

Collins, J.C. & Porras, J.I. (1994) *Built to Last*. New York: HarperCollins.

Copelin, L. (1999a) Bonfire's spine under scrutiny: As A&M deaths climb to 12, search continues for solace, answers. A&M chief vows outside investigation. *Austin American Statesman*, 20 November 1999, pp. A1, A2.

Copelin, L. (1999b) Bonfire was too tall, says memo: Stack was already at 59 feet, in violation of A&M's limit, and was headed higher. *Austin American Statesman*, 16 December 1999, pp. A1, A17.

Copelin, L. (2000) Alumni, students say they'll fight for bonfire no matter the outcome of today's report. *Austin American Statesman*, 2 May, p. A1.

Copelin, L. & Adame, J. (2000) A&M suspends Bonfire: Event could return in 2002, but students won't run it. Bowen: Despite outcry, "I will do what's right." *Austin American Statesman*, 17 June 2000, pp. A1, A11, Days of student-run Bonfire are over.

Davenport, C. (1999) Tributes, not trash talk, set the tone. *Austin American Statesman*, 27 November 1999, pp. A1, A13.

Denison, D. R. (1990) *Corporate Culture and Organizational Effectiveness*. New York: Wiley.

Elsbach, K.D. & Kramer, R.M. (1996) Members' responses to organizational identity threats: Encountering the *Business Week* rankings. *Administrative Science Quarterly*, **14**, 442–476.

Ferguson, H. (1936) *Modern Man: His Belief and Behavior*. New York: Knopf.

Gamboa, S. (2000a) Report: A&M chief concerned by bonfire. *Austin American Statesman*, 4 February, pp. B1, B2.

Gamboa, S. (2000b) Groups seek more time, money for bonfire probe: Report about what caused the log stack to tumble is not expected by 31 March. *Austin American Statesman*, 12 February 2000, p. B7.

Gamboa, S. (2000c) Team forms theory on bonfire collapse. *Austin American Statesman*, 18 March 2000, pp. B1, B7.

Geertz, C. (1970) The impact of the concept of culture on the concept of man. In Hammal, Eugene A. & W.S. Simmons (Eds), *Man Makes Sense*, pp. 47–65. Boston: Little, Brown.

Greenberger, S.S. (2000) Tradition can continue, many say. *Austin American Statesman*, 3 May 2000, p. A11.

Gregory, K.L. (1983) Native view paradigms: Multiple cultures and culture conflict in organizations. *Administrative Science Quarterly*, **28**, 359–376.

Guralnik, D.B. & Friend, J.H. (1966) *Webster's New World Dictionary of the American Language, College Edition*. Cleveland, OH: The World Publishing Company.

Haas, J. (1977) Learning real feelings: A study of high-steel ironworkers' reactions to fear and danger. *Sociology of Work and Occupations*, **4**, 147–169.

Harris, S.G. & Sutton, R.L. (1986) Functions of parting ceremonies in dying organizations. *Academy of Management Journal*, **29**, 5–30.

Haurwitz, R.K.M. (1999a) A&M e-mails discuss future of Bonfire: In message, president says he thinks tradition will continue, but it must be done safely. *Austin American Statesman*, 11 December 1999, pp. B3, B7.

Haurwitz, R.K.M. (1999b) Parents: Bonfire should burn on: Many victims' families say they don't blame Texas A&M, won't sue. *Austin American Statesman*, 12 December 1999, pp. B1, B3.

Haurwitz, R.K.M. (2000) State panel launches inquiry, *Austin American Statesman*, 15 June 2000, pp. B1, B7.

Hight, M. (1999) A&M student reacts: Stunned campus turns inward for some solace. *Austin American Statesman*, 19 November 1999, p. A5.

Hochschild, A.R. (1983) *The Managed Heart: the Commercialization of Human Feeling*. Berkeley, CA: University of California Press.

Hofstede, G. (1980) *Culture's Consequences: International Differences in Work-related Values*. Beverly Hills, CA: Sage Publications.

Kotarba, J.A. & Hurt D. (1995) An ethnography of an AIDS hospice: Toward a theory of organizational pastiche. *Symbolic Interaction*, **18**, 413–438.

Kunda, G. (1992) *Engineering culture: Control and Commitment in a High-Tech Corporation*. Philadelphia: Temple University Press.

LeBlanc, P. (1999) A&M bonfire: The work. Thousands take part in building monument to university's spirit. *Austin American Statesman*, 19 November 1999, p. A7.

March, J.G. (1965) *Handbook of Organizations*. Chicago: Rand McNally.

Martin, J. (1992) *Cultures in Organizations: Three Perspectives*. New York: Oxford University Press.

Martin, J., Feldman, M., Hatch, M.J., & Sitkin, S. (1983) The uniqueness paradox in organizational stories. *Administrative Science Quarterly*, **28**, 438–453.

Martin, J., Knopoff, K., & Beckman, C. (1998) An alternative to bureaucratic impersonality and emotional labor: Bounded emotionality at The Body Shop. *Administrative Science Quarterly*, **43**, 429–469.

McCarl, R.S. (1976) Smoke jumper initiation: Ritualized communication in a modern occupation. *Journal of American Folklore*, **81**, 49–67.

McNamara, B., Waddell, C., & Colvin, M. (1995) Threats to the good death: The cultural context of stress and coping among hospice workers. *Sociology of Health and Illness*, **17**, 222–244.

Moore, D.G. (1982) The committee on human relations in industry at the University of Chicago. *Academy of Management Proceedings*, **42**, 117–121.

Nystrom, P.C. & Starbuck, W.H. (1981) *Handbook of Organizational Design*, Vols 1 and 2. Oxford: Oxford University Press.

Pierce, E. (1999) A crushing wave of wood: A collapsing tower of logs buries a dozen lives at Texas A&M. To Aggies, the annual bonfire is a tradition that goes back 90 years. But should it rise again? *Newsweek*, 29 November 1999, pp. 44–45.

Pirtle, C. III (1999) Days of sorrow, hours of heroism. *Texas Aggie*, December, pp. 2–7.

Prus, R. & Irini, S. (1980) The impact of departmentalization on interoccupational cooperation. *Human Organization*, **27**, 362–367.

Rachman, S.J. (1990) *Fear and Courage*. 2nd ed. New York: Freeman.

Salancik, G.R. (1977) Commitment and the control of organizational behavior and belief. In B.M. Staw & G.R. Salancik (Eds), *New Directions in Organizational Behavior*. pp. 1–54. Chicago: St. Clair Press.

Sackmann, S.A. (1991) *Cultural Knowledge in Organizations: Exploring the Collective Mind*. Newbury Park, CA: Sage Publications.

Schein, E.H. (1985) *Organizational Culture and Leadership*. San Francisco: Jossey-Bass Publishers.

Schein, E.H. (1992) *Organizational Culture and Leadership*. 2nd ed. San Francisco: Jossey-Bass Publishers.

Schneider, B. (Ed.) (1990) *Organizational Climate and Culture*. San Francisco: Jossey-Bass Publishers.

Schwartzman, H.B. (1986) The meeting as a neglected social form in organizational studies. *Research in Organizational Behavior*, **8**, 233–258.

Shah, A. (1999) Rivals draw together at UT: Longhorns, Aggies share words of comfort. *Austin American Statesman*, 23 November 1999, pp. A1, A8.

Siehl, C., Bowen, D.E., & Pearson, C.M. (1992) Service encounters as rites of integration: An information processing model. *Organization Science*, **3**, 537–555.

Smith, A.C. III & Kleinman S. (1989) Managing emotions in medical school: Students' contacts with the living and the dead. *Social Psychological Quarterly*, **52**, 56–69.

Spencer, J. (1999) Grieving for young lives lost: A&M victims mourned at churches across state. *Austin American Statesman*, 22 November 1999, pp. B1, B7.

Sutton, R.I. (1991) Maintaining norms about expressed emotions: The case of bill collectors. *Administrative Science Quarterly*, **36**, 245–268.

Sutton, R.I. & Callahan, A.L. (1987) The stigma of bankruptcy: Spoiled organizational image and its management. *Academy of Management Journal*, **30**, 405–436.

Trice, H.M. (1993) *Occupational Subcultures in the Workplace*. Ithaca, New York: ILR Press.

Trice, H.M. & Beyer, J.M. (1993) *The Cultures of Work Organizations*. Englewood Cliffs, NJ: Prentice-Hall.

Tunstall, W.B. (1985) Breakup of the Bell system: A case study in cultural transformation. In R.H. Kilmanm, M.J. Saxton, R. Serpa, & Associates (Eds) *Gaining Control of the Corporate Culture*, pp. 44–65. San Francisco: Jossey-Bass.

Van Gennep. A. [1909] (1960) *Rites of Passage*. Chicago: University of Chicago Press.

Van Maanen, J. (1973) Observations on the making of policemen. *Human Organization*, **32**, 407–418.

Van Maanen, J. (1991) The smile factory: Work at Disneyland. In P.J. Frost, L.F. Moore, M.R. Louis, C.C. Lunberg, & J. Martin (Eds), *Reframing Organizational Culture*, pp. 58–76. Newbury Park, CA: Sage Publications.

Ward, M. (2000a) Bonfire logs appeared to be leaning, report says: In December, engineers also said ground under pile was sloped. *Austin American Statesman*, 12 January 2000, pp. A1, A10.

Ward, M. (2000b). A&M head says he'll resign if leadership faulted in bonfire: Bowen's comments won't affect inquiry into collapse, Limbeck says. *Austin American Statesman*, 13 January 2000, B1, B8.

Ward, M. & Gamboa, S. (2000a) Reports: Alcohol found at Bonfire: 2 rescuers who saw beer cans. *Austin American Statesman*, 1 February 2000, p. B1.

Ward, M. & Gamboa, S. (2000b) Anatomy of a collapse. *Austin American Statesman*, 3 May 2000, p. A1.

Weber, M. (1947) *The Theory of Social and Economic Organization*. In A.M. Henderson & T. Parsons (Eds), New York: The Free Press.

Weick, K.E. (1993) The collapse of sensemaking in organizations: The Mann Gulch disaster. *Administrative Science Quarterly*, **38**, 628–652.

Chapter 8

Origins and consequences of emotions in organizational teams

Carsten K.W. De Dreu
University of Amsterdam, The Netherlands
Michael A. West
Aston Business School, Birmingham, UK
Agneta H. Fischer
University of Amsterdam, The Netherlands
Sarah MacCurtain
University of Limerick, Ireland

Organizational psychology has long been dominated by the view of employees and their leaders as rational, cool-headed individuals. Individuals are presumed to attempt to act rationally, but to be bounded in their ability to achieve rationality (Simon, 1957). This approach has allowed researchers to predict, a priori, how people will make decisions that are inconsistent, inefficient, and based on normatively irrelevant information. Perhaps more importantly, this approach has allowed scholars to advance prescriptive advice as to how employees should make decisions, how leaders should approach their subordinates, and how people should negotiate and manage their interpersonal conflicts. Indeed, the (bounded) rationality assumption is critical in still leading models of decision making (cf. Beach, 1997; Harris, 1995), work motivation (Porter & Lawler, 1968), leadership (Vroom & Yago, 1988), and conflict and negotiation (Carnevale & Pruitt, 1992; Neale & Bazerman, 1991).

Emotions at Work. Edited by Roy Payne and Cary Cooper.
© 2001 by John Wiley & Sons, Ltd.

The drawback of this approach is that we may overemphasize the conscious, controlled, and thorough aspect of what employees, decision makers, and organizational leaders do, at the expense of the subconscious, automatic, and emotional components of organizational behavior. In their review, Pekrun and Frese (1992, p. 153) noted that they "should not have consented to write an article on work and emotion in a yearly review book ... [because] there is little research that speaks directly to the issue of work and emotion." Although the situation has improved since their review was published (see e.g. Briner, 1999), a thorough search of the relevant electronic databases still yields little research on interrelated topics such as feelings in teamwork and the impact of emotions on negotiation and conflict management. Yet teamwork and conflict management are both crucial for organizational effectiveness and performance, and we not only need to know how employees *should* behave, but also how and why they behave the way they do. A better understanding of automatic, subconscious, and emotional correlates of behavior in organizations is therefore vital.

Rather than focusing on the entire arena of organizational behavior, the current chapter focuses on emotions in teams. Early studies into group dynamics by Kurt Lewin and Leon Festinger, among others, have shown that group processes cannot be fully understood when we ignore the affective component. The assumption underlying this chapter is that emotions can be seen as both the origins and outcomes of social interactions in teams. In other words, group processes may affect emotions, but emotions in turn affect group processes. As we are concerned with emotions and social processes, we will first sketch a general theoretical framework, based on cognitive–motivational theories of emotions, and with special attention to the social aspects of emotions. Second, we will discuss emotions as the outcome of concerns that are part and parcel of group membership, namely our need to belong. The need to belong, we argue, is responsible for group formation, and group cohesion gives rise to various positive and negative emotions. The resulting emotions can be experienced and expressed at an individual level, but also at a group level, creating collective emotions or an emotional atmosphere. Third, emotions in teams, whether individually or collectively experienced and expressed, are in turn assumed to affect group processes, such as group effectiveness or the management of conflicts.

EMOTIONS IN SOCIAL INTERACTION: A THEORETICAL FRAMEWORK

Emotions are considered as multi-component processes, with cognitive, motivational, and behavioral components (Frijda, 1986; Scherer, 1984). Moreover, emotions are not just internal states of mind possessed by an individual, but rather are processes that develop both within and between individuals (e.g.

Manstead & Fischer, in press; Parkinson, in press). For instance, the development of a person's anger may not only be determined by a mere insult by another member of the team, but also by the reactions of the other team members, or by the history of their relationship. The onset, intensity, duration, and expression of the anger thus depends not only on who insulted, but also on the presence of others, the motives that the insulted individual attributed to the actor, the display of any regret by the actor, the status of the actor, and so forth. Moreover, emotions generally do not occur or disappear suddenly. Rather, emotions evolve over time and are strengthened, inhibited, or transformed by the social context in which they occur.

Emotions arise when an individual's or group's concerns are affected (Frijda, 1986). Concerns may refer to everything that is significant for an individual's or group's well-being in the broadest sense of the word, like goals, sensitivities, ideals, or values. The need to create social bonds and the wish to belong to a group or a team is one such concern. Team-related emotions are thus elicited when an event affects their concern as a team member in either a positive or negative way. These events may be non-social, as when an economic change threatens the existence of the organization or particular unit we are working for, or social, as when a colleague's behavior is appraised as positive or negative, cooperative, or competitive. Characteristic of an emotional reaction is that the antecedent events are appraised in specific ways, resulting in an accompanying motive to act and in various physiological changes. For example, the appraisal of an economic downturn as threatening for our work unit is characteristic of anxiety, in this case for being unemployed. This may lead us to take distance from this situation and to scan newspaper advertisements or to approach headhunters recruiting new personnel. The same event may also be appraised in different ways, resulting in different emotions. For example, we may appraise a colleague's competitive behavior as a threat, resulting in anxiety, but also as an attack on our own position, resulting in anger. Different emotion appraisals are assumed to result in different action tendencies (Frijda, Kuipers, & Ter Schure, 1987; Roseman, Antoniou, & Jose, 1996). Action tendencies in turn often come hand in hand with non-verbal expressions, such as smiling or frowning, and with various types of physiological changes, like a fastened heart rate, sweating, or increased muscle tension. Whether action tendencies result in actual actions depends on the ongoing (re)appraisal processes and on the way in which the emotion is regulated. For example, flight attendants are instructed to never show their irritation towards even the most obnoxious clients, and to keep smiling (Hochschild, 1983).

Thus, emotions involve an entire process from appraising an event that affects our concerns, via motivational tendencies, physiological and non-verbal expressions, and behavioral patterns. Emotions are never static and vary according to individual styles, socialization experiences, social contexts, the reactions of others, and so forth. This is due to the fact that every part of this process is permanently, though not always in our full consciousness, subjected to regulation.

Social functions of emotions

The analysis of the emotion process clarifies that emotions are affected by the social context and also influence this social context. Emotions do not occur and are not expressed only because an individual has appraised an event in a certain way, but also because social relations are involved (e.g. Frijda & Mesquita, 1994; Keltner & Haidt, 1999). The elicitation, experience, and expression of emotions generally imply a change in relationships with others. Consider the previous example of a team member being angry because of an insult. When this insult is regarded as a major injustice, the psychological distance between these two team members will increase. In fact, the chances are that their relationship will never be the same because one team member continues to remember the other's insulting act and develops deeply ingrained distrust.

Alternatively, expressing our anger may also serve to repair the hurt relationship, either because it clarifies that we have been insulted (the actor may not have been aware of this) or to prevent similar instances occurring again. Whereas anger obviously implies an attack on a person and thereby creates distance, either temporarily or more permanently, other emotions such as love, happiness, but also regret, shame, or guilt, act to reduce the distance between two people. Nearly all emotions can be described along social dimensions, reflecting a change in social relations, such as distancing, attacking, withdrawing, or approaching. Emotions, and especially the expression of emotions, thus have an important function in the creation, but also in the destruction of social relationships.

As the relation between emotions and groups is concerned, we may distinguish three major social functions of expressing emotions. First, *social bonding* is a fundamental human concern, and emotions serve to create and maintain these bonds. Most positive emotions like joy, love, or empathy enhance social bonds, because they are characterized by the tendency to approach others, and to emphasize the harmonious bond between persons. However, the expression of negative, intra-punitive emotions such as shame and guilt also improves social bonds, because they signal an effort or desire to repair or make up for our faults. The second major function of emotion expression is the signaling of a *need for social support*. The expression of fear or frustration, for instance, displays our powerlessness and inability to cope with a situation, thereby requesting others for help or support. A third important function is the *establishment of our social position*, in terms of power, control, or superiority. The expression of anger, for instance, shows interdependent others their place and imposes our will upon others. Team leaders may affirm their position through the expression of anger or disappointment about the functioning of team members through the expression of pride or forgiveness, and so on.

In sum, emotions are not momentary states, but processes that result from the social context in which they are elicited and that, in turn, influence this social context. Because the existence of a group necessarily implies the presence of specific social relations between group members, emotions are by definition part and parcel of group processes.

BELONGING TO A TEAM AS ORIGIN OF EMOTIONS

Being a member of a team and its concomitant interaction processes implies a human concern that—if affected—gives rise to emotions. The fundamental human drive and pervasive motivation to form and maintain lasting, positive, and significant relationships helps us to understand the functioning of teams at work, and in particular the emotions manifested in work groups. Satisfying the need to belong requires our relationships to be characterized by frequent interaction, temporal stability and likely continuity, mutual affective concern, and freedom from conflict (Baumeister & Leary, 1995). Most current research and theories about functioning teams fail to take account of the fact that the tendency to form strong attachments and, by extension, to live and work in groups has a solid evolutionary basis. Human beings work and live in groups because groups enable survival and reproduction (Ainsworth, 1989; Axelrod & Hamilton, 1981; Barash, 1977; Bowlby, 1969; Buss, 1990, 1991; Hogan, Jones, & Cheek, 1985; Moreland, 1987). By living and working in groups, human beings could share food, easily find mates, and care for infants. They could hunt more effectively and defend themselves against their enemies. Individuals who did not readily join groups would be disadvantaged in comparison with group members as a consequence. "Over the course of evolution, the small group became the basic survival strategy developed by the human species" (Barchas, 1986, p. 212).

The need to belong shapes human behavior and, for our purposes, helps to explain emotional reactions in teams. The absence of one or more of the characteristics of belongingness (frequent interaction, likely continuity and stability, mutual affective concern, and freedom from negative affect) is proposed to lead to disintegration within relationships and teams. Our tendency to concentrate on task characteristics and organizational contexts may often blind us to these fundamental socio-emotional requirements of team-based working. For the benefits of working in teams are not only in improved task performance (West, 1996), but also in intra-psychic and emotional benefits for team members (West & Patterson, 1999).

Early research in social psychology showed how group identification occurs almost immediately when people are randomly assigned to groups, with dramatic behavioral consequences of strong loyalty and in-group favoritism (Sherif, Harvey, White, Hood, & Sherif, 1961; see also Billig & Tajfel, 1973; Tajfel, 1970; Tajfel & Billig, 1974). The tendency of people to discriminate in favor of their own group and to discriminate against members of out-groups is pervasive (Turner, 1985). This in-group favoritism occurs spontaneously and without obvious value to the individual. Research indicates that there is no need for material advantage to the self or inferred similarity to other group members for group identification to occur. However, there is evidence that external threats lead to the creation of firmer bonds within groups (Stein, 1976) and there is evidence that group identification extends to the workplace with stronger identifications with smaller groups within our organizations (Van Knippenberg & Van Schie, 2000).

By recognizing the influence of the need to belong upon the behavior of individuals in teams, we can come to understand something of the range and underlying causes of emotions in teams. Being accepted, included, and welcomed in the team promotes feelings of happiness, elation, contentment, and calm. Being rejected, excluded, or ignored, on the other hand, will lead to feelings of anxiety, depression, grief, jealousy, or loneliness. Thus, we argue that team members' emotional reactions will be evoked by real, potential, or imagined changes in their belongingness to their work team. Real, potential or imagined increases in belongingness will lead to an increase in positive individual and team-level affect. Decreases in belongingness will be associated with threats to the individual and a sense of deprivation leading to negative affect.

Positive emotions

When a new work team is formed, team members tend to experience positive emotions, and the creation of the team is often a cause for celebration. When new members join teams, there tends to be an abundance of positive affect and warm expressions of welcome, reflecting the sense of belonging experienced by existing members and by the new members alike. Indeed, research shows this positive affect itself increases attraction and social bonding within groups (Moreland, 1987).

One of the characteristics of a strong sense of belonging is the sense of mutuality in the relationships. So satisfaction in teams is also likely to be a consequence of both the costs as well as the rewards of team membership. People prefer relationships and teams within which all give and take. For example, Hays (1985) examined relationship satisfaction from the perspective of behaviorism, assuming that rewards would determine people's satisfaction. He found instead that satisfaction was predicted by rewards plus costs, apparently because people prefer relationships and groups in which all both give and receive support and care. Similar results were obtained by De Dreu, Lualhati and McCusker (1994). They asked participants to rate their satisfaction with payment for task performance. Consistent with equity theory (Adams, 1965), results showed most satisfaction when payment was equal to the pay received by a co-worker who performed equally well, somewhat less when pay exceeded that of the co-worker, and lowest when payment was less than that of the co-worker. And Baumeister, Wotman, and Stillwell (1993) report that, for both those who give love without receiving it and those who receive love without giving it, the experience is aversive. Thus, mutuality and reciprocity appears to be necessary for positive affect, and satisfaction will be highest when the sense of mutuality in teams is strong.

Negative emotions

Threats to the need to belong trigger a variety of negative emotions. The influence of the human need to belong is indicated by our strong tendency to respond with distress and protest to the end of relationships (Hazan & Shaver, 1994). We see such phenomena in training groups which come together for only a few days. Group members typically express some resistance to the notion that the group will dissolve. Members promise that they will stay in touch with each other, exchange business cards, and may even plan for reunions. More specific negative emotions, manifested in teams as a consequence of threats to belonging, include anxiety, depression, loneliness, guilt, and grief. We briefly consider each of these below.

Anxiety and jealousy Human beings become anxious at the prospect of losing relationships, and threats of social exclusion may be the most common cause of anxiety amongst work team members. Horney (1945) proposed that our basic anxiety resulted from a feeling of being isolated and helpless in a potentially hostile world. Team members may typically experience anxiety at the prospect of the break-up of the team, the impending ending of a long-running team project, or their transfer to another team (Leary, 1990). Group instability (frequent member changes) and threatened dissolution of the team will also cause anxiety. High levels of conflict too will engender anxiety since team members are likely to develop an anxious watchfulness in anticipation of conflict between team members. Spector, Dwyer and Lex (1988; see also Beehr, Drexler & Faulkner, 1997) indeed report substantial positive correlations between conflict at work, on the one hand, and frustration and anxiety, on the other.

Related to anxiety is jealousy. Pines and Aronson (1983) propose that jealousy is a consequence of the threat or experience of being excluded. Team members will be likely to experience jealousy when they feel that they are excluded by, or less in the favor of, a particularly powerful or attractive team member. In addition, jealousy manifests itself when team members feel that others are more accepted and included in the team than they themselves are. Perceptions of inclusion or exclusion by the team leader are likely to be particularly important. Indeed, from a psycho-dynamic perspective, it would be expected that a good inclusive relationship between a team member and the team leader will reduce the likelihood of angry or defiant behaviour (Belsky, 1979; Miller, Cowan, Cowan, Hetherington, & Clingempeel, 1993).

Jealousy, as a consequence of feeling excluded by the team leader, relates to Leader Member Exchange Theory. According to LMX Theory, leaders form positive relationships with some group members (the "in-group") and less positive and more negative relationships with other group members (the "out-group"). Members who are neglected are likely to feel jealousy and anger at their relative exclusion from the group and a diminution in their sense of belonging.

Depression and loneliness While anxiety and jealousy are immediate emotional reactions to being excluded, a sustained period of feeling excluded and isolated tends to produce feelings of depression. For example, Hoyle and Crawford (in press) found that depression and anxiety were significantly correlated negatively with students' sense of belonging to the university. As such, it is a small step to argue that feelings of depression may be associated with an enduring lack of team membership and a long-term deprivation of our sense of belonging where team members feel excluded or isolated over a period of time, they are more likely to feel depression. The team leader may play a particularly important role in moderating this effect. In malfunctioning teams, members may deliberately make the leader a target of attempts to isolate or exclude, particularly where they perceive s/he has not enabled the team to provide a strong sense of belonging.

Related to depression is loneliness. Human beings feel lonely when their needs to belong are insufficiently met. Jones (1981) has shown that this is not simply a result of lack of social contact. There are no differences in the level of social contact between those who are lonely and those who are not. The crucial factor appears to be spending time with people with whom we are close. It is social isolation rather than size of network that appears to influence loneliness, along with lack of intimate connection (Williams & Solano, 1983). Although people may work in teams, loneliness can still occur if there is no sense of closeness or relative intimacy of contact between team members. Those who work in multiple teams or short-lived project teams, and who thus have many social contacts, may feel loneliness nevertheless because they are prevented from developing close social contacts with other team members. Similar effects are likely to occur amongst team members who work in different locations and manage their interactions via technology-mediated communication such as videoconferencing and email. The relative impoverishment of these communication media will militate against the development of a strong sense of belonging in the team.

Another cause of loneliness, derived from the need to belong, is if initial frequent contact between members of a strong team lapses. Members then have less contact over time, so the establishment of an early sense of belonging is likely to be supplemented by loneliness. Where a team does not establish a sense of belonging early in its life (through the development of the four characteristics of belongingness), the change from frequent to infrequent contact is likely to lead to loneliness among team members.

Finally, depression and loneliness also come with grief, which occurs at the loss of relationships (Lofland, 1982). When couples divorce, even where they mutually agree on the desirability of the end of their relationships, they typically experience grief. In a similar vein, the departure of team members is often an occasion when grief is experienced. This is especially likely when the departing individuals strongly contributed to the sense of belonging in the team, by contributing concern for the well-being of other team members, by interacting frequently or by ameliorating potential or actual conflicts. Perhaps more profound grief is likely to be felt by the departing individual who loses a whole team. Interestingly, and to mitigate grief, team members often promise and even try to maintain contact with the departing team member via social events and through other forms of social contact.

Guilt and shame   Whether intended or not, team members may engage in activities endangering others' sense of belonging, and this may produce feelings of guilt and shame. Vice versa, guilt is sometimes induced in others to cause them to exert more effort to maintain team relationships by spending more time with, or paying more attention to the members in the team (cf. Baumeister, Stillwell, & Heatherton, 1999). Within a team, members may induce guilt in their colleagues when they feel they are spending inadequate time interacting interdependently with other team members, or if they feel they are showing inadequate concern for the well-being of their colleagues. Guilt-inducing signals are especially likely to be directed towards the team leader since s/he carries a greater share of the responsibility for maintaining the sense of belonging in the team. Guilt induction can thus be seen as a response to disturbances or threats to attachments.

Research evidence

Because well-functioning teams fulfill the need to belong, they should produce positive emotions and reduce negative emotions. Recent empirical evidence tends to support this thesis. In a study of the mental health of health-service workers in the United Kingdom National Health Service, West and Patterson (1999) compared those people who worked in teams, those who worked in pseudo-teams, and those not working in teams. Individuals were classified as pseudo-team members when (a) they reported working in a team but without clear team objectives, or (b) they did not frequently work with other members of the team to achieve those objectives, or (c) there were no separate roles, or (d) the team was not recognized by others in the organization as a team. The sample of 2,250 workers completed the General Health Questionnaire and individuals were categorized as "cases" if their scores indicated that they would benefit from professional intervention, because of high stress levels. The results revealed that 35% of those that did not work in teams were cases, 30% of those who were in pseudo-teams were cases, while only 21% of those who worked in real teams were cases. It appears from these data that working in teams is a significant buffer against the stresses of health-service work. Further investigation revealed that the differences between these teams could be attributed to the role clarity experienced by team members, along with the high level of peer support that they experienced. Moreover, working in teams appeared to ameliorate negative effects of organizational level difficulties. The findings extend to studies at the organizational level which showed that, in 54 UK manufacturing organizations, the extent of team working was a predictor of the overall levels of mental health amongst employees (West & Patterson, 1999).

The study by West and Patterson (1999) supported the idea that belonging to a team itself increases positive affect and reduces stress. Other evidence suggests, likewise, that not belonging may be damaging in itself, regardless of enacted support from those around. Cohen and Wills (1985) report that simply being part of a supportive social network reduces stress, even if those in the network do not provide emotional or practical assistance. Moreover, effects may translate from emotional reactions through to immunological and other physiological functioning, particularly among those working in stressful environments, such as health-care workers. Kiecolt-Glaser, Garner et al. (1984) and Kiecolt-Glaser, Richer et al. (1984) found that loneliness was associated with a decrease in immuno-competence, particularly in relation to natural-killer-cell activity and elevations in cortisol levels.

Collective emotions

So far, we have explored the need to belong as the origin for a range of emotions to occur at an individual level. However, emotions may also be experienced and expressed at a group level. One important perspective, developed by George (1996), has been to consider the shared affect of teams at work. She uses the term "group affective tone" to refer to "... consistent or homogenous affective reactions within a group". If, for example, members of a team tend to be excited, energetic, and enthusiastic, then the team itself can be described as being excited, energetic, and enthusiastic. As another example, if members of a team tend to be "distressed, mistrustful and nervous, then the team also can be described in these terms" (George, 1996, p. 78). Such collective feelings are also discussed by Hatfield and colleagues, who have studied a phenomenon they called "emotional contagion". The term "emotional contagion" actually refers to the process under-lying group-based emotions and is defined as "the tendency to automatically mimic and synchronize facial expressions, vocalizations, postures, and movements with those of another person, and consequently, to converge emotionally" (Hatfield, Cacioppo, & Rapson, 1994, p. 5). Thus, the fact that we observe other people's emotions unconsciously produces similar emotions in ourselves.

Collective or group-based emotions may also result from the way in which persons in a group emotionally relate to each other (e.g. whether they trust, fear, or admire each other). This has been described as the "emotional climate" (De Rivera, 1992) of a nation, organization, or group. De Rivera describes various examples of emotional climates that specify the relationships between people in a particular nation-state at a particular period in time, such as a climate of fear (in Chile during the Pinochet regime), of instability (in Russia in the 1990s), or of confidence (when the economy of a country is booming). Such typologies can also be applied to organizations or to smaller groups within organizations, as will be argued later in this chapter.

In conclusion, collective feelings have different sources. First, they may be based on the shared appraisal of an external event (e.g. when they are elated after a good team performance or disappointed after a bad one). But collective feelings may also originate from the history of emotional relationships within a group (e.g. when they have been terrorized by their leader or left in insecurity by an incompetent manager). Collective feelings are assumed to be more than the sum of its parts, in that they produce an emotional atmosphere, an emotional framework upon which future actions of a team are based. These collective feelings may be characterized by a greater intensity and permanency than feelings at an individual level, because appraisal processes (of either an external event or the behavior of other group members) are socially shared, resulting in firm consensus about the injustice, or threat, or whatever the event was that elicited the emotions.

Summary and conclusions

In this section, we reviewed several ways in which group processes may elicit a variety of emotions. Our starting point was the idea that humans have a fundamental need to belong and that group membership promotes positive emotions. A study by West and Patterson (1999) provided initial support for this reasoning, by showing that being a member of a team decreased the likelihood of negative emotions, including depression and loneliness. However, teams have to meet certain criteria in order to fulfill the need to belong and to elicit positive emotions, and, if they do not, a variety of negative emotions is likely to occur. The most important requirements of well-functioning teams seem the provision of a sense of closeness and intimacy among its members, mutuality in relationships (give and take), and the absence of threats of exclusion or isolation. This not only results in positive feelings in each of the group members, but may also create a positive collective feeling, and more generally a climate of solidarity, confidence, security, or hope.

THE CONSEQUENCE OF EMOTIONS FOR TEAM PROCESSES AND EFFECTIVENESS

Positive emotions

How does positive affect influence team behavior and effectiveness? George suggests that, if all or most individuals in a work team tend to feel positive at work (the team has a 'high positive affective tone'), then their cognitive flexibility will be amplified as a result of social influence and other team processes. As a result of these individual- and group-level processes, the team will develop shared (and flexible) mental models. In effect, teams with a high positive affective tone will be creative. Evidence suggests when individuals feel positive they tend to connect and integrate divergent stimulus materials—they are more creative, see interrelatedness among diverse stimuli and use broader, inclusive categories (Isen & Daubman, 1984; Isen, Daubman, & Nowicki, 1987; Isen, Mitzi, Johnson, & Robinson, 1985).

Another example of the influence of collective emotions is provided by studies on team learning. Edmondson (1996) demonstrated differences between teams in a study of hospital patient care, finding significant differences across work teams in their management of medication errors. In some teams, members openly acknowledged and discussed their medication errors such as giving too much or too little of a drug, or administering the wrong drug, and discussed ways to avoid their occurrence. In others, members kept information about errors to themselves. Learning about the causes of these errors as a team and devising innovations to prevent future errors were only possible in teams of the former type.

Edmondson (1996) argues that learning and innovation will take place if team members work in an emotional climate of trust. This manifests in a collective belief that well-intended action will not lead to punishment or rejection by the team. Edmondson calls this "team safety":

> The term is meant to suggest a realistic, learning oriented attitude about effort, error and change—not to imply a careless sense of permissiveness, nor an unrelentingly positive affect. Safety is not the same as comfort; in contrast, it is predicted to facilitate risk.
>
> (Edmondson, 1996, p. 14)

Her research in 53 teams of a large manufacturer of office furniture revealed that safety was the one consistent predictor of team learning, whether self- or observer rated. She concludes that perceptions of team safety will lead team members to engage in learning and risk- taking behavior (i.e. to innovation, Edmondson & Moingeon, 1998).

Positive emotions also influence the interactions between members of *distinct* groups (e.g. in negotiation situations). A classic study was conducted by Carnevale and Isen (1986). They had participants negotiate a transaction involving several issues, some of these being more important to the one party than to the other. In one condition, positive mood was induced prior to the negotiation, while in another condition this manipulation was absent. Results generally showed positive mood to increase the accurate exchange of information, to reduce contentious, competitive behaviors, and to lead to more win–win solutions providing both parties with high gains. In a similar vein Baron, Fortin, Frei, Hauver, and Shack (1990) have shown that positive affect reduces preferences for resolving conflicts through competition and avoidance, and increases preferences for collaboration (see also Forgas, 1998; for a review see Barry & Oliver, 1996).

Taken together, increasing evidence suggests positive emotions, whether individually or collectively experienced (team safety, mutual trust), predict better team processes and performance. Positive affect improves learning, enhances creativity, leads to greater innovation, and reduces conflict. These outcomes in turn are likely to produce new positive emotions, serving to enhance group cohesion and to improve team effectiveness and performance in the long term.

Negative emotions

Group affective tone and team safety are prerequisites for optimal team functioning and performance, but no team is completely free of negative emotions. Working in teams involves, by definition, mixed-motive conflicts, which need careful management. Understanding how people manage conflict, and how emotions influence conflict management, thus is of critical importance.

Conflict in teams occurs when individual team members perceive differences with one or more other team members (cf. De Dreu, Harinck & Van Vianen, 1999). Perceived differences produce psychological states, including feelings, cognitions, and motivations, that in turn produce behaviors intended to intensify, reduce, or solve the tension. Implicit in this definition, then is that conflicts arise out of emotional situations: we may be angry, irritated, or anxious because we do not get what we want, or because we feel insulted. Indeed, Thomas and Pondy (1977) suggested that anger often accompanies conflict, and that the root of organizational conflict lies in the judgements one party makes about why another party behaved in a harmful manner (for empirical evidence see e.g. Allred, 1996; Bies & Tripp, 1995; Tripp & Bies, 1996).

Moreover, the development of conflict situations is determined by the interpretation of the others' behavior and intentions, and this interpretation in turn is highly dependent upon the expression of specific emotions by each of the parties in the conflict. In mixed-motive conflicts people evaluate others' behavior as cooperative or hostile and as dominant or submissive. The way we interpret others' intentions and conflict behavior may reinforce or inhibit our own tendency to engage in collaborating, contending, yielding, or avoiding. When we see the other as dominant and hostile, we may be inclined to either approach the other by contending or by yielding, depending on our own power position. The expression of emotions may contribute to the way we interpret and evaluate others' intentions and behavior. For example, an angry person may be more likely to make hostile attributions, and view others' concessions as a trick rather than a genuine attempt to solve the conflict. In a similar vein, we assume that anxiety and fear bias towards the suspicion of ulterior motives, underlying other team members' ambiguous behaviors. Happy, empathic feelings, on the other hand, are more likely to bias towards the expectation of genuine, prosocial motives underlying others' ambiguous behaviors. Thus, emotions may bias the interpretation of more or less ambiguous conflict behaviors by opposing team members.

The expression of the other party's emotions may also steer the interpretation of the other's intentions and behaviors, thereby influencing our own conflict behavior. Fischer and De Dreu (1999) examined the emotions people attribute to their conflict opponent. They assumed that the inference of the other's emotions strongly determines our own strategy, because emotions inform us about the motives of the other party, and what the other party wishes to achieve at what costs. Fischer and De Dreu provided students with short descriptions of situations in which they were involved in a conflict with someone else. The description ended with a short statement that the conflict opponent was just entering their office and displayed one of the four conflict management strategies (collaborating, contending, yielding, or avoiding). Participants were asked to indicate their ideas about the emotions felt by their conflict opponent. Results showed that opponents who were dominating or avoiding are assumed to be angrier than opponents who were yielding or collaborating. Furthermore, opponents who were yielding are considered to be more anxious or self-blaming than individuals displaying any of the other strategies. Happiness, finally, is most likely to be attributed to opponents who were collaborating.

Emotion expressions not only affect the way in which conflicts develop, but have broader social implications for team cohesion and team performance. For example, Allred, Mallozzi, Matsui and Raia (1997), using a laboratory simulation of a negotiation between an employer and an employee, showed that negotiators who felt high anger and low compassion had less desire to work together in the future, and achieved lower joint gain. That is, anger together with low compassion results in fewer win–win agreements that meet both negotiators' aspirations as much as possible. Interestingly, this effect was particularly strong when the employer rather than the employee felt anger and low compassion, suggesting that power and status differences may boost or attenuate the effects of emotions on conflict management and outcomes.

Recent studies on conflict and team performance (for a review see De Dreu & Van de Vliert, 1997) also suggest a relationship between emotional processes in conflict, on the one hand, and more distal team performance, on the other. These studies typically distinguish between task conflict and relationship conflict. *Task* conflicts are about the distribution of resources, about procedures and policies, and about judgements and interpretation of facts. *Relationship* conflicts concern insights and information that are unrelated to the task, and threaten our personal identity and feelings of self-worth (Pelled, 1995). As a result, research has shown that high levels of relationship conflicts in groups are associated with low team performance and low satisfaction with the group. Task conflict is less threatening to our personal identity, and tends to motivate team members to search for optimal judgements and decisions (for reviews see Amason & Schweiger, 1997; De Dreu et al. 1999; Jehn, 1997). Although more research is needed, we speculate that relationship conflict involving negative emotions such as anger, anxiety and shame and guilt add to a negative emotional climate in a team and that exactly these emotions trigger interaction processes detrimental to team performance.

Summary and conclusions

In this section, we discussed the consequences of emotional processes for behavior and performance in teams. Both individual positive emotions and collective positive emotions, in the sense of mutual trust, have been shown to relate to learning, to divergent, creative thinking, and to innovation in teams. Positive affect in teams may also lead to more constructive conflict management and more mutually beneficial, integrative agreements. However, positive emotions in teams are under permanent threat because working in teams involves mixed-motive conflicts, which are generally overflowing with negative emotions such as anger, fear, guilt, and regret. There is some initial evidence that negative emotions may bias attributions toward suspecting ulterior motivation in others, which is likely to result in hostile and non-cooperative behavior, contributing to a negative emotional relationship between the parties in conflict. In addition, we reviewed evidence suggesting that if conflicts in teams focus on relationship issues, negative consequences may be more severe than when conflicts focus on task-content issues. Moreover, recent evidence suggests that when there is high mutual trust and team safety, task conflict is less likely to escalate into relationship conflict with its concomitant negative consequences for team performance. It may be that positive affective tone in teams induces more tolerant, positive attitudes about others, which helps team members in conflict to stay focused on task rather than relationship issues.

EMOTIONS IN ORGANIZATIONAL TEAMS: CONCLUDING THOUGHTS

In this chapter, we discussed emotions as both the origin and consequence of processes in organizational teams. Our starting point was that the organizational behavior literature has been overly concerned with a rational choice perspective on employee behavior and performance, to the neglect of processes that operate outside of awareness, intentions, and immediate control. Emotions are one strong example of such processes, and our review touched upon key issues in the functioning of individuals and teams in organizations that are substantially related to emotions.

Although basic psychological theory about emotion is developing, and emotions have become a solid field of study in social and experimental psychology, organizational psychology has only recently started to recognize the importance of emotions. As a result, much of the current discussion about emotions in organizational teams lacks a solid empirical basis and the conclusions we draw throughout the chapter should be taken as indications of what might happen or be at stake, rather than firm statements about what is going on in organizational teams. Thus, our review may be seen as a springboard for further theory development and empirical studies. In fact, we believe there is a great need for such activity. Emotions have important social functions in teamwork, and the expression of either positive and negative emotions not only inform us about the functioning of teams, but, at the same time, affect the ongoing processes within a team. Moreover, emotions trigger and steer such critical processes in organizational teams as managing conflict and developing creative and useful ideas for making teamwork more effective.

REFERENCES

Adams, S. (1965) Equity theory. In L. Berkowitz (Ed.) *Advances in Experimental Social Psychology*. New York: Academic Press.

Ainsworth, M.D. (1989) Attachments beyond infancy. *American Psychologist*, **44**, 709–16.

Allred, K.G. (1996) *Judgments, Anger, and Retaliation: A New Perspective on Conflict in Organizations*, Working Paper. International Center for Cooperation and Conflict Resolution, Columbia University, New York.

Allred, K.G., Mallozzi, J.S., Matsui, F., & Raia, C.P. (1997) The influence of anger and compassion on negotiator performance. *Organizational Behavior and Human Decision Processes*, **70**, 175–187.

Amason, A.C. & Schweiger, D.M (1997) The effects of conflict on strategic decision making effectiveness and organisational performance. In C.K.W. de Dreu & E. van de Vliert (Eds) *Using Conflict in Organisations*, London: Sage Publications.

Axelrod, R. & Hamilton, W.D. (1981) The evolution of cooperation. *Science*, **211**, 1390–1396.

Barash, D.P. (1977) *Sociobiology and Behaviour*. New York: Elsevier.

Barchas, P. (1986) A sociophysiological orientation to small groups. In E. Lawler (Ed.) *Advances in Group Processes*, Vol. 3, pp. 209–246. Greenwich, CT: JAI.

Baron, R.A., Fortin, S.P., Frei, R.L., Hauver, L.A., & Shack, M.L. (1990) Reducing organizational conflict: The role of socially-induced positive affect. *International Journal of Conflict Management*, **1**, 133–152.

Barry, B. & Oliver, R.L. (1996) Affect in negotiation: A model and propositions. *Organizational Behavior and Human Decision Processes*, **67**, 127–143.

Baumeister, R.F. & Leary, M.R. (1995) The need to belong: Desire for interpersonal attachments as a fundamental human motivation. *Psychological Bulletin*, **117**, 497–529.

Baumeister, R.F., Stillwell, A.M., & Heatherton, T.F. (1999). Guilt: An interpersonal approach. *Psychological Bulletin*, **115**, 243–267.

Baumeister, R.F., Wotman, S.R., & Stillwell, A.M. (1993) Unrequited love: On heartbreak, anger, guilt, scriptlessness and humiliation. *Journal of Personality and Social Psychology*, **64**, 377–394.

Beach, L.R. (Ed.) (1997) *Decision Making in the Work Place: A Unified Perspective*. Mahwah, NJ: Lawrence Erlbaum Associates.

Beehr, T.A., Drexler, J.A., & Faulkner, S. (1997) Working in small family businesses: Empirical comparisons to non-family businesses. *Journal of Organizational Behavior*, **18**, 297–312.

Belsky, J. (1979) The interrelation of parental and spousal behaviour during infancy in traditional nuclear families: An exploratory analysis. *Journal of Marriage and the Family*, **41**, 749–755.

Bies, R. & Tripp, T.M. (1995) Beyond distrust: "Getting even" and the need for revenge. In R. Kramer and T. Tyler (Eds) *Trust in Organizations*, pp. 246–260. Newbury Park, CA: Sage Publications.

Billig, M. & Tajfel, H. (1973) Social categorization and similarity in intergroup behavior. *European Journal of Social Psychology*, **3**, 27–51.

Bowlby, J. (1969) *Attachment and Loss*, Vol. I, *Attachment*, London: Hogarth.

Briner, B. (1999) The neglect and importance of emotion at work. *European Journal of Work and Organizational Psychology*, **8**(3), 323–346.

Buss, D.M. (1990) The evolution of anxiety and social exclusion. *Journal of Social and Clinical Psychology*, **9**, 196–210.

Buss, D.M. (1991) Evolutionary personality psychology. *Annual Review of Psychology*, **42**, 459–491.

Carnevale, P.J. & Isen, A.M. (1986) The influence of positive affect and visual access on the discovery of integrative solutions in bilateral negotiation processes. *Organizational Behavior and Human Decision Processes*, **37**, 1–7.

Carnevale, P.J. & Pruitt, D.G. (1992) Negotiation and mediation. *Annual Review of Psychology*, **43**, 531–582.

Cohen, S. & Wills, T.A. (1985) Stress, social support and the buffering hypothesis. *Psychological Bulletin*, **98**, 310–357.

De Dreu, C.K.W., Harinck, F., & Van Vianen, A.E.M. (1999) Conflict and performance in groups and organizations. In C.L. Cooper and I. Robertson (Eds) *International Review of Industrial and Organizational Psychology*, Vol. 14, pp. 369–414. Chichester, UK: Wiley.

De Dreu, C.K.W., Lualhati, J., & McCusker, C. (1994) Effects of gain-loss frames on satisfaction with self-other outcome-differences. *European Journal of Social Psychology*, **24**, 497–510.

De Dreu, C.K.W. & Van de Vliert, E. (Eds) (1997) *Using Conflict in Organizations*. London: Sage Publications.

De Rivera, J. (1992) Social structure and emotional dynamics. In K.T. Strongman (Ed.) *International Review of Studies on Emotion*, Vol. 2, pp. 197–219. Chichester, UK: Wiley.

Edmondson, A.C. (1996) Learning from mistakes is easier said than done: Group and organizational influences on the detection and correction of human error. *Journal of Applied Behavioral Science*, **32**, 5–32.

Edmondson, A.C. & Moingeon, B. (1998) From organizational learning to the learning organization. *Management Learning*, **29**: 499–517.

Fischer, A.H. & De Dreu, C.K.W. (1999) Emotion and conflict management, Raw data. University of Amsterdam.

Forgas, J.P. (1998) On feeling good and getting your way: Modd effects on negotiator cognition and bargaining strategies. *Journal of Personality and Social Psychology*, **74**, 565–577.

Frijda, N.H. (1986) *The Emotions*. Cambridge: Cambridge University Press.

Frijda, N.H., Kuipers, P., & Ter Schure, L. (1987) Relations among emotion, appraisal and action tendency. *Journal of Personality and Social Psychology*, **57**, 212–228.

Frijda, N.H. & Mesquita, B. (1994) The social roles and functions of emotion. In S. Kitayama & H. R. Markus (Eds) *Emotion and Culture*, pp. 51–89. Washington: APA.

George, J. (1996) Group affective tone. In M.A. West (Ed.) *Handbook of Work Group Psychology*. Chichester, UK: Wiley.

Harris, E.F. (1995) *The Managerial Decision Making Process*. Boston: Houghton Mifflin.

Hatfield, E., Cacioppo, J. T., & Rapson, R. L. (1994) *Emotional Contagion*. Cambridge: Cambridge University press.

Hays, R.B. (1985) A longitudinal study of friendship development. *Journal of Psychology and Social Psychology*, **48**, 909–924.

Hazan, C. & Shaver, P.R. (1994) Attachment as an organisational framework for research on close relationships. *Psychological Inquiry*, **5**, 1–22.

Hochschild, A. (1983) *The Managed Heart*. Berkeley, CA: University of California Press.

Hogan, R., Jones, W.H., & Cheek, J.M. (1985) Socioanalytic theory: An alternative to armadillo psychology. In B.R. Schlenker (Ed.) *The Self and Social Life*, pp. 175–198. New York: McGraw-Hill.

Horney, K. (1945) *Our Inner Conflicts: A Constructive Theory of Neurosis*. New York: Norton.

Hoyle, R.H. & Crawford, A.M. (in press). Use of individual level data to investigate group phenomena: Issues and strategies. *Small Group Research*.

Isen, A.M. (1984) Toward understanding the role of affect in cognition. In R.S. Wyer, Jr. & T.K. Srull (Eds) *Handbook of Social Cognition*, Vol. 3, pp. 179–236. Hillsdale, NJ: Lawrence Erlbaum Associates.

Isen, A.M. & Daubman, K.A. (1984) The influence of affect on categorization. *Journal of Personality and Social Psychology*, **47**, 1206–1217.

Isen, A.M., Daubman, K.A., & Nowicki, G.P. (1987) Positive affect facilitates creative problem solving. *Journal of Personality and Social Psychology*, **52**, 1122–1131.

Isen, A.M., Mitzi, M.S. Johnson, E.M., & Robinson, G.F. (1985) The influence of positive affect on the unusualness of word association. *Journal of Personality and Social Psychology*, **48**, 1413–1426.

Jehn, K. (1997) Affective and cognitive conflict in work groups: Increasing performance thorugh value-based intragroup conflict. In C.K.W. de Dreu and E. van de Vliert (Eds) *Using Conflict in Organizations*, pp. 87–100. London: Sage Publications.

Jones, W.H. (1981) Loneliness and social contact. *Journal of Social Psychology*, **113**, 295–296.

Keltner, D. & Haidt, J. (1999) Social functions of emotions at four levels of analysis. *Cognition and Emotion*, **13**, 505–523.

Kiecolt-Glaser, J.K., Garner, W., Speicher, C., Penn, G.M., Holliday, J., & Glaser, R. (1984) Psychosocial modifiers of immunocompetence in medical students. *Psychosomatic Medicine*, **46**, 7–14.

Kiecolt-Glaser, J.K., Richer, D., George, J., Messick, G., Speicher, C., Garner, W., & Glaser, R. (1984) Urinary cortisol levels, cellular immunocompetency and loneliness in psychiatric inpatients. *Psychosomatic Medicine*, **46**, 15–23.

Leary, M.R. (1990) Impression management: A literature review and two component model. *Psychological Bulletin*, **107**, 34–47.

Leary, M.R. & Downs, D.L. (in press) Interpersonal functions of the self esteem motive: The self esteem system as a sociometer. In M. Kernis (Ed.) *Efficacy, Agency and Self esteem*. New York: Plenum Press.

Lofland, L.H. (1982) Loss and human connection: An exploration into the nature of the social bond. In W. Ickes & E.S. Knowles (Eds) *Personality, Roles and Social Behaviour*, pp. 219–242. New York: Springer-Verlag.

Manstead, A.S.R. & Fischer, A.H. (in press) Social appraisal. In K.R. Scherer, A. Schorr, & T. Johnstone. (Ed.) *Appraisal Processes in Emotion: Theory, Methods, Research*. New York: Oxford University Press.

Miller, N.B., Cowan, P.A., Cowan, C.P., Hetherington, E.M., & Clingempeel, W.G. (1993) Externalising in preschoolers and early adolescents: A cross study replication of a family model. *Developmental Psychology*, **29**, 3–18.

Moreland, R.L. (1987) The formation of small groups. In C. Hendrick (Ed.) *Group Processes: Review of Personality and Social Psychology*, Vol. 8, pp. 80–100. Newbury Park, CA: Sage Publications.

Neale, M., & Bazerman, M.H. (1991) *Rationality and Cognition in Negotiation*. Boston: Free Press.

Parkinson, B. (in press) Putting appraisal in context. In K.R. Scherer, A. Schorr, & T. Johnstone. (Ed.) *Appraisal Processes in Emotion: Theory, Methods, Research*. New York: Oxford University Press.

Pekrun, R. & Frese, M. (1992) Emotions in work and achievement. In C.L. Cooper and I.T. Robertson (Eds) *International Review of Industrial and Organizational Psychology*, Vol. 7. Chichester, UK: Wiley.

Pelled, L.H. (1995) Demographic diversity, conflict, and work group outcomes: An intervening process theory. *Organization Science*, **7**, 615–631.

Pines, M. & Aronson, E. (1983) Antecedents, correlates, and consequences of sexual jealousy. *Journal of Personality*, **51**, 108–135.

Porter, L. & Lawler, E. III (1968) *Managerial Attitudes and Performance*. Homewood, IL: Irwin.

Roseman, I.J., Antoniou, A.A., & Jose, P.E. (1996) Appraisal determinants of emotions: constructing a more accurate and comprehensive theory. *Cognition and Emotion*, **10**, 241–279.

Scherer, K.R. (1984) On the nature and function of emotion: A component process approach. In K.R. Scherer & P. Ekman (Eds) *Approaches to Emotion*, pp. 293–317). Hillsdale, NJ: Lawrence Erlbaum Associates.

Sherif, M., Harvey, O.J., White, B.J., Hood, W.R., & Sherif, C.W. (1961) *Intergroup Conflict and Co-operation: The Robbers Cave Experiment*. Norman, OK: University of Oklahoma Press.

Simon, H.A. (1957) Rational decision making in business organizations. American Economic Review (September), 493–513.

Spector, P., Dwyer, D.J., & Lex, S.M. (1988) Relation of job stressors to affective, health and performance outcomes: A comparison of multiple data sources. *Journal of Applied Psychology*, **73**, 11–19.

Stein, A.A. (1976) Conflict and cohesion: A review of the literature. *Journal of Conflict Resolution*, **20**, 143–172.

Tajfel, H. (1970) Experiments in intergroup discrimination. *Scientific American*, **223**, 96–102.

Tajfel, H. & Billig, M. (1974) Familiarity and categorization in intergroup behaviour. *Journal of Experimental Social Psychology*, **10**, 159–170.

Thomas, K.W. & Pondy, L.R. (1977) Toward an "intent" model of conflict management among principal parties. *Human Relations*, **30**, 1089–1102.

Tripp, T.M. & Bies, R. (1996) *Seeking Revenge in Organizations: An Exploration into the Hearts and Minds of Avengers*. Paper presented at the Research on Negotiations in Organizations Conference, Duke University.

Turner, J.C. (1985) Social categorization and the self concept: A social cognitive theory of group behaviour. In E.J. Lawler (Ed.) *Advances in Group Processes: Theory and Research*, Vol. 2, pp. 77–121. Greenwich, CT: JAI.

Van Knippenberg, D. & Van Schie, E. (2000). Foci and correlates of organizational identification. *Journal of Occupational and Organizational Psychology*, **73**, 137–147.

Vroom, V. & Yago, A.G. (1988) *The New Leadership: Managing Participation in Organizations*. Englewood Cliffs, NJ: Prentice-Hall.

West, M.A. (1996) Introduction to work group psychology. In M.A. West (Ed.) *Handbook of Work Group Psychology*. Chichester, UK: Wiley.

West, M.A. & Patterson, M.G. (1999) The workforce and productivity: People management is the key to closing the productivity gap. *New Economy*, **6**, 22–27.

Williams, J.G. and Solano, C.H. (1983) The social reality of feeling lonely: Friendship and reciprocation. *Personality and Social Psychology Bulletin*, **9**, 237–242.

Chapter 9

Emotions and organizational control

Stephen Fineman
School of Management, University of Bath, UK

> Organization implies control. A social organization is an ordered arrangement of individual human interactions. Control processes help circumscribe the idiosyncratic behaviors and keep them conformant to the rational plan of the organization.
>
> (Tannenbaum, 1968, p. 3)

Organizations have long been regarded as places where control is of the essence. Indeed, control and organization are, for many observers, synonymous. Writing some 20 years before Tannenbaum, Max Weber, with wistful resignation, laid out his own influential vision of control in the 'ideal' bureaucracy:

> ... the more the bureaucracy is "dehumanized" the more completely it succeeds in eliminating from official business love, hatred, and all purely personal, irrational and emotional elements which escape calculation. This is the specific nature of bureaucracy and it is appraised as its special value.
>
> (Weber, 1946, pp. 215–216)

Yet the image of the rational organization, a place where emotions, the "idiosyncratic", can be controlled out of existence, or at least placed in a safe place, is now a patently naïve one (e.g. see Fineman, 1993, 2000). We do not have to look far to discover that emotions and feeling are deeply woven into organizational fabric and they define and shape all manner of practices—from supervision and decision making to culture and community. Furthermore, both the dimensionality and moral framing of control are markedly more complex than the early organizational writers led us to believe. While some managerial theorists take it as

Emotions at Work. Edited by Roy Payne and Cary Cooper.
© 2001 by John Wiley & Sons, Ltd.

unproblematic that organizations are structurally arranged to bring about "required" behaviours from subordinates (e.g. Fayol, 1949; Ray, 1986), more radical critiques alert us to the way that organizational control can also be deceptive, manipulative, or oppressive, while unwanted controls can be resisted (e.g. Walby, 1989; Calas and Smircich, 1993; Buroway, 1985; Robbins, 1992). Furthermore, control is not an exclusively top–down phenomenon, sealed within obvious organizational boundaries. Organizational control is shaped and transformed interactively through the wider social order of business—such as economic, gender, ethnic and professional expectations.

Against this background, the present chapter addresses three questions concerning emotion and organizational control:

- Are the controllers really in control?
- How do organizations control emotion?
- What are the emotions of control?

But first, some definitional issues. Emotions and feelings mean different things to different writers—as is attested in the various contributions to this book. Some present them phenomenologically, deeply rooted in the individual's familial history and biography (e.g. Hirschhorn, 1988; Kets de Vries, 1991). Some regard them as visceral and physiological expressions (e.g. James, 1884; Schachter and Singer, 1962). For others, they are the consequences of cognitive appraisals (Arnold, 1969; Lazarus, 1980); and still others as socially produced experiences (Averill, 1986; Thoits, 1996; Fineman, 1996a; Hochschild, 1983; Elias, 1994).

In the following account, emotions are regarded as essentially socially conditioned responses; the outward presentation and dramatization of anger, fear, excitement, joy, boredom, and so forth. Emotions are shaped through display rules derived from national, family, educational, professional, and organizational mores, fine-tuned by individual experiences and improvisations in socially regulated settings. Thus, we learn when and where to look sad or glad, fearsome or fearful. It follows that emotions, as dramaturgical devices, can be used strategically as a political resource in interactional settings. So, we may try deliberately to get what we want by feigning anger, surprise, humility, or love. Skilled emotion work lies at the heart of organizational control.

Feeling will be taken as an essentially private, subjective, bodily, experience which has an important signalling function—a personal read-out on how we are doing, coping, or interacting. Feelings may be poignant or diffuse, subliminal or bold, conscious or unconscious. Feelings are often transient. When they are articulated to self or others they are formulated, and possibly transformed, through labels and language—such as: "I feel unhappy", "I feel excited", "I'm in pain". Feeling and emotion need not correlate. Indeed, organized life often requires that they do not, despite calls for more "authentic" emotional expression at work (e.g. Frost, Dutton, Worline, & Wilson, 2000). We may not feel what we show; and there is a delicate balance between sustaining and destabilizing a social order by showing what we feel.

ARE THE CONTROLLERS IN CONTROL?

> Managers get things done through other people. They make decisions, allocate resources and direct the activities of others to attain goals.
>
> (Robbins, 1998, p. 2)

The image of the manager in charge of organizational processes is common, even clichéd, in textbooks on organizational behaviour. It is often accompanied by a recitation of the "four functions" of management: planning, organizing, leading, and controlling (e.g. Schermerhorn, Hunt, & Osborn, 2000, p. 11). Such a tidy portrayal is frequently reinforced by photographs of captains of industry, full-faced and smiling, hands firmly on the organizational tiller.

That "real" management may not be quite so smooth, elegant and controlled was revealed in the early studies of Henry Mintzberg (1973). Mintzberg's managers led a fragmented, crisis-driven life, with much *ad hoc* decision making. So did many of the managers in Studs Terkel's evocative accounts of work in the mid-1970s. In the words of a frustrated plant manager:

> If I could get everybody at the plant to look at everything through my eyeballs, we'd have a lot of problems licked. If we have one standard to go by, it's easy to swing it around because then you've got everybody thinking the same way. This is the biggest problem of people—communication.
>
> (Terkel, 1975, p. 166)

When we get close to the emotionalities of managing, the illusion of control is firmly punctured. Tony Watson's ethnography of Ryland, a large telecommunications organization, makes the point:

> The more I saw of the managers at Ryland, the more I became aware of the extent of human angst, insecurity, doubt and frailty amongst them. I observed managers being rude to their staff, refusing to listen to advice given to them within their departments, curtly announcing unexplained decisions, losing their tempers with people from other departments, creating rows with fellow managers.
>
> (Watson, 1994, p. 178)

Psychoanalytic writers have sought to explain such observations as manifestations of (often) unconscious fears concerning identity, security and self-worth. In search of control in often uncontrollable circumstances, managers are driven to act out their anxieties and insecurities through the demands and prescriptions of their role (e.g. see Gabriel, 2000; Diamond, 1993; Kets de Vries & Miller, 1987; Kets de Vries; 1990; Schwartz, 1990). Unconscious desires and conflicting feelings confound and confuse managers' plans and purposes. Control, in practice, is a perpetual struggle with ourselves as tasks and challenges in the organizational world slip from our grasp, rekindling old fears and vulnerabilities. Feelings of being out of control are never far away. Indeed, some writers argue that such anxieties are exacerbated in post-industrial organizations where many of the old certainties of supply, demand, markets, labour stability, and lines of command have been eroded (Gould, 1993; Gabriel, 2000).

The weight of ethnographic and psychoanalytic evidence (e.g. Van Maanen, 1988; Jackall, 1988; Watson, 1994; Kunda, 1992; Mangham, 1986; Fineman, 1996b) certainly points to a managerial world where attempts to make decisions, allocate resources, and direct the activities of others to attain goals are far from linear or dispassionate. Psychoanalytic writers are fond of viewing people in such circumstances as suitable cases for treatment. The anxieties that undermine rational action and control need to be expunged (Gay, 1988; Diamond & Allcorn, 1987). Whether this is possible or desirable is arguable. Control is also a product of changing expectations that people have about work. New generations of managers begin to expect levels of change and uncertainty that were strange or threatening to their predecessors, adapting to what Douglas Hall (1996) has termed the "protean" career, where an unsettled, frequently changing future has replaced the old certainties of a career for life. When the personal meanings of anxiety are situationally contingent and culturally shaped, they are not easily therapised; nor, perhaps, should they be. They offer managers important signals about the contemporaneous nature of their relationships, along with any echoes from their own past.

Emotionalizing management exposes its frailty. It also suggests that the renditions of control found in many texts on management are, at best, over-optimistic; at worst, misleading. But, while the uncluttered image of managerial control may be a myth, it is an important and powerful one, reproduced through the folklore on management and by those (such as management consultants) who wish to profit from it. The rhetoric of managerial control is just that—one of hope and comforting illusion. The appeal of techniques of control, as evidenced in the ebb and flow of management fashions or fads, lies in their promises and reassurances. When they fail to deliver, there is always another, "better" one, to turn to.

HOW DO ORGANIZATIONS CONTROL EMOTION?

Inculcating the "right" form of emotional expressiveness has long been a formal feature of behaviour control in organizations. From the school classroom to the executive boardroom, the desirability or undesirability of, say, sniggering, showing anger, distress, boredom, disloyalty, joy, disdain, and so forth is controlled through explicit rules from powerful agents (e.g. teachers, bosses, significant peers) or informally through gradual socialization and organizational rites of passage (Stearns & Stearns, 1986). Some settings, such as the military, firmly suppress emotions that threaten the power hierarchy. Yet emotions that are seen to serve some military purpose may be encouraged. For example, yelling in anger in close combat to unnerve the enemy and energize the soldier or, when marching, to vigorously chant in unison to raise morale and maintain the rhythm of physical pace.

In all organizational settings, there are circumstances or physical zones where different emotion rules may prevail. They are places where the organization's direct control and surveillance is less, but where informal norms of what feelings can (and cannot) be expressed will prevail. The physical architecture shapes, to an extent, the emotional architecture where meanings of privacy, confidentiality, secrecy and candidness are differentially moulded and defined (see Fineman, 1996a; Wasserman, Rafaeli, & Kluger, 2000). In the relative privacy of the galley area of the aircraft, the niceties of customer care can be suspended and "real" feelings expressed—passengers may be reviled or mocked (e.g. Hochschild, 1983). In the school staffroom, frustration with students are more openly shared. We witness similar occurrences in restaurant kitchens, coffee areas in organizations, police cars, "confessional" booths in churches, corridors, and work car parks. Such contouring of emotion can be symbolically potent, a way of expressing felt organizational injustices or grievances (such as towards management) to safe, often assenting, audiences. Coded humour can be used to redress power imbalances and express frustration.

It should be stressed that none of these settings are emotion-free ports where "anything goes". Organization is maintained (at best) through complementary expressive zones, where what is or can be emotionally displayed is bounded by the protocols of "proper" work or professional conduct, and by beliefs about the appropriate boundary between the private and the public. Hence, the unease or anxiety when someone, through distress, anger, frustrations or inebriation, "over steps the mark"—such as revealing an intimate personal problem, venting fury or feelings of retribution, declaring a passionate attraction for a co-worker or client.

The emotion engineers

> Some days I just can't do it. There's only so much you can smile and put on a phoney face. Sometimes I'm actually too tired or bored or pissed off at the world to pretend I am happy, but my jobs both require that I pretend that I am really happy all the time.

The person speaking (in Pinder, 1998, p. 111) holds two part-time sales jobs. One is in a store that sells hiking equipment, the other is a restaurant. Both employers expect a warm, friendly, "personal" approach to customers, and, explicitly, service with a smile.

Switch the scene: a McDonald's restaurant[1]. A young, male assistant-manager bounces up to Sal during a pause in her hamburger selling. He is exuberant in his greeting:

MANAGER   Morning Sal! How you feeling today?

SAL   Fine.

MANAGER   Now look, when I say how you feeling, I want you to say "outstanding!".

SAL   OK [Sal looks bewildered].

MANAGER   So how you feeling today!?

SAL   Outstanding.

MANAGER   OK. Really get motivation. I'm telling all the crew today, when I ask them how they feel I want them to say "outstanding!" Go like that with your arms [he throws his arms outwards].

SAL   OK.

MANAGER   So how you feeling today!?

SAL   Outstanding! [she mimics him with obvious feigned enthusiasm].

Both these settings reveal something of emotion engineering in corporations. In each case, the corporation, or its agents, want more than physical and mental labour from their employees; they want emotional labour. Emotional labour, a term coined by Hochschild (1983), describes the way that the outward display of feeling is sold for a wage. It is explicit to the work contract and is institutionalized through highly focused training. So, in the above McDonald's scene, the manager is merely transferring his well-internalized lesson on motivation from his student days at McDonald's "Hamburger University". We see a similar picture in the Disneyland philosophy which requires "Employees with a ready smile and a knack for dealing pleasantly with large numbers of people" (Bright, 1987, p. 111), a vocabulary inculcated, once more, in an enclosed training setting— "Disneyland University" (see Van Maanen and Kunda, 1989).

---

[1] Extracted from a BBC Channel 2 television film for the Open University on "empowerment", 1998.

Emotional labour is now a feature of a growing "smile" industry that ranges from fast food and airline services to the selling of insurance (Leidner, 1999; Ashforth & Humphrey, 1995; Reiter, 1996). The process is a clear, and powerful, attempt to control the way employees present themselves emotionally—for commercial ends. But it also strays into wider, and arguably more sensitive, territory—how employees see themselves and how they feel. So insurance agents are exhorted to "fake it till you make it" (Sturdy, 1998) and airline attendants urged to display that "inside-out" smile, regardless of what obstacle comes their way (Hochschild, 1983). The incursion into self-identity has raised both psychological and ethical questions. Psychologically, there is a fear that the relentless corporate message to "really feel" fine, happy, good about the product, concern for the customer, and so forth, can result in "deep acting" that cannot be simply switched off at the end of the working day. Hochschild (1983), especially, charts such occurrences amongst flight attendants, noting that some become disturbed and confused about their identity. Such observations underline the potential onerousness of emotional labour. However, it appears that emotional labourers do not necessarily all suffer in this manner. Many find ways of insulating themselves from the undesired effects of corporate scripts by "surface acting", even creating a game out of the transaction (Wharton, 1999; Adelman, 1995).

Ethical concerns

For the most part, those who take on the "happy" mantle seem to be remarkably acquiescent, a testimony, perhaps, to the potency of organizational cultural capture (see Bryman, 1999). Open resistance to emotionally engineered jobs appears rare, but there are some recorded instances—such as the "smile strike" by female shopworkers of a Californian supermarket. They claimed that their smiling and eye contact with customers invited unwanted intimacy (Zeidler, 1998). Resistance can also be more quietly and privately expressed—such as through resentment towards management and ambivalence towards the job (Zibart, 1997).

As the service sector comes to dominate Westernized industrialized economies, so does the corporate engineering of emotion. When once the intuitive rapport of the good salesperson was put down to "personality" or "chemistry", it is now an attainable skill or "competence" for all who pass through the corporate emotion sieve. Face-to-face encounters in supermarkets, airlines, holiday firms, utility services, computer sales, restaurant chains, hotels, and so forth are tuned to the corporate script, while managerial surveillance keeps them on track. Telephone sales follows suit with the cultivation of the "telephone smile"—a warm, enthusiastic voice. It is perhaps no coincidence that "resting" professional actors often fill such positions.

The ethics of such emotion control depends on our perspective. For some, it smacks of a new form of exploitation and alienation, especially as many emotion labourers are to be found in relatively low-skilled jobs which are hard to escape from. When regimes of emotion control are enforced through video surveillance, random monitoring of salespersons' calls, or smile police ("mystery shoppers") secretly spying on workers, the ethical propriety of the practice is highly questionable. One UK agency claims to have 2,500 mystery shoppers to call upon, all specially trained for their covert role in monitoring others' emotions (Carty, 1996; see also Macdonald & Sirianni, 1996). What responsibility does the employee's organization hold for the unintended consequences (e.g. stress, suspicion, self-doubt) of the rigid control of emotion enactment?

The cultural transplanting of emotion engineering also raises ethical concerns. To what extent should a Western, urban, and essentially Americanized style of commercial transaction be placed in social–cultural settings where they clearly do not belong? The colonizing economic power of some service industries appears an unstoppable force, bringing with it a form of emotional eugenics. Local employees are selected and shaped to fit the corporate culture, rather than harmonizing the job with the extant national culture. Hence, all Big Macs, anywhere in the world, are to be served with that "outstanding" demeanour. This more than puzzled staff and customers of the first McDonald's restaurant in Moscow, where Soviet-style commercial interactions were typically cursory and coarse. Similarly, cultural discord was largely ignored in the smiling training given to indigenous Inuit staff of a Greenlandic supermarket chain (Jones, 1999). The Inuit have no tradition of greeting each other with a smile or "hi".

In neo-Tayloristic form, or the "McDonaldization" of society (Ritzer, 1993, 1998), there are understandable fears that homogenized consumer products and homogenized emotions go hand in hand, leading to a highly unenriched experience of work. But concerns reach deeper than this. An employee's affective world has long been the subject of organizational shaping and intervention. Indeed, management texts on leadership typically recommend ways of creating "appropriate" feelings in subordinates. In recent decades, however, we have witnessed a wider systematizing and legitimizing of programmes of control. They often take place under the banner of corporate-culture management programs that seek to mould employees' feelings and emotions, even unconscious strivings (Schwartz, 1987a). For some critics, this is a worrying form of managerial totalitarianism (Willmott, 1993).

Indirect emotion control

There are less obvious means by which emotion is controlled in or through organizations. The process of professionalization—such as becoming a teacher, medical practitioner, lawyer, psychiatrist, management consultant, probation officer, police officer, or social worker—inculcates ways of looking, sounding, "being" professional when dealing with others. This is often reached through diffuse, imitative learning, reinforced in a variety of organizational settings—such as professional training establishments, fieldwork, and consulting rooms. The expectations of clients add to the process of emotion shaping. Indeed, both professional and client are complicit in defining the boundaries of each other's appropriate emotional display. So what the patient expects emotionally from the doctor at the surgery is, in part, mirrored in what the doctor expects of the patient. A patient's tears of sadness or distress can be an acceptable feature of the organizational role relationship. But a weeping doctor—either in sympathy or in revealing his/her own anxieties—is likely to compromise or strain the relationship.

A play of expectations, or dance of masks, is part of the intricate social coding of emotion in social interactions (see Ekman & Davidson, 1995; Clark, 1990). While there is normally some improvisational space for the actors involved, the interactional scene is rarely equally balanced, being set by power, gender, and economic relationships (Rose, 1989; Latour, 1986; Harré, 1986; Hearn, 1993). In other words, some organizational members are more able to impress their emotion rules on others because of their dominant position in the wider, socially constructed, rewards system.

... And the body

The way the human body is placed in organizations has long been of interest to employers. Workstations, technology, office space, work breaks all confine and control the body in some form—usually for productive or efficiency purposes. But these arrangements also restrict, facilitate or trigger certain feelings or emotion states—compliance, frustration, resistance, happiness, anger, comfort, embarrassment, envy. The ability to share, to laugh, to talk, to enjoy privacy, to have a pleasant work setting, to be able to change physical position, can affect feelings—of being valued, of status, of loneliness, of variety, of respect. As the organization controls the body, it also, often unwittingly, frames people's emotional experiences of work.

Sometimes the emotional purposes of physical arrangements are intentional and obvious. The prominent position of the receptionist at the expansive front desk, the security guard on the main door, the chief executive in the large panelled room on the top floor are part of the corporate management of symbols that help the incumbent feel, and look, important, authoritative, welcoming, attractive, or significant. Dress and body adornment embellish such processes. Required dress codes have long been part of organized life—the school uniform, the sharp business suit, the brash fast-food apron and hat, the lavish regalia of high-court judges and military officers. Dress not only defines an occupational role and status position, it is also expected to create a feeling and emotional presence amongst its wearers and those with whom they interact—such as pride, fun, fear, awe, respect, seriousness, aggression, submissiveness, or composure.

The branding and theming of many corporate products—from fast food and Disney toys to designer footwear—is now replicated in the "packaging" of the staff who sell them. Many are expected to *be* the emotional image (fun, cool, sexy, comic) of what they sell by wearing the product, or donning its colours or insignia. Any deviations from standardized dress are, managerially, not readily tolerated as they fail to provide the corporately designed stimulus that is expected to rouse the mood to buy in customers.

THE EMOTIONS OF CONTROL

I have suggested that there are various means by which organizations control the feelings and emotions of their employees. But affectivity is not just a simple outcome of various corporate manipulations. The very process of controlling implicates emotions (i.e. emotion is essential, intrinsic, to the control process).

This perspective—on the emotions of control—is reflected in the work of organizational psychoanalysts. For example, the charismatic "pull" of certain leaders can be attributed to the way followers' needs and anxieties interact with the leader's fear of losing control, thrusting the leader to centre stage (Kets de Vries, 1990; Bryman, 1992). The indoctrinal strength of some corporate cultures can be such that employees who do not feel the "right" feelings will experience anxiety, guilt, and shame (Schwartz, 1987a, 1987b; Willmott, 1993)—such as Disneyland employees who feel guilty when they are "too tired to smile" (Van Maanen, 1991, p. 74). These are potent feelings of *self*-discipline and *self*-control, which become a substitute for external agents of control—such as managers, supervisors, and trainers.

The fusing of emotion and control can be demonstrated in other ways. Actors will attempt to influence and control each other through a range of dramaturgical devices—persuasion, extortion, rhetoric, body language. Some of these are everyday, informal occurrences at work; others are shaped by more formal structures, such as performance assessments, appraisal schemes, formal negotiations, interviews, briefings by bosses or supervisors. All such operations are, in practice, emotionalized in manner or form. For example, an interaction may be emotionally toned at the outset—such as through mistrust, apprehension, fear, or excitement. Feelings and emotions will be present in the way impressions are created and judgements made. Controller and controlled are also postured via emotion scripts, the expressive rules of the game for "boss", "subordinate", "woman", "man", "professional", or "expert". Indeed, the actor's place in the economic/ power order will predefine how emotions such as fear, embarrassment, anxiety, or disdain can be received or exploited (see Carr, 1988; Gabriel, 1998).

Underpinning this perspective is the view that much of what we take to be rational in our ways of control is, in fact, impregnated with feeling (e.g. see Damasio, 1994, 2000; Fineman, 1996a). Thinking and feeling, cognition and affect interpenetrate in ways that make action possible. So feeling and emotion are essential to realizing control, rather than an appendage or interference. Moreover, cognitions in organizations are invariably embedded in politicised interests where emotionalized discourses prevail.

The emotionalizing of control is illustrated in the following two case examples. Both highlight, in different ways, how feeling and emotion create both the substance and consequences of control interactions.

An inspector calls

The first illustration is an ethnographic account of the work of a pollution inspector (the notional controller) from the UK Environment Agency. It is an excerpt from a wider study of the author's on the politics and emotions of environmental regulation (in Fineman & Sturdy, 1999; see also Fineman, 1998). Typically, pollution inspectors work face to face with industrial managers to ensure that their production processes comply with the legalities of environmental protection. Many industrial processes require a permit to operate from the Agency, so the dealings with the inspector can be of considerable consequence. The inspector has the power to withdraw a permit, caution, or prosecute a company. Inspectors develop their own style of interaction, with more or less flexibility. Generally, their influence and credibility hinges upon their interpersonal skills and expert knowledge as much as their legal authority.

Alex, the inspector in this account, is experienced in the job. It is his second visit to Starr Polishes. The company manufactures domestic cleaning products and makes much of its environmental credentials. Today, the intention is to discuss the authorization of a new production process, after clarifying some details in their written application. The application was made by Dave, the environment manager—and professional chemist by training—with whom we have an appointment.

> We are 5 minutes late and Alex is irritated with himself:
>
> > Golden rule to be on time. I like to arrive an hour beforehand, and in my car read through the case. We are told that we should have a visit plan.
>
> Starr is using a very toxic, new, chemical—TDI—to produce their air fresheners. The manufacturing process is contained in a sealed area with an extraction system that filters emissions to the atmosphere. Alex wants to get the authorization "exactly right first time" and needs to know more about the way the extraction system works, how the noxious precipitates are processed and diluted, and where monitors to the system are sited.
>
> Alex is tense and authoritative. He tells me that his street credibility is very high with industry:
>
> > which they like. I can impress an operator with my competencies; I have experience with over 100 sites—they don't want someone wet behind the ears.

We are kept waiting in the smart reception area in Starr. This adds to Alex's irritation. He recounts, sympathetically, in a low voice, the story of one angry inspector who "stormed off" after 10 minutes wait. As if to reinforce the point, he shows me his official Agency identity card which, like police identification, confers special powers of entry in an emergency.

We finally get to Dave—who looks preoccupied and harassed. He has recently taken over responsibility for the environment alongside his usual safety and health issues. He and Alex sit across a small table in Dave's office. After some quick, token pleasantries they get down to business.

Alex starts going through Dave's application, line by line. Dave is startled, seemingly unprepared for this. He regains his composure, moves forward in his chair, and takes issue with some of the emission limits and measurement details that Alex is requesting. The atmosphere is soon combative. Given that TDI is a new substance, it is unclear what precise constituents and volume of the compound falls within official guidelines. That gives scope for both parties to argue how best to judge the emission levels, frequency, dilution, measurement, and extraction of TDI. And argue they did.

Alex generally holds his ground as Dave forcefully challenges his premises. Dave becomes frustrated, swinging between compliance and reluctant deference: "Well, what exactly do you want of me?" he says, staring firmly at Alex. Alex coolly responds: "I'm putting a control on you; you need to tell me if you will go along with it".

Dave is keen to have flexibility in the authorization; Alex is pushing for more control: "I'm not in the business of letting you have higher limits; if you change the process we need a mechanism to talk about it. Your measuring instruments must be convertible to guidance notes units".

Dave suddenly reveals that they now have an additional production line, not included in the initial application, which uses TDI. Alex looks surprised and a little angry. He immediately, and curtly, declares that this will delay the whole authorization and he will require more information from Dave.

They spend some time debating the best formula for measuring emissions and Dave unenthusiastically agrees with Alex that micrograms per cubic metre "might be best". This is a different requirement from the previous inspector, so Dave looks resentful about the change. Alex ignores this reaction and ploughs on; he wants emissions expressed so that they can go on the public register rather than be attached to "industrial confidentiality". Dave wearily complies. They discuss the timescale for revised submission. Alex says mid-January; Dave looks pained and says end of January because he's got "vast commitments".

The meeting draws to a close and Alex starts tidying his documents. As he does so, the graphical printouts from the machine that monitors TDI emissions catch his eye—and the discussion starts up again. They begin to argue about interpretation of the graphs, and Alex presses for a different form of monitoring based on "instantaneous limits" rather than the trends currently mapped. Dave looks unconvinced and uncomfortable. Alex persists, firmly pressing his point home: "have you any objections to instantaneous limits? You haven't answered this yet". Dave pauses for thought and responds blandly: "I'll have to come back to you on that".

Two hours have passed and Dave and Alex seem, again, ready to part. Alex then remembers that he has not inspected the extracting system on the roof—he will do it now. Dave looks disappointed, but reluctantly acquiesces. He seems to want an end to the matter.

We don protective clothing and enter the plant. There is a cloying chemical smell as cleaning agents, in neat batches, trundle along a complex of conveyor belts. In a glass box, some 4 metres square, three gooey mixtures are squirted together with TDI to make up the spongy base of air fresheners. There are extractor fans and monitors in the box that are ducted into the flat roof of the factory, which we climb onto. The roof is a cluttered landscape of chimneys, vents, and piping. Dave struggles with his embarrassment: he is not sure which chimney belongs to which process. Alex looks at him, impassively judgemental, calmly taking notes as he clambers around. We then find our way back to the reception area and leave the premises.

An emotion reading

This portrayal is more than a bland description of a professional regulator going through the motions of controlling someone else's behaviour. There is a strong emotional texture that patterns events and commitments. In terms of emotions expressed, there is both variety and dynamic quality: irritation, harassment, impassivity, startle, embarrassment, deference, anger, calmness. The emotional shifts are partly interactional as the parties respond and adjust to each other's conceptions and preconceptions. So the manager's apparent composure, thinly disguising his feelings of overwork, melts into frustration as he responds to the inspector's forcefulness. And the inspector's assertiveness seems, throughout, to be a product of his irritation and pique with the manager from the beginning. The physical settings—reception foyer, closed office, rooftop—frame emotions differently, respectively, "low voice" complaining, to open resistance and anger, to suppressed feelings. Strategic shifts in influence can be interpreted in emotion terms—such as the manager's look of "pain", which wins a minor concession in the timetable, signalling resistance following earlier concessions; the inspector's impassivity and calmness to add further embarrassment to the manager's struggles on the rooftop. And the inspector's assertiveness on "instantaneous limits"— to compound the manager's vulnerability and discomfort.

In emotionalizing the control encounter in this manner, we can see the emotional complexity of responses such as cooperation, acquiescence, compliance, and resistance. We can also see how the feelings held/expressed by controllers and the controlled are both *part* and *product* of "outcomes". Yet psychologizing the situation in this form does only part justice to the event. Both players are conditioned by role postures and emotion scripts that are associated with wider social structures—such as what it is to be an "inspector", "manager", or "professional". Indeed, both appeared exercised by challenges to their identities as competent professionals, expressed in anxieties and defensiveness about their technical judgements. Less transparent is the status contest as each man jostles for the hierarchical position he feels he deserves. The inspector's unease rises as he attempts to gain the respect he desires from the manager, while the manager struggles for more expert information from the inspector. Arguably, the manager's ultimate compliance reinforces his subordination in the face of someone whom he (literally) fears able to prevent production and, in turn, can embarrass him with his superiors and peers.

On being a doormat

This second illustration is rather different. It is a story told by a young, undergraduate student of management after his first industrial internship. It is taken from a compendium of first-hand accounts on the experience of organizational life—its emotions, its politics, its justices and injustices—as related through "innocent eyes", newcomers to the world of work (Fineman & Gabriel, 1996). Geoff, the student and narrator, encounters for the first time, life in a merchant bank in the City of London, and is somewhat shocked by what he finds.

> Many people hold stereotypical views of the merchant-banking environment—arrogant, power-crazed men, working long hours under intense pressures for vast sums of money, burnt-out after short careers. My personal experience after a 6-month placement for Leber's has not dispelled these images.
>
> I worked under Paul, a 30-year-old bachelor on a rumoured salary of over £200,000 p.a. Red Ferrari, a yacht, and a flat in Islington, which he shared with his cat, supported the rumours. I was often required to do personal favours for my boss, which extended beyond work practices and the following was one such favour. He rang me at work one Friday afternoon from Geneva to ask me to "run" his car to Heathrow, so he could travel straight from the airport to visit some friends in Exeter. He felt it would be inconvenient to take a train back to his house first to pick up his car. I was told I could take a taxi back to work. The incident highlighted some fundamental aspects of the organization, its managers, and its culture.
>
> The first striking feature of this incident was the way it highlighted the power structure. Although the bank has a fairly flat hierarchy, managers never hesitated to make their position known by putting me in a position where I could not refuse (mind you, I actually quite fancied driving his Rover

8-series top model, the Ferrari being explicitly out of bounds for me). The incident also showed disregard for my own time; it meant that I had to work unpaid overtime in order to catch up with my work (and on a Friday night!).

To say I was used as a doormat would be an understatement. Paul thrived on *his feelings of domination.* It seemed utterly unnecessary to have me drive his car to the airport. This attitude was common among management and it led to resentment and back-stabbing, which could be seen at all levels of the organisation. The incident did no harm to Paul's ego. Many managers, like him, were status and empire builders, showing extraordinary presumptuousness and arrogance. When asking me to drive his car, Paul classed the task as a "small" favour—in fact, it took me all afternoon. It is characteristic that, when speaking to me on the phone, Paul called me "Geoffrey", as always, although I am known to all else as "Geoff". He likewise insists on calling his secretary Suzanne, although her name is Su and is printed as such on her birth certificate.

When I asked Paul on the phone about flight details and the whereabouts of the keys, his answer was "My secretary has the details", although she had not. I don't think that Paul ever realized or cared about the embarrassing situation he put me in when the rest of the office found out that I had become his personal chauffeur.

I had to go to Paul's house in order to pick up the car (I was under strict instructions not to take the Ferrari, although it was very tempting). I was amazed when I entered his flat. It was completely unfurnished except for the kitchen, a study (with an ashtray full of cigar stubs, obviously the pressure), and a bedroom. The bedroom was full of shirts, ties, suits, but no other clothes. This emphasized how much that work had taken over his life.

At the airport, I left a note with his car keys saying that I had enjoyed driving his car. When Paul came back to the office on Monday, he told me and his colleagues how, on seeing the note, he had been convinced that I had driven the Ferrari. He seriously could not comprehend how I could enjoy driving a car "such as a Rover", said in a jeering voice. I think this final twist summarizes how unable he is to comprehend anyone else, apart from people like himself.

An emotion reading

We do not directly hear the voice of Paul, the "controller", in this story, but we get some insight into the emotions of control through Geoff's perceptions. For a start, there is a picture of an organizational status/power system, male centred, where arrogance and indifference go hand in hand. Unconcern towards others is supported by an economic hierarchy, which favours the wealthiest while cultivating resentment amongst others. The most potent symbol of personal success in the merchant-banking environment is very large financial gain in a short period.

Paul's control over Geoff, it appears, is a product of this culture. His self-aggrand-izement is held in place by making others, lower in the prized economic order, feel uncomfortable and finding ways of exploiting that discomfort.

A cluster of humiliating acts (jeering, embarrassment) subordinate Geoff in ways that he appears unable or unwilling to overtly resist. In Paul's hands, the innocent alteration of people's names, often a mark of affection, smacks of a power trip, "feelings of domination"—his ability, as Geoff sees it, to insult others with impunity.

Geoff's discomfort and resentment are apparent. He loathes being cast in the role of an errand boy, even more so in the light of public embarrassment in the office. His status may be low, but he is a *manager* in training. Yet he still does as he is told. Why? There is an implied fear of losing his job ("I could not refuse"). But there is also a hint of envy of Paul's life, especially the smart, fast car. Could this be Geoff's own life sometime in the future? Geoff's seduction is a helpful emotional basis for Paul's control over him.

IN CONCLUSION

In this chapter, I have sought to demonstrate that feeling and emotion are crucial to organizational functioning; they underpin the very essence of control. They also expose the myth of organizational dispassion and rationality. In different ways, we are all emotion managers, and the tension between private feeling and emotional display is an enduring feature of social organization and the civilization process. Indeed, without it and its ever-simmering dilemmas, organizing would be a markedly less manageable process, despite the humanistic allure to express all that we feel. Emotion work is also organizational work, usually, of the invisible kind.

In making emotion work visible, our social psychology and sociology of organizations is markedly enhanced. It renders control more comprehensible and de-mechanizes it. It also reveals practices that may concern us. The corporate hijacking of emotion is one. As emotion and its control becomes a commodified part of the corporate product, we are witnessing emotion engineering on a grand scale. The employee's feelings and emotions are shaped by market forces to an unusual degree. If employees "adapt" to such conditions, is that a satisfactory state of affairs? Maybe we can tolerate any emotional casualties. Or should we, as social scientists, take a more proactive stance on what we feel is wrong about an employment culture, where emotion is just another variable of the market economy.

REFERENCES

Adelman, P.K (1995) Emotional labor as a potential source of job stress. In S.L. Sauster and L.R. Murphy (Eds) *Organizational Risk Factors for Job Stress*. Washington, DC: American Psychological Association.

Arnold, M. (1969) Human emotion and action. In T. Mischel (Ed.) *Human Action: Conceptual and Empirical Issues*. New York: Academic Press.

Ashforth, B.E. and Humphrey, R.H. (1995) Emotion in the workplace—a reappraisal. *Human Relations*, **48**(2), 97–125.

Averill, J.R. (1986) The acquisition of emotions in childhood. In R. Harre (Ed.) *The Social Construction of Emotions*. Oxford: Blackwell.

Bright, R. (1987) *Disneyland: Inside Story*. New York: Harry N. Abrams.

Bryman, A. (1999) The Disneyization of society. *The Sociological Review*, **47**(1), 25–47.

Bryman, A. (1992) *Charisma and Leadership in Organizations*. London: Sage Publications.

Buroway, M. (1985) *The Politics of Production*. London: Verso.

Calas, M. & Smircich, L. (1993) Dangerous liaisons—"the feminine in management" meets "globalization". *Business Horizons*, **32**,(2), 71–81.

Carr, A. (1988) Identity, compliance and dissent in organizations: A psychoanalytic perspective. *Organization*, **5**(1), 81–99.

Carty, P. (1996) *The Guardian*, 9 October 1996, P. 3.

Clark, C. (1990) Emotions and micropolitics in everyday life: Some patterns and paradoxes of "place". In T.D. Kemper (Ed.) *Research Agendas in the Sociology of Emotions*. Albany, NY: State University of New York Press.

Damasio, A.R. (1994) *Descartes' Error*. New York: Putnam.

Damasio, A.R. (2000) *The Feeling of What Happens*. London: Heinemann.

Diamond, M.A. (1993) *The Unconscious Life of Organizations: Interpreting Organizational Identity*. Westport, CA: Quorum Books.

Diamond, M.A. and Allcorn, S. (1987) The psychodynamics of regression in work groups. *Human Relations*, **40**(8), 525–543.

Ekman, P. and Davidson, R.J. (1994) *The Nature of Emotions: Fundamental Questions*. New York: Oxford University Press.

Elias, N. (1994) *The Civilizing Processes*, Vols 1 and 2. Oxford: Blackwell.

Fayol, H. (1949) *General and Industrial Management* (transl. C. Stores). London: Pitman.

Fineman, S. & Gabriel, Y. (1996) *Experiencing Organizations*. London: Sage Publications.

Fineman, S. (Ed.) (1993) *Emotion in Organizations*. London: Sage Publications.

Fineman, S. (1996a) Emotion and organizing. In S. Clegg, C. Hardy, and W. Nord (Eds) *Handbook of Organization Studies*. London: Sage Publications.

Fineman, S. (1996b) Emotional subtexts in corporate greening. *Organization Studies*, **17**(3), 479–500.

Fineman, S. (1998) Street level bureaucrats and the social construction of environmental control. *Organization Studies*, **19**(6), 953–974.

Fineman, S. (Ed.) (2000) *Emotion in Organizations*, 2nd ed. London: Sage Publications.

Fineman, S and Sturdy, A. (1999) The emotions of control: A qualitative study of environmental regulation. *Human Relations*, **52**(5), 631–663.

Frost, P.J., Dutton, J.E., Worline, M.C., & Wilson, A. (2000) Narratives of compassion in organizations. In S. Fineman (Ed.) *Emotion in Organizations*, 2nd ed. London: Sage Publications.

Gabriel, Y. (1998) Psychoanalytic contributions to the study of the emotional life of organizations. *Administration and Society*, **30**(3), 291–314.

Gabriel, Y. (2000) *Organizations in Depth*. London: Sage Publications.

Gay, P. (1988) *Freud: A Life for Our Time*. New York: Newton.

Gould, L.J. (1993) Contemporary perspectives on personal and organizational authority: The self in a system of work relationships. In L. Hirschhorn and C.K. Barnett (Eds) *The Pychodynamics of Organizations*. Philadelphia: Temple University Press.

Hall, D.T (1996) *The Career is Dead: Long Live the Career!* San Francisco: Jossey Bass.

Harré, R. (1986) *The Social Construction of Emotions*. Blackwell: Oxford.

Hearn, J. (1993) Emotive subjects: Organizational men, organizational masculinities and the (de)construction of "emotions". In S. Fineman (Ed.) *Emotion in Organizations*. London: Sage Publications.

Hirschhorn, L. (1988) *The Workplace Within*. Cambridge, MA: MIT Press.

Hochschild, A. (1983) *The Managed Heart*. Berkeley, CA: University of California Press.

Jackall, R. (1988) *Moral Mazes*. New York: Oxford University Press.

James, W. (1884) What is emotion? *Mind*, **9**, 188–205.

Jones, L. (1999) Smiling lessons end service with a scowl in Greenland. *The Guardian*, 23 October 1999, p. 21.

Kets de Vries, M.F.R (Ed.) (1991) *Organizations on the Couch: Clinical Perspectives on Organizational Behavior and Change*. San Francisco: Jossey Bass.

Kets de Vries, M.F.R. (1990) The organizational fool: Balancing a leader's hubris. *Human Relations*, **43**(8), 751–770.

Kets de Vries, M.F.R. & Miller, D. (1987) Interpreting organizational texts. *Journal of Management Studies*, **24**(3), 233–243.

Kunda, G. (1992) *Engineering Culture: Control and Commitment in a High-tech Corporation*. Philadelphia: Temple University Press.

Latour, B. (1986) The powers of association. In J. Law (Ed.) *Power, Action and Belief: A New Sociology of Knowledge*. London: Routledge and Kegan Paul.

Lazarus, R. (1980) Thoughts on the relations between cognition and emotion, *American Psychologist*, **37**, 1019–1024.

Leidner, R. (1999) Emotional labor in service work. *The Annals of the American Academy of Political and Social Science*, **561**, January, 81–95.

MacDonald, C.L. & Sirianni, C. (1996) *Working in the Service Economy*. Philadelphia: Temple University Press.

Mangham, I.L. (1986) *Power and Performance in Organizations*. Oxford: Blackwell.

Mintzberg, H. (1973) *The Nature of Managerial Work*. New York. Harper & Row.

Pinder, C.C. (1998) *Work Motivation in Organizational Behavior*. Englewood Cliffs, NJ: Prentice-Hall.

Ray, C.A. (1986) Corporate culture: The last frontier of control?. *Journal of Management Studies*, **23**(3), 287–297.

Reiter, E. (1996) *Making Fast Food: From the Frying Pan into the Fryer*. Montreal: McGill-Queen's University Press.

Ritzer, G. (1993) *The McDonaldization of Society*. Thousand Oaks, CA: Pine Forge.

Ritzer, G. (1998) *The McDonaldization Thesis*. London: Sage Publications.

Robbins, S.P. (1992) *Essentials of Organizational Behavior*. Englewood Cliffs, NJ: Prentice-Hall p. 6.

Robbins, S.P. (1998) *Organizational Behavior*. Englewood Cliffs, NJ: Prentice-Hall.

Rose, N. (1989) *Governing the Soul: The Shaping of the Private Self*. London: Routledge.

Schacter, S. & Singer, J. (1962) Cognitive, social and physiological determinants of emotional state. *Psychological Review*, **69**, 379–399.

Schermerhorn, J.R., Hunt, J.G., and Osborn, R.N. (2000) *Organizational Behavior*. New York: Wiley.

Schwartz H.S. (1987b) Anti-social actions of committed organizational participants: An existential psychoanalytic perspective. *Organization Studies*, **8**(4), 327–340.

Schwartz, H.S. (1987a) On the psychodynamics of organizational totalitarianism. *Journal of Management*, **13**(1), 45–54.

Schwartz, H.S. (1990) *Narcissistic Process and Corporate Decay: The Theory of the Organizational Ideal.* New York: New York University Press.

Stearns, P.Z. and Stearns, P.N. (1986) *Anger: The Struggle for Emotional Control in America's History.* Chicago: University of Chicago Press.

Sturdy, A.J. (1998) Customer care in a consumer society. *Organization*, **5**(1): 27–54.

Tannenbaum, A.S. (1968) *Control in Organizations.* New York: McGraw-Hill.

Terkel, S. (1975) *Working.* Harmondsworth, UK: Penguin.

Thoits, P.A. (1996) Managing the emotions of others. *Symbolic Interaction*, **19**(1), 85–110.

Van Maanen, J. (1988) *Tales of the Field.* Chicago: University of Chicago Press.

Van Maanen, J. (1991) The smile factory: Work at Disneyland. In P.J. Frost, L.F. Moore, M.R. Louis, C.C. Lundberg, & J. Martin (Eds) *Reframing Organizational Culture.* Newbury Park, CA: Sage Publications.

Van Maanen, J. & Kunda, G. (1989) "Real feelings": Emotional expression and organizational culture. *Research in Organizational Behavior*, **11**, 43–103.

Walby, S. (1989) *Patriarchy at Work.* Cambridge: Polity.

Wasserman, V., Rafaeli, A & Kluger, A. (2000) Aesthetic symbols as emotional cues. In S. Fineman (Ed.) *Emotion in Organizations*, 2nd ed. London: Sage Publications.

Watson, T. (1994) *In Search of Management.* London: Routledge.

Weber, M. (1946) *From Max Weber: Essays in Sociology.* New York: Oxford University Press.

Wharton, A. (1999) The psychosocial consequences of emotional labor. *The Annals of the American Academy of Political and Social Science*, **561**, January, 158–175.

Willmott. H. (1993) Strength is ignorance; slavery is freedom: managing culture in modern organizations. *Journal of Management Studies*, **30**(4), 515–552.

Zeidler, S. (1998) Don't have a nice day—workers protest smile rule. Los Angeles. Reuters, 16 November.

Zibart, E. (1997) *The Unofficial Disney Companion.* New York: Macmillan.

Part IV

Managing emotions in the workplace

Chapter 10

Helping individuals manage emotional responses

Rose Evison
Consultant, Pitlochry, Scotland

This chapter explores the ways individuals can manage emotional responses in their work situations, for the benefit of themselves and their organization. Strategies reviewed are those which can be awarely learned, and hence developed on and off the job. The development context is the organization, with interventions for facilitating individual learning, set within organizational development. The objectives for managing emotional responses are *the production and enhancement of emotional states associated with optimizing performance, and minimizing emotional states associated with performance decrements or health hazards.* The emphasis is on normal individuals in their everyday work situations. This approach considers managing emotions as embedded in tasks and performance, and integral to all work situations.

I write this chapter as an occupational and counselling psychologist with 25 years experience as an independent consultant in people development. Client organizations have included heavy industry, retail, financial, IT, local government, and helping professionals. Groups and individuals have varied from senior managers to clerks. For the past 15 years, I have integrated managing emotional responses into people-development programmes. When drawing on this experience, I use the word "participants" to describe people on my worksite programmes.

Emotions at Work. Edited by Roy Payne and Cary Cooper.
© 2001 by John Wiley & Sons, Ltd.

DEFINING EMOTIONAL RESPONSES

Affect researchers define *emotions* as "episodic, relatively short-term, biologically based patterns of perception, experience, physiology, action, and communication that occur in response to specific physical and social challenges and opportunities" (Keltner & Gross, 1999). Lists of emotions from different researchers overlap but are not identical.

Emotions are distinguished from *drives* and *moods*. Drives, such as hunger, regulate the internal operating conditions of the organism, whereas emotions regulate the individual's relation to the external environment. Moods are longer lasting, more generalized, affective states. Another distinction is between *state* emotion and *trait* emotion. Affective traits are defined as the general tendency to experience a given mood or emotion state over time, or across situations. Trait affect is associated with the development and progression of chronic disease (Mayne, 1999).

All emotional phenomena which impact on performance and health are potentially of interest. Gross (1999) calls this the *wider affective family*, which includes emotions, moods, *stress responses*, and *emotion episodes* such as worksite bullying. This chapter defines the wider affective family as including all emotionally linked responses. Such responses are detected as emotional thinking, feeling, and acting, along with body reactions like muscular tensions. Individuals apply managing strategies to emotional responses.

WHICH EMOTIONAL RESPONSES NEED MANAGING?

The notion that "rationality is good, emotions are bad" is entrenched in most organizational cultures, including management learning (Fineman, 1997). Despite this, management-development participants, encouraged to explore their experience of emotions at work, discover they have functional and dysfunctional emotional responses. *Functional emotional responses* (FERs) enhance job performance and *dysfunctional emotional responses* (DERs) interfere with job performance. Ostell (1996) suggests that emotional responses are dysfunctional when they have adverse effects on judgements, task performance, relations with others, and individual well-being. Negative and positive emotions both generate FERs and DERs.

DERs which are targeted in emotion management are those resulting from daily work hassles (Zohar, 1999): equipment malfunction, unscheduled change of task assignments, information difficulties, inappropriate behaviour of co-workers. Zohar showed that hassles' severity, as measured by expert ratings, predicts end-of-day mood, fatigue, and subjective workload, and also burnout.

Experts measure work hassles, but individuals spontaneously identify situations in which they produce DERs they wish to change. Categorizing DER experiences assists such identification. Three types are recognizable: *spillovers, intrusions, and rigidities*:

Spillover DERs are emotional responses aroused by one task which spill over into the next. Some jobs entail chronic spillover problems—physicians seeing a new patient every 5 minutes describe spillover problems graphically (Frost & King, 2000).

Intrusive DERs involve attention being taken up by extraneous negative events; memories from last week or future events anticipated.

Rigidity DERs are negative thoughts, feelings, behaviours, body symptoms which individuals recognize as not tied to one event, but recurring in similar situations (e.g. thoughts which are putdowns of self or others, anxious feelings in evaluative situations, shouts of rage over costly errors, tension headaches after meetings).

Rigidities are readily surfaced by asking participants, in a confidential, unevaluated activity, to list things they want to change about themselves. Most listed items are DERs the individuals have experienced for a long time, and have been unable to change despite wanting to. Although one emotional component is often salient, participant exploration shows rigidities are tightly linked complexes of thoughts, feelings, behaviours, and physiology. Everyone, even the most competent, has lots of them. They may be isolated DERs, multiple knots like sexist or racist behaviours, or attributes of individual character. See Stuart (1991) for work with managers in identifying and changing *stress characters*.

The DER categories enable participants to identify moods, negative thinking, out-of-control behaviour, and stress as dysfunctional emotional responses which interfere with performance and health, and need emotion management to change them.

DEFINING DER MANAGING STRATEGIES

A variety of terms relate to managing emotional responses: emotion regulation, affect regulation, mood management, stress management, coping strategies. Gross (1999) discusses *emotion regulation* as "the ways individuals influence which emotions they have, when they have them, and how they experience and express these emotions." Emotion regulation may be *automatic* or *controlled* and *conscious* or *unconscious*.

Emotion regulation addresses any of the major components of emotions: experiential, cognitive, behavioural, or physiological—not just subjectively experienced emotion (*feelings*), as in *affect regulation* studies (Parkinson & Totterdell, 1999). It overlaps with stress management and coping skills. This chapter emphasizes selected emotion-regulation processes: *strategies for managing DERs that improve performance without health hazards,* **and** *which can be awarely learned* *and intentionally applied.* Such processes will be referred to generally as emotion management, and specifically as Dysfunctional Emotional Response Management Strategies (DERMS).

EMOTION MANAGEMENT REPLACES STRESS MANAGEMENT

Emotions are basic-level, experiential human categories which are learned intuitively, and which conceptually link situations, thinking, feeling, and performance (Lakoff, 1987). Stress is a hypothetical concept developed from research, requiring detailed intellectual linking to individual experience. While stress symptoms are emotional effects, stress provides a limited view of emotional responses—one bearing an unknown relationship to experienced emotions. Detecting and measuring stress is done through emotional subcategories like physiological parameters, negative thinking, or feeling. Relating stress to organizational factors uses concepts superordinate to emotion, as in the Sparks & Cooper (1999) meta-analysis of work-strain research. Here *work control* and *work pressure* are the independent variables, and *mental* and *physical health* the dependent variables.

Stress-management programmes tend towards lifestyle interventions, assessed by mental and physical health measures. Organizational interventions are provided in a worksite context, but not embedded in work hassles and performance. Despite the increasing prominence of worksite problems the stress concept has not been fruitful in generating effective organizational interventions with individuals. Murphy (1996), reviewing worksite intervention research, notes a lack of progress since 1988 in addressing information gaps about interventions, and in assessing impacts on collateral effects like improved interpersonal relationships or self-efficacy.

Changing the paradigm from stress management to emotion management provides a stronger theoretical and practical base for interventions. Thus, the psychophysical model of emotion and health reviewed by Mayne (1999) "posits that emotional arousal which is not appropriate to environmental demands (either too little or too much) can damage health." DERMS minimize inappropriate emotional arousal—changing DERs into FERs. Emotion management is easier to learn, implement, and evaluate in worksites than stress management, because the relationships between situations, DERs, and performance are direct. The next section discusses the theory underlying DER generation, to act as a base for a taxonomy of DERMS.

THEORY RELEVANT TO MANAGING EMOTIONAL RESPONSES

An Integrative theory of emotions was first presented in writings on reciprocal-role counselling (Evison & Horobin, 1988), and related to strategies of managing emotions in organizations (Evison, 1988). The theory suggests emotions potentiate motivation and resources for interacting with the environment and surviving, adapting, and developing as individuals and groups. It fulfils the four interrelated elements of functional accounts of emotions (Keltner & Gross, 1999). Basic positive and negative emotions have different and complementary functions inbuilt by evolution. Positive emotions provide optimum conditions for goal-directed learning interactions with the environment. Negative emotions provide optimum conditions for immediate dealing with threats. Basic emotions interact with learning and socialization processes in families, schools, and work (Abe & Izard, 1999; Ashforth & Humphrey, 1995), producing the range of emotional phenomena evident in adults in the work place.

Positive affect emotions

These motivate ongoing mastery of the environment, nurturing of young, and solving long-range problems in living together. Positive emotions enable such goals by organizing maximum attentional and processing capacity, and providing access to the full range of experience and learning. This gives maximum choice over actions, and makes available mental and physical resources as needed. Three basic emotions, *interest*, *joy*, and *love*, motivate and reward exploration, mastery, and relating to others, respectively, because they are pleasurable activities. They blend through learning to produce more complex emotions. Izard (1991) gives detailed research.

Negative affect emotions

These motivate us to deal expeditiously with immediate physical or social threat, unhindered by aware decision making. Automatic processes, compellingly, make threatening stimuli the attentional focus, and provide rapid activation of physical resources oriented to actions specific to the type of threat detected. Acting to master, or escape from, threats is motivated by the pain of not acting. Action choices are limited to the learned repertoire of responses. Five basic emotions are distinguished by characteristic situations, by anatomical, physiological, and muscular activation, and by verbal and non-verbal expressive behaviours. These are *anger*, *fear*, *disgust*, *grief* (Ekman, 1992; Levenson, 1999), and *shame*, the latter facilitating survival through preservation of relationships (Scheff, 1997).

Learning under positive emotions is functional long term

Learning proceeds through experimenting, and using feedback to select from available options behaviours that maximize rewards through goal achievement. Such learning integrates with existing stores of experiences, is available to use behaviourally and symbolically, and can be modified as new situations occur. In contrast, learning under negative emotions is short-term functional but typically long-term dysfunctional. Different learning options produce different types of DERs.

Learning under negative emotions produces rigidities

Such learning is functional in that it occurs when actions minimize pain. Most such learning involves punishment by other people, physical or psychological, producing *conditioned responses—rigidities*, which are long-term dysfunctional.

Learning functional responses via punishment Such learning, occurring frequently in socialization, is less functional than the same learning under positive emotions, because it cannot readily be modified under new conditions. Socialization of shame expressiveness is a potent example as it forms the basis of destructive anger and conflict (Scheff, 1997).

Learning partially dysfunctional responses Holt (1965) observed children learn strategies of fooling the teacher to avoid punishment. This leaves children with DERs driving inadequate learning strategies. In research across five European countries, Evison (1990a) found that trainers' use of behaviours which were reminders of teacher putdowns was inversely correlated with ratings of learning facilitation.

Learning dysfunctional responses Experiments have demonstrated self- or other punitive behaviour readily occurs under punishment conditions (e.g. Martin, 1972; Stone & Hokanson, 1969). In mild forms, this shows in self-putdown and sarcastic DERs—ubiquitous in most organizations.

Learning when no response reduces pain If all responses fail to reduce pain, the inadequate responses occurring when punishment ceases become conditioned. The paradigmatic case is a child victimized by an adult. With strong pain, victims internalize the aggressor's actions as well as their own. When children become adults, they can be triggered into the aggressive role or the victim role. Examples are bullying, sexism, racism, and authoritarian–submissive behaviour in hierarchies. *DERMS facilitate unlearning of the conditioned rigidities.*

Spillovers arise from unmastered threats

When actions to remove threat are unsuccessful but the threat ceases, individuals are left with bodily readiness for action, which only slowly subsides. Subjectively this is paralleled by lingering negative feelings and thoughts. Further emotional responses, triggered before achieving complete reset, build up emotional arousal

(Scheff, 1983) needing even more time to reset. This process constitutes a mechanism for spillovers and for building up stress effects. *DERMS facilitate rapid return to positive emotions.*

Intrusions arise from painful memories

Memories of physical or psychological pain are stored along with memories of situations that produced the pain. Such *painful memories* mean reminders of such unsolved problems are appraised as threat, *restimulating* negative emotions in the present. Recent negative events are highly likely to restimulate DERs as current responses, experienced as intrusions. Thinking about such events triggers emotional pain; hence, problem solving is difficult. *DERMS facilitate maintenance of positive emotions in the presence of restimulations.*

Resets of DERs to positive emotions occur with mastery

The autonomic nervous system operates emotion-supporting processes via the sympathetic and parasympathetic subsystems. "The sympathetic system can be characterised as geared to energy mobilisation and to effective dealing with the environment; the parasympathetic system can be seen as geared to establishing and conserving energy reserves" (Frijda, 1986). The balance between the two is constantly changing. There is sympathetic dominance when arousal is needed for intentional muscular activity, as in many negative emotions, excited activities, and energetic skilled performance as in sports. There is parasympathetic dominance under conditions of relaxed positive emotions, like interest and happiness, and under conditions of helplessness, such as sullen resignation and depressive states.

When threats are mastered, the parasympathetic system acts to conserve energy resources by actively counteracting the sympathetic system effects, reducing heart rate, blood pressure, body temperature, and changing EEG—experienced as the emotion of joy, see Seligman (1975, p. 98). *Thus perceived absence of threat is the prime condition for activating parasympathetic reset of redundant emotional arousal.*

Reset to positive emotions occurs when attention focuses on positive experiences

After fear-related arousal, subjects shown positive emotional stimuli returned to cardiovascular baseline faster than subjects shown neutral or negative stimuli (Levenson, 1999). Levenson discusses this as the *undoing* function of positive emotions. Integrative theory suggests that attentional focus on positive experience signals an absence of current threat, so activates the parasympathetic system. *Using the resetting power of positive experiences is a major DERMS.*

Reset to positive emotions can occur after failure experiences

Redundant emotional arousal also occurs after surviving failure experiences. It is plausible that perception of absence of threat would potentiate parasympathetic reset to positive emotions after failures. This, indeed, occurs, with reset processes specific to each basic emotion, storming for anger, shaking for fear, retching for disgust, crying for grief, and laughing for shame. When observed in children, they are followed by signs of positive emotions. They are rarer in adults, as socialization of emotional expressiveness turns them into sources of shame, and hence ever-present threats. Slow reset of redundant emotional arousal occurs when the natural emotionally expressive processes have been interfered with by punishment. *DERMS facilitate disinhibition of natural reset processes.*

Natural reset processes can be used for unlearning

The term *cathartic reset* is used for processes resetting redundant, emotionally aroused body/mind states to relaxed, alert positive states. Cathartic reset not only resets spillovers rapidly, but can also be used for unlearning the restimulated DERs of intrusions and rigidities. Unlearning requires re-establishing of the reset conditions; namely, restimulation of the original basic emotional response plus awareness of present safety from threat. These conditions are known as *aesthetic* or *optimal distance* (Scheff, 1981) or *balance of attention* (Evison & Horobin, 1988). The latter list detailed methods for achieving reset. After cathartic reset, the positive emotion state provides unpainful access to the failure experiences, so facilitating problem solving—and spontaneous reappraisal of emotion-eliciting stimuli occurs. *Painful memories become memories of pain—an unlearning and relearning process.*

Evidence for cathartic reset

For an emotion theory that incorporates cathartic reset, see Scheff & Bushnell (1984). Research evidence that catharsis is associated with good therapy outcomes is provided by Symonds (1954) and Pierce, Nichols, and DuBrin (1983). A carefully controlled study on cathartic reset (Karle, Corriere, & Hart, 1973) showed initial boosts in blood pressure, pulse, and body temperature were followed by significant drops; these changes, plus EEG changes, corresponded to moving into a rest state while being awake and alert. Fry (1994) summarized much research on mirthful laughter, showing beneficial effects on health. He concluded these arose because an initial sympathetic system boost was followed by parasympathetic activation, with a drop in vital signs often to below the pre-laughter baseline, plus an immune-system boost lasting several hours.

This *stimulation–relaxation* pattern identified by Fry is typical of cathartic reset of all kinds. He notes that "subsequent to the relaxation phase, greater social and psychological animation frequently persists" and "This combination of relaxation and heightened animation follows a pattern indicated in Freud's catharsis theory of humor."

Catharsis is controversial

Efforts to test the cathartic hypothesis have sometimes concluded it was ineffective or dangerous (Bushman, Baumeister, & Stack, 1999). Such experiments have equated catharsis with acting aggressively, and, moreover, fail to establish non-threatening conditions for subjects. Unsurprisingly, encouragement to commit aggressive acts increases rather than decreases hostility towards a target. Bushman also used a hydraulic model of anger catharsis, although Frijda (1986) noted the release of pent-up energy was an outdated metaphor. Lack of understanding of necessary conditions for catharsis also confuses interpretation of experiments concerned with crying (Gross, Fredrickson, & Levenson, 1994). *Cathartic reset forms a basis for DERMS used in organizational development.*

A TAXONOMY OF DERMS

Figure 10.1 adopts the viewpoint of an individual wanting to use DERMS, showing the embedding of DERs and DERMS in performance situations. Some situations are individually defined, like "dealing with a difficult person", and some organizationally defined, like "meetings" or "dealing with customers". Performance behaviour is usually a mixture of DERs and FERs. Managing emotions is about changing DERs into FERs—changing rigid mode responses into flexible mode responses. Changes may be temporary using changing situations or more permanent using methods which result in complete reappraisal of *triggering stimuli.*

Such reappraisal may be achieved by any of the three main DERMS—changing situations, changing DERs, changing performance—as change in one arena results in changes in the others. This basic change strategy framework is one I first used in courses for middle management in Dairy Crest 1982–1985. Since DER-triggering stimuli may be external or internal events (Izard, 1993),

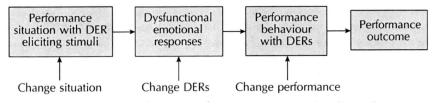

Figure 10.1 Dysfunctional Emotional Responses Managing Strategies

Changing situations	

Problem solving Avoiding having to deal with situations where DERs are elicited.
   Modifying the physical environment to reduce DERs.
   Modifying systems and working practices to reduce DERs.
	Using positive experiences Selectively paying attention to positive aspects of a situation or to positive images.
	
	Using rational reappraisal Using experiences that enable situation reappraisal to reduce triggering of DERs.

Changing DERs	
Disinhibiting emotional controls Using activities that disinhibit emotional controls and release expressive behaviour, using cathartic reset to positive emotions.	**Using humorous reframing** Using humorous reframing of triggering stimuli producing mirthful laughter to provide cathartic reset to positive emotions.
Changing performance	
Increasing job skills Reducing DERs in the relevant tasks. Includes interpersonal skills, decision making, and time management.	**Increasing emotional resilience** Increasing self-efficacy to maintain flexible thinking when problems and difficulties crop up.

Figure 10.2   A taxonomy of DERMS

DERMS can also operate on either external or internal stimuli. This gives the six DERMS categories shown in Figure 10.2.

DERMS categories can be compared with Gross's (1999) five types of emotion-regulatory processes, targeting different points of the emotion-generative process. While there is overlap, the two schemes are not identical—changing DERs does not appear on Gross's list. The next section considers these missing DERMS in more detail.

LINKING EMOTION THEORY TO CHANGING DERs

Feelings labels provide a means of mapping emotional responses onto dimensions of positive affectivity, negative affectivity, and general arousal, as in Figure 10.3. Functional and dysfunctional emotional responses are a dichotomous third dimension, shown in separate columns. Emotional responses are grouped into categories representing different relationships between feeling, thinking, and acting. These categories cover areas of the map, not specific points on the dimensions. The gap between positive and negative affectivity emphasizes they are different dimensions—there is no neutral zone. Neutral affective states are artefacts of narrow definitions of emotional responses—introspection shows many

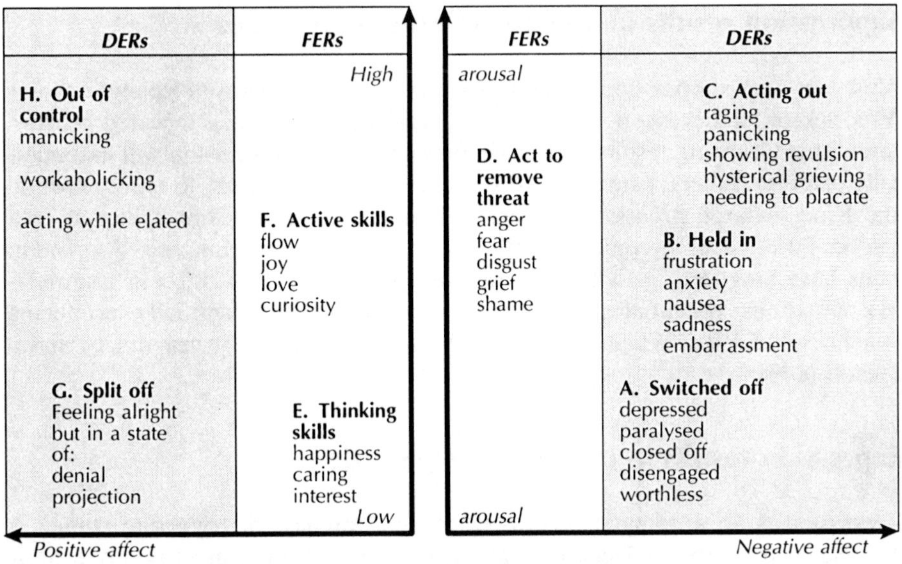

DERs	FERs	FERs	DERs
	High	*arousal*	
H. Out of control manicking workaholicking acting while elated	**F. Active skills** flow joy love curiosity	**D. Act to remove threat** anger fear disgust grief shame	**C. Acting out** raging panicking showing revulsion hysterical grieving needing to placate **B. Held in** frustration anxiety nausea sadness embarrassment
G. Split off Feeling alright but in a state of: denial projection	**E. Thinking skills** happiness caring interest *Low*	*arousal*	**A. Switched off** depressed paralysed closed off disengaged worthless

Positive affect   Negative affect

Figure 10.3 Relationships between feeling, thinking, and acting

fleeting negative thoughts and transient affects, and minor DERs, which affect performance.

Feelings are placed where an average person in the culture experiences them. This is not precise because of individual and cultural differences. An illustrative selection of feelings is shown—representing the normal range of emotional states, not clinical diagnostic syndromes. Connections between thinking, feeling, and acting vary:

- positive FERs have total choice of action with flexible connections;
- negative FERs have limited choice of actions, with narrow ranges of flexibility of connections;
- DERs, positive and negative, have no choice of actions, and rigid connections.

DERMS change DERs into FERs

The objective is to move to zone E—the relaxed alert state with minimum physiological arousal, from which maximum resources can be devoted to chosen goals. Moving to zone E from different starting points can be represented by arrows on the "feelings map" (Evison & Horobin, 1988). This map is used with participants, to facilitate DERM selection. The map can also be used to show all kinds of therapeutic change processes (Evison, 1990b). Strategies addressed by emotion-regulation research—*suppression, repression, reappraisal, rumination* (Gross, 1999)—will be discussed as movements over the map. These all appear to be *DER transformations* (i.e. they substitute one form of DER for another).

Suppression results in autonomic arousal penalties

With conscious suppression of emotional responses, awareness of feelings remains (Fredrickson & Levenson, 1998). When such suppression is a repeated process, conditioned learning results and mechanisms for pain suppression will automatically operate. Generalization of DER-triggering stimuli occurs, to reduce arousal and hence enlarge processing capacity. This process transforms spillovers into held-in DERs: fear becomes anxiety, anger becomes irritation, etc. Short-term gains have long-term penalties. Continuing emotional suppression in restimulative situations potentiates continuing pain reduction, eventually producing switched-off DERs. When extreme, such low-arousal, highly generalized states constitute *burnout*.

Repression results in performance penalties

Repression is an automatic process whereby awareness of triggering stimuli is dissociated from their effects. Individuals lack feelings and direct bodily expression of the DER, but have autonomic arousal. The pain-reduction mechanisms operate to reduce this, so evidence of negative DERs is absent, producing dissociated positive DERs. Clinical and experimental work on repression is discussed by Karon and Widener (1999). They suggest traumas are remembered when people can learn to avoid them and repression operates when traumatic events are unavoidable. However, processing capacity is needed to keep material repressed, so avoidance of restimulating situations means lowered performance in affected areas of life.

Reappraisal may be repression

Gross (1998), studying reappraisal, found instructions to keep a "detached and unemotional attitude" while watching a disgusting film resulted in lower levels of self-reported feelings and objectively observed expressiveness, but not of physiological responses, compared to watching without instructions (other experimenters have similar findings). Disgust is a basic emotion, and probably strong, disgusting stimuli cannot be reappraised. To carry out "distancing" instructions, subjects dissociate, producing the "repressive" pattern of results. Reappraisals of this "distancing" kind occur in the socialization of doctors and nurses (Smith & Kleinman, 1989) and result in health hazards and long-term loss of sensitivity to feelings.

Rumination is failed emotion regulation

Rumination is widely described as conscious and controlled. However, it leads to deterioration in performance and increase in physiological stress indicators, with higher levels of dispositional rumination leading to greater likelihood of developing depressive symptoms (Gross, 1999). Rumination consists of unintentional intrusive DERs, which occur when individuals are paying attention to current problems, leading to switched-off DERs when prolonged.

DERMS are processes for moving into zone E

Possibilities are (1) switching to zone E directly using positive experiences, relaxation, meditation or (2) using cathartic reset—moving from zones A, B, or C to experiencing zone-D emotions, along with experiencing safety from threats (i.e. some attention in positive FERs). Effective DERMS vary with DER characteristics:

- *A. Switched-off DERs* characteristically present as generalized negative thinking, resistant to efforts to change attentional focus (Murphy et al., 1999). Direct switching to FERs by focusing on positive experiences, or reappraising, is very difficult. Adding physical energy, to transform to held-in DERs, makes cathartic-reset DERMS available. Laughter increases arousal, so reset via laughter is effective.
- *B. Held-in DERs* are associated with stress feelings, thoughts, and muscular tensions from controlling the impulses to action. Switching directly into FERs is often possible, to get on with tasks effectively. To use cathartic reset, DERMS that add arousal and disinhibit tensions are effective (see the section entitled Disinhibiting emotional controls on p. 256).
- *C. Acting-out DERs* present as destructive behaviour that fully occupies attention. Direct switching to FERs is very difficult though possible, as when counting to ten before saying anything when suddenly enraged. Effective cathartic-reset DERMS reduce arousal and gain attention to present safety—often needs unambiguously supportive interruption of the behaviour.
- *G. Split-off DERs* are the result of repressive processes, keeping negative feelings and thoughts out of awareness. Individuals, being unaware they have these DERs, are not motivated to change. The repressed negative DERs need tackling, which falls outside the scope of this chapter.
- *H. Out-of-control DERs* have redundant arousal, reducing processing capacity and hindering focusing of attention. This interferes with thinking tasks (e.g. Sinclair (1988) found mild elation interfered with an appraisal task). Arousal reducing DERMS are effective (see the section entitled Using positive experiences on p. 254). Cathartic reset is not possible for positive emotions.

The next sections will discuss specific DERMS. Problem solving and increasing job skills strategies are familiar so not discussed. Cathartic-reset strategies are limited to practical methods found useful in organizational contexts. Following the model in Figure 10.1, experimental research quoted as supporting particular DERMS uses measurements of performance change in real task situations.

USING POSITIVE EXPERIENCES

Isen and Baron (1991), reviewing research in everyday and worksite settings, show that inducing positive affect by small everyday experiences, in everyday situations, with unaware subjects, produces major effects on interpersonal and cognitive skills. Subjects with induced positive affect are more able than controls to: be cognitively flexible; integrate information; generate alternatives; offer help to others; seek win–win negotiating solutions; and are less likely to do harm to themselves or others. Similarly, Estrada, Isen, & Young (1997) showed distorted or rigid thinking in professional tasks was less likely after induced positive affect. Recalling positive images also has supportive evidence:

- Schwartz, Fair, Salt, Mandel, & Klerman (1976) found electromyography of forehead muscles registered relaxation during happy imagery.
- Isen and Baron (1991) cite three studies where positive affect mitigated work-related stress: use of calm, modulated voice tone; imagining pleasant and calm scenes; building enjoyable activities into schedules.
- Martin, Moritz, & Hall (1999) note five studies with athletes using positive images to reduce physiological arousal (e.g. imagining yourself in a favourite, relaxing place).

Using positive experiences in worksites can be done in many ways: positive memories; positive images; pleasant environments; pleasurable activities; positive strokes from others. However, rapid resetting of spillovers or intrusions at work needs individuals learning to reliably pay concentrated attention.

Paying concentrated attention to positive memories

The strategy involves listing positive memories for 2–3 minutes, moving quickly from one to another to prevent intrusions. Learning is done by listing aloud in reciprocal role pairs (RRPs) with a non-intervening, non-judgemental partner (see my activities "Increasing positive feelings", "Supportive pairs introductions" and "Recent enjoyments" in Kirby, 1993). Increasing skill potentiates availability from increasingly negative feelings. Finding *random pleasant memories* is the easiest topic. However, skills need to progress to finding positives embedded in difficult situations to change mood in relating to the difficulties.

Even with naive participants, listing positive memories produces facial changes corresponding to reported increases in positive feelings in 90% of participants. When participants rate positive and negative feelings before and after 3 minutes of listing "random pleasant memories", increases in positive feelings and decreases in negative feelings are significant (Evison, unpublished research).

Developing conditioned positive associations

This strategy involves building a personal, positive image of yourself, anchored to a place providing positive sensory experiences of all kinds. Moving between this *special place* and difficult situations is imaged. Special-place positive feelings, and individuals' strengths and skills, are associated with touching a real object that can be carried around, or that exists in a working environment subject to crises. The image and associated positive emotions can be accessed via touch in difficult situations. This approach was developed and applied by Sargent with nuclear power plant engineers (Blum & Sargent, 1980).

USING RATIONAL REAPPRAISAL

Reappraisal means modifying the evaluation of situations to eliminate triggering of DERs. Reappraisal is associated with cognitive methods for changing negative thinking. However, "despite its wide currency, even the hypothesis that cognitive strategies may be used to decrease negative emotion ... has a surprisingly modest empirical foundation" (Gross, 1999).

Bevington (1999) trained work groups using Beck's methods for changing negative attributions. Improved handling of team outputs was found. However, although strength of belief in negative thoughts dropped, associated negative feelings showed much less change. Such *cognitive substitution* training appears unsatisfactory in emotion management. Given control groups had no training, successes can be attributed to a Pygmalion effect inducing greater application to the work tasks involved, with reinforcement from better performance. This seems an inappropriate application of clinical methods to organizations having fewer payoffs than working with job skills and effective emotion management.

The usual target of cognitive strategies is rigid negative thinking. This can comprise blinkers of past successes or straightjackets of past failures. Blinkers are functional learning that becomes dysfunctional when situations change, and which becomes rigid under stressful conditions (Nystrom & Starbuck, 1984). Straightjackets are rigidities. Cowen (1952) illustrated these two types in problem-solving experiments. Blinkers can be unlearned if safe learning conditions are provided, as demonstrated in the Amway Company (Pratt & Barnett, 1997). Rigidities cannot be modified by normal learning processes, the unlearning needs different conditions—*therapeutic change* rather than *educational change* as described by Evison (1994) (see the section entitled Humorous reframing on p. 257 for organizational methods).

Rational reappraisal is reframing of situations. For successful reframing individuals need:

- personal experience which supports the new frame of reference;
- trust in the person presenting the new frame;
- new successful experience using the new frame.

Linking new experiences to new frames of reference is a normal part of organizational training. New experiences need supplying if they are not in participants' repertoires. Experiencing successful behaviour needs to be part of the training— *attitudes change in line with successful behaviour*.

Applying this to training for using emotion-management strategies, the experience that supports new frames of reference is either surfaced by participants or provided by development activities. Two crucial reframings are:

- some emotions are functional and others are dysfunctional;
- everyone has rigid responses, run by emotions interfering with performance.

Such reframings are reinforced, and embedded in participants' jobs, by activities in which participants experience emotion-management successes using strategies that can be used on the job.

DISINHIBITING EMOTIONAL CONTROLS

Gross (1998) showed that when emotion is suppressed rather than expressed sympathetic autonomic tone is elevated. He linked this to research showing ongoing emotional suppression is associated with hypertension and coronary artery disease. Typical socialization in organizations reinforces suppression of negative emotional expression. Fortunately, there is folk wisdom which says letting out feelings is healthy. Crying, laughing, and venting regularly appear in studies of coping strategies and affect regulation research (Parkinson & Totterdell, 1999). However, in our anti-cathartic culture, few people understand cathartic-reset conditions, so such strategies frequently fail.

Temporary disinhibition to deal with spillovers and intrusions is achieved by shaking or stretching to loosen muscle tensions. Sighing, groaning, and yawning are also helpful techniques (see my activity "Active relaxation" in Kirby, 1993). More permanent results with intrusions can be achieved by cathartic reset.

Writing is a disinhibition strategy, as it anchors people to a safe present while they re-experience a past event, providing optimum distance possibilities and hence cathartic reset. A meta-review by Smyth (1998) of *written emotional expression* research shows that writing about traumatic life events improves health indices. The prevailing "inhibition" theory suggests failure to confront traumatic events requires physiological effort, and results in long-term cumulative stress

(Pennebaker & Beall, 1996). Duncan and Gidron (1999), who use a cathartic-reset model, have investigated how to minimize hazards and maximize benefits, and have developed a promising written guided-disclosure protocol.

Spera, Buhrfeind, & Pennebaker (1994) found that people who wrote about their feelings concerning losing their jobs were more likely to secure re-employment than were controls. As such writing takes only 15 minutes a day for 3 to 5 days, it could prove valuable for helping people deal with incidents of worksite violence. Moreover, research with police and firefighters shows priming effects of previous violent experiences on incidence of post-traumatic stress—so expressive writing during induction training would hopefully reduce trauma frequency.

Self-reflective therapeutic writing has been used for ten years to train doctors, nurses, and counsellors—to use for themselves and to offer to patients (Bolton 1999a). Bolton found that individual writing, with group sharing as an option, enhances possibilities of processing negative experiences. "Writing is a staged process involving reading, redrafting, editing, and sharing only when the writer is ready ... so the writer can afford to say more to the silent page" (Bolton, 1999b). Explicit examples of catharsis are mentioned. The use of professional self-reflecting writing in organizations has possibilities for integrating managing emotions with real tasks.

I teach participants to vent safely and successfully, to deal with spillovers on the job, and with intrusions off the job. A typical strategy is to think of a recent negative incident, and seek to express key negative thoughts in a forcefully spoken sentence, with vigorous body movements helping to express the feelings (working in a safe place, not with people causing the upset). For example, after being on the receiving end of malicious questions in a meeting, the person might be saying "You insensitive bastards". Processes are learned in RRPs, with a coach role to encourage disinhibition and interrupt aggressive acting out. Training courses set up safe conditions, and teach participants the observational and experiential differences between cathartic reset and acting out. Reinforcement of aggression is avoided by using actions that do not duplicate aggressive ones (e.g. tearing up cardboard boxes or slapping a soft surface with both hands simultaneously).

USING HUMOROUS REFRAMING

Mirthful laughter has beneficial effects, regardless of the laughter's cause (Fry, 1994). Health services have utilized health-promoting laughter by introducing clowns, laughter rooms, and laughter trolleys (Buxman, 1991). These interventions use laughter as a therapeutic treatment, which appears equally applicable in stress management. Some organizational consultants are using laughter to facilitate creative thinking.

The interpersonal effects of laughter are also relevant in worksites. Retzinger (1991) in her videotaped study of marital quarrels found laughter, following being shamed, was associated with positive outcomes for the relationship, as was sharing of feelings. Aggression or hiding were the alternative responses, which were associated with destructive conflict. This is congruent with laughter being the cathartic reset of shame, explaining the findings that mirthful laughter provides benefits in easing tensions and building respect between people. There are also implications for conflict management in organizations.

A naturalistic study of Air Training Corps leaders showed intelligence, attractiveness, and humour correlated with transformational leadership, with $r = 0.88$ for sense of humour the highest (Taylor & Brown, 1999). While humour is usually considered a special talent, Foot (1996) considers it a social skill that can be encouraged and learned.

Humorous reframing as a DERMS is based on individuals producing laughter in work tasks, to tackle negative thinking and encourage creativity. Lefcourt and Martin (1986) experimentally studied the moderating effects of humour on the relation of negative life events to mood-disturbance measures. Scales and tasks measuring *production of humour* under stress were associated with the least mood disturbance.

A major theme in humour research is that laughter results from incongruity. Nerhardt described humorists as skilled in producing rapid switches in frames of reference, allowing listeners to distance themselves from the immediate threat of a problem, and therefore to reduce the often paralysing feelings of anxiety (Foot, 1996) (cf. Scheff's "optimum distance" for producing cathartic reset). Humorous reframing uses incongruity to enable individuals to laugh about their negative thoughts, feelings, and personal attributes. I have taught humorous reframing for many years for worksite use.

Encouraging laughing instead of getting stuck

This eases anxieties and builds trust in groups, and is part of changing routinely judgmental cultures into supportive ones. Changing behaviour in public settings is usually embarrassing and shaming. Providing a group with humorous reframing tools, such as *Yippee, a mistake!* facilitates change.

Developing humorous reframing

This involves two types of skills:

- producing effective reframings—many methods help here (e.g. ridiculous opposites, boasting about inadequacies);
- working with reframings to produce laughter—a loud cheerful stating of a reframing is needed to embody it, while retaining awareness of the DER being worked on.

Pairs and group activities are used for learning, with participants producing negative thinking related to work tasks—about themselves, others, or situations. This work imports directly into worksite situations using reframings already practised, along with methods for working with new negative thoughts.

INCREASING EMOTIONAL RESILIENCE

Emotional resilience is the ability to handle disconfirming experiences with minimum reduction in flexible thinking and acting. Emotional resilience equates to self-efficacy. Increasing any aspect of self-efficacy such as magnitude, strength, or generality improves performance (Smith, 1999). The term *affirmational resources* (Steele, Spencer, & Lynch, 1993) will be used to refer to the total effects of these self-efficacy factors. Research has established significant performance differences between individuals who are high and low on self-efficacy. High self-efficacy individuals concentrate more on tasks, spend more time working at overcoming problems, and so achieve more, reinforcing their self-efficacy (Vrugt, 1996). Increasing self-efficacy increases application to tasks and overcoming problems. Affirmational resources may be increased by:

Using an outside expert. When success potential is directly or indirectly affirmed, self-expectancy and objectively measured performance increase significantly— Pygmalion and Galatea effects (Eden & Ravid, 1982).

Using "personal example models". A personal-example model (Eden & Kinnar, 1991) is someone who is already successful at a task or career that other individuals aspire to, *and* who emphasizes to the aspiring others that they have the same capabilities, and can successfully overcome learning difficulties, and move from their current position to success following the models example. Eden and Kinnar compared the effectiveness of the same people acting as personal-example models with experimental groups, and factual information sources for control groups in a real-life situation of encouraging volunteering for special military service units. The personal-example modelling was more effective, particularly with lower self-efficacy individuals.

Using affirmational resources from another life area. Steele et al. (1993) reviewed studies which showed that irrelevant affirmational resources, if immediately available, can diminish effects of disconfirming experiences, and demonstrated this finding in their own experiments.

Using Motivational General Mastery [MG-M] imagery. A key experiment by Feltz and Riessinger showed that participants instructed to use MG-M imagery had higher and stronger self-efficacy expectations for their sporting performance than non-imaging participants (Martin et al., 1999). Martin and Hall, studying golf training, found such effects only occur with MG-M imagery, not other types of performance imagery, and were mediated through higher self-expectations and more practice time (Martin et al., 1999).

"*Taking ownership*" *of mastery experiences.* Smith and Nye compared cognitive–
affective stress-management training to stress inoculation. The former was
equally effective in reducing test anxiety and general trait anxiety; significantly
more effective in increasing general self-efficacy; and uniquely effective in fos-
tering significant shifts towards an internal locus of control (taking ownership)
(Smith, 1999). Smith suggests that athletes need facilitating to *take ownership*
of their coping skills and achievement, and he gives examples of facilitative
statements such as "You ought to feel some real pride in the way you've
worked to master these skills".

Strengthening affirmational resources, increasing access to them when needed,
and adding to them by taking ownership of daily achievements are collectively
termed *working from strengths.* Learning is needed to enable individuals to
develop skills for the worksite—to assemble their affirmational resources before
starting new tasks or tackling difficulties, and to note achievements as reinforcing
and adding to resources. Learning activities use RRPs with listing aloud.
Examples: *My strengths and skills*; *My recent achievements.* Such activities are
much harder than listing positive experiences, as many shaming rigidities intrude
(e.g. "Musn't boast" or "I'm inadequate"). These rigidities are dealt with by
encouraging lots of laughter.
    The interpersonal environment is crucial in confirming or disconfirming affir-
mational resources, so training and worksite environments need affirming cultures
to support change. Participants typically require reframing of learning and
achievements to include all steps forward, however small, and skill development
in appropriate interpersonal behaviours.

MANAGING DERs IN LEARNING SITUATIONS

Spillovers, intrusions, and rigidities all occur in learning situations, so individual
management of emotions is necessary for learning. Furthermore, most organizational learning situations involve groups whose members interfere with each
other's learning, often providing strong reinforcement for shame DERs. "Evaluation apprehension is thought to cause group members to censor their performance
so as to adhere to group norms" (Craig & Kelly, 1999). This apprehension
provides ever-present DERs.
    Under stressful conditions, group members direct attentional resources
inwardly rather than outwardly—producing narrowing of group attention and
degrading of group thinking. Such effects are mitigated by working interdependently (Driskell, Salas, & Johnston, 1999). Although training courses are not
work teams, high levels of outward attention and positive affect are required
for sharing of experiences and linking these to new frameworks.
    Many interventions which help individuals manage emotions will be learned on
training courses, providing an immediate context for participants to practise what

they are learning. Facilitation of adult learning by trainers correlates with high ratings of empathy, genuineness, success promotion, respect, student involvement (Aspy & Roebuck, 1976). Evison (1990a) and Evison and Lindley (1991) showed high-rated trainers had high ratios of positive relating behaviours (showing respect, affirming learning abilities, appreciating achievements) to negative relating behaviours (using putdowns, evaluating, using threat reminders).

George (1996) argues that high positive *work group affective tone* impacts positively on team mental models, decision making, prosocial behaviour, withdrawal behaviours, and group-member well-being. I have used the strategy of setting up supportive learning groups with high positive affective tone, joint responsibility for climate, and interdependent learning activities in development courses since 1982. A crucial element is having the group opt into a supportive learning contract to maximize positive emotions. Participants agree to:

- set themselves challenging learning goals;
- support other people's learning;
- avoid putdowns and negative judgements of others and self;
- keep all personal information confidential;
- use humorous reframing to defuse the negative effects of contract infringements and training errors.

A second element is RRPs work, with participants alternating between doing their own work and a coaching role (Gray, 1999). This promotes taking ownership of their own work and achievements, and increases general self-efficacy by promoting the development of *inner coaches*. A third component is developing skills in positive relating behaviours (Evison, 1990c). This approach has participants taking responsibility for affective climate and facilitative group behaviour—turning the training group into a team whose task is to maximize everyone's learning.

Synectics has a similar approach, which has been applied in training and team environments in organizations for many years to increase creativity and innovation. Users are clear about which positive and negative behaviours facilitate supportive climates, and individual ownership of problems is promoted (Ceserani & Greatwood, 1995).

The above models of worksite training cultures differ markedly from the favoured group life-cycle model: forming, storming, norming, performing, adjourning (Dainow, 1998).

IMPLICATIONS FOR EMOTION MANAGEMENT INTERVENTIONS

Emotion management in organizations is a more fruitful paradigm than stress management. This does not imply throwing out stress management *in toto*, rather subjecting it to critical assessment from the viewpoint of the new paradigm. Research is needed into emotion-management strategies and interventions that can effectively facilitate individuals managing emotions in organizations. Some tentative conclusions.

Increasing job skills has a double payoff

Bruning and Frew (1985) compared the physiological effects of exercise, meditation training, and management-skills training (goal setting, time management, conflict resolution, dealing with people). Whilst all three interventions led to improved physiological indicators, management-skills training was clearly the best option. Given job skills improve performance along with health; assessing whether more job skills would lead to fewer DERs seems the first requirement in selecting interventions. Research studies evaluating emotion-management interventions need to include a developing-job-skills control group.

Using positive experiences is cost effective

Relaxation and meditation are known to have beneficial effects (Murphy, 1996). However, learning to use positive experiences has larger physiological and psychological effects in a shorter time. Moreover, it is easier to integrate with daily work, both to move out of spillovers and to maximize thinking skills. Additionally, sharing of positive experiences in work groups builds trust and better relationships.

Increasing emotional resilience increases payoffs

Interventions incorporating self-efficacy activities have more lasting effects than similar programmes that do not integrate self-efficacy aims. Vrugt (1996) compares an exemplary self-efficacy programme with otherwise similar cognitive–behavioural programmes. Similarly, Caplan, Vinokur, Price, and van Ryn (1989), using self-efficacy training with unemployed groups, showed the job-seeking self-efficacy of those still unemployed after 4 months was higher than controls; whereas Proudfoot, Guest, Carson, Dunn, and Gray (1997), using cognitive–behavioural training (CBT) with unemployed groups without self-efficacy components, found the benefits of the training had dissipated for those CBT and social support group trainees still unemployed after 3 months.

Adding changing-DERs strategies increases payoffs

Integrating rapid reset strategies with other DERMS increases payoffs (e.g. using bi-modal activities (Evison, 1994), integrating unlearning and learning, as in *bi-modal critical incident role plays*). Participants select a situation they will encounter in the near future, decide on the crux where they usually behave inadequately, and move between rehearsing what to say, in one place, and disinhibiting the interfering negative thoughts and feelings, in a separate place. Disinhibition is followed by affirming their own competence, and then moving back to rehearsal. Movement between rehearsal (learning) and disinhibition (unlearning) modes is rapid, and noticeable skills change occurs with each cycle. Mastery imagery is automatically developed, and keyed to a relaxed alert body posture. Such activities, embedded in real situations, lend themselves to evaluation research that includes performance changes.

Organizational theory and methodologies are mandatory

For maximum impact on organizations, emotion management needs separating from clinical theory and practice—from stress management, CBT, and cognitive–analytical therapy (CAT) as used by Walsh (1997). Models, vocabulary, and methodologies need to be naturalized into organizational contexts. For example, calling rigid mode responses *blocks* and changing DERs *block-breaking* provides a basis for acceptable models applicable to all worksite situations. Using natural observational categories for diagnoses, and combining DERMS with skill-learning methodologies, needs training but does not require therapy skills (Evison, 1990c). I have already developed organizational trainers to integrate emotion-management activities into routine training, replacing the need for clinical practitioners.

Organizational integration is required

Emotion management is for everyone at a worksite and is relevant to all job and task skills, so needs embedding in all change processes, not restricted to replacing stress-management courses. Such replacement training, covering all the main DERMS can be useful (for such activities in a stress-management context see Evison, 1986). A recent course developed by me showed positive changes on the occupational stress inventory (Gray, 1999). However, this approach confines emotion management within a psychopathology model likely to minimize useful impact on organizations.

Integration will be more successful if all types of training courses include identification of blocks and use of appropriate DERMS. Such courses have been run in organizations by me in assertiveness, coaching, counselling, and trainer skills, and in several management-development variants.

Implications for emotion-management research

Assessment of appropriateness of emotion-management interventions must take organizational systems, individual skills, and DERs into account. Research needs to compare before-and-after task performance, and changes in DERs, using repeated measurements on individuals, not cross-sectional data gathering. Non-intrusive physiological measurements like saliva or sweat analyses need including as checks on self-reports (Schofield, Ferguson, & Ray 1997). Major differences in learning due to varying group affective climates, and levels of facilitative conditions from trainers, mean rigorous studies must standardize these at high levels. Effective implementation of strategies being evaluated also needs standardization of content and process. Caplan et al. (1989) covered the last two points in an exemplary fashion.

REFERENCES

Abe, J.A.A. & Izard, C.E. (1999) The developmental functions of emotions: An analysis in terms of differential emotions theory. *Cognition and Emotion*, **13**, 523–549.

Ashforth, B. & Humphrey, R. (1995) Emotion in the workplace: A reappraisal. *Human Relations*, **48**, 97–125.

Aspy, D.N. & Roebuck, F.N. (1976) *A Lever Long Enough*. Washington, DC: National Consortium for Humanizing Education.

Bevington, J. (1999) *Cognitive Management: Using Cognitive Therapy to Facilitate Organisational Change and Learning*. Unpublished Ph.D. thesis, Department of Psychiatry, University of Edinburgh.

Blum, R.B. & Sargent, T.O. (1980) Use of the bimodal theory in reactor crisis. *Proceedings of the American Nuclear Society/European Nuclear Society*, **11**.

Bolton, G. (1999a) Stories at work: Reflective writing for practitioners. *The Lancet*, **354**, 243–245.

Bolton, G. (1999b) *The Therapeutic Potential of Creative Writing*. London: Jessica Kingsley.

Bruning, N.S. & Frew, D.R. (1985) The impact of various stress management training strategies: A longitudinal experiment. In R.B. Robinson & J.A. Pearce (Eds) *Academy of Management Proceedings*, pp. 192–196. San Diego, CA: Academy of Management.

Bushman, B.J., Baumeister, R.F., & Stack, A.D. (1999) Catharsis, aggression, and persuasive influence: Self-fulfilling or self-defeating prophecies? *Personality and Social Psychology*, **76**, 367–376.

Buxman, K. (1991) Make room for laughter. *American Journal of Nursing*, December, 46–51.

Caplan, R.D., Vinokur, A.D., Price, R.H., & van Ryn, M. (1989) Job seeking, reemployment, and mental health: A randomised field experiment in coping with job loss. *Journal of Applied Psychology*, **74**, 759–769.

Ceserani, J. & Greatwood, P. (1995) *Innovation and Creativity*. London: Kogan Page.

Cowen, E.L. (1952) The influence of varying degrees of psychological stress on problem-solving rigidity. *Journal of Abnormal and Social Psychology*, **47**, 512–519.

Craig, T.Y. & Kelly, J.R. (1999) Group cohesiveness and creative performance. *Group Dynamics: Theory, Research, and Practice*, **3**, 243–256.

Dainow, S. (1998) *Working and Surviving in Organisations: A Trainer's Guide to Developing Organisational Skills*. Chichester, UK: Wiley.

Driskell, K.E., Salas, E., & Johnston, J. (1999) Does stress lead to a loss of team perspective. *Group Dynamics: Theory, Research, and Practice*, **3**, 291–302.

Duncan, E. & Gidron, Y. (1999) Written Emotional Expression and Health: Evidence for a new "Guided-Disclosure" technique. *Proceedings of the British Psychological Society*, **7**, 29.

Eden, D. & Kinnar, J. (1991) Modeling Galatea: Boosting self-efficacy to increase volunteering. *Journal of Applied Psychology*, **76**, 770–780.

Eden, D. & Ravid, G. (1982) Pygmalion versus self-expectancy: Effects of instructor- and self-expectancy on trainee performance. *Organizational Behavior and Human Performance*, **30**, 351–364.

Ekman, P. (1992) An argument for basic emotions. *Cognition and Emotion*, **6**, 169–200.

Estrada, C.A., Isen, A.M., & Young, M.J. (1997) Positive affect facilitates integration of information and decreases anchoring in reasoning among physicians. *Organizational Behavior and Human Decision Processes*, **72**, 117–135.

Evison, R. (1986) Self-help in preventing stress build-up. *The Professional Nurse*, **2**, March, 157–159.

Evison, R. (1988) Effective stress management = Management of inappropriate negative emotions. *The Occupational Psychologist*, No. 6, 5–15.

Evison, R. (1990a) *Encouraging Excellence in Trainer Classroom Delivery*. Unpublished research report to the European Educational Services Division of Digital Equipment.

Evison, R. (1990b) *Building the Theoretical Underpinnings to Counselling's Diversity*. Paper presented at the BPS Special Group in Counselling Psychology Annual Conference.

Evison, R. (1990c) *Developing Total Quality Working Relationships; An Open Learning Package for Change Agents in the Computer Industry*. Pitlochry: Change Strategies.

Evison, R. (1994) Applying counselling psychology in organisations. Paper accompanying Division of Counselling Psychology Workshop "Exploring Personal Blockbreaking". *Proceedings of the British Psychological Society*, **3**.

Evison, R. & Horobin, R. (1988) Co-counselling. In J. Rowan & W. Dryden (Eds) *Innovative Therapy in Britain*, pp. 85–109. Milton Keynes: Open University Press.

Evison, R. & Lindley, K. (1991) *What Do Effective Trainers Do to Achieve Results?* Paper presented at BPS Occupational Psychology Annual Conference.

Fineman, S. (1997) Emotion and management learning. *Management Learning*, **28**, 13–25.

Foot, H.C. (1996) Humour and laughter. In O.D.W. Hargie, (Ed.) *The Handbook of Communication Skills*, 2nd ed., pp. 259–285. London: Routledge.

Fredrickson, B.L. & Levenson, R.W. (1998) Positive emotions speed recovery from the cardiovascular sequelae of negative emotions. *Cognition and Emotion*, **12**, 191–220.

Frijda, N.H. (1986) *The Emotions*. Cambridge: Cambridge University Press.

Frost, C.D. & King, N. (2000) Physician heal thyself—the emotional demands of general practice. *Proceedings of the BPS Occupational Psychology Conference*, **6**, 17–22.

Fry, W.F. (1994) The biology of humour. *Humor: International Journal of Humor Research*, **7**, 111–126.

George, J.M. (1996) Group affective tone. In M. West (Ed.) *Handbook of Work Group Psychology*, pp. 77–93. Chichester, UK: Wiley.

Gray, S. (1999) Professional partnering: A peer support system in the workplace. Does it reduce the indicators of stress in neuro-rehabilitation staff? *Proceedings of World Congress of Neuro-Rehabilitation*, **2**, 3.

Gross, J.J. (1998) Antecedent- and response-focused emotion regulation: Divergent consequences for experience, expression, and physiology. *Journal of Personality and Social Psychology*, **74**, 224–237.

Gross, J.J. (1999) Emotion regulation: Past, present, future. *Cognition and Emotion*, **13**, 551–573.

Gross, J.J., Fredrickson, B.L., & Levenson, R.W. (1994) The psychophysiology of crying. *Psychophysiology*, **31**, 460–468.

Holt, J. (1965) *How Children Fail*. London: Pitman.

Isen, A.M. & Baron, R.A. (1991) Positive affect as a factor in organizational behavior. In L.L. Cummings & B.M. Straw (Eds) *Research in Organizational Behavior*, pp. 1–53. Greenwich, CT: JAI.

Izard, C.E. (1991) *The Psychology of Emotions*. New York: Plenum Press.

Izard, C.E. (1993) Four systems for emotion activation: Cognitive and non-cognitive processes. *Psychological Review*, **100**, 68–90.

Karle, W., Corriere, R., & Hart, J. (1973) Psychophysiological changes in abreactive therapy—study 1: Primal therapy. *Psychotherapy: Theory, Research and Practice*, **10**, 117–122.

Karon, B.P. & Widener, A.J. (1999) Repressed memories: Just the facts. *Professional Psychology: Research and Practice*, **30**, 625–626.

Keltner, D. & Gross, J.J. (1999) Functional accounts of emotions. *Cognition and Emotion*, **13**, 467–480.

Kirby, A. (1993) *A Compendium of Icebreakers, Energizers and Introductions*. Aldershot: Gower Press.

Lakoff, G. (1987) *Women, Fire and Dangerous Things: What Categories Reveal about the Mind*. Chicago: University of Chicago Press.

Lefcourt, H.M. & Martin, R.A. (1986) Sense of humor as a moderator of life stress. In *Humor and Life Stress: Antidote to Adversity*, pp. 48–63. New York: Springer-Verlag.

Levenson, R.W. (1999) The intrapersonal functions of emotion. *Cognition and Emotion*, **13**, 481–504.

Martin, D.G. (1972) *Learning-based Client-centred Therapy*. Monterey, CA: Brooks/Cole.

Martin, K.A., Moritz, S.E., & Hall, C.R. (1999) Imagery use in sport: A literature review and applied model. *The Sport Psychologist*, **13**, 245–268.

Mayne, T.J. (1999) Negative affect and health: The importance of being earnest. *Cognition and Emotion*, **13**, 601–635.

Murphy, L.R. (1996) Stress management techniques: Secondary prevention of stress. In M.J. Schabracq, J.A.M. Winnubst, & C.L. Cooper (Eds) *Handbook of Work and Health Psychology*, pp. 428–441. Chichester, UK: Wiley.

Murphy, F.C., Sahakian, B.J., Rubinsztein, J.S., Michael, A., Rogers, R.D., Robbins, T.W., & Paykel, E.S. (1999) Emotional bias and inhibitory control processes in mania and depression. *Psychological Medicine*, **29**, 1307–1321.

Nystrom, P.C. & Starbuck, W.H. (1984) To avoid crisis, unlearn. *Organizational Dynamics*, **12**, 53–65.

Ostell, A. (1996) Managing dysfunctional emotions in organisations. *Journal of Management Studies*, **33**, 525–557.

Parkinson, B. & Totterdell, P. (1999) Classifying affect regulation strategies. *Cognition and Emotion*, **13**, 277–303.

Pennebaker, J.W. & Beall, S.K. (1996) Confronting a traumatic event: Towards an understanding of inhibition and disease. *Journal of Abnormal Psychology*, **95**, 274–281.

Pierce, R.A., Nichols, M.P., & DuBrin, J.R. (1983) *Emotional Expression in Psychotherapy*. New York: Gardner Press.

Pratt, M.G. & Barnett, C.K. (1997) Emotions and unlearning in Amway recruiting techniques—promoting change through "safe" ambivalence. *Management Learning*, **28**, 65–88.

Proudfoot, J., Guest, D., Carson, J., Dunn, G., & Gray, J. (1997) Effect of cognitive-behavioural training on job-finding among long-term unemployed people. *The Lancet*, **350**, 96–100.

Retzinger, S. (1991) *Violent Emotions: Shame and Rage in Marital Quarrels*. London: Sage Publications.

Scheff, T.J. (1981) The distancing of emotion in psychotherapy. *Psychotherapy: Theory, Research and Practice*, **18**, 46–53.

Scheff, T.J. (1983) Toward integration in the social psychology of emotions. *Annual Review of Sociology*, **9**, 333–354.

Scheff, T.J. (1997) *Emotions, the Social Bond, and Human Reality: Part/Whole Analysis*. Cambridge: Cambridge University Press.

Scheff, T.J. & Bushnell, D.D. (1984) A theory of catharsis. *Journal of Research in Personality*, **18**, 238–264.

Schofield, L.A., Ferguson, J., & Ray, S. (1997) Physiological measurement of the response to and recovery from stress during a selection procedure. *Proceedings of the BPS Occupational Psychology Conference*, **3**, 275–280.

Schwartz, G.E., Fair, P.L., Salt, P., Mandel, M.R., & Klerman, G.L. (1976) Facial muscle patterning to affective imagery in depressed and nondepressed subjects. *Science*, **192**, 489–491.

Seligman, M.E.P. (1975) *Helplessness: On Depression, Development, and Death*. San Francisco: W.H. Freeman.

Sinclair, R.C. (1988) Mood, categorisation breadth, and performance appraisal: The effects of order of information acquisition and affective state on halo, accuracy, information retrieval and evaluations. *Organizational Behavior and Human Decision Processes*, **42**, 22–46.

Smith, A.C. & Kleinman, S.L. (1989) Managing emotions in medical school: Students' contacts with the living and the dead. *Social Psychology Quarterly*, **52**, 56–69.

Smith, R.E. (1999) Generalization effects in coping skills training. *Journal of Sport & Exercise Psychology*, **21**, 189–204.

Smyth, J.M. (1998) Written emotional expression: A meta-analytical review. *Journal of Consulting and Clinical Psychology*, **66**, 174–184.

Sparks, K. & Cooper, C.L. (1999) Occupational differences in the work-strain relationship: Towards the use of situation-specific models. *Journal of Occupational and Organizational Psychology*, **72**, 219–229.

Spera, S., Buhrfeind, E., & Pennebaker, J.W. (1994) Expressive writing and job loss. *Academy of Management Journal*, **37**, 722–733.

Steele, C.M., Spencer, S.J., & Lynch, M. (1993) Self-image resilience and dissonance: The role of affirmational resources. *Journal of Personality and Social Psychology*, **64**, 885–896.

Stone, L.J. & Hokanson, J.E. (1969) Arousal reduction via self-punitive behavior. *Journal of Personality and Social Psychology*, **12**, 72–79.

Stuart, R. (1991) Characterising stress: Part 2. The emergence and loosening of stress characters. *Journal of European Industrial Training*, **15**, 8–13.

Symonds, P.A. (1954) A comprehensive theory of psychotherapy. *American Journal of Orthopsychiatry*, **24**, 193–207.

Taylor, H. & Brown, A. (1999) Make 'em laugh: The importance of humour in leadership. *Proceedings of the BPS Occupational Psychology Conference*, **5**, 254–255.

Vrugt, A.J. (1996) Perceived self-efficacy, work motivation and well-being. In M.J. Schabracq, J.A.M. Winnubst, & C.L. Cooper (Eds) *Handbook of Work and Health Psychology*, pp. 389–390. Chichester, UK: Wiley.

Walsh, S. (1997) Using the unconscious to explore organizational vicious circles. *Proceedings of the BPS Occupational Psychology Conference*, **3**, 227–229.

Zohar, D. (1999) When things go wrong: The effect of daily work hassles on effort, exertion and negative mood. *Journal of Occupational and Organizational Psychology*, **72**, 265–283.

Chapter 11

Organizational management of stress and destructive emotions at work

Cary L. Cooper
Lancaster University Management School, Lancaster, UK
Susan Cartwright
*Manchester School of Management, University of Manchester
Institute of Science and Technology (UMIST)*

INTRODUCTION

Any organization that seeks to establish and maintain the best state of physical, mental, and social well-being of its employees needs to have policies and procedures that comprehensively address the management of emotions at work. These policies should include procedures to manage stress, based on the needs of the organization and its members, and should be regularly reviewed and evaluated.

TYPES AND LEVELS OF INTERVENTION

There are a number of options to consider in looking at the prevention of destructive emotions or stress at work. These are termed primary (e.g. stressor reduction), secondary (e.g. stress management), and tertiary (e.g. employee assistance programs/workplace counselling) levels of prevention, and they address different stages in the stress process (Sutherland & Cooper, 2000).

Primary prevention is concerned with taking action to modify or eliminate sources of negative emotion or stress inherent in the work environment, and thus reduces their negative impact on the individual. The "interactionist"

Emotions at Work. Edited by Roy Payne and Cary Cooper.
© 2001 by John Wiley & Sons, Ltd.

approach to stress (Cox, 1978; Edwards & Cooper, 1990) depicts stress as the consequences of the "lack of fit" between the needs and demands of the individual and his/her environment. The focus of primary interventions is in adapting the environment to "fit" the individual. Elkin and Rosch (1990) summarize a useful range of possible strategies to reduce workplace stressors:

- redesign the task;
- redesign the work environment;
- establish flexible work schedules;
- encourage participative management;
- include the employee in career development;
- analyse work roles and establish goals;
- provide social support and feedback;
- build cohesive teams;
- establish fair employment policies;
- share the rewards.

A number of general recommendations for reducing job stress have been put forward in a report by US Government's National Institute for Occupational Safety and Health in the National Strategy for the Prevention of Work Related Psychological Disorders (Sauter, Murphy & Hurrell, 1990). A few of these recommendations include:

Workload and work pace. Demands (both physical and mental) should be commensurate with the capabilities and resources of workers, avoiding underload as well as overload. Provisions should be made to allow recovery from demanding tasks or for increased control by workers over characteristics such as work pace of demanding tasks.

Work schedule. Work schedules should be compatible with demands and responsibilities outside the job. Recent trends toward flexitime, a compressed work week, and job sharing are examples of positive steps in this direction. When schedules involve rotating shifts, the rate of rotation should be stable and predictable.

Job future. Ambiguity should be avoided in opportunities for promotion and career or skill development, and in matters pertaining to job security. Employees should be clearly informed of imminent organizational developments that may affect their employment.

Social environment. Jobs should provide opportunities for personal interaction, both for purposes of emotional support and for actual help as needed in accomplishing assigned tasks.

Job content. Job tasks should be designed to have meaning and provide stimulation, and an opportunity to use skills. Job rotation or increasing the scope (enlargement/enrichment) of work activities are ways to improve narrow, fragmented work activities that fail to meet these criteria.

Primary intervention strategies are often a vehicle for culture change. Obviously, as the type of action required by an organization will vary according to the kinds of stressors operating, any intervention needs to be guided by some prior diagnosis, stress audit, or risk assessment to identify the organizational-, site-, or departmental-specific problems responsible for employee stress.

Secondary prevention is essentially concerned with the prompt detection and management of experienced stress by increasing awareness and improving the stress-management skills of the individual through training and educational activities. Individual factors can alter or modify the way employees exposed to workplace stressors perceive and react to this environment. Each individual has their own personal stress threshold, which is why some people thrive in a certain setting and others suffer. This threshold will vary between individuals and across different situations and life stages. Some key factors or "moderator" variables that influence an individual's vulnerability to stress include their personality, their coping strategies, age, gender, attitudes, training, past experiences, and the degree of social support available from family, friends, and work colleagues.

Secondary prevention can focus on developing self-awareness and providing individuals with a number of basic relaxation techniques. Health-promotion activities and lifestyle-modification programs also fall into the category of secondary-level interventions.

Stress education and stress-management training serve a useful function in helping individuals to recognize the symptoms of stress, and to overcome much of the negativity and stigma still associated with the stress label. Awareness activities and skills training programs designed to improve relaxation techniques, cognitive coping skills, and work/lifestyle modification skills (e.g. time-management courses or assertiveness training) have an important part to play in extending the individual's physical and psychological resources. They are particularly useful in helping individuals deal with stressors inherent in the work environment that cannot be changed and have to be "lived with" like, for example, job insecurity. Such training can also prove helpful to individuals in dealing with stress in other aspects of their life (i.e. non-work related). However, the role of secondary prevention is essentially one of damage limitation, often addressing the consequences rather than the sources of stress which may be inherent in the organization's structure or culture. They are concerned with improving the "adaptability" of the individual to the environment. Consequently, this type of intervention is often described as "the band aid" or inoculation approach, because it is implicitly assumed that the organization will not change but continue to be stressful; therefore, the individual has to develop his/her resistance to that stress.

Tertiary prevention is concerned with the treatment, rehabilitation, and recovery process of those individuals who have suffered or are suffering from serious ill health as a result of stress. Interventions at the tertiary level typically involve the provision of counselling services for employee problems in the work or personal domain. Such services are either provided by in-house counselors or outside agencies in the form of an employee assistance program (EAP). EAPs provide counselling, information, and/or referral to appropriate counselling treatment and support services. Originally introduced in the USA to tackle alcohol-related problems, the concept of workplace counselling has since assumed a significantly wider focus. Such services are confidential and usually provide a 24-hour telephone contact line. Employees are able to voluntarily access these services or, in some cases, are referred by their occupational health function. The implementation of comprehensive systems and procedures to facilitate and monitor the rehabilitation and return to work of employees who have suffered a stress-related illness is another aspect of tertiary prevention.

There is evidence to suggest that counselling is effective in improving the psychological well-being of employees and has considerable cost benefits. Based on reports published in the USA, figures typically show savings to investment rates of anywhere from 3 : 1 to 15 : 1 (Cooper & Cartwright, 1994). Such reports have not been without criticism, particularly as schemes are increasingly being evaluated by the "managed care" companies responsible for their implementation and who frequently are under contract to deliver a preset dollar saving (Smith & Mahoney, 1989). However, evidence from established counselling programs which have been rigorously evaluated, such as those introduced by Kennecott in the USA and the UK Post Office, resulted in a reduction in absenteeism in 1 year of approximately 60%. In the case of the UK experience (Cooper & Sadri, 1991), measures taken pre- and post-counselling showed significant improvements in the mental health and self-esteem of the participating employees. However, there was no improvement in levels of employee job satisfaction and organizational commitment. Similarities were found in a recent national evaluation of employee-assistance programs in a variety of UK companies (Highley & Cooper, 1996).

Like stress-management programs, counselling services can be particularly effective in helping employees deal with workplace stressors that cannot be changed and non-work-related stress (i.e. bereavement, marital breakdown, etc.), but which nevertheless tend to spill over into work life.

A COMPARISON OF INTERVENTIONS

Whereas there is considerable activity at the secondary and tertiary level, primary or organizational-level (stressor reduction) strategies are comparatively rare (Murphy, 1984; Murphy & Cooper, 2000). This is particularly the case in the USA and the UK. Organizations tend to prefer to introduce secondary and tertiary level interventions for several reasons.

There is relatively more published data available on the cost benefit analysis of such programs, particularly EAPs (Berridge, Cooper, & Highley, 1992). Those traditionally responsible for initiating interventions (i.e. the counselors, physicians, and clinicians responsible for health care), feel more comfortable with changing individuals than changing organizations (Ivancevich, Matteson, Freedman, & Phillips, 1990).

It is considered easier and less disruptive to business to change the individual than to embark on any extensive and potentially expensive organizational development program—the outcome of which may be uncertain (Cooper & Cartwright, 1994). They present a high-profile means by which organizations can "be seen to be doing something about stress" and taking reasonable precautions to safeguard employee health.

Overall, evidence as to the success of interventions, which focus at the individual level in isolation, suggests that such interventions can make a difference in temporarily reducing experienced stress (Sutherland & Cooper, 2000). Generally, evidence as to the success of stress-management training is confusing and imprecise (Elkin & Rosch, 1990), which possibly reflects the idiosyncratic nature of the form and content of this kind of training. Some recent studies that have evaluated the outcome of stress-management training have found a modest improvement in self-reported symptoms and psychological indices of strain (Sallis, Trevorrow, Johnson, Howell, & Kaplan,1984; Reynolds, Taylor, & Shapiro, 1993), but little or no change in job satisfaction, work stress, or blood pressure. Participants in a company-wide program, for example, reported improvements in health in the short term (i.e. 3 months post-intervention), but little was known about its long-term effect (Teasdale, 1996). Similarly, as discussed, counselling appears to be successful in treating and rehabilitating employees suffering from stress, but as they are likely to re-enter the same work environment, they continue as dissatisfied in their job and no more committed to the organization than they were before, so potential productivity gains may not be maximized. Firth-Cozens and Hardy (1992) have suggested that, as symptom levels reduce as a result of clinical treatment for stress, job perceptions are likely to become more positive. However, such changes are likely to be short term if employees return to an unchanged work environment and its indigenous stressors. If, as has been discussed, such initiatives have little impact on improving job satisfaction, then it is more likely that the individual will adopt a way of coping with stress which may have positive individual outcomes, but may have negative implications for the organization (i.e. taking alternative employment).

The evidence concerning the impact of health-promotion activities has reached similar conclusions. Research findings, which have examined the impact of lifestyle changes and health habits, provide support that any benefits may not necessarily be sustained. Lifestyle and health-promotion activities appear to be effective in reducing anxiety, depression, and psychosomatic distress, but do not necessarily moderate the stressor–strain linkage. According to Ivancevich and Matteson (1988), after a few years 70% of individuals who attend such programs revert to their previous lifestyle habits. Furthermore, as most stress-management programs or lifestyle-change initiatives are voluntary, this raises the issue as to the characteristics and health status of those participants who elect to participate. According to Sutherland and Cooper (1990), participants tend to be the "worried well" rather than the extremely distressed. Consequently, those employees who need most help and are coping badly are not reached by these initiatives. In addition, access to such programs is usually restricted to managers and relatively senior personnel within the organization. Given that smoking, alcohol abuse, obesity, and coronary heart disease are more prevalent among the lower socio-economic groups, and that members of these groups are likely to occupy positions within the organizational structure which they perceive afford them little or no opportunity to change or modify the stressors inherent in their working environment, the potential health of arguably the "most at risk" individuals is not addressed. Finally, the introduction of such programs in isolation may serve to enhance employee perceptions of the organization as a caring employer—interested in their health and well-being—and so may contribute to create a "feel good" factor which is unlikely to be sustained if the work environment continues to remain stressful.

Secondary and tertiary level interventions have a useful role to play in stress prevention, but as "stand-alone" initiatives they are not the complete answer, unless attempts are also made to address the sources of stress itself (Cartwright, Cooper, & Murphy, 1995). Cardiovascular fitness programs may be successful in reducing the harmful effects of stress on the high-pressured executive, but such programs will not eliminate the stressor itself, which may be over promotion or a poor relationship with his/her boss (Cooper & Cartwright, 1994). Identifying and recognizing the problem and taking steps to tackle it, perhaps by negotiation (i.e. a "front end" approach), might arguably arrest the whole process. If, as has been discussed, experienced stress is related to the individual's appraisal of an event or situation, an organization can reduce stress by altering the objective situation (e.g. by job redesign).

A further limitation of secondary and tertiary level interventions is that they do not directly address the important issue of control. This is particularly critical in terms of the health of blue-collar workers. Research has shown (Karasek, 1979) that jobs which place high demands on the individual, but at the same time afford the individual little control or discretion (referred to as "decision latitude"), are inherently stressful. Stress-management training may heighten the awareness of workers to environmental stressors which may be affecting their health, but because as individuals they may lack the "resource" or "positional" power to change them, they arguably exacerbate the problem.

Again, there is not a great deal of research evidence that has evaluated the impact of primary level interventions on employee health and well-being. However, what exists has been consistently positive, particularly in showing the long-term beneficial effects (Quick, 1979; Jackson, 1983; Kompier & Cooper, 1999).

Treatment may often, therefore, be easier than prevention, but it may only be an effective short-term strategy. In focusing at the outcome or "rear end" of the stress process (i.e. poor mental and physical health) and taking remedial action to redress that situation, the approach is essentially reactive and recuperative rather than proactive and preventative.

In summary, secondary and tertiary levels of intervention are likely to be insufficient in maintaining employee health without the complementary approach of primary/stressor reduction initiatives. Secondary and tertiary level interventions may extend the physical and psychological resources of the individual, particularly in relation to stressors that cannot be changed, but those resources are ultimately finite. Tertiary level interventions, such as the provision of counselling services, are likely to be particularly effective in dealing with non-work-related stress. Evidence from workplace counselling programs (Cooper & Sadri, 1991) indicate that approximately a quarter of all problems presented concerned relationships outside of work. Organizations considering counselling schemes should recognize that counselling is a highly skilled business and requires extensive training. It is important to ensure that counselors have recognized counselling skills training and have access to a suitable environment that allows them to conduct this activity in an ethical and confidential manner (Berridge et al. 1992).

THE WIDER IMPLICATIONS OF CREATING HEALTHY WORK ORGANIZATIONS

The previous sections have emphasized the importance and potential costs–benefits to the organization of introducing initiatives to reduce stress and promote employee health and well-being in the workplace. Action to reduce stress at work is usually prompted by some organizational problem or crisis (e.g. escalating rates of sickness absence or labour turnover). Consequently, actions tend to be driven by a desire to reduce or arrest costs (i.e. problem-driven-negative motives) rather than the desire to maximize potential and improve competitive edge (i.e. gains-driven-positive motives). The danger of this type of approach is that, once sickness absence or labour turnover rates stabilize at an acceptable level, interventions may lose their impetus and be considered no longer necessary. It has to be recognized that stress is dynamic and, in a rapidly changing environment, is unlikely to ever disappear completely, but needs to be regularly monitored and addressed. Organizations need to consider stress prevention not only as a means of cost reduction or containment but also as a means of maintaining and improving organizational health and increasing productivity. The costs of stress and the collective health and wealth of organizations and their workers is of great importance to society as a whole (Cooper, Liukkonen, & Cartwright, 1996). Occupational stress is not just an organizational problem but a wider societal problem which is ultimately shared by UK plc and by all members of the EU, both directly and indirectly, through increased taxation and state health-insurance contributions or diminished living standards, as a result of loss of competitive edge. This final section is therefore concerned with the extent to which consolidated action and policies at UK and EU levels can address the problem of stress at work. It considers ways in which policymakers can encourage and provide information and incentives to responsible organizations to instigate and maintain stress-intervention strategies.

Risk assessment

Legislative differences in health and safety matters within individual member states of the EU would seem to influence practices, interpretation, and employer attitudes. The framework Directive on Health and Safety (89/391) embodies the concept of risk assessment which makes it mandatory for organizations within the 15 member states to assess the health and safety risks to its workers. In terms of employer obligations, the important points of this Directive are:

- the provision of protective, preventive, and emergency services;
- comprehensive information in the area of health and safety; and
- full consultation and participation rights to workers on matters affecting workplace health and safety.

Stress represents an occupational risk to health. The assessment of psychosocial factors relating to health is substantially different from assessing physical hazards in the working environment, which has been the traditional domain of the Labour and Factory Inspectorate and those responsible for health and safety within an organization. Concerns have been expressed (Wynne & Clarkin, 1992) as to the shortage of sufficiently trained personnel and the adequate provision of training in many countries to undertake the traditional task of occupational health and safety. Not surprisingly, there is likely to be even greater skills and training deficiency in the area of psychosocial factors pertaining to health.

Therefore, to provide appropriate guidance and increase organizational awareness of these factors, investment is needed to provide comprehensive, professional, and universal training for existing labour and factory inspectors. Alternatively, there should be a move toward more interdisciplinary teams, which include an expert trained in this field. This training should also be extended to managers and employee representatives within companies. By introducing regular risk assessments in this area, this would help organizations understand and monitor factors that may negatively affect employee health and psychological well-being. Health and safety authorities in the UK and EU member states have a major role to play in either conducting risk assessments themselves or providing appropriate advice and support to organizations to enable them to perform their own assessment.

Economic incentives

Typically, organizations respond to statutory legislation by implementing the minimum requirements to conform to the law. Rather than merely punishing "bad practice", the more effective way of encouraging "good practice" is to reward it. This could take the form of providing tax incentives for validated health and safety expenditure incurred by organizations as discussed in the recent European Founding publication (Bailey, Jorgensen, Kruger & Litske, 1994).

Another option is to more directly link risk-assessment and stress-prevention strategies to insurance premiums. Currently, the cost of employee accidents and compensation for injuries and illness and negligence is met by a variety of insurance bodies in both the public and private sector. Insurance premiums may be levied as a flat rate or vary according to the claims experience of the industry sector or the individual organizations. When premiums are linked to the claims experience or past accident history of the individual organization, employers become more aware of the true cost of their actions. If an employer is penalized by an increased premium as a result of a high accident rate, they are likely to take steps to address and improve the situation. However, there are drawbacks to such arrangements. For example, employers may put pressure on employees not to pursue claims or report accidents. Claims experience shows data-based costs can give a distorted picture when there is a large payment made for a long-term disability or fatality. Similarly, experience based solely on accident frequency rates may unfairly penalize an organization which has a lot of relatively inexpensive minor accidents compared to an organization with fewer, but which result in a more severe and costly outcome. These issues are particularly relevant to small and medium-sized enterprises. Most importantly, experienced-based insurance ratings focus on historical record, and so do not take into account the efforts an organization may be making to reduce future risk. However, there would perhaps be some benefit in insurance providers pooling their collective experiences and statistics on an industry basis to help identify particular business sectors which might benefit from more specifically targeted health and safety initiatives.

A more effective and fairer way in which organizations could be rewarded for the efforts in creating more healthy working environments would be to link incentives to stress audits and the presence of stress intervention programs. A rather similar scheme, the Work Injury Reduction Program (WIRP), is currently being trialled in Alberta, Canada. Employers who have voluntarily opted to join the scheme are required to undergo an annual audit of their management systems. This audit focuses on six areas: corporate leadership, operations, human resources, facilities and services, administration and health, and safety information and promotion.

The organization's performance is scored out of a possible 2,000 points to provide an index of progress. Employers are required to take action on the results of this audit and to report recommendations to qualify for financial incentives. The potential exists for large companies to receive incentives as high as $2 million.

Specific assistance for Small and Medium-Sized Enterprises (SME)

The low participation of SMEs in stress-prevention and health-promotion activities is another source of concern, because SMEs form a major proportion of business for example, in Europe some 40% of companies employ less than 20 people and around 60% with less than 50 (Bailey et al., 1994). This may be due to lack of resources, lack of skilled personnel, and/or lack of access to information. Time and financial costs are more problematic for smaller companies. The pricing structure of employee assistance programs means that these kinds of services are generally not available on an individual basis to SMEs. Training provided by external agencies is significantly more limited and difficult for SMEs. Certainly, the provision of more government-funded training opportunities and easier and more open access to information and courses specifically targeted at SMEs would help in this respect.

Another possible way in which SMEs could access professional help and expertise would be for companies to combine to share the costs of preventative services, along the lines of group practice models operating in some EU member states (e.g. The Netherlands). In The Netherlands, all employees have access to a panel of professionals who will provide them with occupational health and health and safety services. These services are funded by levies paid by the organization, based on the size of their workforce. In Sweden, prior to 1995, all organizations paid a levy into a central fund, the Working Life Fund, which provided employers with access to professional help and expertise on work-related health issues, which they could call upon for advice on organizational problems. In addition to providing information and guidance, the Working Life Fund undertook specific projects at the corporate level. The combination of these two kinds of services to provide assistance to both employees and employers would be greatly beneficial to SMEs.

More information and research

The level of research activity in the area of occupational stress and stress prevention varies considerably from country to country, as does the level of organizational activity. Much more research is needed, particularly studies that evaluate the long-term effectiveness of stress intervention strategies. There is also much to be learned from the dissemination of more practical case studies or organizational practice and experience in stress prevention. Stronger industrial links between the business community and academic institutions can promote this type of activity, particularly when there is some joint investment.

The conventional sources of research funding provided through government research grants awarded to academic institutions are increasingly limited. This suggests that alternative sources of funding may be needed to ensure that the research activity keeps pace with the demand for knowledge.

Endnote

This article was drawn from a report published by the authors for the European Foundation for the Improvement of Living and Working Conditions, entitled Stress Prevention in the Workplace.

REFERENCES

Bailey, S., Jorgensen, K., Kruger, W., & Litske, H. (1994) *Economic Incentives to Improve the Working Environment*. Dublin: European Foundation for the Improvement of Living and Working Conditions.

Berridge, J., Cooper, C.L., & Highley, C. (1992) *Employee Assistance Programmes and Workplace Counselling*. Chichester, UK: Wiley.

Cartwright, S., Cooper, C.L., & Murphy, L.R. (1995) Diagnosing a healthy organization: A proactive approach to stress in the workplace. In G.P. Keita & S. Sauter (Eds) *Job Stress Intervention: Current Practice and Future Directions*. Washington, DC: APA/NIOSH.

Cooper, C.L. & Sadri, G. (1991) The impact of stress counselling at work. *Journal of Social Behavior and Personality*, **6**(7), 411–423.

Cooper, C.L. & Cartwright, S. (1994) Healthy mind, healthy organizational—a proactive approach to occupational stress. *Human Relations*, **47**(4), 455–471.

Cooper, C.L. Liukkonen, P., & Cartwirght, S. (1996) *Stress Prevention in the Workplace*. Dublin: European Foundation for the Improvement of Living and Working conditions.

Cox, T. (1978) *Stress*. London: Macmillan.

Edwards, J.R. & Cooper, C.L. (1990) The person-environment fit approach to stress: recurring problems and some suggested solutions. *Journal of Organizational Behaviour*, **11**, 293–307.

Elkin, A.J. & Rosch, P.J. (1990) Promoting mental health at the workplace: The prevention side of stress management. *Occupational Medicine: State of the Art Review*, **5**(4), 739–754.

Firth-Cozens, J. & Hardy, C.E. (1992) Occupational stress, clinical treatment, change in job perception. *Journal of Occupational and Organizational Psychology*, **95**: 81–88.

Highley, C. & Cooper, C.L. (1996) *An Assessment of Employee Assistance Programmes in the UK Industry*. London: Health and Safety Executive.

Ivancevich, J.M. & Matteson, M.T. (1988) Promoting the individual's health and well-being. In C.L. Cooper, & R. Payne (Eds) *Causes, Coping and Consequences of Stress at Work*. Chichester, UK:Wiley.

Ivancevich, J.M., Matteson, M.T., Freedman, S.M., & Phillips, J.S. (1990) Worksite stress management interventions. *American Psychologist*, **45**, 252–261.

Jackson, S.E. (1983) Participation in decision making as a strategy for reducing job related strain. *Journal of Applied Psychology*, **68**, 3–19.

Karasek, R.A. (1979) Job demands, decision latitude and mental strain: Implications for job design. *Admin. Science Quarterly*: **24**, 285–307.

Kompier, M. & Cooper, C.L. (1999) *Preventing Stress, Improving Productivity*. London: Routledge.

Murphy, L.R. (1984) Occupational stress management: A review and appraisal. *Journal of Occupational Psychology*: **57**, 1–15.

Murphy, L.R. & Cooper, C.L. (2000) *Healthy and Productive Work: An International Perspective*. London and New York: Taylor & Francis.

Quick, J.C. (1979) Dyadic goal setting and role stress in field study. *Academy of Management Journal*, **22**, 241–252.

Reynolds, S., Taylor, E., & Shapiro, D.A. (1993) Session impact in stress management training. *Journal of Occupational and Organizational Psychology*: **66**, 99–113.

Sallis, J.F., Trevorrow, T.R., Johnson, C.C., Howell, M.F., & Kaplan, R.M. (1984) Worksite stress management: A comparison of programmes. *Psychology of Health*, **1**, 237–255.

Sauter, S., Murphy, L.R., Hurrell, J.J. Jr. (1990) A national strategy for the prevention of work related psychological disorders. *American Psychologist*, **45**, 1146–1158.

Smith, D. & Mahoney, J. (1989) McDonnell Douglas Corporation's EAP produces hard data. *The Almacan*, 18–26.

Sutherland, V.J. & Cooper, C.L. (1990) *Understanding Stress*. London: Chapman & Hall.

Sutherland, V.J. & Cooper, C.L. (2000) *Strategic Stress Management*. London: Macmillan Books.

Teasdale, E. (1996) Stress management within the pharmaceutical industry. In C. Cooper, P. Liukkonen, & S. Cartwright (Eds) *Stress Prevention in the Workplace*. Dublin: European Foundation for the Improvement of Living and Working Conditions.

Wynne, R. & Clarkin, N. (1992) *Under Construction: Building for Health in the EC Workplace*. Dublin: European Foundation for the Improvement of Living and Working Conditions.

Chapter 12

Emotion and offices at work

Ian Donald
Department of Psychology, University of Liverpool

THE ENVIRONMENT IN CONTEXT

Emotions are an important yet neglected area of organizational and work psychology. As Fineman (1993a) has noted, when work on organizations is looked at in detail, the people are presented as emotionally anorexic.

> They have "dissatisfactions" and "satisfactions", they may be "alienated" or "stressed", they will have "preferences", "attitudes" and "interests" ... we find little or no mention of how feeling individuals worry, envy, brood, become bored, play, despair, plot, hate, hurt, and so forth.
>
> (Fineman, 1993a, pp. 9–10)

The same can be said of the majority of studies looking at office designs and their relationship to the people that work in them.

Office environments are not a popular topic of research within mainstream organizational and work psychology; the field's leading UK periodical, the *Journal of Occupational and Organizational Psychology*, has carried only one article (Donald, 1994a) on office environments in the last 20 years. Closely related disciplines such as engineering psychology, ergonomics or human factors, pay more attention to the environment, but are even more likely to neglect emotion. Textbooks on organizational and work psychology show a similar picture to journals, typically limiting the extent of the domain to ergonomics and equipment design (e.g. Arnold, Cooper, & Robertson, 1998).

Environmental psychologists as a group have, on the whole, been ahead of work and organizational psychologists in putting emotions on their theoretical and research agenda (cf. Russell & Snodgrass, 1987). Unfortunately, those

Emotions at Work. Edited by Roy Payne and Cary Cooper.
© 2001 by John Wiley & Sons, Ltd.

examining office designs have tended to ignore emotion. As a recent review of papers that have been published in the *Journal of Environmental Psychology* over the last decade pointed out, most articles concerned with offices adopt a deterministic framework, were carried out on student populations, used office simulations rather than real offices, considered basic performance criteria for assessing the impact of offices, and showed few statistically significant relationships (Donald, 1999). With one or two possible exceptions, emotional factors were absent from this work. Part of the reason for this is a focus on the *characteristics* of offices rather than *events* that are associated with work environments.

There are a great many office studies looking at satisfaction in relation to various characteristics of the environment including lighting (e.g. Kenz, 1995; Veitch, 1997), noise (e.g. Kjellberg, Landström, Tesarz, Söderberg, & Åkerlund, 1996) and so on. Useful work has also examined outcomes such as Sick Building Syndrome (e.g. Hedge, 1987; Hedge, Erickson, & Rubin, 1996) and environmental stress. Yet, few look at emotion and what goes on behind the mask of rationalism and determinism. Office research, then, follows that conducted in organizational and work psychology, in which feelings are translated into stress and satisfaction (Briner, 1999a). However, these constructs are often considered "theoretically inadequate and of very limited practical use" (Briner, 1999a, p. 325) for understanding employees' affect.

None of this would really matter if office environments were of little importance. There is a strong argument to suggest, however, that workplaces may potentially impact on everyday life to as great or greater extent than almost any other building type. Whilst offices are a relatively recent phenomenon, their potential impact has grown dramatically. In 1850 only around 1% of the working-age population worked in offices. By 1950, this number had risen to 10%. Over the next 25 years the figure had grown to 40%, and had reached 53% by 1981. It was estimated during the 1980s that more than 70% of the working population would occupy offices by 1999 (Craig, 1981; Kleeman, 1986). Writing a decade ago, Vischer (1989) painted a more graphic picture of what this means in North America:

> Some thirty million adults go to work every day in office buildings in North America. For white-collar workers who work an average productive life span, this means that about one third of their lives between the ages of twenty and sixty is spent in these environments.
>
> (Vischer, 1989, p. 1)

If attention is not paid to people's emotions in relation to offices, or if their emotions are actively suppressed, a vast number of people are going to spend a large part of their lives in an emotionally barren landscape. Moreover, for many organizations the cost of housing the work force is often second only to the cost of that workforce. Clearly, even purely in financial terms, it is crucial that organizations have environments that help people to achieve their full potential.

A BRIEF LOOK AT EMOTION

Before going on to examine the potential role the environment can play in employees' emotions, it is worth briefly clarifying the concept of emotion and the ways in which it features in work life. One important distinction, which will be relevant in the later parts of this chapter, is between the *experience* of emotion and the *expression* of emotion (Briner, 1999b).

Most research on the expression of emotion centres on Hochschild's (1983) concept of *emotional labour*, which Putnam and Mumby (1993) describe as "the way roles and tasks exert overt and covert control over emotional displays" (Putnam and Mumby, 1993, p. 37). They go on to point out that:

> organizations continue to manage hearts by calling on employees to exhibit forced niceness, phoney smiles and suppressed anger ... the expressed feelings of flight attendants are set by management to evoke passenger commitment. Employee training manuals urge clerks to express concern for customers, to make their voice warm and friendly, and to prevent emotional leakage of frustration and impatience.
> (Putnam and Mumby, 1993, pp. 37–38)

Most researchers apply the concept of emotional labour to services industries where there is clear contact between an organization and its clients. However, Mann (1999) estimates that emotional labour is evident in approximately two-thirds of all workplace communication.

Furthermore, Briner (1999b) notes that almost all supervisory or managerial jobs require the suppression of some emotions and the display of others. This could be conceived of as *intra-organizational emotional labour*. The difference between Hochschild's (1983) emotional labour and intra-organizational emotional labour is that in the latter the control of emotional expression is part of the day-to-day interaction within an organization, whereas with emotional labour the expression is both more overt and a central characteristic or part of the job (Briner, 1999b). However, the same psychological processes are likely to be experienced in relation to both types of emotional labour, though less formally within an organization, and so the consequences for the well-being of employees are also likely to be the same.

Experienced emotion is a more straightforward concept, and simply refers to the feelings an employee has as a result of some event or events that take place during their work. The sources of experienced emotion may be task generated or a product of a particular social interaction or situation at work (Briner, 1999b). Another way of thinking about social situations is as *events*. Briner notes that the focus of most approaches to well-being at work is on job characteristics rather than events. Furthermore, according to Weiss and Cropanzano (1996) it is events rather than characteristics that are of most importance to emotion within organizations (Briner, 1999b). This difference is paralleled in office research where there has been a clear focus on the environmental characteristics of the office rather than the events that they facilitate or the events that take place as part of the management and design of offices.

Emotional labour, intra-organizational emotional labour, and experienced emotion are all related to the environment of offices. Before going on to consider these in detail, it is useful to examine the historic context of office design and its relationship to organizational theory.

OFFICES IN THE AGE OF REASON

Until the latter part of the eighteenth century there were few purpose-built offices, and those that did exist were small, often converted rooms of domestic premises. With the growth of organizations and the need to house large numbers of workers there was a shift to purpose-built office blocks, the construction of which had been made possible by technological advances. At the same time the growth of organizations also led to the development of theories of organization and work. In effect, organizational theory and office design have evolved together, and not surprisingly the "emotionally anorexic" models used at the start of the 1900s to understand workers' behaviours appear to have dominated office design and research, producing similarly "emotionally skinny" or "malnourished" environments.

The end of the 1800s and the start of the 1900s saw the coalescence of the work of a number of independent writers into classical organizational theory. Although not a consciously organized body of work, classical theorists did share underlying assumptions and a general paradigm of human and organizational functioning. While there were many contributors to classical organizational theory, the ideas of Max Weber and Frederick Taylor were arguably amongst the most influential.

Central to Weber's (1947) theory of organization is the concept of bureaucracy. In essence, Weber proposed that organizations could be classified in terms of the extent to which they fulfilled characteristics of a bureaucratic ideal. Some of the principal features of this ideal are specialization or division of labour, hierarchy of authority, the use of written rules and regulations, the rational application of rules and procedures (Arnold et al., 1998), impersonal (formal) interpersonal relations, and meritocratic advancement (Sharma, 1982). The essence of the theory was that work is, or at least should be, "organized and conducted on an entirely rational basis" (Arnold et al., 1998, p. 4); that is, without emotion or emotional display.

Taylor's (1911) "theory" of scientific management had a slightly different focus being concerned principally with motivation and the nature of work. Like Weber though, scientific management made no provision for human emotion, needs or potential. It was argued that there is a single best and most efficient method of performance for each task, that tasks could be reduced to minute elements, and that they should be simplified as much as possible. Further, individual discretion, it was argued, should not be allowed. Employees were viewed as extrinsically motivated and so intrinsically lazy, working only under supervision and motivated by financial gain alone. It was believed that when given the appropriate conditions, people would work to their optimum efficiency. Consequently the focus of research and management at the time was on establishing the appropriate working conditions, which led to the need to collect detailed information on the most minute aspects of work tasks. The absurd level of detail reached is evident from research findings of the time. For instance, it was discovered that to open and close a file drawer takes 0.04 of a minute, opening a central drawer is a little quicker at 0.026 of a minute, and to get up from a chair takes 0.033 of a minute (Becker, 1981).

While these accounts are caricatures of detailed theories, they do provide an adequate skeleton for discussion. Additionally, while it can easily be seen that the foci of Weber and Taylor are different, there is considerable common ground between the two writers. As Sharma (1982) argues, almost "all the concepts from scientific management were similar to those in Weber's bureaucratic model" (Sharma, 1982, p. 124). Similarly, the implications for the environment and person-organization relations that accrue from both theories are fundamentally common, and both remove emotion from the office.

Perhaps the most important characteristics of the classical theories are their subjugation of the individual and individual expression to the primacy of the formal organization. In a major review of research on psychological aspects of office and factory environments, Sundstrom (1986) points to three basic environmental implications, which derive from classical theories. These will be discussed further in later sections, but it is worth mentioning them here.

First, *symbols of office* relate to Weber's bureaucracy. Status markers were not, however, thought of as means of developing motivation or feelings of success and pride amongst workers. Instead symbols reflect and communicate organizational hierarchy, aiding organizational functioning. The form that symbols could and still do take are varied and many. They include, for example, the position someone sits in relation to a window, the direction faced in the office, the size of a person's workspace or desk. Referring to the work of Wotton (1976), Sundstrom (1986) provides a good example of environmental status markers in an organization:

> In the Canadian Ministry, the deputy minister receives a minimum of seven windows, assistant deputy ministers get six, directors have four, and the luckier of the less senior officers make do with a three-window bay.
>
> (Wotton, 1976, p. 35)

The second and third environmental implications drawn by Sundstrom (1986) are *economy of motion* and *visual accessibility*. Both of these environmental considerations are derivatives of scientific management. Economy of motion requires ready access to equipment and others with whom contact is needed for efficient workflow. It also implies the tight control of movement. The Taylorist view that workers are intrinsically lazy points to the need for close supervision, which requires an office to be designed in such a way as to allow visual accessibility. The constant monitoring prevented the unwanted expression of emotion by the workforce, though it is likely to have resulted in negative but hidden feelings. In effect, employees were always "front stage" where their emotions had to be kept in check.

In relation to the previous consideration of emotions, the on-show nature of these offices probably resulted in intra-organization emotional labour, and, perhaps, the stresses associated with it. While some involved in emotional labour, such as aircraft cabin crew, may take breaks "back-stage", similar relief is not possible within large open offices.

In addition to Sundstrom's list of implications, other factors can be added, including the need to delineate space, thereby differentiating various functional and hierarchical groups. The image of the organization, and its primacy, may also be communicated to the individual worker via physical means. Moreover, there are features that by implication should be avoided. The requirement of using only official, formal channels of communication suggests the need to prevent informal gatherings. Consequently, meeting places, the coffee machine culture, need to be controlled.

Taylor's principles were originally applied to manual and factory work. They were soon transferred to business organizations and offices, where Weber's ideas were also incorporated. Examples of office designs that reflect the classical approach to organizations show how these ideas permeated design (Duffy, 1980) and office practice (Braverman 1974). Frank Lloyd Wright's Larkin building, built in 1904, demonstrates the straitjacket form an office could take when designed along the principles of scientific management and bureaucracy.

Duffy (1980) gives a detailed description of the building and its place within the history of office design. However, it can be seen from Figure 12.1, slogans on the walls espouse corporate values, desk layout is tight and rigid in planning, women and men are sharply segregated within the same office space and a supervisor can monitor workers' behaviour. Spatially, the building expresses the unity of the organization, and the cathedral-like interior reinforces the dominance of the organization over the individual.

If the image of the building is not sufficient, the furniture it contained reinforced the control of the workers. Referring to the clerical desk from the Larkin Building shown in Figure 12.2, Duffy (1980) describes how "the seat hinged to the clerical desk restricts freedom of movement, saves space and is entirely rational, and effectively expresses the degradation of the clerk" (Duffy 1980, p. 268).

Referring to Gerth and Mills (1958), Fineman (1993a) notes that Weber's ideal bureaucracy focussed on efficiency unsullied by "love, hatred and all purely personal and emotional elements" (Fineman, 1993a, p. 9). Such a focus is very apparent in the Larkin and other buildings of the time, which reflect and symbolize the suppression of workers' emotion. It is all too easy to imagine the feelings that are likely to be engendered by the experience of working each day in such an environment. Clearly, the psychological needs of the workers were purposively excluded from the workplace. It would be expected that from this position "things could only get better".

Figure 12.1   Interior of the Larkin Administration Building, Buffalo, New York, 1904

NEW LABOUR AND A NEW OFFICE LANDSCAPE

The Hawthorne Studies achieved almost legendary status within psychology. However, the aim of the researchers who conducted the first of the studies was

Figure 12.2 Clerical desk, Larkin Administration Building, Buffalo, New York.

relatively straightforward and humble. Their objective was simply to identify the optimum physical working conditions necessary to achieve maximum productivity. Within the framework provided by Taylor, the results were, to say the least, surprising. The researchers increased lighting levels, and, as may be expected, the workers increased their productivity. However, amongst numerous experimental manipulations, they also found that when lighting was reduced to a level where the workers could hardly see, productivity continued to rise, or at least did not fall. It became clear from these and other findings that workers and work groups were more complex than Taylor and his contemporaries had suggested. Furthermore, the research results tended to be taken to imply that the physical environment at work was of little importance for efficiency and productivity.

The conclusions of the Hawthorne experiments have been summarized by many writers. In brief, the principal findings were that workers define their own roles and norms, which may be different to those prescribed by the organization; people are motivated by more than purely financial reward; employees work as collectives, often with informal leaders who can neutralize the power of formal leaders; communication within an organization needs to be two-way and participation is important in decision making (Sharma, 1982). Clearly, from this perspective people are social beings with higher order needs and emotions. It is not sufficient, therefore, to provide workers with an environment that is purely rational, or to expect its impact to be direct and simple. In some senses, the Hawthorne Studies shifted the focus from characteristics of the work environment to events within that environment.

The consequent development of humanistic approaches to organization and work had the potential to allow the inclusion of emotional factors in the workplace. As Roethlisberger (1949) wrote when describing the Hawthorne studies:

> Gradually and painfully the experimenters had been forced to abandon this (economic man) conception of the worker and his behavior ... they found that the behavior of *workers could not be understood apart from their feelings* or sentiments.
> (Roethlisberger, 1949, p. 19) (emphasis added)

The new theories that evolved out of the Hawthorne and other studies clearly had a potential to impact on both workers and their environments. After all, the approaches were given the title of the *human relations* movement, so suggesting the possibility of humanizing office environments. That emotion continued to be absent from the agenda of most researchers is perhaps explained by the view that in reality the new human relations approach represented a refinement and expansion of the classical doctrine rather than a fundamental abandonment of it. For example, Clegg and Dunkerley (1980) argue that "The innovations of the 1960s did not, in fact, challenge Taylorist division of labour ... they were neo-Taylorist rather than anti-Taylorist." (Clegg and Dunkerly, 1980, p. 514). Whether the human relations movement represented old wine or new, one thing is for sure, it was certainly contained in a very different bottle.

A revolution in the design of offices coincided with the development of humanistic theory. The design concept of Bürolandschaft (office landscaping), introduced from Germany, marked a major shift in the design of work environments. It is difficult today to appreciate quite how surprising this new concept was, but the writings of designers who were its witnesses make clear the design's radicalism, as Duffy (1979, p. 54) reveals:

> Many architects will remember very well the shock of seeing office landscaping for the first time. In the early '60s the essence of office design was to stack homogenised net lettable areas into Miesian towers. Nothing had prepared us for those curious German drawings which actually showed *desks* (original emphasis), hundreds of desks, randomly arranged in great open spaces ... Their look burned itself into the retina, an image never to be forgotten.

The design concept came with a set of rules and rationales as to how and why a layout should take its form and relate to an organization. The designs also had wide-ranging implications for organizational structure, democracy, and practice (Duffy, 1979).

Bürolandschaft design was open plan, but did not simply follow the organizational chart (Lorenzen & Jaeger, 1968) or basic workflow, as did earlier offices such as the Larkin Building. The design was meant to be a tool that took into account the *affective* bonds that hold organizations together; "for the first time in office planning, attention was drawn to the distinction between the informal and the formal organisation" (Duffy, 1974, p. 115). The new emphasis was on communication rather than workflow (Duffy, 1974), and communication was not to be a one-way supervisor to subordinate flow, it was to travel across departmental boundaries, across status levels, often circumventing intermediary personnel. As part of the new approach, places for informal meetings were provided to facilitate informal contact. Rather than using the environment to constrain employees' preferred behaviour, as classical theory required, the new approach aimed at channelling it into an organizationally useful form.

Along with less formal communications, one of the most significant features of Bürolandschaft was that private offices and status markers were considered inefficient and were excluded. The linear juxtaposition of desks was replaced by an irregular arrangement of workspaces that could be moved around the office area as required. In essence, the subordination of conventional issues of privacy and status, it was argued by proponents of the design, in favour of communications flow, would lead to increased productivity. Clearly, the new offices were a far cry from the confined, controlled and regulated offices required by classical theory. As Duffy wrote:

> If physical barriers come down, and desks are arranged loosely according to need not status in the manner of office landscaping, true cooperation towards a common goal is likely to be encouraged if not engendered.
>
> (Duffy, 1974, p. 115)

Despite the "brave-new-world" of freedom and democracy in the workplace, in reality the offices produced post-Bürolandschaft were fundamentally the same as those prior to the concept's introduction. The design's diluted form meant that the revolution was limited.

> In Holland the best known office building of the decade, Centraal Beheer, is open plan but is nevertheless entirely heretical in terms of the rules about lighting, circulation, depth of space which once were so fundamental. In the United States there are plenty of open plan offices and much discussion of office landscaping but it would take a very subtle mind to distinguish between what is part of the old American tradition of open office planning and what has been imported from Europe.
>
> (Duffy, 1979, p. 55)

All was not well in the offices of Eden. The occupants soon began to complain of distractions, excess noise, and a lack of privacy (e.g. Hedge, 1982, 1986). These dissatisfactions, along with the original claims of the proponents of office land-scaping, spawned the growth of research and interest in the office environment and its impact on employees. Yet, as Sundstrom's (1986) comprehensive review shows, there remained little interest in workers' emotions.

Discontent also emerged amongst designers. Duffy (1974), for instance, noted that a reprehensible aspect of the Bürolandschaft movement was that all organiza-tions should be equally participative and equally landscaped. This disregard for the uniqueness, or at least dissimilarity, between organizations foreshadowed concerns found in current theories and views on the nature of organization and work. As Dipboye, Smith, and Howell (1994, p. 20) note:

> An understanding of the true complexity of work organizations began to emerge, and the insufficiency of simplistic prescriptions such as those offered by either classical management theory or the human relations movement became apparent. One cannot ensure effective management by making workers happy and capitalizing on informal group processes any more than one can by planning and directing their every move. How an organization should be designed and run for best results depends on a host of considerations at the individual, group and macro-organiza-tional levels.

In terms of offices, the contingency theory approach suggests that it is inappropri-ate to impose a prescribed set of design rules. Offices should be a part of and reflect the uniqueness of the specific organization that is to be housed within it. It is consequently inappropriate, for instance, to remove status symbols if that does not fit within the general culture of the company. Furthermore, the office needs to be able to meet the changing requirements of the organization. In other terms, design should be contextually appropriate, flexible, responsive, and organic (Donald, 1994b). Recent research has shown that there are a host of emotional factors that relate to this responsiveness.

GETTING EMOTIONAL

The description of office design and its relationship to employees has shown the absence of emotion as an overt consideration by work and organization theorists, as well as designers. So far, offices have been considered in relatively functional ways, how they contribute directly to work, and how emotion has not been a part of the thinking in the area. Some allusion has been made to other factors that are emotional in tone, such as the subjugation of the worker to the organization. In the remainder of the chapter more overt links between emotion and offices at work will be made. Their tie into contingency theory and the concomitant need to situate design within its organizational context will also be considered. To under-stand further the role of offices, and to identify how emotion fits within it, a theoretical and conceptual framework is useful.

The essence of this framework is a reworking of the old saying about sticks and stones breaking bones while words cause little hurt. It is clear from everyday experience that while the sticks and stones may do physical damage, it is words that create most emotional hurt. The same is true at work. While the basic sticks and stones of the physical environment may relate to the physical aspects of tasks, it is often what the environment 'says' that is likely to impact upon workers' emotions.

Taking this perspective, Ellis (1986) has noted the importance of workers' perceptions of the social and organizational context in which they work. In doing this, Ellis placed his research within the theoretical framework of symbolic interaction. As he explains:

> (the) physical environment is viewed not as an independent variable that evokes human responses, but as a medium for symbolic communication in the course of social interaction ... A variety of media, both verbal and nonverbal, may be used in such social communication, and the physical environment is an important nonverbal medium of communication. As such, it acquires symbolic value, in addition to its purely functional significance.
>
> (Ellis, 1986, p. 228)

In Ellis's view then, the physical environment and the way in which it is managed have the potential to speak to those who work within it, in the same way as the gestures, verbal intonations and words of colleagues and bosses do.

The symbolic communication process of the environment can work in many ways and in relation to different populations. The organization, explicitly or implicitly, can speak to both its workforce and the outside world through the design and management of its offices. In return, the workforce can communicate with their organization through the same medium. For workers, using the environment in this way may be less risky than voicing their opinions directly in a context in which emotions are seen as a weakness, or even undesirably female (Hearn, 1993). In the remainder of this chapter, a number of examples of these processes will be given. These examples will consider both the expression of emotion, or emotional labour, and the experience of emotion.

Giving emotion some status

Status within an organization is something to be taken seriously (Katz & Kahn, 1978). The rationality of Weber and Taylor required recognizable status distinctions reflected in the physical environment. With the introduction of Bürolandschaft designs, status was considered something that should not have a manifest environmental form. Contingency theorists would probably argue that whether status symbols should be part of an office design depends on the specific organization.

The all-or-nothing approach to status found in classical and humanistic theory ignores the importance of the organizational context of the office environment. For instance, when an organization that traditionally had clear environmental representations of hierarchy moves from cellular to open plan offices many workers express feelings of great dissatisfaction. There may be many reasons for this, but one is likely to be that the removing of an individual's status markers can imply demoting and devaluing them, which can lead to negative emotions. In Briner's (1999b) terms, such environmental changes could be considered emotionally laden. While Briner (1999b) considers emotionally laden experiences, such as feeling valued or devalued, as not being emotions, he does contend that they are a central part of affective work experience.

While the removal of status symbols can have a negative emotional effect, through one mechanism or another, the consequences of strict adherence to status symbols and standards can also be emotionally and functionally negative. For instance, adherence can prevent the organization being able to respond to changing needs, and lead to frustration by hindering people from doing their work.

Environmental status symbols *per se* are neither emotionally good nor bad. It is the context of an organization's culture, traditions and norms that define the appropriateness of status symbols and people's reactions to them. In a sense, the way in which an environment is read and experienced depends on the symbolic language used in a particular place or organization.

Becker and Steele (1995) note that despite the move to a more egalitarian use of space during the 1960s, most offices continue to show status demarcations. They go on to provide an example of how emotive and frustrating it can be to work within a status defined office. When interviewing members of a research group, Becker and Steele (1995) describe one such incident:

> One of them spoke with great emotion about how bad it felt to be hamstrung in her work by bureaucratic indifference and game playing. She had needed a particular piece of equipment to run a series of tests ... There was just such a machine sitting two doors away from her in a vacant workspace ... she was not authorized to use it because of her level in the hierarchy. *She spoke with tears in her eyes about the frustration of wanting to do a good job* and being arbitrarily blocked from doing it.
> (Becker and Steele, 1995, p. 39) (emphasis added)

In this case, there are quite strong negative emotions created by the maintenance of environmental status. The converse of this response can also be evident in offices where negative emotions may be experienced as a result of the removal of environmentally-based status distinctions.

Once status markers are part of an organization, removing them is not a simple matter. Many studies have shown that when employees are relocated from private or small group offices to open-plan spaces they express a good deal of dissatisfaction. The dissatisfaction is usually expressed within a functional, rational, non-emotional framework. The expressed views of employees are usually taken at face value, with little effort exerted in looking below the surface, where emotion is as likely to be the force behind the dissatisfaction.

Hedge (1986), for instance, observes that many studies have identified problems with less status driven designs, and that their findings have shown a "remarkable consensus". Identified as typical is the loss of visual and conversational privacy, visual and aural distractions, interruptions and ambient conditions (Hedge, 1986). Whilst these problems are likely to be present and have a direct impact on work, it is also probable that there are emotional issues related to a lack or removal of status. To some extent this view is supported by Hedge's (1986) observation that those in supervisory and managerial positions typically view open-plan offices less favourably than other workers. Whilst there may be functional reasons for this, such as a greater need to concentrate, it is supervisory and managerial workers who are also most likely to feel a loss of status; moreover, they are the group who are more likely to have previously occupied private offices.

Most of the work considered by Hedge is quantitative, questionnaire-based research. Qualitative research has also shown how angry managers can be when moved to open offices, along with how the environment can be used by employees to communicate with their organization. This communication by employees is particularly important when they do not feel able to directly express their emotional response to an event.

Research carried out by Donald (1991) demonstrates the suppression of emotion, in this case anger, and its channelling into rational complaint. One participant, a department manager, interviewed during the research described numerous functional problems with his workplace. Moreover, and much to the annoyance of more senior members of the organization, he had posted bright yellow sticky notes all over the glass partitions around his workspace, apparently to prevent colleagues accidentally walking into them and causing themselves injury. On close examination, many of these difficulties appeared either unimportant or curiously unlikely to create the problems described.

During the course of a lengthy interview, the reasons and motivations behind the manager's feelings and actions became more apparent, and were clearly born of emotion. Prior to the move to a new office, the interviewee had spent many months and a great deal of time and effort with members of his department identifying their functional environmental needs. These had been presented to the space planners, designers and facilities managers. Yet despite all his work, the resulting design of the space showed that little attention had been paid to his efforts. Furthermore, the manager had been moved from a private office to a more "efficient" partitioned open office.

The manager was clearly angry at what he saw as the reduction in his status, and the organization ignoring his requirements. Essentially, there was an experience of inequity in the social exchange between the manager and the organization, which quite possibly broke the psychological contract between them, but certainly suggested that he was less valued than he had previously been. It was not possible for him to express his anger and frustration without appearing almost childish within the rational world of work. Consequently, the manager expressed his emotions by breaking rules and retaliating symbolically, whilst at the same time producing an organizationally acceptable, rational explanation for his action.

While this may seem relatively trivial, for those involved it was an issue of great frustration and conflict, and one that created a good deal of stress for both the department manager and the facilities management team. What is also evident from this example is that it would not be possible to resolve the apparently functional problems the manager had with his environment without addressing the deeper, more emotionally based issues; the problems were related to *events* rather than environmental *characteristics*.

The presentation of organizations in everyday life

The Larkin building considered earlier was clearly designed and run within the framework of classical theory and its demands for segregation of function, control, and economy of motion. It was also designed according to what Donald (1994b) describes as the work aesthetic. Looking at such an office in the early 1900s, it would have been quite apparent that the organization was efficient and rational, and so by implication were its employees.

The image created by an office's appearance is often the consequence of a great deal of work on the part of both designers and managers. Becker and Steele have indicated why this is considered effort well spent:

> Clarity of statements (images) ... can help members identify with and strengthen their commitment to the system, and it can help outsiders know how to relate to the organization. Clarity of identity can also be a help in attracting and keeping people who are essential to the system.
>
> (Becker & Steele, 1995, p. 30)

In their discussion of the importance and nature of the image created by an organization using the physical environment Becker and Steele (1995) go on to suggest two ways in which an image can be created. The first is to allow the look of the office to develop out of the day-to-day work and organizational processes, and perhaps emotions; essentially form following function. The second possibility is to create an image and fit work processes within it. Becker and Steele strongly support the approach of "making workplaces that reflect your goals and work style, thereby letting the image speak for itself." They further argue that:

> Doing it the other way around requires too much "staging" of scenes for the benefit of observers. This places too much pressure on workers to follow scripts so they look right in terms of the desired image, which in many instances is different from getting on with doing a good job.
>
> (Becker & Steele, 1995, p. 30)

Though not previously conceptualized in this way, the idea that the outward appearance of an office puts pressure on the workforce ties directly into research and writing on emotional labour.

Offices and emotional labour

A number of researchers have considered emotional labour in terms of the façades that employees are required to construct in order to portray a particular emotion or to hide other feelings. Yet, few have considered the way in which the physical environment of workers may also be manipulated to create a similar facade. Likewise, the consequences of *environmental–emotional labour* have rarely been considered.

Tied into to the concept of environmental–emotional labour is the issue of employees' personalization of their workspaces. While it is unlikely that personalization will directly enhance the efficiency of an employee, it is likely to have a significant impact on the emotional experience of work. Moleski and Lang (1986), for instance, argue that "corporate office design must consider appropriate means by which a worker may personalize the work environment, communicate an expression of self, and indicate his or her position in the organization" (Moleski & Lang, 1986, p. 18). Sundstrom (1986) makes a similar point, noting that personalization is of importance to an individual in establishing their self-identity in the workplace, and that the freedom to personalize a workspace depends on the "policies of the organization and decisions made by local executives" (Sundstrom, 1986, p. 219).

One group that has a major impact on personal expression and the image of an environment once an office has been built is the facilities managers. Facilities managers are responsible for the process by which the internal environment of such settings as offices is organized in relation to people, technology, and activities (Becker, 1981; Donald, 1994b). Their belief as to how an office should look has a significant impact on the day-to-day experience of office workers.

In a longitudinal study of offices Donald (1994b) examined the views of facilities managers and their impact on the offices they managed. During an interview in one organization the issue of the desired appearance was directly addressed:

> My background was in stores, and what was instilled into me was cleanliness, tidiness and product availability. To me this means standard configurations. It may look slightly boring, but it's neat, it's tidy, and what more do you want?

Not only do some facilities managers wish to create an office aesthetic that may consequently impact on workers' experience, they can also have their own emotional reaction when their aims are thwarted. Another facilities manager described by Donald (1994b) clearly demonstrates the point:

> This is a marvellous new place. You get people changing things, sticking balloons up and so forth. It lowers the whole tone. This is personally offensive to me having put so much work into it.

From this research it seemed apparent that organizations and facilities managers were trying to create a work aesthetic of orderliness and efficiency. Donald (1994b) argued that the reason behind this was a belief that the aesthetic is symbolic of an effective and productive environment. A remarkably similar point has been made by Briner (1999b) in relation to visible, expressed emotions in the workplace.

A further reason why employers might want employees to display particular emotions is that … (the employer) may believe that the way the employee feels is related to their performance. The employer's perhaps implicit reasoning here is that if an employee looks happy they probably also feel happy which means they will work more effectively.

(Briner, 1999b, p 330)

While the image created by the appearance of an office is important to organizations and their facilities managers, attempts to create and maintain that image may have a less than positive impact on the workforce. For instance, in Donald's (1994b) study one employee related that:

Standardized furniture makes it look better … but it's very impersonal. It's better psychologically to be able to personalize, to put things on screens. Rules about not putting things up are OK, but it depersonalises.

Not allowing the expression of self-identity in an office has the potential to create a degree of stress amongst a workforce. It can also lead to other, more simple and direct emotional responses such as boredom.

The worst part is you're in an office every day. It's ideal to get out occasionally, changes of faces, a change of scenery. It doesn't matter how good an office is, if you're going into it every day, at some stage you're going to get bored.

It is clear from these comments that it is the emotional experience of boredom rather than any simple difficulty with the office design that is directly hindering the ability to work. The importance of this experience should also not be underestimated. The person quoted had resigned from her job; a contributory factor was her experience of the environment. Ironically, after resigning she was given a number of temporary positions and tasks within the company. This new role provided greater environmental and work variation, which resulted in her reconsidering her decision to leave. Boredom is a significant emotion that is rarely considered, but is behind much of the work directed towards job enhancement and enrichment.

In order to maintain a particular work aesthetic or face, an organization may develop numerous techniques. One of the more common is the *clear desk* policy. Such policies usually require that workers clear away and file all their documents at the end of the working day. This can have the direct effect of interrupting the day-to-day flow of a person's work, but can also be frustrating if the rules and the environment are not congruent. For instance, workers may be criticised and "told off" on a daily basis for not adhering to a company's clear desk policy (Donald, 1994b). Yet when the office space is examined, it is often apparent that there is simply not sufficient space at employees' workstations for them to store their work. The constant criticism leads to many workers feeling frustrated and angry (Donald, 1991).

Like the departmental manager described on p. 294, the emotional aspect of work being described here is *experienced* emotion. There is a further point to be made that relates to the distinction that Briner (1999b) makes between emotions that are experienced because of the work task compared to those that arise out of social interaction. In the examples given here, the difficulties and emotions are generated not by the characteristics of the environments themselves, but by the way in which they are managed, and the processes that brought them about.

The impact of emotional labour is thought to be stressful as a result of dissonance between what a person feels and what they are allowed to express (Zapf, Vogt, Seifert, Mertini, & Isic, 1999). It is perhaps taking it a little too far to suggest that a great emotional dissonance is generated by the look of an office, but in attempting to achieve a work aesthetic an organization can have a negative impact on its workforce's emotions. Donald (1994b), for example, found the outcome of the rules and regulations used to maintain a particular environmental image was apathy, frustration, and conflict. The day-after-day experience of these emotions is unlikely to be organizationally efficient or individually healthy. One employee, quoted by Donald, succinctly expressed her view on the work aesthetic, commenting, "I'd rather work efficiently out of a slum than inefficiently out of an up-to-date office."

Shedding emotion on light

The final, brief example comes from Ellis's (1986) work on lighting. This is particularly interesting as lighting is perhaps the one aspect of office environments that has received the most attention from the rationalists and determinists. Beyond the possibility that most people do not like fluorescent lighting, it could be thought that there would be little by way of emotional interest. One of the few psychological studies to directly address this issue showed this not to be the case.

In a series of case studies Ellis (1986) demonstrated the interaction of functional, aesthetic, and symbolic qualities of the introduction of new lighting in two organizations. There are a number of interesting findings from Ellis's work that have significant implications for design and research, but which have, apparently, yet to be understood by environmental and organizational researchers.

The first of Ellis's observations fits well within the present discussion. He notes that the acceptance of lighting schemes in the organizations he studied was a function not only of the lighting characteristics, but again the processes or events that brought them about. Ellis describes how there was resistance to new lighting forms and negative feelings expressed towards them. The opposition seemed to be due to feelings about the organizations themselves, and what the users saw as a lack of participation. Supporting this view, Ellis found that greater participation resulted in higher levels of acceptance.

The research also found that aesthetic qualities, principally determined by colour rendering and contrast, affected "mood and state of mind", which in turn influenced attitudes and feelings to work, and as a consequence of that, absenteeism from the office. That some users felt the lighting was inadequate, not because of its objective characteristics, but as a result of management and organizational factors, is important. As Ellis notes, "a user who believes that the lighting ... is inadequate, for whatever reason, is likely to experience and report that inadequacy (e.g. headaches or eye strain) and behave accordingly" (Ellis, 1986, p. 243). It is possible that Ellis's view has some explanatory power in relation to such a phenomenon as Sick Building Syndrome (SBS), and therefore has implications for studies that seek to understand SBS by examining the purely physical aspects of the environment at work.

Another of Ellis's interesting findings is in relation to the way in which different groups of users perceived the lighting and developed what he termed "brand loyalty". In one of his studies two different types of lighting were introduced on two different floors of the same organization's offices. One group, who had been given halide lamps, described their lighting as "bright" and "businesslike", whereas they perceived the other group's sodium-based light as "gloomy" and likened it to a boutique or disco. The sodium group on the other hand felt rather differently describing their lights as "warm" and "homey" and the metal halide lamps as "cold" and "clinical". What is interesting about the feelings of the two groups is the way in which they interpret the objective characteristics of the lighting.

A NOTE ON RESEARCH METHODS

One of the important implications to arise from Ellis's (1986) work is in relation to the research methodologies employed to study environmental conditions in the workplace. Towards the start of this chapter it was noted that most research on offices assumes a rational and deterministic model of person–organization–environment relations. Throughout this chapter it has been seen that much lies below the surface of the impact of environmental conditions on workers' feelings. Ellis reiterates this view. However, an examination of research on offices shows how inadequate much current research is. A great deal of the research uses questionnaires and measures of the physical characteristics of the environment. Few delve deeply into workers' views or examine the organizational context. It is clear that to more fully understand the relationship between offices and emotions, there is a need to broaden the research domain and, quite probably, shift to a more qualitative approach to research. Unfortunately qualitative research is time consuming and difficult to publish in many academic psychology journals.

Numerous writers on emotions at work (e.g. Briner, 1999b; Fineman, 1993b) have argued for qualitative and narrative-based approaches to research. One reason for this is the importance of *events* rather than *task characteristics*, or in the present case, *environmental characteristics*, in the generation of employee's emotions. As Briner (1999b) argues, for example, "it is the *relationship* between the person and their context and how it unfolds that is of central interest in understanding emotion rather than proximal causes and immediate effects" (Briner, 1999b, p. 337). In addition to a need for qualitative data, research using longitudinal research designs are thought to be useful so as to "track over time the ebb and flow of transactions" (Briner, 1999b, p. 340). Donald's (1994b) research, which used both a narrative and longitudinal approach, resulted in many insights that would not have been apparent from other methodologies.

In terms of office research in general, it was noted at the start of the chapter that most studies are carried out using simulated environments and artificially selected, often student, populations. Research of this sort divorces the physical environment from its social and historic context, thereby removing any possibility of considering the impact of events. What is left is emotionally sterile research into environmental characteristics.

THE FUTURE OF OFFICES

There is much speculation about the future of office environments. As with previous attempts to predict what will happen with offices (e.g. Kleeman, 1986), the future is likely to be tied into and made possible by technology. For example, with the development of telephone and Internet banking along with other services there is likely to be a growth in call centres. If they follow the majority of current practice, the "offices" occupied by call centre workers are likely to make the Larkin Building appear positively cosy. Currently these environments are often barren landscapes dictated by reason and devoid of emotion. The impact they are likely to have on their inhabitants is clear. Fortunately, some organizations are beginning to recognize the problems of battery workers.

In some ways there may be a return to the past with office design turning full circle, becoming once again a converted domestic premises. One development that has long been predicted and is increasingly taking place is teleworking or homeworking. According to Turner and Myerson (1998), there are now one million employed or self-employed tele-workers in the UK, representing a saving of around 1.2 billion pounds in commercial rents and rates. The worldwide figure for teleworkers is around 20 million, with this number set to rise to 200 million within the next 20 years (Turner and Myerson, 1998).

The idea of increasing numbers of the workforce using part of their home as an office raises some interesting issues in relation to emotion. The home is a place far more imbued with emotions than is the corporate office. It could be said that it is a place where the rationality of work is not at home. However, much interest is in the technology of homeworking and the control and monitoring of homeworkers. Issues of trust are important here; as are the emotional reactions to having behaviour at home monitored by an employer.

Questions are also raised about the possibility and problems of separating "home life" from work. In essence, what much of that discussion is about is how to partition emotion from reason. Open-door policies, so often praised in organizations, are problematic when it is the worker's children that feel free to walk into their boss' office for an informal discussion. The Bauhaus architect Mies van der Rohe once famously described the office as "a machine for working in" (Turner & Myerson, 1998). While people may accept working in a corporate machine, they are unlikely to be so enthusiastic about their home being turned into one.

After more than a century of office design and management, rationality and reason remains the dominant ethos. Whether emotions will be allowed into the vast expanses of IT sheds, or driven from parts of people's homes, remains to be seen. Either way, what will lie at the real heart of an organization will be the way its employees feel.

REFERENCES

Arnold, J., Cooper, C., & Robertson, I. (1998) *Work Psychology: Understanding Behaviour in the Workplace*, 3rd edn. London: Financial Times Professional.

Becker, F. (1981) *Workspace: Creating Environments in Organisations*. New York: Preager.

Becker, F. & Steele, F. (1995) *Workplace by Design: Mapping the High-performance Workscape*. San Francisco: Jossey-Bass.

Braverman, H. (1974) *Labour and Monopoly Capital*. New York: Monthly Review Press.

Briner, R. (1999a) The neglect and importance of emotion at work. *European Journal of Work and Organizational Psychology*, **8**, 323–346.

Briner, R. (1999b) Introduction. *European Journal of Work and Organizational Psychology*, **8**, 321–322.

Clegg, S. & Dunkerley, D. (1980) *Organisation, Class and Control*. London: Routledge and Kegan Paul.

Craig, M. (1981) *Office Workers' Survival Handbook: A guide to Fighting Health Hazards in the Office*. London: BSSRS.

Dipboye, R., Smith, C., & Howell, W. (1994) *Understanding Industrial and Organizational Psychology: An Integrated Approach*. London: Harcourt Brace.

Donald, I. (1994a) The structure of office workers' experience of organizational environments. *Journal of Occupational and Organizational Psychology*, **67**, 241–258.

Donald, I. (1994b) Management and change in office environments. *Journal of Environmental Psychology*, **14**, 21–30.

Donald, I. (1991) Managing the organic office. *Building Services: The CIBSE Journal*, **13**, (8), 28–30.

Donald, I. (1999) *Organizational Context and the Environment*. Paper presented at Looking for Environmental Psychology in the UK, London, 16–17 December 1999.

Duffy, F. (1974) Office Design and Organisations: 1. Theoretical Basis. *Environment and Planning B*, **1**, 105–118.

Duffy, F. (1979) Bürolandschaft '58-'78. *The Architectural Review*, *CLXV*, January, 54–58.

Duffy, F. (1980) Office Building and Organisational Change. In A.D. King (Ed.) *Buildings and Society: Essays on the Social Development of the Built Environment*. London: Routledge and Kegan Paul.

Ellis, P. (1986) Functional, Aesthetic, and Symbolic Aspects of Office Lighting. In J.D. Wineman (Ed.) *Behavioral Issues in Office Design*. New York: Van Nostrand Reinhold.

Fineman, S. (1993a) Organizations as Emotional Arenas. In S. Fineman (Ed.) *Emotion in Organizations*. London: Sage Publications.

Fineman, S. (1993b) An Emotion Agenda. In S. Fineman (Ed.) *Emotion in Organizations*. London: Sage Publications.

Gerth, H.H. & Mills, C.W. (1958) *From Max Weber: Essays in Sociology*. New York: Oxford University Press.

Hearn, J. (1993) Emotive Subjects: Organizational Men, Organizational Masculinities and the (De)construction of 'Emotions'. In S. Fineman (Ed.) *Emotion in Organizations*. London: Sage Publications.

Hedge, A. (1982) The Open-Plan Office: A Systematic Investigation of Employee Reactions to their Environment. *Environment and Behavior*, **14**, 519–542.

Hedge, A. (1986) Open versus Enclosed Workspaces: The Impact of Design to Employee Reactions to Their Offices. In J.D. Wineman (Ed.) *Behavioral Issues in Office Design*. New York: Van Nostrand Reinhold.

Hedge, A. (1987) Office health hazards: An annotated bibliography. *Ergonomics*, **30**, 733–772.

Hedge, A., Erickson, W., & Rubin, G. (1996) Predicting sick building syndrome at the individual and aggregate levels. *Environmental International*, **22**, 3–19.

Hochschild, A.R. (1983) *The Managed Heart: Commercialization of Human Feeling*. London: University of California Press.

Katz, D. & Kahn, R. (1978) *The Social Psychology of Organizations*. Chichester: Wiley.

Kenz, I. (1995) Effects of indoor lighting on mood and cognition. *Journal of Environmental Psychology*, **15**, 39–51.

Kjellberg, A., Landström, U., Tesarz, M., Söderberg L., & Åkerlund, E. (1996) The effects of nonphysical noise characteristics, ongoing task and noise sensitivity on annoyance and distraction due to noise at work. *Journal of Environmental Psychology*, **16**, 123–136.

Kleeman, W.B. (1986) The Office of the Future. In J.D. Wineman (Ed.) *Behavioral Issue in Office Design*. New York: Van Nostrand Reinhold.

Lorenzen, H.J. & Jaeger, D. (1968) The office landscape: A systems concept. *Contract*, **9**, 164–173.

Mann, S. (1999) Emotion at work: To what extent are we expressing, suppressing, or faking it? *European Journal of Work and Organizational Psychology*, **8**, 347–369.

Moleski, W.H. & Lang, J.T. (1986) Organizational goals and human needs in office planning. In J.D. Wineman (Ed.) *Behavioral Issues in Office Design*. New York: Van Nostrand Reinhold.

Putnam, L. & Mumby, D. (1993) Organizations, Emotion and the Myth of Rationality. In S. Fineman (Ed.) *Emotion in Organizations*. London: Sage Publications.

Roethlisberger, F. (1949) *Management and Morale*. Cambridge MA: Harvard University Press.

Russell, J.A. & Snodgrass, J. (1987) Emotion and the Environment. In D. Stokols & I. Altman (Eds) *Handbook of Environmental Psychology*, Vol. 1. New York: Wiley.

Sharma, R.A. (1982) *Organisational Theory and Behaviour*. New Deli: Tata McGraw-Hill.

Sundstrom, E. (1986) *Work Places: The Psychology of The Physical Environment in Offices and Factories*. Cambridge: Cambridge University Press.

Taylor, F.W. (1911) *Scientific Management Comprising Shop Management, the Principles of Scientific Management, Testimony Before the Special House Committee.* New York: Harper and Row.

Turner, G. & Myerson, J. (1998) *New Workspace, New Culture: Office design as a catalyst for change.* Aldershot, UK: Gower.

Veitch, J. (1997) Revisiting the performance and mood effects of information about indoor lighting and fluorescent lamp type. *Journal of Environmental Psychology*, **17**, 253–262.

Vischer, J.C. (1989) *Environmental Quality in Offices.* New York: Van Nostrand Reinhold.

Weber, M. (1947) *The Theory of Social and Economic Organisation.* Translated by A.M. Henderson & T. Parsons. New York: The Free Press.

Weiss, H. & Cropanzano, R. (1996) Affective events theory: A theoretical discussion of the structure, causes and consequences of affective experiences at work. *Research in Organizational Behaviour*, **18**, 1–74.

Wotton, E. (1976) Some considerations affecting the inclusion of windows in office façades. *Lighting Design and Applications*, **6**(2), 32–40.

Zapf, D., Vogt, C., Seifert, C., Mertini, H., & Isic, A. (1999) Emotion at work as a source of stress: The concept and development of an instrument. *European Journal of Work and Organizational Psychology*, **8**, 371–400.

Chapter 13

Future work and its emotional implications

Peter Herriot
The Empower Group, London, UK

There appear to be two ways in which this chapter title might be addressed. The first would elaborate the trends in the nature of work which have been identified recently, assume their continuance to yet more pronounced forms, and draw some implications for the likely emotional impact upon employees. So, for example, the increasing variety and flexibility of employment contracts might be argued to likely result in increased feelings of job insecurity. The second approach, which is the one I will take, is to reverse the order of the elements of the title. In other words, I intend to take a particular stance on the nature of emotions and then look at some fundamental issues in the employment relationship of the future in the light of this analysis.

EMOTIONS ARE SOCIAL

Emotions are dependent upon social relationships; that is, they are "socially constructed" (Harré, 1986). They originate with others, refer back to the self, and always take others into account (Denzin, 1984). This general statement is not intended to deny that emotions have biological and physiological substrates. Rather, it affirms that the meanings which we put on this substrate, the way we experience it, and, indeed, its very activation, are the result of our social relationships.

Emotions at Work. Edited by Roy Payne and Cary Cooper.
© 2001 by John Wiley & Sons, Ltd.

How then do social relationships form our emotional experience? Social relationships are conducted through the playing of social roles in particular situations. Such role playing is imbued with social meaning, which is often expressed
by language during the social exchange. Hence the "symbolic interactionist"
approach argues that the way in which we construe and experience our
emotions is a result of the symbolic meanings we encounter during our playing
of our social roles in daily life (Rosenberg, 1990; Hochschild, 1990). However, this
emphasis on language and symbols should not lead us to the conclusion that we
simply learn to attach verbal labels to our emotional experiences. Rather, we learn
what it is that we are supposed to feel in particular situations, how to interpret it
to ourselves, and how appropriately to express it (Greenwood, 1992).

Different cultures hold different values regarding how social relationships
should be conducted, and hence about which social roles should be played, by
whom, and how. As a consequence, they embrace different forms of emotional
experience and expression (White, 1993). The most fundamental value distinction
is that between individualism and collectivism (Triandis, 1995), which is demonstrated in a wide range of social behaviour. Because of their values in favour of
mutuality and reciprocity in specific role relationships, collectivists' emotions tend
to be focused on others, and for the duration of the social exchange. They therefore favour such emotions as empathy or embarrassment. Individualists, on the
other hand, are more concerned about themselves, and hence may be more likely
to feel, for example, angry or proud. Their emotional experiences may last longer,
since the self is more permanent (though not static) than a social situation.

Thus emotions are both formed by social relationships and are expressed within
them. The same is true of the self-concept. I treat the self-concept as a mental
structure within which various elements coexist. These elements may relate to
identity (e.g. occupation, family, gender, religion) or they may be evaluative in
nature, such as self-esteem and self-efficacy. However, to speak of structure does
not imply stasis. Rather, the self is continually being reformed as a result of social
relationships. However, it is also dynamically related to those relationships, since
it in turn affects their nature and course. For it is the nature of the self which
determines our responses to others' words or actions; and it is our responses
which affect the course of the ongoing social episode, and hence the relationship
itself (Hinde, 1997).

How, then, are emotions, social relationships, and selves related? One answer is
to suggest that emotions are an integral part of the development and the expression of the self; that is, the emotions which we learn to express in particular social
situations are incorporated into our view of our selves. We observe ourselves
feeling and expressing certain emotions strongly or often, and believe ourselves
to be a person with those emotions. Others confirm our view by their reactions to
our emotional expressions, which we note and internalize. Hence, emotions help
both to construct our selves and to express them (Haviland & Kahlbaugh, 1993).

Indeed, it is possible that certain features of relationships are associated with
certain emotions, and, thence, with certain central elements of self. For example,
power and status in relationships (Kemper, 1991,1993) may be associated with

guilt and shame (Scheff, 1990), and, hence, with such elements of identity as gender and self- esteem (Hochschild, 1983).

In sum, emotions are an extremely important element in the formation and expression of the self, and, hence, in the course of social relationships.

EMOTIONS, SELVES, AND THE EMPLOYMENT RELATIONSHIP

Given this account of emotion as a social phenomenon intimately connected to relationships between parties with selves, how may we relate emotions to the future of work? The approach which I will adopt here is to consider the future of work as largely synonymous with the future of the employment relationship. Thus, the employment relationship is to be seen as an example of a social relationship, with all that this implies for the impact of emotion upon the selves of the parties to that relationship, and upon the relationship itself.

This social psychological view of the employment relationship is largely different from the perspectives of those who have traditionally studied it. Both industrial-relations scholars (e.g. Blyton & Turnbull, 1998) and organizational, sociological, and political theorists (see Clegg, Hardy, & Nord, 1996) have emphasized the *employment* element of the employment relationship at the expense of the *relationship* element. They have stressed the unique nature of employment, with its simultaneous requirement both for control and also for collaboration. They have consequently failed to appreciate sufficiently that employment is a relationship between persons, and, therefore, that aspects of other relationships may be relevant to this particular case.

However, when we do apply the social psychological analysis of emotion, selves, and social relationships outlined above to the employment relationship, considerable explanatory benefits become apparent.

First, anchoring the employment relationship in specific interactions in time between persons allows us to bypass the highly contested constructs of "the individual" and "the organization" which have confounded analysis hitherto. The parties to any employment relationship are, first, top managers. It is they who determine such things as the range of employment contracts available, and it is they who initiate structural change, such as downsizing or mergers and acquisitions. It is such decisions as these, together with the explanations and justifications given for them, which are likely to have major impact upon the other party to the employment relationship: each employee (Herriot, Hirsh, & Reilly, 1998). The other party is thus not "the individual" in abstract, but rather each and every individual employee. Hence, by definition, there exist a wide range of employment relationships in any organization. And those relationships are based not upon abstract political or sociological theory but upon a history of social interactions in real time between real people.

Now, of course, the relationship may mostly be conducted through intermediaries: line managers, negotiators, union representatives, and so on. Furthermore, it may be conducted virtually via communications technology rather than face to face in person. Nevertheless, it is a relationship between persons. Moreover, it is important to realize that the relationship may be conducted through action episodes just as much as through exchanges of words or symbols. Hence an action of top managers, such as the board discarding a chief executive, may be invested with a variety of meanings by employees seeking to make sense out of an ambiguous situation (Weick, 1995; Isabella, 1990).

The second advantage of this social psychological analysis is that it allows access to the selves of these persons. Selves both form and are formed by any social relationship, including the employment relationship. Of course, the dynamic balance varies. For some people and in some cultures, the employment relationship is of major concern (Meaning of Work International Research Team, 1987), and, hence, its nature and progress may affect the self profoundly. For others, it is of less importance, and their existing selves may determine their contribution to the relationship rather than the reverse. Moreover, the relative power of the parties may affect this dynamic balance. Top managers may put a lot of effort into socializing the values of the organization into employees (Anderson & Ostroff, 1998). Employees, on the other hand, may have relatively few resources with which to resist this pressure and affirm their selves (Ackroyd & Thompson, 1999).

Third, a role for emotion in the employment relationship now becomes clear. Emotions which arise from specific interactions between the parties in the employment relationship may affect both the selves of the parties and the relationship itself. Consider, for example, the spate of recent and now regular downsizings in organizations. There is considerable evidence of feelings of anger on the part of employees that the psychological contract which they thought that they had with top managers (Rousseau, 1995) has in their view been broken (Brockner, 1988). Furthermore, many felt guilty about surviving when their colleagues were made redundant. These feelings are likely to have affected their selves, especially in terms of their self-esteem and their self-efficacy. Likewise, top managers engage in a variety of ways with the task of making employees redundant (Kets de Vries & Balazs, 1997). They have to cope with being survivors themselves, being responsible for the downsizing, and being blamed by employees for being responsible. Many respond with a variety of self-defence mechanisms: rationalization, splitting, or dissociation, for example. Or else they simply continue resilient and hardy, maintaining their self-esteem through the plaudits of shareholders and colleagues at their own level.

A final important contribution of the social constructivist perspective to the understanding of the employment relationship is the recognition that different cultures, with different social values, engage in different forms of relationship. These differences are expressed at work in different sorts of social behaviour within the social episodes that create the employment relationship (Erez & Earley, 1993). For example, since they value social relationships highly, employees from a collectivist culture are more likely to seek a strong identification and a long-term relationship with their employer than are individualists. Hence, they are more likely to be willing to adapt their selves to the employer's expectations, and to comply. Because of the importance of membership and socialization, collectivists are more likely to blur the boundaries between business relationships and private life. Hence, there may be fewer elements of their selves from which collectivists exclude their employer. Individualists, on the other hand, only identify with their employer if s/he continues to meet their aspirations. They expect a much more transactional form of relationship in which roles and tasks and accountabilities are spelt out. And they seek to draw clear boundaries between their work identities and the rest of their selves.

An important cultural development is the trend away from collectivism and towards individualism (Triandis, 1995; Giddens, 1991). Hence, if top managers are looking for employment relationships which incorporate the values of collectivism, but employees globally are becoming more individualist, then the employment relationship is likely to face major problems.

This cultural trend exemplifies the following general issues for the employment relationships of the future, expressed in social constructionist terms:

- To what extent are the expectations of top managers likely to be compatible with the selves of employees?
- To what extent are employees likely to be willing to change their selves, and hence their values and social behaviour, so as to accord with these expectations?
- Or to what extent will they be prepared to comply with them behaviourally, whilst defending their selves and their values against their employers?
- To what extent will employees succeed in affecting the nature of their employment relationship, so that it remains compatible with their selves?

Clearly, these are not issues which can be resolved in one way or another. Rather, the social constructionist position would understand most relationships as both affecting and being affected by the selves of the parties. However, in a case such as that of employment where one of the parties, top management, usually holds the balance of power, attention is rightly focused upon possible changes in the selves of the weaker party: employees. Hence, any evaluative discussion of the outcome for selves will need to devise criteria for acceptable changes in employees' selves; for example, do the changes in employees' selves induced by their employment relationship permit them to retain their integrity? However, this will at least be a counter to managerialist assumptions that the only thing that matters is the business success of the enterprise.

The role of emotions in our consideration of the employment relationship of the future now becomes clearer. If emotions both help to form selves and also to express them, then we need to consider the impact of emotions upon employment relationships from two perspectives. First, employees will experience emotions in response to top managers' expectations and actions. *What emotions will they*

experience, and what effects upon their selves are those emotions likely to have?
Second, employees may express these emotions, or, on the other hand, they may
not. If they do, *what effects upon the employment relationship are such expressions
likely to have?* And if they do not, *what effects will such non-expression have?* I will
address these questions by examining three current and likely continuing expectations of top managers in larger organizations: the expectations for compliance,
difference, and change. I will conclude with some implications for the relationship
itself.

RELATIONSHIPS, EPISODES, EVENTS, AND EMOTIONS

Before I do so, however, I need to expand upon the limited account of emotions in
the context of the employment relationship which I have given so far. I will rely in
particular on the reviews of Fineman (1996) and Briner (1999).

Emotions are feeling responses to *specific events* (e.g. the reception of a notice
of redundancy or the notification of a promotion). As such they are short lived,
relative to other psychological phenomena (e.g. attitudes). They are more specific
than the generalized feeling states which work and organizational psychologists
have hitherto spent so much time investigating: job satisfaction, stress, and well-
being.

The English language presents us with a wide range of emotion labels: loyalty,
involvement, fear, anger, guilt, shame, envy, pride, pity, anxiety, disgust, admira-
tion, excitement, exhilaration, anticipation, irritation, foreboding, relief, and
boredom, to name but a few. It is worth noting that not all of these emotions
are always florid and loudly expressed: we speak of being "quietly proud", for
example, where overt expression of pride might be deemed inappropriate; or we
may express boredom by falling asleep or switching off. Indeed, we are capable of
not expressing our emotions at all, merely of feeling them internally. It is also
worth noting that the existence of a multiplicity of emotion labels does not mean
that all of them are widely distinguished by individuals as they interpret their own
or others' experiences. Nor does it mean that people who speak languages with
fewer emotion labels experience, or can distinguish, fewer emotions.

However, social events occur in a context (Weiss & Cropanzano, 1996). Their
immediate context is the *social episode* of which the event is a part. So, for
example, the reception of the redundancy notice is a part of an episode
between top managers and the redundant employee. This episode may have
started with top managers communicating to all employees an urgent need to
cut costs before the end of the financial year. Employees responded differentially.
Some co-operated with local management in economizing, others communicated
their anxieties about the possible implications of the message to their union
representatives. In response to these responses, top management announced
that redundancies would be carried out in those businesses which had not met

their cost-cutting targets. Employees' representatives in these businesses responded by proposing economies which, they and their members were convinced, removed any need for redundancies. Top managers acknowledged receipt of these proposals, but almost immediately informed employees via their representatives that their accountants had demonstrated to their satisfaction that the required economies would not accrue. They had no option but to declare redundancies. The reception by many individual employees of redundancy notices was the next event in the episode.

Clearly, it is hard to establish when an episode begins and when it is at an end. Perceptions as to what is an episode may differ between the parties, although in this case both would probably agree that the episode consisted of the downsizing exercise. But what is important is that the appraisal by the employee of the notification event, and the emotion that s/he felt, will be profoundly affected by the other events in the episode. If those other events had succeeded in persuading the employee that redundancies had been forced upon top management by overwhelming external competition, for example, then the feeling might have been one of resignation. As it is, given the sequence of events outlined above, the employee is perhaps more likely to have experienced anger and disgust than resigned acceptance.

However, the context to the expression of emotion is broader than this episode. It also includes all the *other episodes* which the employee has experienced during his or her employment with the organization. If top managers have previously demonstrated a responsive attitude to employee concerns, then it is possible that employees will believe their justifying statement that redundancies are the only way of achieving cost reductions, and that cost reductions are essential to the organization's very survival. On the other hand, if these explanations are not believed, the apparent betrayal of trust built up over time may result in yet stronger feelings of anger (Brockner, Tyler, & Cooper-Schneider, 1992).

The state of *the employment relationship* at any point in time is thus a function of a history of social episodes between the parties. These episodes have consisted of a series of events, in response to each of which the parties may have experienced different emotions. These emotional experiences will have become incorporated into their selves and their perceptions of the relationship, and hence will affect their responses in subsequent episodes.

How does this incorporation of feelings into the self occur? We observe ourselves experiencing certain emotions within the employment relationship; we note the responses of others to our expression of those emotions; we check, against our knowledge of social norms, whether it was appropriate for us to express them in that particular situation. In brief, we monitor our emotions and others' responses to them. Thus, it is our thoughts and feelings about our feelings which enable us to incorporate those feelings into our selves.

As a history of episodes and events accumulates in the experience of an individual employee, they may have experienced certain emotions much more frequently than others (e.g. fear and anger more often than pride and involvement). Thus, the selves of the parties and their perceptions of the relationship will be affected by their regular experience of, and reflections upon, these particular emotions. Perhaps the end of an episode is a crucial point for the reflection on events and our reactions to them, which results in their incorporation into the self. And the added realization that we have responded with the same fear and anger to previous events in previous episodes may affect the relationship more profoundly.

It is with this analysis in mind that I consider the three forms of expectation which I predict top managers will hold ever more strongly in the future: expectations for compliance, difference, and change. These expectations will be consistently and repeatedly expressed by means of action or communication events embedded in a series of episodes. Hence, the emotions with which employees respond to these events are themselves likely to be frequent and consistent. They are, therefore, likely to affect profoundly employees' selves, or their actions in the employment relationship, or both. It should then be possible to address the three questions posed at the end of the previous section regarding the effects of the expression or non-expression of emotions upon employees' selves and upon the employment relationships of the future. For we will have suggested the nature of employees' probable emotional responses to employers' expressed expectations, and their likely effects.

THE COMPLIANCE EXPECTATION

Most management commentators see organizations moving towards flexibility and away from control. They anticipate flexible mutual and organizational support as the dominant internal cultural orientation; and creative innovation as the dominant external, market-facing orientation. The typical employee in such organizations is autonomous, creative, and supported by a team. They will be developing themselves continuously, and, therefore, by virtue of their enhanced employability, they will be enjoying a "boundaryless" career (Arthur & Rousseau, 1996).

Continuing with this model of culture (Quinn, 1988), I argue that the opposite is likely to be the case for most employees in most organizations; that is, the fundamental move is away from flexibility and towards control. Internally, the dominant cultural orientation will not be support but rules; externally, it will not be innovation but rather goals and targets. Let us give these cultural orientations more specificity:

- *Support* highly values affiliation, participation, cooperation, mutual trust, team spirit, and individual growth. Informal communication and decision making are the order of the day, feelings and ideas are expressed freely, and individual commitment is emphasized
- *Innovation* involves searching for environmental information, anticipating change, creative thinking and activity, openness to change, and willingness to experiment and take risks. Involvement and commitment from employees is assumed and expected

- *Goals* is about rationality, competitiveness, performance indicators, performance management, accountability, contingent rewards, and the efficacy of such processes as appraisal. Its artefacts include mission statements, objective setting, and budget targets
- *Rules* emphasizes hierarchy, authority, order and stability, compliance, responsibilities, procedures, job descriptions, rules, and discipline.

The move towards goals and rules is exemplified in the growth of call centres, which are currently the fastest growing occupation in the UK and employ nearly 3% of the working population. *Rules* require call-centre employees to stick rigidly to the decisions which the expert system software in their computer dictates. Total compliance is required, since deviations from the system are, in the long run, less profitable. The operative may feel that they know special details about the client which would enable them, for example, to give an insurance quotation which is better suited to both client and insurer. This opportunity for initiative and autonomy has to be steadfastly ignored.

Call-centre employees are also tasked with clear *goals*. They have to complete so many calls per day, and there is a limit to the time they are allowed to spend on each call. The time they spend off the phone, the time it takes them to pick up the phone when it rings, even what they say to every customer, is recorded and can be listened to contemporaneously or subsequently.

The pendulum in this and many other sectors appears to be swinging firmly towards control and away from Zuboff's (1988) alternative function for technology: "informating", that is, most employees are not expected to use the information acquired about their work behaviour to understand their own work or the customers better and to improve their performance as a consequence. Data is monitored centrally rather than locally to extract trends, etc., and the 5% of cases with which the expert system fails to deal are referred to Head Office.

Moreover, the fastest growing jobs in the USA are in janitorial, custodial, medical, sales, and restaurant occupations. Only 6% of jobs in the USA are of such a technical level as to require two or more years of higher education (Perrow, 1996).

Any shift towards a cultural orientation of rules immediately presents top managers with a serious problem. For there is clear evidence that support and, to a lesser extent, goals and innovation in cultural orientations are positively related to organizational commitment (Vandenberghe & Peiro, 1999). Thus, paradoxically, organizations which move towards rules and away from support and innovation are actively inhibiting the normative commitment which they seek to impose.

Top managers have two options with regard to this increase in rules and goals as means of control. First, they can make clear that this is, indeed, the direction which they are taking in their relationship with the majority of their employees, and give the reasons why they believe it to be necessary. Then, at least their actions and their words agree. Alternatively, they can continue with the rhetoric of empowerment (Argyris, 1998), whilst steadily moving towards greater control. What are the likely emotional responses to these two options?

The requirement to comply, and to comply with the utmost precision and without any exception, is likely to arouse *hostility* in individualists (and thus to the majority of employees in most Western countries).

Individualists tend to "view themselves as independent of collectives; are primarily motivated by their own preferences, needs, rights, and the contracts they have established with others; give priority to their personal goals over the goals of others; and emphasise rational analyses of the advantages and disadvantages of associating with others" (Triandis, 1995, p. 2). They consider themselves to have a unique personality, to be independent of, and distinct from others. They tend to have high self-esteem.

The incompatibility of these features of individualist selves with the expectation of compliance is evident. Rules have to be followed by everyone; all are the same in this regard, and there is no room for the desired autonomy, nor for the realization of their own preferences or goals. *Frustration* as well as hostility is, therefore, a likely emotional reaction. If, however, the requirement for compliance is limited to those elements of work where it is essential, and if there is plenty of opportunity to gratify their own preferences outside the work relationship, then a transactional relationship of compliance in exchange for reward is feasible. But this has to be a bilateral transaction rather than a unilateral imposition.

The expectation for compliance is much more likely to elicit a favourable emotional response from collectivists. Collectivists "see themselves as parts of one or more collectives ... (and) are primarily motivated by the norms of, and duties imposed by, those collectives; are willing to give priority to the goals of these collectives over their own personal goals; and emphasize their connectedness to members of these collectives" (Triandis, 1995). Collectivists would like to describe themselves as dutiful and cooperative. Given the stability of their relationships, collectivists tend to have consistent selves which change relatively little over time (in marked contrast to individualists, who may tend to treat their selves as a reflexive project to which they can apply a "makeover" when they wish). Clearly, all these elements of their selves make compliance a much more realistic expectation for collectivists.

However, there are two major caveats which argue against the fantasy-led policy recommendation to locate all the major parts of large organizations in collectivist cultures! The first is the requirement for collectivists to construe themselves as part of the company as a collectivity before they give it their loyalty and compliance. If for any reason (especially their perception of the company as embodying individualist values) they withhold this commitment, then the benefits to the employer will not follow. The second caveat is the trend away from collectivism towards individualism, gradually diminishing the potential population from which compliant employees can be drawn.

So the likely response of some, but not all, to a requirement for compliance is one of *frustration and hostility*, although there are certain actions which top managers can undertake to reduce its probability. The second option for top management is to continue with the rhetoric of empowerment whilst enforcing compliance. This is not really an option, since the most likely emotional response from employees to this approach is one of mistrust. Obvious gaps between rhetoric and experienced reality are one of the quickest ways of inducing feelings of *mistrust and cynicism* (Kramer, 1996). Mistrust and cynicism rule out the use of rational persuasion and the transactional contract as strategies for inducing compliance.

The increasing expectation of compliance, then, will probably result in hostility in individualist cultures, and, depending upon top managers' actions, may also result in mistrust and cynicism. Hostility will lead to an increased perception of the self as "one of us" as opposed to "one of them" (top management) (Kelly & Kelly, 1991), and will therefore sharpen the differences between the parties. Mistrust and cynicism will, in addition, create the need for a re-establishment of trust over the long term, before a productive and reciprocal employment relationship can be enjoyed.

Thus the expectation of compliance will be expressed by top management more and more frequently in the episodes of interaction with employees. The events within these episodes will increasingly arouse emotions of hostility, and possibly mistrust and cynicism. These in turn will affect employees' views of their selves, and, in particular, of their selves in respect of the employment relationship. These perceptions will affect their actions, which will generally put a greater strain on the employment relationship than currently exists.

THE DIFFERENCE EXPECTATION

Recent findings in the human-resource management literature (Huselid, 1995; Becker & Huselid, 1998) have indicated that the use of certain human-resource (HR) processes by organizations has resulted in improved bottom-line perform-ance. The implication has been drawn by some commentators that organizations will survive and prosper by achieving benchmark standards of excellence in these processes.

This outcome is highly unlikely. Competitive excellence is achieved not by doing the same as other organizations, but rather by doing something different. Advantage is likely to accrue from the unique ways in which people processes and business processes are related to each other and embedded in the day-to-day operations of the organization (Lepak & Snell, 1999). It is likely to depend upon unique social capital (Nahapiet & Ghoshal, 1997). Hence, rather than organizations becoming more like each other in terms of their employment re-lationships, the reverse is true: there will be increasing differences *between* organizations.

The same picture of increasing diversity also applies to employment relation-ships *within* organizations. Here the variety of employment contracts will probably continue to proliferate, ranging from temporary employees from employment agencies, through operatives working part time or shiftwork and professionals on fixed-term project contracts, to those from whom the organisation hopes to develop its top managers (Emmott & Hutchinson, 1998; Brewster, 1998). The mutual expectations of the parties to these relationships are vastly different. The temps are expected to get up to speed and learn the organisation's systems; the operatives are expected to make the transition to new employment contracts and maintain their motivation; the professionals have to do a professional job without supervision, but within time and budgetary constraints; the favoured core need to be totally committed and willing to learn fast.

Members of each of these categories of employee will have their own expectations in return. For example, part- timers will expect the flexibility to suit them as well as their employer; the favoured few will leave unless they get development opportunities (Winter & Jackson, 1999). Hence, within organizations, employees will be aware that colleagues enjoy markedly different employment relationships to their own.

If employees compare their own employment relationship with those of others within the same organization, or with those enjoyed in other organizations, then feelings of *inequity* are likely to rise. For differences in outcomes, despite similar inputs, will become evident (Pearce, 1993). As the range of comparisons increases, so these feelings become more probable. Related feelings of *procedural and interactional injustice* (Folger & Cropanzano, 1998) may also increase, as employees from less favoured groups perceive the superior HR processes and the more respectful treatment which others more fortunate than themselves receive.

As with the compliance expectation, there is an added complication, however. Top management may employ rhetoric which implies that a single and favourable employment relationship is enjoyed across the organization. Metaphors of family, crusade, club, or citizenship are all likely to be counterproductive, however (Herriot, 2001). The existence of favoured sons or rejected children argues against family. Contracted mercenaries are hardly likely to share the crusading vision. Club servants perceive only too clearly the gap between themselves and the members. And equal and democratic rights for citizens are hardly universal. When top managers employ metaphors from employees' own experience, they run an added risk of inducing feelings of cynicism and mistrust, as employees supply from their own experience the flip sides of these metaphors: family feud, play-acting crusaders, exclusive and privileged minority, and oligarchy or dictatorship.

Hence, feelings of inequity or injustice may be accompanied by *mistrust and cynicism*. On the other hand, it is perfectly possible that employees may experience feelings of gratitude and loyalty if the benefits of their employment contract are mutual and reciprocal (and, therefore, probably, if they have been negotiated). Yet, in order to achieve such reciprocity, top managers will need to understand the selves of employees and their vulnerability. For example, they will need to recognize that:

- occupational identities are likely to be threatened if employees are moved away from their core skill set;

- family identities may be at risk if temporal flexibility is required without consideration of employees' needs;
- the self-esteem of agency staff or part-timers is endangered if they are treated as second-class citizens.

The difference expectation, then, is in a sense an extension of the compliance expectation. Not only will the majority of employees be expected to comply; they will be expected to do so even when they realize that there are other employees who enjoy very different relationships, and of whom very different expectations are held. Once again, given the increase in individualist values, feelings of inequity and injustice are likely to become more salient for employees. The perception of our selves as wronged, and of top managers as oppressors, is therefore more likely, with consequent damage to the employment relationship. Top management's main hope for the future appears to be to engage in reciprocal dealing with individual employees, so that their needs are met as well as the organization's. As a consequence, comparisons of their own treatment and outcomes with those of others become less probable, and so do feelings of inequity and injustice.

THE CHANGE EXPECTATION

To argue that control, rather than innovation, will be the experience of most employees was bold. To suggest that organizations will at some stage cease to change at their present feverish rate is to court ridicule. Commentators agree that as the technical, economic, social, and political environments change ever faster, so will organizations if they are to hope to survive within them.

Yet the evidence hardly supports this social Darwinist assumption. It is not so much the survival of the fittest that is the order of the day. Rather, it is the survival of the biggest (Baum, 1996). It is not organizations which cut themselves back so as to become "lean and mean" which survive and prosper (Cameron, Freeman, & Mishra, 1993); nor is it those which explicitly seek to change their culture (Beer, Eisenstat, & Spector, 1990). It is those which grow. And the more mature the market, the better the larger and more staid organizations perform (Nelson, 1994).

Moreover, the bulk of the evidence also demonstrates that radical organizational change is extremely dangerous (Davis & Powell, 1992). Reliability and accountability of performance, sunk costs, and organizational memory are all at risk, and the rapid development of new philosophies, roles, policies, processes, and practices is often beyond organizations' capabilities. An organization loses legitimacy if it decides to change its goals; it risks losing control if it changes its authority systems; it puts operations at risk if it changes its core technology; and it stands to lose its cash cows if it changes its markets.

Finally, it is evident that the grounds for undertaking radical change are socially derived rather than based on rational considerations. In other words, they are determined largely by fashion. The benchmarking and imitation of so-called excellent companies demonstrates the search for legitimate justifications for change initiatives about the effectiveness of which there is seldom any reliable evidence (Tolbert & Zucker, 1996). Legitimating institutional support buttresses certain interventions (e.g. certificating institutions for total quality management). The personal networks of top managers, oiled by the fruitful and creative minds of management consultants, provide further ideas for change and its legitimation.

Thus both structural and programmatic change is often of dubious benefit to the organization and to some extent a matter of fashion or fad (Huczynski, 1993). On the other hand, top managers are often judged in terms of their willingness to create radical change, and, in particular, in terms of their readiness to cut costs through redundancies or mergers and acquisitions. It is worth noting that, as the sequence of radical changes has progressed over the past two decades, it has become more and more difficult to implement them at ground level. This should point top management towards the implication that the enthusiasm for change amongst employees may not equal their own. Indeed, in the end, change initiatives can become mere play-acting for the sake of the external audience, becoming totally decoupled from what is happening on a day-to-day basis inside the organization (Tolbert & Zucker, 1996).

In such a context, we may ask what employees' emotional reactions are likely to be to an event which has become more frequent as downsizing episodes recur: top management's announcement of the next restructuring. After all, many change initiatives threaten elements of the selves of employees. Compulsory redundancy, for example, can assault a wide range of identities: identification with the organization; identification with our own work group; identity as family breadwinner; self-esteem; and sense of agency. A culture-change programme can result in a response of reactance (unwillingness to be manipulated), or loss of self-esteem ("they are not satisfied with me as I am").

In the light of such potential threats to their identity, it would not be surprising if employees felt *anxious and insecure, resentful, and mistrusting*: anxious and insecure because they might suffer; resentful because top managers do not appear to understand or care about the impact of change upon them; and mistrustful of top managers' competence and motives, given the previous history of change initiatives. They could also, over the longer term, come to feel *helpless and despairing*, as they seem to themselves to have lost any capacity to influence what happens to them.

On the other hand, it is possible that many could feel very different emotions: *excitement and even exhilaration* as the prospect of new activities and new career opportunities opens up before them; *relief* that something has been done to address obvious business issues; and so on. However, it is those higher up the organization who are most likely to have favourable responses to change. Nevertheless, it may still be possible to engage all levels of employee positively in change, for example, by involvement, preparation, transparency of process, and a clear rationale (Guest & Peccei, 1992).

Such engagement is rendered far less likely, however, by the rhetoric with which managerial discourse has surrounded change. Using the evolutionary metaphor, change (and therefore the change which we are making) is inevitable, and the only two possibilities are adaptation or extinction. People who disagree with the direction or the detail of change are stigmatized as obstructive, or as dinosaurs incapable of change. Change initiatives are presented as part of an overall strategy, when it is easy for employees to see them, rightly or wrongly, as knee-jerk reactions to unforeseen external events. They are pictured as opportunities for learning, and thus for increasing employability, when for many the outcomes are more work for the same rewards. Cynicism and distrust are once again the likely outcome of rhetoric, as world-weary and media-sophisticated employees note the reality gap and marvel that top management should think them so naive.

Once again, top-management rhetoric renders far worse an employment relationship which could potentially be rescued. For whilst anxiety can be allayed and resentment disarmed, mistrust is a major long-term problem.

IMPLICATIONS FOR THE EMPLOYMENT RELATIONSHIP

The trends in top management's expectations which I have outlined above certainly do not lead us to entertain an optimistic outlook regarding the employment relationship for most employees. The expectation of compliance is apt to result in feelings of frustration and hostility; that of difference, feelings of inequity and injustice; and that of change, feelings of anxiety and insecurity, and possibly resentment and helplessness as well. As these feelings recur, and as employees reflect upon them and incorporate them into their selves and their view of the employment relationship, that relationship is itself likely to change for the worse. Yet, there are ways to lead people through these expectations. The need for compliance can be justified and areas of autonomy can be provided; relationships based on reciprocity can be negotiated; and even change initiatives can be successful if conditions of involvement and mutual commitment are met.

Yet, the fundamental problem is that there exists in many organizations a previous history and a current practice of attempts at rhetorical persuasion by top management (Legge, 1995). This rhetoric seldom meshes in with employees' experience. The rhetoric of empowerment is directly contradicted by the requirement for compliance. The rhetorical metaphors of family, crusade, club, or citizenship, which imply unity and equality, are negated by the increasingly varied deals available to different groups within the organization. And the rhetoric of social Darwinism comes up against the awkward fact that leaner does not mean fitter but merely meaner.

It is this gap between rhetoric and reality which leads to mistrust and cynicism on the part of employees, and therefore presents the greater threat to the employment relationship. For the reestablishment of trust in a relationship, once it has been lost, is a long and difficult task. It requires the practice of dialogue; that is, the attempt to understand the selves of employees by eliciting and listening to their accounts of their experience; and the willingness to reveal our own selves. The practice of rhetoric is actively hostile to dialogue, for it has the purpose of persuading the other to adopt a particular perspective. It becomes a branch of marketing, treating the employee, like the customer, as a consumer (du Gay, 1996).

The continued managerial use of rhetoric will result in yet greater cynicism, a cynicism which will permit employees to play-act the emotional responses that are expected of them. Many of them are already working in service occupations which require them to put on certain emotional performances on demand (Hochschild, 1983). The cynicism of playing at soldiers serves to add to this existing assault upon their authenticity and integrity.

Yet, whilst in this chapter I have hopefully avoided the trap of managerialist optimism, I have also avoided the dark pessimism of what we might term the literature of oppression. Top managers and employees still have options for action, despite the constant and often conflicting demands of the stakeholders of the business. Top managers have to lead their colleagues into the practice of dialogue with employees, so that the episodes of the employment relationship result in positive emotions which enhance top managers' and employees' selves and improve their relationship.

REFERENCES

Ackroyd, S. & Thompson, P. (1999) *Organisational Misbehaviour*. London: Sage Publications.

Anderson, N.E. & Ostroff, C. (1998) Selection as socialisation. In N. Anderson & P. Herriot (Eds) *International Handbook of Selection and Assessment*. Chichester, UK: Wiley.

Argyris, C. (1998) Empowerment: The emperor's new clothes. *Harvard Business Review*, 76(3), 98–105.

Arthur, M.B. & Rousseau, D.M. (1996) The boundaryless career as a new employment principle. In M.B. Arthur and D.M. Rousseau (Eds) *The Boundaryless Career*. New York: Oxford University Press.

Baum, J.A.C. (1996) Organisational ecology. In S.R. Clegg, C. Hardy, & W.R. Nord (Eds) *Handbook of Organisation Studies*. London: Sage Publications.

Becker, B.E. & Huselid, M.A. (1998) High performance work systems and firm performance: A synthesis of research and managerial implications. *Research in Personnel and Human Resource Management*, 16, 53–101.

Beer, M., Eisenstat, R., & Spector, B. (1990) Why change programmes don't produce change. *Harvard Business Review*, 68(6), 158–166.

Blyton, P. & Turnbull, P. (1998) *The Dynamics of Employee Relations*, 2nd ed. London: Macmillan.

Brewster, C. (1998) Flexible working in Europe: Extent, growth, and the challenge for HRM. In P. Sparrow & M. Marchington (Eds) *Human Resource Management: The New Agenda*. London: Financial Times and Pitman.

Briner, R.B. (1999) The neglect and importance of emotion at work. *European Journal of Work and Organisational Psychology*, **8**, 323–346.

Brockner, J. (1988) The effects of work layoffs on survivors: Research, theory, and practice. In B.M. Staw and L.L. Cummings (Eds) *Research in Organisational Behaviour*, Vol. 10, pp. 213–255. Greenwich, CT: JAI.

Brockner, J., Tyler, T.R., & Cooper-Schneider, R. (1992) The effects of prior commitment to an institution on reactions to perceived unfairness: The higher they are, the harder they fall. *Administrative Science Quarterly*, **37**, 241–261.

Cameron, K.S., Freeman, S.J., & Mishra, A.K. (1993) Downsizing and redesigning organisations. In G.P. Huber and W.H. Glick (Eds) *Organisational Change and Redesign*. New York: Oxford University Press.

Clegg, S.R., Hardy, C., & Nord, W.R. (1996) *Handbook of Organisation Studies*. London: Sage Publications.

Davis, G.F. and Powell, W.W. (1992) Organisation and environment relations. In M.D. Dunnette and L.M. Hough (Eds) *Handbook of Industrial and Organisational Psychology*, Vol. III. Palo Alto, CA: Consulting Psychologists Press.

Denzin, N.K. (1984) *On Understanding Human Emotion*. San Francisco: Jossey-Bass.

du Gay, P. (1996) *Consumption and Identity at Work*. London: Sage Publications.

Emmott, M. & Hutchinson, S. (1998) Employment flexibility: Threat or promise? In P. Sparrow & M. Marchington (Eds) *Human Resource Management: The New Agenda*. London: Financial Times and Pitman.

Erez, M. & Earley, P.C. (1993) *Culture, Self-identity, and Work*. New York: Oxford University Press.

Fineman, S. (1996) Emotion and organising. In S.R. Clegg, C. Hardy, & W.R. Nord (Eds) *Handbook of Organisation Studies*. London: Sage Publications.

Folger, R. & Cropanzano, R. (1998) *Organisational Justice and Human Resource Management*. Thousand Oaks, CA: Sage Publications.

Giddens, A. (1991) *Modernity and Self-identity: Self and Society in the Late Modern Age*. Cambridge: Polity Press.

Greenwood, J.M. (1992) The social constitution of emotion. *New Ideas in Psychology*, **10**, 1–18.

Guest, D. & Peccei, R. (1992) Employee involvement: Redundancy as a critical case. *Human Resource Management Journal*, **2**(3), 34–59.

Harré, R. (1986) *The Social Construction of Emotions*. Oxford: Blackwell.

Haviland, J.M. & Kahlbaugh, P. (1993) Emotion and identity. In M. Lewis and J.M. Haviland (Eds) *Handbook of Emotions*. New York: Guilford Press.

Herriot, P. (2001) *The Employment Relationship: A Psychological Perspective*. London: Routledge.

Herriot, P., Hirsh, W., & Reilly, P. (1998) *Trust and Transition: Managing Today's Employment Relationship*. Chichester, UK: Wiley.

Hinde, R.A. (1997) *Relationships: A Dialectical Perspective*. Hove, UK: Psychology Press.

Hochschild, A.R. (1983) *The Managed Heart: The Commercialisation of Human Feeling*. Berkeley, CA: University of California Press.

Hochschild, A.R. (1990) Ideology and emotional management: A perspective and path for future research. In T.D. Kemper (Ed.) *Research Agendas in the Sociology of Emotions*. Albany, NY: New York State University Press.

Huczynski, A.A. (1993) Explaining the succession of management fads. *International Journal of Human Resource Management*, **4**(2), 443–464.

Huselid, M.A. (1995) The impact of human resource management practices on turnover, productivity, and corporate financial performance. *Academy of Management Journal*, **38**(3), 635–672.

Isabella, L.A. (1990) Evolving interpretations as a change unfolds: How managers construe key organisational events. *Academy of Management Journal*, **33**, 7–41.

Kelly, J. & Kelly, C. (1991) Them and us: Social psychology and the new industrial relations. *British Journal of Industrial Relations*, **29**(1), 25–48.

Kemper, T.D. (1991) An introduction to the sociology of emotions. In K.T. Strongman (Ed.) *International Review of Studies on Emotion*, Vol. I. Chichester, UK: Wiley.

Kemper, T.D. (1993) Sociological models in the explanation of emotions. In M. Lewis & J.M. Haviland (Eds) *Handbook of Emotions*. New York: Guilford Press.

Kets de Vries, M.F.R. & Balazs, K. (1997) The downside of downsizing. *Human Relations*, **50**(1), 11–50.

Kramer, R.M. (1996) Divergent realities and convergent disappointments in the hierarchic relation: Trust and the intuitive auditor at work. In R.M. Kramer & T.R. Tyler (Eds) *Trust in Organisations: Frontiers of Theory and Research*. Thousand Oaks, CA: Sage Publications.

Legge, K. (1995) *Human Resource Management: Rhetorics and Realities*. London: Macmillan.

Lepak, D.P. & Snell, S.A. (1999) The human resource architecture: Toward a theory of human capital allocation and development. *Academy of Management Review*, **24**(1), 31–48.

Meaning of Work International Research Team (1987) *The Meaning of Working*. New York: Academic Press.

Nahapiet, J. & Ghoshal, S. (1997) Social capital, intellectual capital, and the creation of value in firms. *Academy of Management Best Paper Proceedings*, 35–39.

Nelson, R.R. (1994) The co-evolution of technology, industrial structure, and supporting institutions. *Industrial and Corporate Change*, **3**, 47–64.

Pearce, J.L. (1993) Toward an organisational behaviour of contract labourers: Their psychological involvement and effects on employee co-workers. *Academy of Management Journal*, **36**(5), 1082–1096.

Perrow, C. (1996) The bounded career and the demise of civil society. In M.B. Arthur and D.M. Rousseau (Eds) *The Boundaryless Career*. New York: Oxford University Press.

Quinn, R. (1988) *Beyond Rational Management: Mastering the Paradoxes and Competing Demands of High Performance*. San Francisco: Jossey-Bass.

Rosenberg, M. (1990) Reflexivity and emotions. *Social Psychology Quarterly*, **53**, 3–12.

Rousseau, D.M. (1995) *Psychological Contracts in Organisations*. Thousand Oaks, CA: Sage Publications.

Scheff, T. (1990) Socialisation of emotions: Pride and shame as causal agents. In T.D. Kemper (Ed.) *Research Agendas in the Sociology of Emotions*. Albany, NY: New York State University Press.

Triandis, H. (1995) *Individualism and Collectivism*. Boulder, CO: Westview Press.

Tolbert, P.S. & Zucker, L.G. (1996) The institutionalisation of institutional theory. In S.R. Clegg, C.Hardy, & W.R. Nord (Eds) *Handbook of Organisational Theory*. London: Sage Publications.

Vandenberghe, C. & Peiro, J.M. (1999) Organisational and individual values: Their main and combined effects on work attitudes and perceptions. *European Journal of Work and Organisational Psychology*, **8**(4), 569–581.

Weick, K.E. (1995) *Sensemaking in Organisations*. Thousand Oaks, CA: Sage Publications.

Weiss, H.M. & Cropanzano, R. (1996) Affective events theory: A theoretical discussion of the structure, causes, and consequences of affective experiences at work. *Research in Organisational Behaviour*, **18**, 1–74.

White, G.M. (1993) Emotions inside out: The anthropology of affect. In M. Lewis & J.M. Haviland (Eds) *Handbook of Emotions*. New York: Guilford Press.

Winter, J. & Jackson, C. (1999) *Riding the Wave: the New Global Career Culture*. Redhill, UK: Career Innovation Research Group.

Zuboff, S. (1988) *In the Age of the Smart Machine*. London: Heinemann.

Chapter 14

Inner technology: emotions in the new millennium

Ayman Sawaf, Harold H. Bloomfield, and Jared Rosen
Whole Life Publishing, San Rafael, CA

EMOTIONAL INTELLIGENCE (EQ): THE INNER TECHNOLOGY OF THE NEW ERA

Human business has evolved in exponential ways through technological advances such as the ability to transport people anywhere in the world, as well as dispatch a message to anyone instantly through the global telecommunications network. Within the shadow of the glory of mankind's material evolution lurks the ageless abyss of suppressed human emotions. People's underlying unresolved emotional dynamics continue to contaminate the evolutionary and business potential of societies. Greed, jealousy, fear, and rage continue to generate hatred, war, and the repression of free thought.

As the information age flourishes in the realm of global commerce, it will be of great necessity to balance the technological intelligence with the expansion of knowledge that nourishes the human spirit and liberates the universal language of emotions. As computer technology entered into every industry and paradigm, transforming them to higher levels of productivity and profitability, so will emotional intelligence in the years to come. Emotional intelligence or EQ is the breakthrough inner technology for the 21st century because emotions are a primary source of human energy and information that is essential. The development and education in the *self-science* of EQ is of critical value at this juncture in human evolution.

Emotions at Work. Edited by Roy Payne and Cary Cooper.
© 2001 by John Wiley & Sons, Ltd.

In the past millennium, having a high IQ was the indicator of an intelligent person. Many people with high IQs were employed to deliver well-thought-out solutions to the vast challenges of civilization. Frequently, ingenious solutions to these challenges were only temporary and generated new problems. For example, the smart discovery of the hydrogen bomb was thought to be a final solution to global conflict. This discovery only created new problems, with the need for additional solutions. The belief of using atomic weapons to create peace through fear has left the world in a precarious position. The proliferation of a global nuclear arms race is now the new problem with a more challenging need for a solution.

When choosing the individuals who will deliver the solutions to the problems of this new millennium, emotional intelligence or EQ needs to be considered an equal partner to IQ. This equal blend of EQ and IQ is the recipe of for creating long-lasting *resolution* to global problems as opposed to volatile *solutions*. Being "smart without heart" is a dangerous disposition for the fundamental challenges required during this tenuous phase of our civilization.

EQ is a vital factor in think-tank settings and brainstorming sessions. This is articulated by Cooper and Sawaf (1997) in their book *Executive EQ*:

> In meetings and other group settings where people come together to collaborate, there is a strong sense of group IQ, the sum total of intellectual knowledge and skills in the room. However, it turns out that the single most important element in group intelligence is not the average, or highest IQ, but emotional intelligence.

EMOTIONAL LITERACY: APPLICATIONS FOR PARENTING AND EDUCATION

As computers entered our modern society in the last half of the 20th century, people progressively found it imperative to learn computer skills. Twenty years ago, students who used computers needed to be proficient in a computer language that required a certain level of aptitude. With the introduction of user-friendly personal computers, students of this current age use computers like a pencil and slide ruler of yesteryear.

In a world where academic literacy and computer literacy is rapidly becoming the norm, emotional literacy will also become commonplace in order for human beings to grow and develop the consciousness to face the challenges of the future.

Emotional literacy is one of the best investments that we can make as a culture. Becoming emotionally literate is learning the alphabet, grammar, and vocabulary of our emotional life.

As emotional literacy is progressively introduced into the school rooms and living rooms of our society, children will learn to be more comfortable with their authentic nature and inspired to develop their innate creative attributes. It is critical to invest in educating prospective parents in the value of emotional self-awareness and honesty of expressiveness. In past generations, emotionally illiterate parents have been a source of discouragement and psychological wounding for their children. In contrast, emotionally literate parents can foster a generation of healthy, happy, and productive people.

As we start the 21st century, our culture has struggled with the complex problems that have resulted from broken families. Dysfunctional relationships are destroying individuals, and families. In his book *Making Peace With Your Parents*, Bloomfield (1983, p. 49) observes that: "Many of us grew up in families in which it was not all right for children to get angry." This suppressed anger translates into deep-seated resentments that alienate family members. The inheritance of emotional illiteracy has been a primary factor in their disintegration of cohesive families.

Emotional literacy will support parents in developing and retaining deeply bonded relationships with their children. Through emotional literacy, we can educate young people that a healthy and intimate relationship such as a marriage can be forged and adhered to through a mutual commitment to consciously respect each other's feelings.

Becoming resistant to dealing with the emotional challenges of a committed relationship is a ticket for a rocky ride and a potential breakdown of the relationship. Training people to have the emotional skills to use in all of their personal and professional dynamics will be a priceless asset.

Our ability to raise healthy, emotionally literate children is perhaps the greatest profit we can achieve. In an era where we have drug czars, mandatory drug testing, and drug education as the solutions to the childhood drug epidemic, we need to carefully scrutinize the underlying precursor to this phenomenon. One of the primary reasons children take drugs is to fill the emptiness that they are experiencing on an emotional level. Drugs, when used chronically, block painful feelings and anesthetize the feelings.

With the horrors of the 6 o'clock news mirroring the consequences of emotional illiteracy, a voice is being heard in the wilderness shouting "save our children". Do you ever wonder why well-educated children from affluent American homes go to school and shoot their classmates? Who is to blame? Blame is usually a symptom of denial. We all know that children who perform such atrocious acts are the victims of emotional illiteracy. They are embodying the accumulative effect of suppressed emotions such as rage, depression, grief, and fear.

Who is responsible for perceiving the emotions of a child? Who can sense that a child has a lot of suppressed rage? And, if someone can read such deeply intense emotions, are they emotionally fluent enough to address the condition in a non-judgmental and healthy way. This is certainly a clarion call to mobilize emotional-literacy educators and establish emotional literacy as a primary language taught in all early education curriculums.

THE EMOTIONALLY INTELLIGENT WORKPLACE

In the workplace, emotional intelligence is an essential reality that is being progressively addressed. Commonly, workers who do not have the skills to listen to their own internal feelings are, thus, more prone to make decisions based on unresolved fears, guilt, and resentment.

With the successful introduction of EQ training into the business world, we will be able to identify and measure its profitability. In the future, businesses will feel less awkward providing EQ training, whereas, during the past century, educating workers about their emotions was characterized as provocative. Year by year, the organizational development and training industry will continue to transform EQ training out of the theoretical and into the practical.

These training programs will be in conjunction with EQ profiling. Essi Systems/Q Metrics of San Francisco (Cooper, 1997) has pioneered the first extensively researched, nationally norm-tested, statistically reliable measurement system for emotional intelligence. The EQ Map™ is a metric tool for plotting an individual's emotional strengths and vulnerabilities, and for identifying their personal and interpersonal patterns for success.

Currently, thousands of executives have been profiled using the EQ map (Cooper and Q Metrics, 1997), and the results are being compiled in a database to determine the correlation between emotional intelligence and competency. As EQ profiling becomes more valued within the business community, corporate consultants will learn how to diagnose the culture of a company and have a delineation of what is lacking and what is needed within the emotional intelligence of their workforce.

High EQ businesses will see their workers as human capital instead of human resources, as they continually invest in their employees' self-development. Business leaders will learn that the more they appreciate their employees the greater the business appreciates in value. The resultant profit will be delivered through greater team coherence and productivity, as well as emotionally content employees.

In the 21st century corporate climate, there will be a shift away from the traditional vertical hierarchy of not questioning authority, to a more horizontal approach of listening to real feelings from within the workforce. This is currently visible in smaller creative organizations and is partially due to the more relaxed workplace environment. In larger organizations, on-site training programs that focus on communication and self-development have paved the way for an atmosphere of increased emotional honesty.

Caring about the employee's emotional condition will impact decisions about the architectural design and general environmental considerations (Ryerson, 1999). For example, greater understanding about the effects of color and lighting on the emotions of the workers will be commonplace. This new direction will transform sterile business environments into warm, pleasant surroundings. The integration of indoor waterfalls, aromatherapy, and other ambiance-oriented enhancements into the workplace will be known to bolster increased productivity and health within the employees.

The attitude that you must leave your personal life at home before coming to work is based on denial and idealism. To be able to consistently be yourself in all settings is the template for an emotionally fit society. This does not discount the need for healthy boundaries. Many people need a degree of autonomy at work. Autonomy and emotional honesty can go hand in hand. In other words, you can effectively express your emotions with your co-workers without choosing to disclose the details of your personal life.

These new emotionally intelligent skills must be modeled by the leaders of their organizations. Changing the attitude of the corporate climate will change the nature of competition. Industry leaders who fear potential failure in their future may misuse the inherent healthy aspects of competition and fall victim to jealousy and anger. A business leader who is jealous of the competition can foster bitter and resentful sentiment toward their competitor. For example, this can appear as negative advertising. Such a business would focus on cutting down their competitor instead of focusing on presenting their product with joy and pride.

This scenario is similar to a common dynamic that plays out in sibling rivalry. Frequently, siblings compete for the love and attention of their parents. This pattern of competition is carried into their adulthood with their colleagues, as they strive for external validation from others. Successful individuals are those who can generate self-esteem internally, as well as be open to feedback externally. Your self-identity needs to be free from obsolete parental influences. The common incentive to be successful in order to disprove a doubting parent can generate a lifelong experience of self-sabotage. Such a person might achieve financial wealth, but the distorted subconscious motivation of proving their abilities to their unsupportive parents will not address the abysmal feelings underlying their drive.

EMOTIONAL INTELLIGENCE AND HEALTH

Traditional, 20th century Western science made the assumption that emotions are exclusively controlled and stored in the brain. In recent decades, many pioneers in the life sciences have presented new vantage points that are beginning to close the gap between the brain, the body, and the emotions.

One of the most respected researchers in the area of the mind/body connection is Dr Candace Pert. Dr Pert is a research professor at Georgetown University Medical Center and the former Chief of Brain Chemistry at the National Institute of Health. She has proven that all cells throughout the body have receptors for a string of amino acids called neuropeptides. Neuropeptides are produced in the brain. The receptors link the brain to the entire body, thus establishing what could be a body/mind integrated system. Dr Pert hypothesizes in her ground-breaking book *Molecules of Emotions* (Pert,

1997, pp. 140–141) "Maybe these peptides and their receptors are the biochemical basis of emotions." Since these peptides exist in the heart as well as the gut, this could possibly explain why we sometimes check in with our heart or gut before making decisions.

In his best-selling book *The Heart's Code* (Pearsall, 1998), Dr Paul Pearsall makes the case that the heart is more than a pump. Through his compiled research, Pearsall presents how the heart communicates, as well as stores, information. Citing case studies from heart-transplant recipients, Dr Pearsall portrays how these recipients began experiencing emotional qualities and sometimes even vivid memories congruent with their donor's lives. One of the most compelling stories involves a child who received a donor heart from another child, who was murdered. In this case, the heart recipient began to have vivid nightmares about the murderer of her donor. Her descriptions of the murderer were so accurate that the police were able to correctly identify him.

At the Institute of HeartMath® in Boulder Creek, California, researchers (Institute of HeartMath) have been studying the patterns of the heart, to gain insight into the relationship between heart rhythms and emotional and psychological states. The Institute has developed training programs that teach techniques for increasing the coherence in the rhythmic patterns of heart-rate variability. The researchers have documented dramatic positive shifts in the participants' ability to reduce stress and deal more effectively with difficult situations while practising the techniques. Some of the physiological benefits recorded were improved balance in the nervous system as well as enhanced immunity. In direct juxtaposition, they discovered a correlation between what they describe as "negative emotions" and disorder in both the heart's rhythms and the autonomic nervous system.

As the health-care industry becomes more educated about the empirical evidence of the emotions' direct effects on health, stress medicine is becoming more recognized as one of the most important disciplines for eradicating chronic illness. Health-care providers are slowly beginning to shift their focus from using methods to repair the damage of unhealthy emotional energy to implementing proactive approaches, such as the methods developed by the Institute of HeartMath. These approaches will teach people how to channel emotional energy through their bodies in ways that are regenerating and vitalizing to their physiology.

The past models used to explain the emotions are rapidly becoming outdated. The old paradigm separated the body, mind, and emotions. The new body/mind paradigm invites us to be aware of how our thoughts, feelings, and cells are all part of one seamless whole.

EMOTIONS AS INNER FIRE

The acronym FIRE stands for Feelings Information Responsibility and Energy (Bloomfield, Sawaf, & Rosen, 2000). As we begin this new millennium, we will rediscover this fire and learn to temper it. We will learn to use its light to illuminate the darkened regions of human consciousness, as well as learn to transport its warmth into our daily communication and community building.

At the beginning of the 20th century, a medical doctor named Sigmund Freud began the ensuing process of developing an independent scientific discipline that revolved around analyzing the latent emotional content of his patients. Thus, the field of psychotherapy was born. During the past several decades, psychotherapy, working with "sick patients", has been integrated into modern pop culture. Emotional literacy programs for the 21st century will begin to shift the perspective of using therapy to repair emotional trauma to a new paradigm of perceiving emotions as energy and information. As people become more emotionally intelligent, they will learn to identify the signals that emotional energy is transmitting to them.

For example, when they feel fear, they will know that the fear is giving them information to pay attention and be concerned. People will choose to feel and process their emotions for the purpose and benefit of receiving information. Imagine going through your day consciously perceiving and expressing your feelings as they appear. Instead of sitting around feeling bored, as soon as you felt boredom you would instantly receive the message "it is time to learn a new skill".

As people resonate with the concept of "emotions as information", they will shift from avoiding their feelings to realizing the necessity to glean the information out of their feelings. Individuals will have their own "emotional information system". Such a system will foster the transformation of feelings into action. For example, when individuals feel anger, they can be informed that their reality is not the way they like it. This is a call for them to take responsibility and act to change it. If they feel jealousy, that emotion can transmit the information that they need to question the issue of ownership that is the cause of such jealousy.

Misconceptions about emotions will become destigmatized as individuals become masters of their emotional expression. One of the first misconceptions that needs to be changed is that some emotions are good and some are bad. This polarization of emotions has encouraged us to avoid the so-called negative emotions. Three of the most commonly defined negative emotions are anger, fear, and jealousy. These emotions have been behind the scenes of the grand drama of human evolution. From the great works of art to the great wars, these three emotions have motivated intense human interaction.

When the alliance of fear, jealousy, and anger are expressed together, they can ruthlessly be used to unleash the horrors of war. For example, if a world leader feels the fear that he will not succeed in leading his people, he may feel jealous of another nation that has what he feels is missing for his people such as oil or other commodities. He then might feel anger toward that nation and begin to ferment anger within his people, eventually driving them into the fervor of war.

This interface of fear, anger, and jealousy can be deeply rooted in early childhood memories. For example, when a child wakes up alone in a room, he may feel fear. The child cries out for its mother. If there is no response, the baby may begin to feel jealous that its mother is paying attention to someone else. The baby may become frustrated and angry and its crying intensifies into an angry cry.

Many times these primal emotions are suppressed as our parents discipline us to be in more control of our emotions. This is a direct result of the parents' fear of their own emotions being projected onto their children. The emotional challenges of parents is articulated by Dr Harold H. Bloomfield in his book *Making Peace With Your Parents* (1983, pp. 84):

> Parenting is never easy. In the process of wanting to influence, guide and protect their children, parents may habitually or only at times, resort to a variety of emotional weapons that have negative psychological consequences.

The problem with learning to control emotions is that this can sometimes be against our healthy human nature. *Intense emotions need to be effectively expressed or they will become unbearably constrictive.* Have you ever seen someone trying to hold back rage or terror. It looks like they will literally explode.

REFINING RAW EMOTIONS INTO HIGHER OCTANE ENERGY

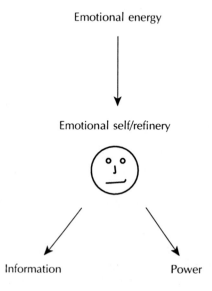

Emotional energy

Emotional self/refinery

Information   Power

The three root emotions of fear, jealousy, and anger have one thing in common, which is that they are generally compressive emotions. These emotions have a powerful internal charge that contracts tightly within the individual feeling the emotion. It is similar to a tyre being pumped up with air; the more you feel the raw emotion of fear, jealousy, and anger, the tighter you feel the constriction. If you keep pumping your self up with the emotion, like a tyre you will begin to spring a leak or eventually burst. Suppressed anger, fear, and jealousy can potentially lead you to dramatic or violent reactions if not consciously addressed and expressed.

Compressive emotions will feel constrictive until they are discharged through self-expression. Through intentionally expressing the emotional energy within the three root emotions of fear, anger, and jealousy in constructive ways, you can expand into the higher octaves of each of these three emotions. These higher octaves are the virtuous qualities (such as passion, compassion, and discipline) that will assist you in building greater character, emotional resilience, and inner strength. It is important to learn to invite these emotional allies into your conscious awareness, rather then having them covertly infiltrate your emotional life.

Emotions that have a tendency to be more compressive or constrictive can be reversed through healthy expression into feelings of expansiveness and freedom. The formula for transforming a compressive or constrictive emotion into an expansive emotion follows four basic steps:

1 Identify the emotion you are feeling;
2 Feel the energy of the emotion thoroughly;
3 Refine the raw energy of the emotion and outwardly express the emotion in a healthy way;
4 Get the message that is being transmitted by the feeling.

The three root emotions of anger, fear, and jealousy are important allies when transformed into their higher octaves, which increases success and vitality. To illustrate how you can refine emotions, consider the analogy with an oil refinery. When you draw raw crude oil out of the ground it is too impure to use, therefore it goes through a refining process. When the oil is refined to gasoline, it can then be used to power your car.

In a similar light, when you feel raw anger, it is many times too impure to express. Many times people feel anger and impulsively express the raw anger only to regret the rash words used. When you can identify the feeling of anger and internally process and express it, the anger will be experienced with greater self-awareness. For example, if your friend angers you by something s/he says, you may wish to go into another room and allow yourself to feel the pure force of your anger.

You have consciously identified that you are upset and you have chosen not to suppress it, yet you are allowing yourself the opportunity to refine the anger to its higher form such as courage and passion. When you return to verbally express your feelings to your friend, your communication is more clear and potent. By defusing the lower frequency of the anger you are inviting your friend to respond in a more emotionally mature and fluid way as well.

In this coming new era, as technology plays an increasing role in our lives, it will be important to attend to the humanistic values of sincere and heartfelt communication. To learn and practise the language of emotions through direct interpersonal communication is a critical path for healthy human evolution.

BUILDING ALLIANCES WITH YOUR EMOTIONS

The best way for people to learn a new language is to use it. As people become more familiar with their feelings, they will learn to build dynamic relationships with their emotions. They will conjure emotions at will, as they draw upon the refined emotional spectrum. For example, a person going on a job interview can invoke the resonance of joy as they walk into the interview. The person does this by imagining themselves happy in their new job, or by remembering a time that they were confident and proud in a job they enjoyed.

Instead of needing to heal the details of their past by releasing the emotions of bygone days, they can begin to explore new relationships with their feelings and work them out in their daily life. For example, individuals who were taught that anger is bad, and have, therefore, avoided expressing anger most of their lives, can choose to learn about anger and align to the healthy aspect of this emotional energy. They can familiarize themselves with the full range of this emotional expression that they once avoided. When they become angry in the future, they will be able to work with the anger in a more fluid and thorough way. This proactive approach will support them in reconditioning their responses and reactions to anger as it appears in their daily lives.

GOING INTO THE FUTURE TO CREATE THE PRESENT WITH THE BACKDROP OF THE PAST

Our thoughts truly do create our reality. Henry Ford needed to go into the future in his mind to conceive the idea of the automobile. At the present time, he designed the automobile with the past image of the horse and carriage in his mind. Similarly, our emotions project us into the future and carry our past memories with us as we create our life on a daily basis.

Imagine a person going on a job interview who is tightly wound up with the anxiety and fear of future failure. By referencing the past and carrying that image of failure into the future, the interview will be tainted. A key to utilizing your future fears in a positive way is to consciously construct the potential scenario in your mind, and use your imagination and emotional energy to transform your fear into compassion.

The first step to transforming your fear of failure is to feel the fear thoroughly. While you are feeling the raw energy of the fear, imagine yourself in the job interview and conjure the worst case scenario in your mind. For example, imagine that you get so nervous your word-finding ability is disabled and you get stuck on trying to communicate a simple thought. As you imagine this you will amplify the fear to its maximum intensity and feel the other emotions that surface. Finally, you are able to discharge the fear.

Once you have defused the tense energy and enter a more neutral inner state, you can begin to collect the intrinsic information from the imaginary experience. You can gain insight into your worst fears and then begin to see the areas you need to focus on to sharpen your skills. You now have entered a state of feeling compassion for yourself. You become more understanding and caring for yourself.

GETTING INTO YOUR EMOTIONS WITH HONESTY

Regarding your emotions, you have to go in to get out. You have to spend time slipping into the fabric of the emotions. It's similar to trying on clothes. Some clothes are tight and itchy while others are a loose fit and comfortable. If an emotion is constrictive, the first step to addressing it, is to feel the emotion thoroughly, and then make the choice to transform it. If you feel angry and hurt and want to move on to joy and love, you must first feel through the layers of the hurt and anger before a true change can take place. This is what is meant by "you've got to go in to get out."

Direct communication tills the field for intimate relationships with people. Consider this metaphor which illustrates what can happen when you are honest with people. When you till a field big clumps of earth and rock are uncovered where there once was a smooth and level surface. Similarly, in the beginning of a relationship everything may appear smooth, but when you tell the truth, you can turn up hurt, hostility, or even rage. This can be a big risk to take, and for most people they prefer not taking the risk and keeping the illusion going that the relationship has meaning.

For many people with unspoken secrets, it is normal to tell little white lies and sometimes routine lying becomes the norm. People rationalize that the reason they are lying is to protect themselves or others from getting hurt. This is the biggest lie! An example of this pattern is when lovers are deceptive about having a secret affair with someone else. The reason most people are not honest with others is they are fearful of being judged or abandoned.

Choosing apparent loyalty over truth can create resentment. We have seen it all too many times. Those who are loyal to a leader who is clearly violating the will of others and acting irresponsibly, but fail to listen to their internal voice of integrity, are choosing loyalty over honesty.

THE END OF BEING GUILTY FOR FEELING EMOTIONS

Like all of the emotions, guilt is neither good or bad. Guilt has an intrinsic value at its onset, but prolonged guilt can be destructive to yourself and those whom you project guilt on. When you begin to feel guilt, it can facilitate a natural ability to feel concern. For example, you missed your daughter's piano recital and feel concerned that her feelings are hurt. Your concern is related to disappointing someone you care about.

The deceptive aspect of guilt is when you feel guilty for having certain emotions. Have you ever told yourself that you should not be sad, jealous, or angry? Guilt can camouflage emotions such as anger, hurt, jealousy, or fear. Guilt broadcasts the message: "You don't have the right to feel guilt, because it is your fault" to your subconscious mind, commonly causing the authentic feelings to subconsciously submerge. In such cases, you use guilt as a numbing device.

The consequence of suppressing the feeling is that it can sit inside you and ferment, causing you to marinate in old guilt. These ruminations can send you into a depressed state, since guilt and depression thrive on each other.

Guilt is frequently self-generated and can deny you of your truth as it whispers a litany of "should" and "should not" into your inner mind. Guilt can be insidiously fed from self-judgement. For example, if you have a self-judgement that you are too fat and shouldn't eat any of that cake, guilt can barricade you from having and enjoying the cake. Yet, guilt likes to feed on guilt. Therefore you will most likely eat the cake so that you can have more to feel guilty about. This is double guilt. Guilt Trip Number 1: "I should not have any of that cake". Guilt Trip Number 2: "I can't believe I ate the cake, I feel so guilty." Double the guilt, double the misery!

Guilt has a tendency to hang on to the past, disregarding the possibility of self-forgiveness. Life is for learning and our past mistakes are lessons that help us grow and change. Often, when people have guilt for the actions of their past, they continue to perpetuate similar behavior in the present. Most of the time, guilt does not help you learn. As a culture, we need to grieve the damage we have collectively bestowed upon the Earth and then move forward without guilt.

Guilt is often unexpressed sorrow. If you allow yourself to surrender into the feeling of sorrow by regretting the reason you feel guilty, you will be able to move through the guilt much more effectively. The next time you experience guilt, allow yourself to feel if there is any unexpressed sorrow that needs to be realized. Many times, guilt can be repressed shame. Become aware of the source of the shame so that you can prevent further unconscious reactions to the guilt.

Guilt can also be the result of distorted thinking. Commonly, people that self-blame see problems and crises as their own fault. Frequently, these people tend to make a catastrophe out of things and discount the positive nature of events.

They anticipate disasters and assume the worst, while ignoring the positive influences they have on events. Even in the absence of evidence, they focus on the negative impact they had on the event.

Guilt can be used to bolster our self-image in a distorted way. Feeling guilty can be an illusionary way of demonstrating our responsible nature. Such people foster a sense of self-importance by generating more and more anguish upon themselves. Generally, the burden of guilt is a barrier to future success. Guilt gives people excuses to avoid present challenges by filling their minds with burdensome thoughts about past failures. This gives people a way to rationalize failure. One of the challenges of the new century is to let go of the collective rumination of the failures of the past century.

THE END OF FEELING SHAMEFUL FOR BEING ALIVE

Shame has been a virus of the soul as it generates feelings of hopelessness within its victim. Shame can erode a person's self-esteem and self-worth leaving them feeling worthless. Our self-esteem is measured by our achievements in the external world, whereas our self-worth relates to our basic inherent value. In life, we periodically suffer blows to our self-esteem while we retain a healthy self-worth.

The first step to overthrowing the desecration of shame is to recognize and accept your essential truth: The shame you've internalized has produced suffering and despair, but *it is not who you are*. You are perfect exactly the way you are with all of your imperfections and worthy of all of the riches of life. Your existence on this planet has value and purpose. The second step to discharging shame is to vigilantly become aware of the internal voice of shame that taunts you unmercifully. By developing the ability to identify the inner beliefs and messages, you can stop them in their tracks and replace the destructive messages with life-affirming truths.

Now we have moved into the new millennium, it will be of great value to use these two steps when reflecting on the shame of humanity. We can begin by shaking of the nihilistic beliefs that humanity is inherently evil, and begin to accept that we as a species are in a perfect stage of evolution with all of our imperfections. We have been learning as we evolve and the sooner we discharge our collective shame, the sooner we can begin to build a planetary society with love as our highest standard.

THE END OF HIDING FROM GRIEF AND SORROW

Grief is the emotion associated with loss and feelings of separation. When you lose a loved one through death, grief can roll in like a heavy fog bringing profound feelings of abandonment. Grief is experienced in the body often as a dynamic energy that produces the catharsis of crying, or sometimes as an inert state of emotional numbness commonly described as depression.

Every moment someone in this world is facing grief and loss. With the instant access of global news inundating us through the proliferation of electronic media such as the internet and 24-hour cable news television networks, the sordid details of the trauma of the hour are virtually inescapable. Sometimes the stories touch our hearts and draw us into the grieving process. In the past couple of years, with the tragic death of such young, vital, and compassionate figures as Princess Diana and John Kennedy Jr, millions of people have participated in a global grieving process. Sometimes people become numb to the "tragedy of the day" circulating through the global brain, and build a case for their disappointment and disillusionment for society at large.

As we become a more emotionally intelligent society, we will place great value on encouraging individuals to embrace their grief and sorrow, instead of demanding that they "get on with their life". Having policies that demand that a person returns to work shortly after the death of a loved one fosters denial and many times aborts the natural grieving cycle.

As we reflect on the past century, we see a modern society predominately run by men. One of the legacies of this male-dominated era that needs to be transformed is the characterization of sensitive men being soft and weak. Generally, in our society, men have been taught to suppress their tears and control their feelings. This has held men as emotional hostages, who are frequently afraid to authentically experience their deeper and darker feelings.

True sorrow is an experience of "letting go". To let go is to accept the circumstances that have fallen into your life and accept the pain that accompanies these conditions. It is important to surrender into the feeling of sorrow and allow the feelings to wash through you until you feel the joy that awaits you on the other side as you become unencumbered by past pain.

FORGIVENESS DELIVERS LOVE

By getting to know sorrow intimately, we as a society will cultivate the quality of compassion and forgiveness. This will evoke more love in our hearts to share with others. What does it mean to forgive? Well, let's breakdown the word into its two syllables: for-give. Emotional energy flows in two directions—it fills you up or empties you. Forgiving is a process of emptying yourself of emotional pain. When you forgive yourself, you open up to receive love. Love is for-giving and once you clear the emotional pain that blocks your loving nature, you will restore the flow of love.

In this new society, we will harness the ability to forgive ourselves and this will set us on the path of naturally forgiving others. When we forgive, we transcend our limited self and tap into the divine nature of our higher self.

The higher self is the aspect of ourselves that can see the bigger picture, and does not need to control the circumstances of our reality. The higher self resonates with the quality of pure love.

Love is the highest criterion in life. It is the weights and measure of a happy and meaningful life. When you take your last breath, what will really matter? Certainly not how many material things you acquired. What will matter is how much you have loved and received love.

All love begins with self-love. Loving others without love for self can result in bitterness and resentment. Love is the master emotion. Your physical heart is the master electrical oscillator of your body. It sends out the most powerful electromagnetic field that affects all systems in your body. Your emotional heart sends out a powerful field of love that can unify any other emotion. Love is a force that generates wholeness. When you feel love, you feel whole.

Emotions such as anger and grief generate feelings of separation. It is important to feel these emotions so that you can return to the homeostasis of love. After a good cry or scream, your emotions can transform into the condition of feeling whole. When love is freely moving through you, you feel passionate about life.

EMOTIONS AS THE MODEM TO THE SOUL

In the past, the "spiritual life" was regarded as a solemn and austere lifestyle. To contact the spiritual dimension, you would retreat into silence and stillness. The pulse of modern society was in direct juxtaposition to the spiritual domain. In the near future, creating alliances with the soul and spirit will be the quintessence of success as a unique spirituality is beginning to flourish. This is a spirituality of activity and connectivity that is accessed through the emotional reciprocity of everyday life.

During this new age, the process of enlightenment will be practically understood as growing toward your full human potential. A fluency in the language of emotions will be seen as a gateway into the most unlimited and unconditioned aspects of your being. Far from a state of self-delusion, self-denial, or escapism, emotional intelligence represents the ultimate development of what are generally considered the most valuable qualities of human life: kindness, compassion, generosity, intelligence, creativity, and freedom.

The extraordinary dimensions of the spirit will become more and more tangible through the ability to use the emotions as the modem to the soul. Imagine your soul communicating to you through your heart, inspiring you to live a congruent life between your spirit and your emotions. Imagine the delight of hearing your soul signal to you "you've got mail", as you feel divine inspiration guiding your feelings in your daily decision-making process.

The birth of the information age is a catalyst to inspire us to understand we are more than just our material reality, we are spirits playing in a world of matter. This understanding will be cherished as the most valuable information and will propel us into a society that values consciousness, spirituality, and emotions as the greater world currency. This is the dream of an enlightened planet that sits in our hearts as a dormant seed ready to germinate.

REFERENCES

Bloomfield, H.H. (1983) *Making Peace With Your Parents*. New York: Ballentine Books.
Bloomfield, H.H., Sawaf, A., & Rosen, J. (2000) *Emotional Power*. San Francisco: Whole Life Publishing.
Cooper, R.K. & Q. Metrics (1997) *EQ Map*. San Francisco, CA: AIT and Essi Systems.
Cooper, R.K. & Sawaf, A. (1997) *Executive EQ*. New York: Grosset/Putnam.
Institute of HeartMath *Research Overview*. Online at:
    http://www. Heartmath.org/ro/hro/hintro1.html
Pearsall, P. (1998) *The Heart's Code*. New York: Broadway Books.
Pert, C. (1997) *The Molecules of Emotion*. New York: Scribner.
Ryerson, K. (1999) In conversation with Ayman Sawaf, San Francisco, CA.

Conclusion

The title of this book *Emotions at Work* was chosen to suggest two of the main aims of the book. They are to describe current research on the processes that are at work in the production of emotions, and to do the same for research on emotional/affective occurrences in work organizations. With hindsight, it is obvious that the title is not accurate enough. It should have read "Emotions, moods, and temperament at work", for many of the chapters illustrate the difficulty of maintaining the conceptual distinctions that differentiate them, and the need to consider them all in any serious attempt to understand emotional processes, or the outcomes of them in work organizations.

Alongside this observation there is a regular reference to the complexity of understanding emotional life and its relationship to cognitive experience and behaviour. Another consistent theme is the importance of achieving better understanding, both for improving people's physical and emotional health, and for improving the management of people in work organizations. The chapters also contain many references to the need to acknowledge that the health of the workforce and the health of the organization are intimately connected. The final common strand is the call for more and better research.

Despite the self-criticism that pervades the book it contains many suggestions about ways forward to achieve both the scientific aims and the practical aims of authors, whose main concerns are improving the way organizations manage emotions, moods, and temperaments. All the authors advocate another aim of the book, which was to extend consideration of emotions outside the narrowness of stress or job satisfaction which dominated much organizational research in the last half of the 20th century. We believe the book has succeeded in meeting these aims, though it is obvious from the conclusions of most of these chapters that the content of similar books will be rapidly expanded during the decades to come. One gap in the contents is a chapter on qualitative studies of emotions in organizations, but this arose because we failed to get anybody to write it. This is partly due to a paucity of such work as noted by Howard Weiss and Art Brief, and Steve Fineman does refer to much of the work that has been done, but this sort of research will undoubtedly increase. Both human insight and technology will have important roles to play in these research projects of the future, but in the new millennium, the "e" in e-commerce is as likely to endure as "emotion" as "electronic".

August 2000

Roy Payne and Cary Cooper

Index

Lightning Source UK Ltd.
Milton Keynes UK
05 October 2010

160776UK00001B/21/P